THE CITIZEN'S WAGE

JAMES G. SNELL

The Citizen's Wage:
The State and the Elderly in
Canada, 1900–1951

UNIVERSITY OF TORONTO PRESS
Toronto   Buffalo   London

© University of Toronto Press Incorporated 1996
Toronto Buffalo London
Printed in Canada

ISBN 0-8020-0737-6 (cloth)
ISBN 0-8020-7792-7 (paper)

Printed on acid-free paper

Canadian Cataloguing in Publication Data

Snell, James G.
  The citizen's wage: the state and the elderly in
Canada, 1900–1951

  Includes bibliographical references and index.
  ISBN 0-8020-0737-6 (bound). ISBN 0-8020-7792-7 (pbk.)

  1. Aged – Government policy – Canada – History –
20th century. 2. Aged – Services for – Canada –
History – 20th century. I. Title.

  HQ1064.C3S54 1996   305.26'0971   C95-932153-5

University of Toronto Press acknowledges the financial assistance to its publishing
program of the Canada Council and the Ontario Arts Council.

This book has been published with the help of a grant from the Humanities and
Social Sciences Federation of Canada, using funds provided by the Social Sciences
and Humanities Research Council of Canada.

To Neil Colman and David Miller,
and in memory of John Stricks (1942–1993)

Contents

viii   Contents

Figures and Tables

Abbreviations

AO	Archives of Ontario
AOAPS	Alberta Old Age Pensioners' Society
APS	Alberta Pensioners' Society
BCARS	British Columbia Archives and Records Service
CVA	City of Vancouver Archives
NA	National Archives of Canada
NSPU	Nova Scotia Pensioners' Union
OAP	Old Age Pension
OAPO	Old Age Pensioners' Organization
OAPOBC	Old Age Pensioners' Organization of British Columbia
OAPOS	Old Age Pensioners' Organization of Saskatchewan
P	*Pensioner*
PAM	Public Archives of Manitoba
PANB	Public Archives of New Brunswick
PANL	Public Archives of Newfoundland and Labrador
PANS	Public Archives of Nova Scotia
QUA	Queen's University Archives
SA	Saskatchewan Archives
UWO	University of Western Ontario, Regional History Collection
VM	Violet McNaughton Papers, SA
WP	*Western Producer*

Introduction

This book examines the changes and continuities in the lives of the elderly during the first half of the twentieth century – a period in which there were massive structural alterations in the policies and programs shaping their lives. These years saw the founding of distinctive institutions for the elderly, the rise of mandatory retirement, and the initiation of a range of public programs, most notably old age pensions. This study does not attempt any detailed analysis of the political processes through which these various policies and programs were considered and initiated; there are already a number of studies that give us some insight into these developments.[1] Instead, it investigates both the impact of those programs on the lives of the recipients and the ways in which the elderly and sometimes their families responded to them. Overall, the book discusses the ways in which old people's and society's appraisal of aging and the aged changed in the years 1900–51.

Although Canada is used as a case study, similar issues and responses concerning the elderly can be found in all Western countries in this period. Of course, the timing and the character of local actions and reactions varied, influenced as they were by the local political culture and the timing of industrialization, among other factors. Still, the questions posed and the problems confronted are universal among industrialized nations, and are central to the recent history of both the elderly and the modern welfare state.

Writing in 1949, an English sociologist argued that the relatively recent development of state programs for the elderly signalled a recognition of the social rights that were inherent in their citizenship status. The nineteenth-century poor law had treated the claims of the elderly poor as an alternative to citizens' rights, explicitly denying recipients any claims they might have to suffrage, for example. Those who derived support from the state and who did not contribute directly to state coffers could not participate in the responsible political processes of the state. But by the early twentieth century these views were changing. The new public programs designed to assist the needy elderly treated the claims on public support as part of a citizen's rights, and not as infringing on the recipient's civic status. The new residential institutions for the needy elderly at the turn of the century were the first sign that society was beginning, however meagrely, to recognize publicly the needs of the dependent elderly as a distinct group. This development was part of a broader one that would see all the elderly receiving 'a citizen's wage,' in the form of an old age pension, by mid-century. Social rights that had become divorced from the status of citizenship were now being defined as inherent in that status for all members of society, a view that resulted in the creation of 'a universal right to real income which is not proportionate to the market value of the claimant.' The elderly were primary beneficiaries of this new way of thinking.[2] While elderly citizens' wages took such substantial forms as the Old Age Pension (OAP) and medical care, the ideological basis of their claim to aid was best captured by the new name adopted for them – *senior citizens.*

Changing perceptions of the status of the elderly were fundamental to the development of state assistance programs. 'The guiding principle' behind the demand for these programs in western Europe and North America, commented John Myles, 'was that social provision should reflect the equality of citizenship that exists among individuals in the political sphere in a democratic society, not the inequalities produced by the market. Democracy was being called on to assert itself in the form of a citizen's entitlement to an equal share of the society's wealth.' Members of the society were turned into 'social citizens,' in the words of Martin Kohli, with claims for the provision of material continuity throughout their life course. Although claims to an *equal* share of a society's wealth were not endorsed, in all Western countries the claim to a minimum share came to be widely accepted. That minimum share consistently fell below basic subsistence levels, but the provision of a universal old age pension nevertheless recognized the fundamental claims of the elderly members of society to the right to support from that society. Indeed, as Myles pointed out, the apparent contradiction between the low level of support provided and the universal character of that support was a product of the structural tension between a capitalist economy and a protective, democratic polity. During the first half of the twentieth century, the welfare state began to provide the economic infrastructure and much of the material base for old age, creating from one perspective a new dependency of the needy elderly on the state.[3]

Equally important to the development of formal support for the elderly were the changing role and perception of the state. The demands of the First World War drew the state into ever greater involvement in directing the economy and ordering the lives of Canadians. With the economic problems of the early 1920s, the role of government expanded further, then grew to a far greater extent as a result of the economic and climatic disasters of the 1930s. The Second World War was a 'total war,' drawing all the country's residents into its vortex and requiring the state to intrude into the daily economic and social lives of Canadians to a previously unheard-of degree. Postwar reconstruction maintained this level of state involvement, even expanding it further in some areas.

The new provisions for the elderly matured in the context of other state programs in the first half of the twentieth century. Provision for various sectors of society played an increasingly prominent role in state policy. Early in the period, Canadian workers began to receive compensation for accidents and injuries, and later for unemployment as well. Benefits for military veterans and their dependants, provided before the First World War by charities, became the responsibility of the state in its aftermath, and the level of those benefits slowly expanded through the 1920s. State aid was extended to another social sector with the introduction of mothers' allowances in the 1920s, a development reinforced by the introduction of family allowances in 1944. What was more, with the entrenchment of the income tax, all citizens became aware that their individual contributions to the local economy and society were matched by individual contributions to the state, creating a sense of reciprocal obligation in the minds of many. The expansion of taxable fields and of areas of public concession to state control (such as wartime rationing and wage controls) implied a greater obligation by the state to the public. There was a new relationship between citizens and the state, in which the state had an increasing claim on private resources, and individuals came to expect state aid when in need.

Throughout the first half of the twentieth century, public rhetoric continually referred to the elderly as the pioneers of contemporary society – those who had given their labour and their health to open up the Canadian frontier and to develop the modern Canadian economy. This sentimental claim on society was exceeded, however, by a much more fundamental claim. The elderly had not only helped to build modern Canada, but, during their working lives, had contributed directly to the state programs that had benefited others. Now many of the elderly were in need, and, as citizens, they had built up new rights. Old age had come to be viewed as a social problem beyond the control or capacity of the individual – like unemployment or workers' injuries – and the state now had an obligation to help 'from the cradle to the grave' all citizens who shared such problems.4 This culture of entitlement profoundly shaped the claims of the elderly to a citizen's wage.

Although the senior citizens of the 1930s and 1940s did not use the term 'citizen's wage,' they did articulate and assert a new sense of citizenship and a firm claim to entitlement. Spreading across a broad spectrum of the elderly, and of society at large, by the 1940s, the culture of entitlement provided the basis for a new sense of identification and self-worth among the elderly. It was part of a process in which aging itself began to be redefined across society at large.

Exploring the linkage of individual experience, institutional change, program initiation, and structural factors, this book examines the working out of the characteristics of the citizen's wage from the point of view of the Canadian elderly and their families, who were themselves primary actors in the dynamic process.5 Yet this was a more complex process than simply solving the contradictions between capitalism and democracy as they manifested themselves through this problem. Myles emphasized the importance of politics and of its class content in explaining the particular development of the Canadian welfare system directed at the elderly. There were additional factors and actors that played important roles in the historical process.

The elderly themselves, both the organized minority and the unorganized but not always inarticulate majority, were major participants in the shaping of the various public programs. These elderly were by no means a monolithic group, and age alone did not define their status. The elderly can be divided into several overlapping groups, by sex, chronological age, birth cohort, ethnicity, region, and social class. These subgroups responded to the political and social environment in various ways, reflecting their particular needs and interests. Other age groups also played a significant part in shaping the state programs that addressed the elderly, and these groups reflected the tensions that existed in other communities, tensions similar to those experienced by the elderly. As well, attitudinal factors, particularly regarding the perceived character of old age and the changing role and capacity of the state, were influential in the development of state programs for the elderly.

Although 'the citizen's wage' is a convenient catch-phrase for those programs (which were misrepresented in some earlier literature as non-problematic),6 they in fact comprise much more than just the Old Age Pension, which is, of course, the most important and most basic of them all. The adoption of a universal old age pension in Canada in 1951 was the culmination of several decades of struggle and of policy initiatives, beginning with the public and private provision of residential institutions for elderly persons. The recognition of society's obligation to provide for the residential needs of a small number of needy elderly was the first step in the integration of the dependent elderly into the nation's citizenry. Once the OAP was in place, in took two decades of conflict and adjustment before the new programs for the elderly and the traditional principles of personal and familial responsibility meshed. The elaboration of a number of new social services for the elderly in the late 1940s, including medical care and recreational facilities, reflected an even broader definition of the claims that 'senior citizens' had upon society. This range of programs is a manifestation of the changing position of the elderly within twentieth-century society, and of the evolving social and political construction of old age.

In analysing the multifaceted construction of old age, this book follows a straightforward organization. Following an introductory section, chapter 2 looks at the first direct state response to the needs of the elderly – the provision of residential institutions. Chapter 3 shows how this response was accompanied by a continuing authoritative emphasis on the family as a fundamental source of support for the elderly. Chapter 4 examines how the elderly employed their property to protect themselves and their families, and chapter 5 investigates how, when the OAP threatened to interfere with traditional property-based practices, the elderly acted to thwart that interference while taking maximum advantage of the OAP itself. The OAP quickly became the focus of considerable activity by the needy elderly, who sought to represent themselves individually and collectively in the most appropriate possible light (chapter 6). The result, as reflected in chapter 7, was a gradual shifting of state OAP policies, reflecting the changing perceptions of the elderly as a group and of the role of the state.

The analysis undertaken in this study relies heavily on records generated by the interaction of the elderly with the various state programs aimed at shaping their lives. These are the same sources that would be used for a more traditional political or legislative history of the topic, for the problem with studying the history of any group such as the elderly is the central one of sources. As different state programs for the elderly proliferated in the first half of the twentieth century, the elderly themselves inevitably interacted with those programs, generating information about themselves that is now available to historians. Such sources by no means tell the whole story about the elderly and the continuities and changes in their lives during that period, but they do allow us to glimpse some aspects of what it was to be elderly in that time. Records are usually available for the elderly individual only at the point of interaction with the state institution or program, making it difficult to place the interaction within the broader context of the individual's life course. Historians, however, learn early in their careers to accept the notion that not every question can be answered, or at least answered fully.

During this period, the majority of the elderly tended to be inarticulate, particularly about the emotional content of their lives. But the new state programs gave a minority of the elderly an avenue for expressing their views, and thereby allowed us glimpses into their lives. By the 1930s and 1940s, a new sense of group identity encouraged a more direct expression, though one shaped by the predominantly political ends of the pensioners' organizations that gave the elderly their own collective, public voice.

During the first half of the twentieth century the elderly consciously became a distinct group, 'senior citizens.' Their new self-image, as well as the perception of them held by other age groups, was shaped by structural factors, particularly demographic and economic. But they were also shaped by the new public programs aimed at the elderly. The Old Age Pension program, especially, assigned the dependent elderly a different status and a relatively secure and stable source of cash income, often for the first time in their lives (particularly in the case of women). Many, though by no means all, of the barriers based on race or gender were superseded by a program implicitly aimed at some form of equality, and certainly at a minimum standard of living for all elderly Canadian residents.

This pension program gave many elderly a more positive identity and an enhanced sense of their 'rights' as members of the society. A state program directly shaped the identity, not just of the recipients but also of potential recipients and of the elderly in general. As a result, the elderly began to organize their own associations, and to meet together for both social and political purposes; most importantly for our purposes, they began to speak for themselves. The voice of the elderly that is mediated through government sources can thus be balanced by the voice of particular elderly spokespersons addressed to the elderly, the state, and society at large. By mid-century the elderly citizens of Canada had staked their claim to a new status in their society and had won the day. The senior citizenry, through the state and public programs, had successfully claimed a new and secure place in the polity. The interactive process through which this was carried out had, at one and the same time, altered the character and role of the state and reshaped the self-image and the daily lives of the elderly.

Research in this area is dependent largely on state records documenting the interaction of the elderly with state programs and institutions. Because of the nature of these sources, there is a particular emphasis (perhaps even an overemphasis) on factors pertaining to the state in the ongoing process of the construction of old age. It has been essential to set out the context of the available information by elaborating on the nature of the various state programs and the bureaucratic processes that gave them operational life. But I have tried to keep that context to a minimum. Anyone interested in details of the history of any of the programs themselves would be better served by a study with just such a primary aim – for example, Kenneth Bryden's *Old Age Pensions and Policy-Making in Canada* (Montreal, 1974), which discusses both government annuities and old age pensions. Also helpful for the early history of old age pensions is *Old Age Pensions in Canada*, published by the Department of Labour in 1929. Though not directly concerned with the elderly, the early history of Canadian veterans' pensions offers a number of interesting parallels with the OAP and is ably detailed in Desmond Morton and Glenn Wright's *Winning the Second Battle* (Toronto, 1987). No intensive study has yet been written on the various other components of state policy regarding the elderly, though James Struthers's *The Limits of Affluence: Welfare in Ontario, 1920–1970* (Toronto, 1994) is a valuable and welcome addition to the literature.[7]

The present book, by concentrating on the elderly themselves, builds on existing studies of Canadian public policy and on historical investigations of the elderly in other societies. In the period under study, not only were public policy and attitudes changing, but the elderly gradually gained a new sense of their own self-worth and of their claims on society. The records used here permit an analysis of at least some of the behaviour of the elderly as they, along with family and neighbours, adapted to their changing place in a modern state. Because of the nature of the available sources, the working class predominates in this study, and the middle class is strongly underrepresented. It is important to understand, however, that although the working class was strikingly persistent in its struggles to protect its elderly members, the middle class echoed some of the same ideas, if somewhat less vigorously. Old age was being redefined across the class structure.

If the class character of this study is reasonably clear, the same cannot be said about ethnicity. The records employed here did not facilitate an analysis of ethnicity as a factor in the history of aging. The study of that factor must be left to others, but there can be little doubt that it will reveal significant variations in the discovery of senior citizenship among the different ethnic and racial groups in Canadian society.

Access to certain archival collections was granted on condition that the identities of private individuals be concealed; I have extended the same privacy to all individuals whose activities in a private capacity are recorded in the research collections. Thus, for example, the identity of any elderly person writing privately on his or her own behalf to any state or charitable official has been concealed; where it was desirable for stylistic reasons to provide a name for an individual, I have assigned a pseudonym that conveys the ethnic background of the original name. The identity of elderly people acting publicly on their own behalf or on behalf of the elderly as a group, as in the case of the Old Age Pensioners' Organization, has not been protected.

A note about terminology: I have tried to avoid using terms anachronistically. For example, the term 'seniors' is avoided in discussions of events predating the 1940s, when the term achieved currency. However, for the sake of convenience, although Newfoundland did not join Canada until 1949, I have included Newfoundlanders in the term 'Canadian' where appropriate throughout the study, rather than employing the stylistically clumsy 'Canadians and Newfoundlanders.'

This study has some methodological parameters that should be articulated. The nature of the records employed made a life-course definition of the elderly, as opposed to a calendar definition, impossible.[8] I have not defined the terms 'elderly' or 'aged' with any consistency in this study. Early twentieth-century society itself could not decide what age cohorts to include within such terms. According to some studies, age discrimination in hiring affected people even in their mid-thirties; unemployment rates reveal the differing treatment of workers fifty years of age and older. Women were often expected to retire at the age of sixty, men at the age of sixty-five. The Canadian Old Age Pension was available to those aged seventy or older, while the Newfoundland Pension began at the age of seventy-five. Rather than choose any one of these age boundaries, I have allowed the definition of elderly to vary with the themes and topics involved. In discussions pertaining to the OAP, the elderly are defined as seventy or older. Relief programs had no such specific age boundary, so I expanded my definition to include those aged fifty or older. With respect to all elderly, nationwide, I have combined a 'macro-level' analysis of all the processes involved with specific 'micro-level' studies of some of these processes in an attempt to capture both the broad and the specific characteristics of the elderly as well as of the state programs. Such an approach offers the best opportunity for capturing the varying dynamics of the discovery of senior citizenship in Canada in the first half of the twentieth century.[9]

Acknowledgments

I have acquired a debt of gratitude to many during this book's long gestation. Leslie Snell first stimulated my interest in the elderly during her own research and work as a gerontologist. Many of my colleagues in the Department of History, in the Gerontology Research Centre, and elsewhere offered encouragement and support along the way. The research was funded largely by a grant from the Social Sciences and Humanities Research Council of Canada. An early research grant from the Gerontology Research Centre of Guelph helped to get the project under way initially.

Several people contributed their research skills: Rozlyn Cluett, Catherine Gauld, Marion Hoffer, Tricia Jarvis, David Larsen, and Shelley Woods. A number of archivists and archives offered vital support: Brian Young at the British Columbia Archives and Records Service; John Smart at the National Archives of Canada; the Archives of Ontario; Ed Phelps at the Regional History Collection at the University of Western Ontario; the Saskatchewan Archives in both Regina and Saskatoon; Shelley Smith at the Public Archives of Newfoundland and Labrador; and John McLeod at the Public Archives of Nova Scotia.

A number of colleagues contributed far beyond the usual support. Bettina Bradbury, Chad Gaffield, Craig Heron, Greg Kealey, James Struthers, and Catharine Wilson offered extended comments and suggestions on a first draft of most or all of the manuscript, helping me to reconsider my ideas significantly. Ellen Gee, Shirley Tillotson, and Joe Tindale read specific sections or helped me to address particular problems. C.G. Gifford generously shared transcripts of interviews with activists in the seniors' movement. Laurel Doucette helped to introduce me to and shared her knowledge of pertinent material contained in the Memorial University of Newfoundland Folklore Archives. James Struthers allowed me to read his excellent treatment of OAP policy in a pre-publication draft of *The Limits of Affluence*. Kris Inwood brought a number of useful publications by economic historians to my attention. Several people cooperated in interviews: Josephine Arland, Philip Grabke, and Stanley Knowles. Many seniors responded to my request for accounts of their family's interaction with their grandparents.

Finally, I want to acknowledge the support of three other individuals. For many years and throughout my training and development as a scholar I have benefited from the intelligence, support, and friendship of my three undergraduate roommates. Their interest in history has always been minimal, but their steadfast encouragement and companionship have spanned many years and many miles. I appreciate this opportunity to acknowledge my gratitude to them and my affection for them.

THE CITIZEN'S WAGE

1

Daily Lives

For several decades now we have been acutely aware of the elderly in our society. Their numbers are growing and their political influence is becoming more apparent. We are becoming more aware of the particular needs of the elderly, and more concerned with responding positively and meaningfully to those needs, in the certain knowledge that we will be members of that group ourselves some day, if we are not already. Inevitably, this awareness and concern have provoked scholarly study, concentrated within gerontology and geriatrics, and this scholarship has contributed greatly to our knowledge of aging and the elderly.

Historians, perhaps typically for their discipline, were relatively slow to join in the search for knowledge about the elderly. This was attributable, on the one hand, to the discipline's concentration on other, more traditional interests – a focus that was disrupted by the fundamental challenges posed by social historians in the 1960s – and, on the other hand, to the paucity of traditional sources. By the very nature of being old, the historical elderly as a group were relatively small in number and overrepresented among the powerless – the poor, the ill, the indigent. Recently, however, using new methods and posing new questions, historians in a number of countries have begun to turn to the history of the elderly, hoping to add to our knowledge of that social group and to contribute some much-needed perspective to the growing pool of knowledge about aging and the aged.

As with the history of the family in general (within which the history of the elderly is usually categorized), historians have made important discoveries, overturning contemporary assumptions about the past. It is now well established that in the Western world the nuclear family has predominated at least since the 1500s. Probably fewer than 20 per cent of families at any one time fitted the model of an extended, three-generational family that had been assumed to be so common.[1] Attempts to depict the history of the elderly as one of persistent decline have also come under successful attack. Despite a contemporary urge to assume the previous existence of some sort of golden age of the elderly, when respect, deference, and well-being were the norm, no evidence has been found to support this picture. Instead, studies have shown that the old have often suffered both physically and economically, and that families at times were unable or unwilling to take in elderly relatives. In short, for both women and men in the past, old age was often a difficult time.[2] But this is not to argue that the nature of aging and of being old has not changed. While there is a great deal of continuity in the history of the elderly, there has also been considerable change.

A number of recent studies have contributed to expanding our knowledge of the history of the elderly. Several historians have argued that attitudinal forces were central to the changing position of the elderly in the nineteenth and twentieth centuries. Such studies give primary importance to the role of ageism, focusing on the centrality of a society's attitudes towards old age. Though the subject of some disagreement, historians now tend to argue that the status of the elderly declined across the nineteenth century. Prior to that time, the elderly were regarded as potentially useful members of a society in which they were active participants. There was no presumption that the aged shared particular negative physical or social characteristics simply because of their advancing years. During the last decades of the nineteenth century, especially in the United States, the elderly were increasingly regarded as obsolescent. 'The unprecedented disesteem for the elderly reflected and resulted from the impact of new scientific, bureaucratic, and popular ideas converging with innovations in medical practice, the economic structure, and American society itself,' argued W. Andrew Achenbaum. Although these attitudes about the elderly arose independently of any observable changes in the actual position of the elderly, the perceptions were increasingly reflected in very real processes of systemic discrimination. In the early decades of the twentieth century, those discriminatory processes resulted in significant changes in the economic and social conditions of the elderly.[3]

Succeeding studies have examined some of those discriminatory processes. Physicians, who before the 1800s, had not perceived age to be related in any direct way to disease, now developed new understandings of senescence. They came to see old age as a pathological state, the direct cause of significant health problems and a time when 'the body, drained of its energy, simply wasted away.' As one American doctor commented in 1850, old age was 'that stage of life in which the vital forces show unequivocal marks of languishment and decline, where the elasticity of youth and vigor of mankind are followed by a condition in which are manifest symptoms of decay in all parts, both in body and mind.' Medical professionals now defined old women and old men as patients in constant need of medical attention.[4] In Canada, advertisements for patent medicines early in the twentieth century reflected such perceptions, as in the case of 'Dr. Chase's Nerve Food,' which was made in Toronto and advertised across the country; one ad was boldly entitled 'The Weakness of Old Age':

As the years go by the blood gets thin, watery and impure, and fails to supply the nourishment required to keep vitality at high water mark. Circulation gets bad, and the nervous system suffers. Besides the pains and aches, besides the weakness and dizziness, there are feelings of numbness which tell of the approach of paralysis and locomotor ataxia.[5]

Decrepitude had come to be regarded as a natural and inevitable characteristic of old age.

This medical model of aging was paralleled by a sociological model. A social pathology of aging came to be accepted by social workers (both with and without professional training) and early social scientists. Experts increasingly differentiated the old from the rest of society, removing children and young adults from previously non-age-specific institutions of support. Others, such as Charles Booth in England, linked the condition of the elderly with poverty and dependency, under the impact of industrialization and urbanization.[6] By the turn of the twentieth century, geriatrics had become a recognized medical speciality and institutions focusing on the elderly had been established. The elderly had come to be recognized as a distinct social group, simply because of their advancing years and the social and physical characteristics that flowed 'inevitably' from age.

Several other historians have focused our attention on structural, rather than attitudinal, processes. Many of these processes are examined in the context of the specific structures investigated in this book, but two deserve discussion here. Brian Gratton, in *Urban Elders*, studied the demographic characteristics of the Boston elderly in 1890–1950 and the structural processes to which those elderly were exposed.[7] The elderly became a 'social problem' in that period not because of ageism, he argued, but because of demographic shifts and the marginal economic position of working-class families, which undermined their ability to continue to care for the elderly informally. The declining birth rate lowered the ratio of elderly to adult children, so that the burden of care for elderly parents fell on increasingly fewer children; the shrinking real income of the lower strata of the working class across the period reduced many families' ability to assist the elderly. For Gratton, the structural change in families' capacity to care for the aged is the key to the status decline of the elderly. Private charity and public welfare in Boston were so deliberately unattractive that the needy elderly were forced to seek support through continuing employment (whose availability declined only after 1930) and outdoor public relief. Using their increasing political power, Boston's immigrant groups and working class of all ages forced the local government to develop helpful assistance programs through outdoor relief. These new welfare programs allowed the elderly to develop new residential and retirement strategies now common among the elderly.[8]

In more recent work, Gratton has gone on to challenge traditional depictions of the economic problems of the elderly in early industrialization. Offering convincing evidence of the average elderly person's financial well-being, Gratton has forced historians to ask more focused questions about the impact of industrialization. Although individual wages declined in later adult life, the household income of the elderly remained high, and the elderly were able to rely on the support generated by assets accumulated across the life-course. The elderly in general were not the economic victims of industrialization.[9]

William Graebner's study of mandatory retirement in the United States appeared before the publication of Gratton's findings about the economic position of the elderly.[10] Nevertheless, Graebner's work is useful in demonstrating the meshing of negative attitudinal factors with particular structural forces. Though the specific timing of the various stages of the history of retirement was often fixed by the political and constitutional environment in which it was set, other elements of the history were international. This is particularly true for organized labour, which connected many Canadians to their fellow workers in the United States. Driven by newly authoritative perceptions of the inefficiency of older workers, capital and organized labour sought means by which the elderly could be easily removed from the office and the plant floor. Corporate capital developed private pension and retirement plans to ensure the loyalty of younger workers and to rid companies of unwanted older workers; the process of disengagement from older workers could be depersonalized and made less painful (at least for the company) by developing policies of automatic unemployment at a set age. To make this process more palatable, this mandatory, continuing unemployment would be known by the euphemism 'retirement.' Seeking to protect the jobs of younger workers, organized labour cooperated with this development and pushed the state to develop a complementary program of old age pensions. In short, Graebner argued that mandatory retirement developed in the United States not out of a concern for the welfare of the elderly, but out of structural changes in employment patterns and a calculated political decision by organized labour and the state to place a priority on the employment of younger adults.

What is particularly striking about these developments is that Graebner uncovered no resistance among the elderly (though it is not clear how much he looked). It was as if the dependent elderly, already marginalized within the workforce, often in desperate social and economic circumstances and subjected to an increasingly hegemonic perception of the 'uselessness' of the elderly, settled for what they could get – public and private pensions – rather than challenging such basically discriminatory processes. As others have pointed out, the adoption of retirement was slow and gradual, the idea being more widespread than its practice, but new attitudes and processes pushed elderly workers to shift their work patterns, 'stepping down' to less remunerative and less demanding employment.[11]

This apparent acceptance nicely captures the mix of attitudinal and structural factors which constructed aging in the early twentieth century. In the first half of the century, elderly Canadians faced the long-standing problems of the aged in new circumstances. As Gratton and Graebner revealed, the paid workplace altered structurally, marginalizing some elderly workers and eventually forcing many into an increasingly common and age-specific retirement. Across this time period, and particularly in the 1940s, private pension plans – and a government annuity program – helped to redefine old age, not only providing financial support for the retired but also articulating and legitimating a view of old age in which the elderly and paid work were incompatible. At the same time, municipal and provincial governments in Canada established residential institutions for a small proportion of the elderly – those who were indigent and without family or friends to assist them. These old age 'homes,' often still known locally by their earlier title of 'poorhouse,' were important substantial and visual statements of the elderly's increasing public association with such characteristics as dependency, poverty, and helplessness.

At the turn of the century, old age was only beginning to be redefined and constructed as a new social category. There was as yet no consensus on the definition of the elderly. Age itself was not as important a criterion for public or private assistance as health, physical and mental capacity, and self-sufficiency. People were judged to be 'old' when they were no longer able to care for themselves adequately, and when their physical capabilities were perceived to be markedly declining. Old age was gendered; women, presumably on the basis of being 'the weaker sex,' were assumed to become elderly earlier than men. Increasingly across the first half of the twentieth century, age itself became the central criterion in the definition and construction of old age. A new consciousness of time and of age permeated Western society, with particularly important consequences for the elderly. By mid-century one was automatically old at the age of sixty-five, without regard to sex, social class, race, or ethnicity. The definition of old age was applied universally, and public processes, led by state and private pension programs, had been the most powerful elements in articulating the new views of old age.[12]

A number of overlapping programs assisted the elderly in Canada. Prior to the twentieth century, society relied largely on the family to care for the needy. Those without a family or friendship network to fall back on could resort to state-run or charitable residential institutions or on outdoor relief measures, all of which operated without much regard to age and which offered only minimal subsistence. Across the first half of the twentieth century these programs and institutions became increasingly age-specific, many singling out the elderly as targets of particular concern whose advanced age rendered them 'helpless victims.' In striking contrast, the first new state program of the twentieth century, the 1908 annuities program, was based on an assumption that workers could be trained to help themselves and to protect themselves against poverty in old age. What both approaches shared was a paternalistic attitude to the elderly.

The seemingly contradictory character of these two approaches was repeated in two other major state policies. Regulations and new legislation across the first half of the twentieth century insisted repeatedly and aggressively on the primacy of familial responsibility for the elderly. On the other hand, social and political commentators increasingly discussed the provision of a state-funded and state-operated old age pension program for those dependent elderly without adequate family assistance. First discussed at a significant level by the middle of the first decade of the new century, the proposed Canadian Old Age Pension program was a reaction to the initiation of similar programs elsewhere and to the imminent founding of the United Kingdom's program in 1908. Newfoundland responded by initiating its OAP program in 1911, but Canada delayed. While Nova Scotia appointed a royal commission to consider such a plan, and organized labour repeatedly articulated its support for an OAP, the best that Canada could do was appoint a parliamentary committee to investigate the idea.[13] No Canadian OAP program was established at that time.

But the topic was not easily ignored. Organized labour continued sporadically to keep the subject before the public. Industrial unrest and economic distress in the years following the end of the First World War contributed to increasing political interest in the idea, culminating in another parliamentary investigation of such a program in 1924–5. Finally, the federal parliament adopted old age pension legislation in the spring of 1927.[14] The new pension plan was state funded, non-contributory, and means tested; maximum benefits, which were available to women and men seventy years of age or older, were set at $20 per month, where the recipient received other income of no more than $125 yearly (allowing a maximum total income of $365 a year); any assets owned were given an income-producing value based on the purchase of a government annuity, and this fictive income was included in the applicant's total income as though it was in fact received. A pension bureaucracy determined each applicant's assets and income, judged the applicant's eligibility, and calculated the monthly payments. There were narrow citizenship and residency requirements.

Initially, the federal government paid 50 per cent of the benefits, leaving the remainder to provincial and local governments. Provincial enabling legislation was necessary in each jurisdiction, so implementation of the scheme was spread across the ensuing ten years – British Columbia in 1927, Saskatchewan and Manitoba in 1928, Alberta and Ontario in 1929, Prince Edward Island in 1933, Nova Scotia in 1934, and New Brunswick and Quebec in 1936. Each province provided the bureaucracy for administering the pensions, though several sought to 'cut corners' financially by using an existing bureaucracy (such as the Workmen's Compensation Board in British Columbia, Alberta, and Manitoba).

Over the following years the plan was altered in significant ways, though the fundamental philosophy of a means-tested, non-contributory plan was not changed in the legislation. Most important were the early increase in federal support and the eventual rise in individual benefits. In 1931 the federal share of the pensions rose to 75 per cent, making it easier for several of the less-well-to-do provinces to join the program. Beginning in 1942 some provinces (British Columbia and Alberta being first) began to pay a supplemental allowance, usually up to $5 monthly (Nova Scotia offered a means-tested $10 monthly), though the maximum income allowed was not altered. Eventually only Quebec, Prince Edward Island, and New Brunswick were not paying such an allowance. In 1943 the federal government raised the basic monthly payment to a maximum of $25, though again the maximum allowable yearly income remained $365. In 1947 the maximum basic monthly payment was increased again, this time to $30, and then again in 1949 to $40, supplemental provincial allowances usually remaining available beyond these maxima. In 1947 the citizenship and residency requirements, which had proven too strict for some applicants, were relaxed, and the maximum allowable income was raised to $600 for a single or widowed pensioner and $1080 for a married pensioner.

Although these changes were important, the elderly themselves and their families pressured the bureaucracy and the legislatures for a more fundamental rethinking of the program. The result was informal abandonment of several central regulations on which the 1927 program was based. Reclaiming from a pensioner's estate the total pension funds paid generally ended in the late 1940s; insistence on adult children's primary support responsibilities for their parents diminished notably; and the payment level and the maximum allowable income became much more generous. Across the OAP program's first two decades, an increasingly larger proportion of the elderly began to receive this citizen's wage. Other pressures combined to encourage a public and political debate on the program's legislative framework. The result was the 1951 reform of the OAP program. Universality dominated the new Old Age Security program; all persons aged seventy or older would receive a monthly pension cheque automatically. Those aged sixty-five to sixty-nine would be eligible for support under the means-tested Old Age Assistance scheme. Both programs, effectively reflecting both the new and the old in state policy, came into effect on 1 January 1952.

By 1951 the elderly had 'come of age' in Canada. Society had recognized their needs with a proliferation of programs and ideas in the 1940s and with a universal old age pension. These developments were driven by a number of forces, not the least of which were the elderly themselves, as Gratton points out. In Canada they had organized themselves into an influential political movement, which played a role in the movement towards universality and in beginning the reduction of the pensionable age to sixty-five. The unorganized elderly had been even more active in affecting their own lives. They played a role in forcing institutions to change, increasingly leaving behind the traditions of the poorhouse. They calculatingly, if sometimes naively, used their own property, both real and other, to ensure that their lives were lived out as best they could be. And they did what they could to ensure both their own independence, wherever possible, and their continuing place in their own extended family. These changes, the power exercised by the elderly, and their altered status are best captured by the new name for the elderly which came into vogue in the late 1940s.

The term 'senior citizens' has now acquired a certain disrepute. Many elderly resent the somewhat patronizing attitude on the part of the non-elderly and the sense of separateness it implies. But at mid-century the term 'senior citizen' represented hard-won 'rights' and status of which the elderly were justifiably proud. The citizen's wage had been established. If the pride and defiance of the first half-century are less necessary by the 1990s, it is a sign of the solid victories of the 1930s and 1940s and of the continuing changes experienced by the elderly in the second half of the twentieth century.

Other historians have agreed that the first half of the twentieth century was a period of prime importance in the history of the elderly. Graebner locates the central political and labour force changes in the United States in the 1930s and 1940s. Gratton found that, in the same period, there occurred 'a struggle over a new system of age relations' and that, by 1950, Boston 'had witnessed fully the transformation by which old age becomes a social rather than simply a familial or personal concern.'[15] In Canada the full recognition of a new 'social problem' involved both changing perceptions of the elderly and innovative programs and policies that struggled to give substance to those new perceptions in the face of a deeply entrenched ageism. That ageism, of course, did not end in 1951, but a powerful, fresh set of attitudes continued to develop. Newly entrenched programs and policies regarding old age interacted with the elderly in succeeding years to shape and reshape the character of aging.

Family and Demography

Attitudes towards aging in the first half of the twentieth century were complex, and they were not always compatible or consistent. Although only limited support and aid were formally provided, the elderly were increasingly regarded as a distinctive group, sharing a common set of characteristics and problems. It was a time of life that was, as Carol Haber has argued, increasingly seen in negative terms, a period when problems overwhelmed advantages, and when those problems tended to be viewed in medical terms.[16]

At the same time there was a romantic element to perceptions of old age, as though the elderly were particularly privileged, overcoming the forces of nature to live a long life. Euphemisms for aging were beginning to be adopted – witness the 1937 'Golden Mile Club' in Toronto. In October 1940, with the Second World War fully occupying the minds and energy of most Canadians, Ellen Carroll of North River, Newfoundland, turned 113 years of age. It was an occasion for great celebration. A reception was held at the local school, and radio stations VONF and VONH broadcast the proceedings. A number of government figures and religious dignitaries attended the reception, and messages of congratulations were sent by the king and queen, several politicians, and a number of churches. Mrs Carroll received 113 one-dollar bills from the Commission of Government, flowers, and a rocking chair, tokens of the community's respect for her reaching such a venerable age and reminders of the character of being old. For the community as a whole, indeed for all of Newfoundland, the event held a more than transitory importance, according to at least one observer, who claimed that the celebration had brought unity to divided groups, promising future harmony and a recovery of national status.[17] Such was the romantic vision of aging. The reality was much more varied.

Demographic patterns structured the reality of aging.[18] While the number of elderly increased throughout the nineteenth century as the Canadian population grew, the proportion of elderly changed only slowly (see figure 1.1). Waves of immigration played an important role in maintaining a relatively youthful national population. By 1931, however, the census revealed that the elderly were becoming a larger portion of Canadian society. Whereas persons aged sixty and over represented just under 8 per cent of the population in 1901, they constituted more than 11 per cent by 1951, and the size of the 50–59 age cohort promised increasing prominence of the elderly in the future. Throughout the first five decades of the twentieth century, the number of those aged 65–74 grew faster than the number aged seventy-five or more. The majority of the elderly population was male throughout the period; only among the relatively small cohorts aged eighty or more did females predominate numerically (see figure 1.2).

Several factors are important in explaining the increase in the proportion of elderly in the Canadian population. The birth rate was falling significantly, particularly in the more settled provinces. The general fertility rate for Canada slumped from 203 in 1851 to 145 in 1901, and then to 87 in 1941; completed family size declined from 4.1 children for parents born in 1871 to 2.9 children for parents born in 1911.[19] The net decline in fertility resulted in an increase in the elderly's share of the total population, but other factors partially offset this trend. The effect of significant levels of immigration was to increase disproportionately the number of young and middle-aged adults. At the same time, the life expectancy of Canadians was changing. Much the greatest decline in mortality rates occurred among infants, partially cushioning the impact of declining fertility. This reduction in infant and child mortality accounts for an important portion of the general rise in life expectancy for both sexes.

Adult life expectancy rose steadily across the time period. Both sexes experienced this change, though the gap between the two sexes slowly widened.

FIGURE 1.1 Canadian elderly population, 1871–1981*

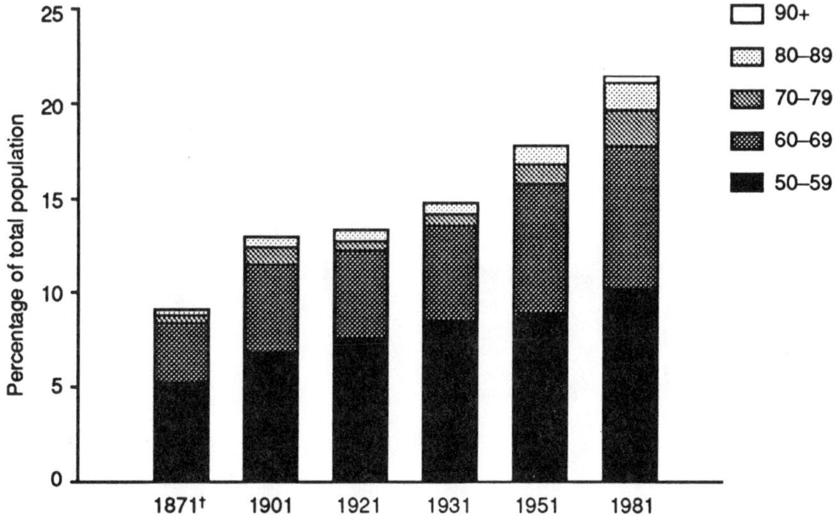

* Excluding Newfoundland and Labrador until 1951
† For 1871, the age categories were slightly different and somewhat ambiguous: 91+,
   81–91, 71–81, 61–71, 51–61.

Sources: *Census of Canada, 1871*, II, table 7; *Census of Canada, 1951*, I, table 19; *Census of Canada, 1981*, table 1

In 1931 young Canadian adults had a considerable life expectancy. A young male at the age of 20 could expect to live to the age of 66.54, while a young female of the same age could expect to live to 69.21. For older adults, the difference between the sexes remained. A woman at age 50 could expect to live to 74.14, 2.11 years longer than could a man at that age. For adult males, life expectancy had been rising consistently at least since Confederation; the average 20-year-old male in 1951 would live 8.77 years longer than his 1901 counterpart. For women, the comparable figure (9.41) emphasized the expanding gap between the sexes. Across the twentieth century, more people could expect to reach old age, and their experience of old age itself would be extended on average.[20]

The changing fertility rate affected the elderly in three other significant ways. First, as long as the birth rate remained high, children continued to be born to parents often in their forties. Active child-rearing continued well into later life, so that many elderly were not free of children living at

FIGURE 1.2 Elderly population by sex, 1871–1981*

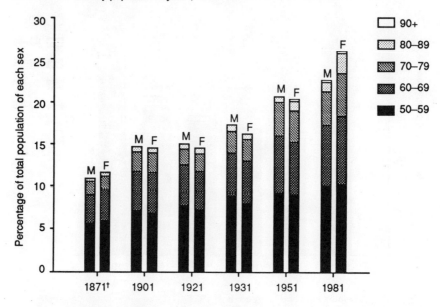

* Excluding Newfoundland and Labrador until 1951

† For 1871, the age categories were slightly different and somewhat ambiguous: 91+, 81–91, 71–81, 61–71, 51–61.

Sources: *Census of Canada, 1871*, II, table 7; *Census of Canada, 1951*, I, table 19; *Census of Canada, 1981*, I, table 1

home. David Gagan reported that in 1881 in Peel County, Ontario, for example, three-fifths of the fathers of the community were more than fifty-five years old before they ceased to be the parents of very young children. In each of the 1851, 1861, and 1871 census years, at least 35 per cent of the married women aged 65–69 had more than two older unmarried children still at home.[21] Later, with declining fertility, earlier marriage, and more concentrated child-bearing, children tended to be born earlier in the parents' lives and to have left the parental home before their parents reached old age.[22] Second, it was increasingly likely for an adult child to have a surviving parent. Last children were born earlier on the average, so the age gap between parent and child was smaller. With declining child mortality, that child was more likely to reach adulthood. However, once the parent reached old age, there were fewer siblings to share the burden of care. Third, as adult life expectancy rose, there was a lengthening duration to the parent-child relationship, what some scholars have called 'co-biography.' These characteristics were to become more pronounced in the years after 1951.[23]

The elderly were not evenly distributed across Canada (see figure 1.3). There were significantly higher ratios of elderly to the general population in the Atlantic provinces, those with perhaps the weakest financial resources to respond strongly to the needy elderly's wants. The outmigration of working-age people had skewed local demography. Indeed, when a government commission investigated the possibility of establishing an old age pension scheme for Nova Scotia workers in 1908, the commissioners recommended against such a program, not because it was a bad idea, but because it was already too late: the province by this time had the highest proportion of elderly in Canada, and the program would be too costly to implement.[24] Ontario, too, had a higher proportion of elderly than did the nation as a whole. The four western provinces, being the most recently settled, had a markedly lower proportion of elderly until the 1951 census. British Columbia stands out, however, as experiencing the greatest change in the percentage of elderly residents. Its rapidly aging population helps to explain the special public position of 'the elderly problem' in that province. Quebec, in contrast, witnessed the least change in the elderly percentage of its population, because the fertility rate in Quebec did not decline at the rate experienced in the other provinces. Thus, the timing of response to the various problems of the elderly might be expected to differ somewhat from province to province in relation to the number and proportion of the elderly population.

For the country as a whole, several characteristics of the elderly population can be determined. The elderly were most likely to live in rural areas. While younger rural people tended to move to urban communities seeking employment opportunities (leaving their parents in the rural districts), older urban people frequently migrated back to rural areas in retirement or semi-retirement; when older people in retirement left their farms, they often did not move far away, but simply to a nearby village. By the 1941 and 1951 census years this rural concentration had ended nationally for all but the oldest (post-80) cohorts.[25] This rural-urban difference in age distribution affected the two sexes differently. Men found greater job opportunities in rural areas, and women in urban areas, resulting in a skewed sexual distribution for all adult cohorts.

Rural-urban differences are reflected in the slight information available on the income level of the elderly in the first half of the twentieth century. A Nova Scotia royal commission on old age pensions in 1928–30 attempted to interview 100 per cent of the elderly in four counties and in the city of

FIGURE 1.3 Provincial distribution of the elderly, 1901–51

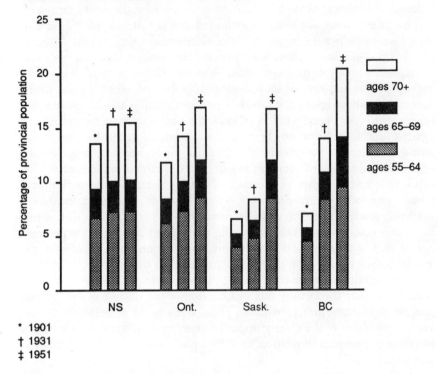

* 1901
† 1931
‡ 1951

Source: *Census of Canada, 1951* (Ottawa, 1953), X, table 9

Halifax. As a result, 4713 persons aged seventy or more were interviewed. When questioned about their income level, it became clear that conditions varied considerably among the various counties and between the city and the countryside (see figure 1.4). The rural counties of Hants, Richmond, and Shelburne compared quite unfavourably with the urban and industrial sectors of the province, as represented by the city of Halifax and by Cape Breton County, where the city of Sydney and the great steel plants of the area dominated. The commission reported 'many persons' in Cape Breton County receiving pensions from the British Empire Steel Company.[26]

In posing its questions to the elderly, the royal commission demonstrated the prevailing image of the elderly as poor. By asking about income, rather than total wealth, it ignored the assets accumulated across a lifetime, particularly if the assets produced no direct income. The data is based on

FIGURE 1.4 Annual income for Nova Scotia elderly, 1929*

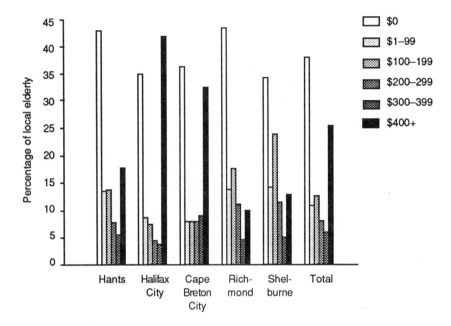

* Elderly aged seventy or more with a reported annual income of less than $400 (calcu-
lated by dividing a couple's total income evenly between the two spouses)

Source: *Report of the Commission Appointed to Consider Old Age Pensions* (Halifax,
1930), 6

self-reporting, despite an obvious advantage to underreporting, yet the report depicted the elderly as facing considerable financial problems. While
the percentage of the elderly with moderate income, or better, varied greatly
between Halifax/Cape Breton County and most rural areas, the percentage
with no income whatsoever varied little. In every jurisdiction surveyed by
the royal commission, a majority of the elderly had an annual income of
less than $200; the numbers with no income at all were quite alarming.
Given this level of poverty, it is striking just how many of these needy elderly were actually able to cope on their own. Of those with incomes between
$200 and $399, 80 per cent remained self-supporting, as did 62 per cent of
those with incomes between $100 and $199. This independence suggests
just how important such assets as land and houses were to the economic
survival of the elderly. Below $100, aid from others was essential for most,

though 22 per cent of those with incomes between $1 and $99 reported no support from other sources.

Where support was forthcoming, children were the principal source for all income groups. In 71 per cent of the cases where the elderly relied on partial or full support, children were the major source. Relatives were the major source in 13 per cent, and friends (presumably including neighbours) in 8 per cent of the cases. Organized charity, both public and private, stepped in as the major source of support for the remaining 8 per cent.[27] There is no indication as to how representative this was of the elderly poor across the country.

Among all forms of family support, marriage was the most important source of assistance. Marital status played a strikingly constant role among the elderly. In the years for which aggregate data are available, approximately 75 per cent of the female elderly aged 50–59 and 60 per cent of those aged 60-69 were married. By ages 70-79, however, death of the husband had made widowhood a more common phenomenon; while approximately 37 per cent were still married, slightly over 50 per cent were widowed. For women aged 80-89 and 90 or over, widowhood was even more common, being the status of 73 and 83 per cent, respectively. As might be expected given the lower life expectancy for men and the older age of husbands in most couples, marriage was even more common for older men, and widowhood correspondingly less frequent.[28] Marriage was a prevalent and vital source of support for the elderly of both sexes throughout the period under study, though this support was significantly more available to older men than to older women.

Most of the elderly had living children. Though the aggregate census reports do not provide such information, the Nova Scotia royal commission on old age pensions reported the number and general proximity of the children in 1928–30 for the elderly poor in that province (see table 1.1). Three-quarters of those interviewed had living children. It is striking that those children with just one or no siblings were much more likely still to be residing in Nova Scotia than were the children of larger families. While inheritance prospects and family property would have been important in persuading many adult children to remain near their parents, so too may have been a sense of obligation to assist their parents.[29] Whatever the motivation, a significant majority of the elderly Nova Scotia poor had children residing in the same small province, and thus available for potential assistance and support, despite the considerable out-migration experienced over many decades. At the same time, a full quarter of the elderly interviewed had no surviving children and thus lacked a vital source of assistance.

TABLE 1.1 Number and location of children of Nova Scotia elderly, 1929*

	Total number of children per family						
	0	1	2	3	4	5	6+
No. of families	na	313	346	320	306	184	319
No. of elderly interviewed	700	350	400	373	352	218	374
No. of children in NS	na	271	536	666	850	598	1,467
No. of children elsewhere in Canada	na	9	23	45	77	48	101
No. of children in U.S.	na	33	133	247	290	271	696
No. of children elsewhere	na	0	0	2	7	3	6
Total no. of children	0	313	692	960	1,224	920	2,270

* Elderly aged seventy or more with a reported income of less than $400 (calculated by dividing a couple's total income evenly between the two spouses).
Source: *Report of the Commission Appointed to Consider Old Age Pensions* (Halifax, 1930), 9–11

Indeed, among the elements of reality missing from the recorded celebration of Ellen Carroll's birthday in 1940, none matched the significance of family in the lives of the elderly. In the first half of the twentieth century, family remained a primary resource of the elderly, as it had for centuries past. Marriage partners were the most important familial resource, but spouses were usually aging together, and their physical and economic ability to assist each other was slowly (and sometimes not so slowly) declining. Adult children, in contrast, represented a potent source of aid. Adult children tended to be near the peak of their earning capacity and could help their parents physically. Adult grandchildren, too, participated in the familial assistance of the elderly, often in quite significant ways. Those elderly without children or grandchildren turned to siblings and their children and, though the claims on familial resources were less authoritative in these instances, many elderly gained substantial and sometimes long-term help from nieces or nephews. The elderly enjoyed the benefits of a pervasive familial culture that prescribed to family members a mutual responsibility for one another.

In the early twentieth century, elderly Canadians employed familial resources as a vital element in their survival strategies. Family members could share housing owned by the elderly in return for labour or income; more than one generation could exploit the productive capacity of the elderly's property while contributing labour and skills that reflected age, gender, and physical ability. When they lacked sufficient property, the elderly could join a family member's household, contributing emotional support, casual labour, and domestic and nurturing skills. If and when the elderly reached the point where ill-health reduced them to nearly complete dependence, most could still rely on the generosity of family to take them into care for their remaining years. Family members sacrificed for one another and supported each other emotionally, economically, and physically, and this care was vital to the elderly as they coped with the problems of survival.

This reliance of the elderly on their children, grandchildren, and other relatives was particularly well developed among primary producers and the working class. Farming/fishing and working-class children assisted, aided, and interacted socially with their elderly parents more often than middle-class children. The stronger intergenerational emotional attachments in farming and working-class families arose from 'long-standing patterns of concrete material interdependencies between the generations.' Proximity was a vital factor in intergenerational sociability and material aid, and both adult generations in primary-producing families and working-class families tended to live close to each other. The 'accumulated trust of a lengthy history of mutual assistance' was fundamental to the interaction among the elderly and their families in these classes.[30] For them, family had long been a vital and often the most reliable source of support across the life-course.

The records used here do not permit any conclusions about the typicality of different forms of family support or of the social characteristics of the participants.[31] The forms employed depended on the health and on the economic and familial circumstances of both of the primary generations involved. Anecdotal evidence suggests that both elderly males and elderly females used their accommodation to assist their adult children; both female and male children, married and unmarried, expended considerable resources caring for aging parents, sometimes moving 'back home' and other times taking the parent into the adult child's home. Family members often deliberately lived close to elderly relatives so as to be readily available to them, and at other times the elderly moved near a settled child.[32] Some families compensated for distance by having one or more members move in with the elderly relative, occasionally or regularly depending on circumstances. Mutual support and care were the constant ends of such behaviour.

For several centuries, the majority of the elderly had relied on the extended family and other household arrangements for shelter. No general examination of the Canadian elderly has yet been undertaken in this regard,[33] but the patterns in comparable societies are clear.[34] In the turn-of-the-century United States, only a small proportion of the elderly aged sixty-five or more lived alone or with only their spouse – 29 per cent of married elderly and just 11 per cent of unmarried elderly – in contrast to the large majorities living in such circumstances in the 1980s. In 1900 the majority of the elderly lived with one of their children. Other relatives, such as siblings or their children, were a significant source of shelter: 7 per cent of the married elderly and 13 per cent of the unmarried elderly lived with such kin. Almost as many elderly in 1900 resided in non-kin households, such as boarding houses. Elderly of the middle class were more likely than those of the working class to live with adult children, but whether this was because of a different family culture or because of wealth is unclear. In short, most elderly lived with others, usually with family members. What is more, this pattern had not changed greatly over the later decades of the nineteenth century.[35]

Considerable reliance on co-residence with children or other kin did not, however, affect the formal status of the elderly as much as might be expected. Where married and particularly unmarried children were present in the household, the elderly tended to remain head of their household or the spouse of the head, though the loss of headship status tended to rise with age. This strong tendency to maintain headship of a household was not a product of adult children's obligation to maintain their parents in an independent household, but rather resulted from the strength of the elderly's own position. Given the general tendency for homeownership to rise consistently with age, much of this co-residence is likely to have taken place in residences owned by the elderly. It was the death of one's spouse, particularly for elderly women, that most affected household status.[36]

Several characteristics dominate the anecdotal evidence of the familial culture that enveloped the lives of most elderly in the early twentieth century. First, reciprocity was a dominant feature of much of this familial interaction. The elderly did not simply accept help, but exchanged support for their own contributions. Frequently the elderly offered the performance of significant reproductive and productive labour, such as childcare, housekeeping, or gardening, often making their own home the site of the family economy. Serial reciprocity was common. One woman recalled, for example, that her husband's parents had agreed to care for an elderly aunt and uncle who themselves had raised her husband's father; her parents-in-law 'were asked to move to their Uncle's farm and a large home and for a number of years looked after them. This Uncle and Aunt, later, moved to town, but my husband's Mother was still expected to stay with them weeks at a time, even though she had family of her own at home, who needed her.'[37] Reciprocity could move in both directions between two generations, across an entire lifespan, or could involve future compensation by a succeeding generation.

As this account makes clear, family care for the elderly often entailed significant sacrifice by family members. Some sons remained at home or moved back to look after parents; others built or purchased new homes that were sufficiently large to allow their parents to move in with them. More often, however, the daily sacrifices were made by adult women and their children. When elderly parents moved into a married child's home, it was the wife's job to care for them and to expand her own reproductive work to include them, whether she was their daughter or daughter-in-law. When parents became bedridden or incapable of coping with stairs, a major room in the house – most often the downstairs parlour – was turned over to them and the burden of care fell almost totally on the wife, occasionally relieved by neighbours, other relatives, or grandchildren. The physical and emotional strain of this arrangement is suggested by some persons' recollections that their mothers, having cared for their ill parents-in-law for many years, promised in the 1940s never to live with their own children.[38] Children, who were often called upon to give up a bedroom when a grandparent moved in, also lost some opportunities for boisterousness and self-expression.

A common family strategy for coping with a dependent elderly relative was to share the burden of support among several family members. In the case of one old Ontario couple in 1910, their adult children (three sons and three daughters) agreed that the parents would live with a married daughter in London, while the others would contribute $0.50 a week each to help with the costs; after a time, however, the contributions ceased, and the married daughter was left to shoulder the burden herself.[39] For many families, support in kind rather than in cash was easier to provide. Thus, the elderly person would rotate among the homes of family members willing and able to take her in. This was a method of care used most frequently when there was just one surviving parent. On a semi-regular basis, the parent would move from one child's home to the next, so that all shared in the burdens and benefits of the parent's care. This was easiest when the adult children were settled and lived in reasonable proximity, but examples were found of children as far apart as Toronto and New Jersey, and Winnipeg and Toronto, taking part in such exchanges.

This form of care required considerable cooperation among the adult children, and could be quite taxing on the elderly. In some instances this procedure would be agreed upon among all concerned, and the rotation would be on a reasonably regular basis. An eighty-one-year-old retired farmer described one such arrangement in the 1920s: 'I have received my board and lodging from my [married] son and [married] daughter, with whom I have lived as a member of their respective families during the past few years; I pay them nothing and they treat me as a member of their respective families.'[40] Such a bald description masks the emotional and physical demands that such care made on all concerned.

At other times the rotation would be irregular and would vary with the needs and characteristics of the elderly parent and the host families. An old woman had lived with one married daughter in Montana for ten years, beginning in the late 1890s, before moving on to another married daughter in London, Ontario. After five years the daughter was no longer able or willing (it is unclear which) to continue to look after her now ninety-two-year-old mother. After a stay in hospital, the old woman moved in with a younger friend, and then sought city support to enter a nursing home. The Montana daughter was angry with her sister for sending 'her *own mother*' to a home, but was quite unwilling to take her mother back: 'My God isent it awful to *think* a Daughter would try to do such a thing with her own mother. She evidently *cant* be Human I know she [the mother] is awful hard to get along with ... my Husband is getting up in years & he says he will *absolutely* not have her back hear again ... so what am I to do.'[41] Her own part in this apparent violation of familial obligations weighed on the daughter's mind.

The elderly could also move among other relatives, particularly siblings and their children. A seventy-year-old unmarried woman, for example, had lived with her unmarried brother in Petrolia, Ontario, keeping house for him; she had no assets or income of her own, except for some furniture. When her brother took ill and lost his job, she moved in with her widowed sister.[42] The chairman of the Manitoba OAP board described a somewhat less attractive, more irregular alternative: 'impecunious old folks ... who have been battered from pillar to post and [were] eking out a subsistence living in one Province with a nephew, and in another with a daughter and again elsewhere, with a son, each relative apparently putting up with the old people as long as possible and then purchasing train fare to the next point of call.'[43] In any such scenario, the vulnerability and relative impotence of the elderly is striking.

Still, there were a number of positive elements to this familial culture of support. The elderly often made important contributions to the life of their children's families. Many grandchildren remembered the stays of their grandparents with great affection. Resident grandmothers and grandfathers frequently played significant supplementary roles as nurturers, reading or telling stories to the children, playing quiet games with them, taking them on outings for which the parents did not have time, and imparting behavioural and spiritual lessons. When the elderly lived on their own, they often hosted family dinners on such increasingly central family occasions as Christmas. Short visits to the homes of their children could be times for the renewal of old emotional ties with their children and the creation of new ties with young grandchildren. Other contributions were much more substantial. While still well, elderly parents offered a safe haven for children or grandchildren in distress. Many elderly parents aided their children financially in various ways – turning over the farm or business to them, helping them buy their own home, or offering reproductive work to a widowed son or daughter or an unmarried child, allowing them to maintain full-time paid work. Such help could be crucial to the maintenance of the family, and shaped the lives of the elderly as well.

The recollections of one woman years later help to capture some of the climate of intergenerational support in the early twentieth century. In the 1920s her maternal grandfather, a gardener, was permanently injured at work in Pennsylvania and was forced to return to his family in Guelph, Ontario, for care. He moved in with his married daughter:

Grandfather was always a 'working member' of the family for he never let his disability stand in his way. He brought his gardening skills to brighten our gardens and he worked every summer in the one 'lot' we had on Woolwich St. In the winter he cleared the snow and kept the furnace fired up for our comfort. He had a healthy appetite. I can remember my father saying it was a pleasure to heap his plate at dinnertime.

If Mother were ever out when we returned from school, Grandfather was there to look after us and he was usually the one to read to us the stories of Uncle Wriggley and Raggedy Ann & Andy. At Christmas he would take us to find and cut down a tree, make wreaths and help us decorate the home for the season.

Another daughter and a son lived in the same locale, and the two sisters shared in the care of their father in his final days.44

But it is important not to romanticize these close intergenerational relations. The elderly gained support, and often respect, affection, and a positive role for themselves. But much of this support entailed dependence. While children certainly came to depend on elderly parents for some forms of assistance, the flow of aid and resources was disproportionately towards the needy elderly. This placed many elderly in an even more dependent position and made them vulnerable to their family. In the above quotation, for example, the father's comment about the grandfather's large appetite could be heard either positively or negatively – as expressing genuine pleasure in sharing or as a reminder not to become too great a drain on the family's resources. Moving in with an adult child entailed a loss of freedom for the elderly parent. But there was a loss of freedom for the hosts as well, particularly the housewife involved. When one remembers the considerable extra work involved in such situations as well as their uncomfortable character, it is not surprising that tension and conflict could result.

There could be considerable regret among the elderly that they had to impose the burden of co-residence and care on their adult children. One seventy-four-year-old widower rotated among his three sons and one daughter; when asked in 1932 what result this support and the absence of any earlier OAP application had had on his children, he replied: 'hardship on them.'[45] Care for elderly parents entailed considerable labour and personal sacrifice; it brought into the household dependent persons who could not help but feel (and resent) their position of weakness and who were often more than willing to offer advice on childcare or domestic work. There was the potential for much unhappiness in such situations.

These problems, and indeed aging in general, had a gendered character. There were slightly more old men than old women, but women predominated increasingly among the very old – those who tended to be most in need of assistance. There was a tendency for older women to reside in urban centres, accounting for their disproportionate numbers in urban old age homes. Elderly women were much more likely to become widowed, the death of their spouse exacerbating the problems of poverty, isolation, and dependence. Although both sexes relied on family for assistance, their position within the extended family likely varied considerably. Older men often retained control of property, giving themselves continuing power, but they lacked the range of skills to contribute to family members taking them in; those men without property were particularly vulnerable.

It is as yet unclear to what extent older women continued to be left propertyless when widowed, and when these women gained the greater protection inherent in being joint owners of the marital home and in being the primary beneficiary in their husbands' wills. It seems likely that most older women lacked the power and benefits derived from property, particularly in the early decades of the twentieth century, and were more likely to be economically dependent. They did, however, have a considerable range of domestic skills to offer the household that took them in, although those skills could be as much a source of competitive friction as assistance. Older women tended to have even less access to paid labour than older men, increasing their vulnerability. For both sexes, changes in the structures of work and retirement exacerbated their vulnerability.

Work and Retirement

The social organization of work had long played an important role in the construction of old age. A fundamental change began to take place in general employment patterns and behaviour, directly affecting the organization of the work of the elderly. Here was perhaps the greatest and most significant change for the elderly in the early twentieth century – the best example of processes undermining existing traditions regarding old age. In the late nineteenth century people entered old age gradually, without abandoning the normal duties of adult life. By the mid-twentieth century this was less true. Early in the century, employment patterns for the elderly were already altering for both sexes in two important ways: a slowly growing tendency towards modern retirement,[46] whether mandatory or not, from the labour force, and a more rapid and continuing deskilling or ghettoization of the paid work associated with the elderly.

Stepping down from productive work was not a new phenomenon in the twentieth century, but its characteristics certainly changed. In the past, persons had coped with the effect of aging on their capacity to work in a variety of ways. The middle class gradually slowed their work pace and hours, and shifted their assets into income-producing revenue, controlling the timing and rate of these changes themselves.[47] The rural elderly followed a similar pattern, slowly handing over tasks and ownership to adult children who were expected to maintain their parents throughout old age. Where children were unavailable, many elderly farmers rented their fields or their entire farm, living off the income. Workers used borrowing and saving to smooth consumption over the life-cycle as the earning capacity of the family changed. Skilled or semi-skilled workers often shifted or were shifted into less onerous jobs as their skills were made redundant by new production processes and as their own physical abilities no longer enabled them to perform various elements of their original tasks. Studies of the late nineteenth-century workplace reveal that on the shop floor the pace of work and the allocation of tasks accommodated the abilities of older workers on a continuing basis.[48] This was particularly apparent in the paternalistic environment of many small factories and shops in the period. In short, the economic character of old age before the twentieth century was multifaceted, combining a tendency to greater and more intense exploitation of personal resources and assets along with supplementary paid labour, usually at unskilled and part-time work.

However, several developments in the late nineteenth and early twentieth century did not augur well for the elderly paid worker. The increasing size of many businesses and industries created an employment environment in which the individual needs of workers, including older workers, were much less easily accommodated. The complexity of the workplace, the number of workers, and new principles of management tended to produce a work environment that was less able and less interested in dealing with the needs of individual workers simply because they were older or had worked there for a long time. Most famous of these new management principles was the efficiency dogma of Frederick Taylor, known as Taylorism. The popular studies of Taylor and his disciples persuaded management in particular that effective and productive work depended most importantly on physical efficiency and on the rapid repetition of simple tasks; by emphasizing mere physical ability and by de-emphasizing skills and knowledge, Taylorism attacked the primary weakness of older workers and undermined their greatest assets. The result was a growing desire on the part of management to ease older workers out of the workplace.

By the early twentieth century, older workers found themselves in a changing environment. Observers were less likely to recognize the skills and abilities that the elderly offered, and the idea of a specific age of retirement became more and more authoritative. In the early years of the century there was no consensus as to what that age should be. It was a Canadian, Sir William Osler, who in 1905 issued one of the most famous and most extravagant pronouncements applying many of the central tenets of the new medical perceptions of aging to the workplace and sanctioning the removal of the elderly from an active role in the economy and the society. While age forty marked the beginning of an individual's 'comparative uselessness,' Osler informed his audience, that uselessness was fully established by the age of sixty. It would be of 'incalculable benefit' to society 'if, as a matter of course, men stopped work at this age.'49 Such attitudes particularly shaped public expectations regarding the elderly. A provincial government memo in 1929 painted a very uninviting picture of old age:

When men and women are approaching the age of 70 the transition from independence to dependence is inevitable for a substantial percentage of our population. Through ill advised investment they find their property gone, friends have passed away or removed, relatives are few, sons and daughters are scattered or are busily engaged in rearing their own families. With ambition collapsed the remaining few years of life are far from encouraging to contemplate. With loss of health and hope many faithful workers are swept into the unemployment and inevitable dependence on public assistance. The demand for younger and more active workers for modern industrial pursuits renders it increasingly difficult for aged people to secure work even at a low wage. Being trained for occupations which no longer exist coupled with waning adaptability they are victims of circumstances largely beyond their control.[50]

Yet despite such negative attitudes and the development of discriminatory processes in the workplace, the evidence suggests that the average elderly continued to work and that their economic condition was better than that of younger cohorts.

There is ample evidence that turn-of-the-century industrialization had no sudden impact on employment of the aged. In the United States, 94 per cent of men aged 55–64 and 79 per cent aged 65–74 were employed in 1900; for those aged seventy-five or over, 55 per cent were in paid employment. A similar pattern, though at a much lower level, is apparent for women.[51] While such figures mask other important changes in the character of employment, they reveal the continuing ability of most elderly to find paid work. At the turn of the century, most of the elderly maintained themselves through labour force participation, and there was no dramatic, age-specific point at which one became 'too old to work.' In the absence of private pension plans for almost all workers, those older workers who had been unable to accumulate significant savings during their working lives were forced to continue to work as a matter of survival.

Income alone remained at a significant level, at least for men. In an examination of the reported income of the urban elderly in 1901 Ontario, Edgar-André Montigny found that, while the income covered a wide range, the average for the three communities studied varied little. The average reported income for male elderly in the cities of Brockville, Kingston, and St Catharines in 1901 was between $389 and $404.[52] When household income and accumulated savings and assets are added, the majority of the elderly did not experience the negative impact of industrialization as described by concerned social reformers.

The first detailed study of elderly and retiring workers in a major Canadian business demonstrated that the new economic and attitudinal forces had a limited and gradual impact. Workers at the Canadian Pacific Railway shops enjoyed the potential protection of a company pension plan beginning in 1903. At first a non-contributory plan awarded at the discretion of the company to workers with a minimum of ten years' service, and who had begun working for the company before the age of forty, the pension program paid benefits to only half the company's workers with at least twenty years' service. By the 1920s, coverage had risen to two-thirds of the same group, and then to three-quarters by the late 1930s. When the plan converted to a contributory basis and a higher level of benefits in 1937, more than 90 per cent of workers joined the program, membership thereafter being involuntary. Employment patterns demonstrated no discernible discrimination towards older workers, despite a dramatic aging of the company workforce; the CPR continued to hire considerable numbers of workers aged forty years or older. If the primary intent of the pension plan was management's desire to influence worker behaviour, the company did not employ the program with great effectiveness. Only in the 1930s did the age of leaving the company by older workers begin to cluster around the mid-sixties, with a marked reduction in departures by men in their fifties. It was not until the 1940s that the modern pattern of retirement emerged: about half of all departures were by workers in their mid-sixties; most workers left because they retired; and most who retired had a company pension.[53]

Nevertheless, the negative factors in the workplace were real, and labour leaders and social workers in particular drew attention to those factors. In doing so, such spokespersons assumed a paternalistic role on behalf of all elderly workers, rather than the minority actually suffering from these factors. The problem was that paid work for some older persons did become more difficult to find as the stigma associated with the quality of older workers became more authoritative. Where work was available it tended to be lower paid and was often sporadic, as older workers tended to become marginalized. Some older men found themselves limited to unskilled work as casual day labourers or as janitors, a common job ghetto for the elderly; older women had even fewer opportunities for paid work, finding some jobs as domestics of various sorts. But contemporary observers sympathetically exaggerated the problems. In 1912 the Trades and Labour Council of Sydney, Nova Scotia, complained that workers were assigned 'to the "scrap pile" at the first sign of age.' Quebec's chief factory inspector emphasized both the age discrimination and the physical vulnerability of older workers: 'In our cement mills, match factories, white paint mills, you look in vain for people sixty-five years of age. They are cut off before that age. Time and disease have done away with the necessity of pensioning them.'[54] Such comments exaggerated the negative impact of industrialization on the elderly in general and helped to entrench an image of the elderly as economically vulnerable and dependent.

A minority of elderly suffered economically (not that this was unique to industrialization), as the individual stories of elderly persons desperately seeking work in the period confirm.[55] Some elderly complained of systemic discrimination that denied employment to the aged, though the age varied at which the discrimination was most acutely felt. An old man in Kitchener, Ontario, protested in 1929 that people more than seventy years of age 'are not wanted to work any more. every person wants young people these days to work for them.' In the same year a seventy-year-old Toronto housepainter commented: 'I am active & willing to work, but am turned down & told I am to old. I have no private income & find it very hard to live on the little I make with living [costs] so high.'[56]

When a seventy-three-year-old man wrote from Vancouver in 1925 asking the provincial government to help him find light employment, the government responded by instructing him how to obtain welfare from the city. While insisting that it was employment that primarily interested him, the old man also indicated that he had accepted the limitations placed on his employment opportunities:

I do not ask for charity. I think I made it clear in my former letter that I am willing to work, provided I am given employment which I am capable of performing. Would it not be possible to give me a position as Assistant Janitor or watchman at one of the public buildings in Vancouver or at the University of Point Grey? Surely there must be some work which an old man like myself can do when he is willing to earn his daily bread![57]

The old man's acceptance of the elderly's marginalized position is as striking as his desire to work. However much some found such ambition to work admirable, the plain fact was that in the absence of public and private pension plans, continuing employment was essential to survival, and certainly preferable to the meagre provisions of local relief.

Where work was available, the traditional paternalism of the employer was considered less justified. An OAP application in northern Ontario received unanimous approval in 1930, as the local board explained: 'This man was merely kept on working for the Corporation [of Timmins] for charity sake as he did not really earn that amount of money [$420] and had they not employed him they would have had to support him.'[58] In the emerging values of the period, the more formal state support through the OAP was considered more appropriate. In the days before a public pension program, work available to the elderly was all too often a matter restricted to a limited spectrum of jobs and the 'generosity' of those controlling the employment. The president of the British Columbia Conservative Association in Victoria wrote to the provincial premier on behalf of an elderly party supporter who was unable to find work 'on account of his age.' Surely the incumbent 'chinaman' in a short-term job at the Jubilee Hospital could be fired and the old man given the job in his place.[59] Various types of discrimination – both ageist and racist – used employment practices to sustain their ends.

The less formal employment of older women was somewhat less vulnerable to market influences. Some older women rented parts of their houses or took in boarders; others did sewing and mending or took in washing. Unmarried older women sometimes were able to gain food and shelter by becoming housekeepers for a brother or some other male relative who lacked domestic skills. A single woman in her mid-seventies lived with her unmarried, older brother on a rented farm; he was now an invalid, cared for by her. 'I have been raising a few chickens and taking in washing, doing a little knitting etc,' but aging was taking its impact: 'I find my strength is failing me and if I am entitled to the [OA] pension I will be more than glad.' Instead, as this example suggests, older women's work was more directly affected by the physical constraints of aging.[60]

But the relative absence of formal market forces did not protect older women from serious economic problems. Census reports suggest, for example, that women were more vulnerable to less substantial but no less powerful social forces than were men. In 1941 a striking 30 per cent of older, unemployed women reported that they no longer had an occupation, compared with less than 1 per cent of older, unemployed men. Older women workers were persuaded that they no longer had a claim on employment, while older men were not prepared to concede this about themselves. The age bias began earlier for women workers than for men.[61] Both sexes experienced the same structural forces in aging, but gender constantly shaped the impact of those forces.

Once retirement became a 'popular' and customary solution to aging, most men appear to have retired around the age of seventy, but there was certainly flexibility to meet individual circumstances. By the 1930s, if not earlier, the age of sixty-five was projected as the appropriate retirement age for men, while the age of sixty was often agreed upon for women. Workers with long-term employment with one employer could expect some form of compensation at retirement – usually a bonus, but in some occupations a regular pension payment. The setting of the amount of payment was usually entirely in the hands of the employer, and it could be altered at any time. This happened to an eighty-nine-year-old widower, who had worked for forty years for the city of Collingwood; at retirement he was granted a pension of $10 weekly, but in 1929 this amount was arbitrarily cut in half.[62]

What is most important about this authoritative belief in retirement was that there were few formal mechanisms of financial support for those retiring. Company pension plans were uncommon and were only slowly being adopted by various businesses from the 1920s on. The early plans tended to be non-contributory and discretionary, one more instrument in the hands of management in seeking to create and maintain the sort of workforce needed.[63] These early pension schemes also contained no spousal benefits, underlining widows' vulnerability. Personal pension plans were overwhelmingly within the financial capacity of only some segments of the middle class, as the early history of the government annuity plan revealed. Cooperative schemes, such as the occupation-based friendly societies and mutual aid societies of the late nineteenth century, were entirely incapable of meeting the massive demands created by the changing work environment and employment patterns. State pension plans were slow in coming, particularly in North America. The result was that those retiring usually did so only involuntarily, since they tended to lack sufficient alternative sources of support.

For the entire workforce, private pension plans covered few workers, and most retiring individuals fell back on their own assets. Studies of the savings capacity of American workers in the late nineteenth and early twentieth centuries indicate quite clearly that most workers and their spouses built up assets that helped to sustain them in old age. Much of their savings could be found in home ownership, a vital resource in old age; not only was their own home important for shelter, but it could produce both income (through rental of rooms or as a site for cottage industry) and food (from small gardens or facilities for such animals as hens). In Canada, at least, much of this housing stock was substandard, particularly in rural areas.[64] Other savings were vested in the education and training of the workers' children, who later contributed portions of their labour and/or their earnings as long as they continued to live at home. Although workers' individual earnings tended to peak in their thirties, the household income continued to rise as adult children became significant members of the family economy. In the 1930s and 1940s many elderly testified to the centrality of their children's financial contributions to the acquisition of the parents' home and the paying off of the mortgage. Direct savings too were possible, as many elderly benefited from industrialization.[65]

Although many elderly succeeded in accumulating savings, not all did. Nor was the amount saved necessarily sufficient to meet the needs of individual elderly. Many elderly had to rely on family. But many families, particularly among the lower strata of the working class, had fewer resources to share than in the past. Urbanization and the restriction of private urban food production, of the sort so important to sustaining families in the nine-teenth century,[66] made it more difficult for some adult children to offer sub-stantial support to their parents and elderly relatives. At the same time, the sense of familial obligation to older people may well have altered (though not necessarily diminished) with population mobility, suburban nuclearity, and stronger assumptions about the state's responsibility for the elderly.

One of the Canadian state's earliest responses to the dilemma of the im-pact on the elderly of the changing character of work was to implement a self-help program. Based on contemporary views of the lack of foresight among most workers and on the belief that most workers had excess in-come that could be diverted to provide security many years later in old age, the federal government established an annuities scheme in 1908.[67] Any Canadian resident could purchase an immediate or a deferred annuity, to a maximum of $600, to begin payment when the annuitant reached a prede-termined age. As a matter of convenience, payments could be made through local post offices. Though it was hoped that workers would protect them-selves against privation in old age, the scheme was for several decades a major disappointment. Workers often had little excess income, and, when they did, diverting it to distant returns was not necessarily the most rational use of that income.

Instead, the government annuities scheme aided two social groups to a limited extent. First, some older people at the point of retirement used their savings in a lump sum to purchase a lifetime annuity. Second, younger persons, almost always middle class, purchased one or more deferred plans to ensure a steady income in old age; purchases through lump sums and through regular periodic payments were both common. Over the first two decades of the scheme to 1927, an average of considerably fewer than five hundred annuity contracts were signed each year; almost 50 per cent of these were by residents of Ontario. During the 1930s the number of con-tracts rose consistently and greatly.[68] The payments for many of these contracts lapsed when the annuitant ran out of excess income. As a scheme to encourage provident savings among individual workers, the government annuities program was a failure. For the middle class, however, it was of some importance, particularly after the maximum total in annuities for each individual was raised to $1000 in 1913 and to $5000 in 1920, before being lowered to $1200 in 1930. By the 1920s and 1930s the rates being charged were out of date with actuarial projections and had become somewhat of a bargain, so that middle-class annuitants found it worthwhile to take out the maximum in government annuities before turning to private annuity programs for any additional coverage. Lacking private pension plans to protect themselves in old age, a small number of individuals – teachers, clergymen, farmers, physicians, civil servants, merchants – purchased government annuities.[69] Though this sort of protection against old age was important for those who could afford the immediate costs, the government annuities program failed to meet its aim of providing an alternative to paid work for older workers and their dependants.

What is more, the program failure and the increasingly unstable and declining income of the elderly poor were exacerbated by the rising cost of living. The cost of living was relatively low in the years before the First World War, peaked in 1920, and remained high throughout the 1920s, fuelled particularly by food and clothing prices. Throughout the 1920s, the price index was at least double what it had been in 1900. In the mid-1930s the cost of living slipped, before rising again during the Second World War. At the end of the war the cost of living jumped dramatically, reaching its highest point in the entire half century; again, the price of food and clothing rose higher than prices in other categories. At the same time, the standard of living aspired to by most Canadians rose; consumer expenditures (calculated in constant dollars) almost doubled across the half century, rising constantly except for a period of non-growth in the 1910s and a decline during the 1930s. Over the half century, Canadians tended to spend a lower proportion of their income on food and clothing and a relatively steady proportion on shelter and household operation; greater shares of income were devoted to transportation, to tobacco and alcohol, and to personal and medical care.[70] For the needy elderly, with shrinking employment opportunities and declining income, the high and rising cost of living and their own expectations of consumption made life potentially very difficult, despite their relative security regarding housing.

By 1951, significant changes in the work patterns of the elderly were well under way. Private pension plans covered many more workers through their employers, and the idea of mandatory retirement at the age of sixty-five had gained a great deal of authority. Elderly workers, particularly women, had little or no leverage in the labour force. Their cause had been abandoned by organized labour, which fully supported – indeed promoted – the idea of mandatory retirement. Most of society now depicted the elderly as casual labourers, working at 'light jobs' suited to their reduced physical capacities for 'pocket money' to supplement their income from various pension programs. It was thus acceptable to shift elderly workers to such job ghettos as janitors, security guards, or housekeeping and to pay them at minimal levels. The proportion of each elderly age cohort in the paid work force declined between 1941 and 1951. While age sixty-five was already of considerable importance, particularly for men, in determining the timing of retirement, age seventy was much more powerful. Women's description of their status is quite distinct. By 1951 a far higher proportion of women adopted the label 'retired' than had previously registered as working.[71] This suggests a new-found status associated with retirement. Women, who had been occasional workers over their adult lives and who might well have listed themselves as 'keeping house' in an earlier census, now adopted the label of retired, even though they likely continued to keep house. Retirement had achieved a new and honourable status among the elderly, as had old age itself (see chapter 7).

Judging by the evidence available for 1951, income distribution was predictably skewed, again particularly for elderly women. While elderly male workers at the age of sixty-five began to make up a disproportionate share of the lower income brackets, men's wage levels were only a pale reflection of the discrimination evidenced in elderly women's wage levels. By the age of seventy, women who found it necessary to work were paid at very low rates, as employers could presumably now rely on such support mechanisms as the Old Age Pension to supplement the wages paid. Elderly women were almost twice as likely as elderly men to consider themselves workers unable to find remunerative work. For men, there was a greater divide between ages 60–64 and 65–69 than there was for women. While there was increasing agreement that men ought to stop work at age sixty-five, there was some uncertainty as to just what the retirement age for women should be – sixty, or sixty-five, or something else.[72]

In short, much was changing in the lives of the elderly in the first half of the twentieth century. Understanding the demographic parameters and the workforce experience of those lives is the first essential step in examining those changes. Structural processes accompanied attitudinal forces at every step of the way. At times one mitigated the effect of the other, but more often the two reinforced one another, as the elderly came to share distinct demographic patterns that were both a product of and grounds for the new perceptions of the elderly. For women, old age was different in part than for men, though much was also the same. There is also evidence that ethnicity, social class, and geographical location played a significant role in determining the character of old age. Through it all, society at large and the state struggled to respond to some of the demands and issues raised with the growing awareness of the elderly as a new 'social problem.'

2

Institutionalizing the Dependent Elderly: The First Old Age Homes

The vast majority of Canadian elderly maintained themselves through private, informal means. They often lived in their own homes, supporting themselves by working part-time and by slowly expending a lifetime's accumulated assets. One of the assets on which they relied particularly was family support. Parents had used family assets to train, educate, and maintain their children, and that investment could now be called on for assistance when the elderly were in need. Elderly parents could rely on adult children for physical and financial support when necessary, even to the extent of claiming full-time shelter and sustenance from them. Most adult children readily accepted the obligation to assist or care for elderly parents when they were in need. For the elderly, family was the most important resource available.

But there was a small proportion of the Canadian elderly that lacked adequate personal and familial resources to sustain them through old age. Among the elderly it was this group that first attracted significant public attention, particularly at the end of the nineteenth century with public revelations by social investigators such as Charles Booth and Seebohm Rowntree in England. The elderly dependent poor, scrounging for survival in the industrializing cities and roaming the rural countryside as 'vagrants,' roused the concern of politically and socially influential elements in Canada regarding the apparently changing character of old age. The most common response to the perceived needs of these elderly was the creation of state or quasi-state residential institutions that would shelter those elderly without any alternative means of support. But these nascent old age homes were more than simply shelters. In their physical character, their language and their environment these 'total institutions' gave expression to new views of old age which in the beginning marked the elderly as less than full citizens.

Though certainly not the most important statements of these new views, these institutions were chronologically first and, for some time, the only physical expressions of this new view of the elderly in local communities. It is appropriate to begin with an examination of these old age homes and to establish the context of their role among the elderly.

The Early Poorhouse Tradition

In the long-established traditions of charity in the Western world, the dependent elderly were among the most common recipients of attention and aid. Historically, the needy elderly had received charitable support not because of their age but because of their social condition. Poor laws and charitable institutions such as hospitals had long focused on those who were physically or mentally disabled or incapacitated (whether through illness or impairment) – such as the 'crippled,' the imbecile, the dying – and on those who were consistently destitute. Old age itself was not a criterion for garnering social assistance, because old age was not yet socially constructed in such a way that it was automatically associated with dependency or incapacity. Though the elderly may have been disproportionately represented among those receiving charitable aid, that assistance was the result of incapacity or destitution rather than old age itself.[1]

With the arrival of significant numbers of Canadian immigrants in the eighteenth and early nineteenth centuries, the social and political leaders of colonial society responded to the social distress among the newcomers in two major ways. In some instances outdoor relief was organized, through such groups as the Emigrant Society of Fredericton and the Halifax Poor Man's Friend Society and through local governments. A more common state response was the founding of residential institutions, usually know as poorhouses.[2] This mixture of public and private initiatives resulted in programs to deal with the dependent poor in all the British North American colonies during the first four decades of the nineteenth century. These programs aimed to help a variety of poor: orphans, deserted children, the incurably ill, and the 'friendless' and homeless elderly and infirm.[3]

By the 1860s, concern for the dependent poor was widespread enough to sustain a debate in Ontario concerning the founding of a network of county poorhouses.[4] In 1866 new legislation required all Ontario counties with more than 20,000 inhabitants to build a poorhouse, but the mandatory element was removed in 1868. In response, a network of houses of refuge was slowly established across southwestern Ontario, matching the existing poorhouses scattered across New Brunswick, Nova Scotia, and Newfoundland. These Ontario poorhouses were located in a relatively rural setting and always included a farm, where the male residents worked and which produced food for the home and for sale; female residents worked at domestic chores, such as mending bedlinen and clothing. By 1875 there were only four urban poorhouses in Ontario: two in Toronto and one each in Kingston and Hamilton. To help recoup the rising costs of operating such institutions, provincial legislation allowed municipalities to receive and hold real and personal property of a resident and, at the resident's death, to sell the property and apply the proceeds to the cost of maintaining the resident during the years spent in the home.

What was consistent among all these varied responses to the dependent and indigent members of society was the almost complete absence of sub-categories. The poor were simply that. Though individuals might be included among the poor for different reasons, once there those reasons did not result in separate groupings except as regards sex. Most strikingly for the purposes of this discussion, both the institutional and the charitable responses focused on the poor as a social group without regard to age; the elderly were generally not singled out for any special attention. These early poorhouses contained what one Canadian study has found to be 'a varied and complex population.' The inmate population was not stable, being in a constant state of flux both demographically and individually. Elderly women and men sought the shelter of these institutions because, in the face of illness or destitution, such persons lacked family or informal community alternatives and because they were increasingly marginalized in local labour markets. Physically or mentally handicapped persons of all ages and both sexes resorted to institutional support because they were unable to support themselves and had lost the informal support of their family for a host of reasons. Young women and children found themselves in a dependent position primarily because of the loss of a primary male breadwinner, temporarily or otherwise; young men, other than those handicapped, usually entered a poorhouse only on a temporary basis when they had been so seriously injured that they were unable to work and lacked a family-based alternative. These were institutions for the marginalized poor and vulnerable of the working class. Many of the inmates used these poorhouses as a means of coping with a particular crisis or set of crises; once the crisis had passed, either for the individual or for their family, the inmate moved on.[5]

Beginning in the late 1870s and extending steadily across the 1880s and 1890s, there was a considerable expansion of institutions aimed at the poor, and increasingly each specialized in a particular social element – orphans, unwed mothers, lunatics, or the elderly. At least as important as new views of childhood and of appropriate treatment of unwed mothers were new perceptions of aging and medical understandings of senescence. Both public and private institutions were involved, and they strongly reflected the religious division between Protestants and Roman Catholics. In some instances, such as in Ottawa, an institution directed at orphans found itself in a position where a few elderly women needed help, resulting eventually in the establishment of a second institution – hence the founding of the Refuge Branch of the Ottawa Protestant Orphans' Home.[6] Such developments serve as important reminders that the lines of responsibility among institutions remained somewhat blurred.

Not all types of institutions existed in every region, so even where distinctions began to be drawn among different categories of dependants, the institutional infrastructure did not yet allow their full expression. Thus, where asylums existed, they often housed the aged of reduced mental capacity who could fit easily into the regimented character of a house of refuge; poorhouses housed the insane and 'orphans'; jails contained the aged and the unemployed. The heterogeneous character of some such institutions lasted well into the twentieth century in some regions. Surveys of New Brunswick welfare systems in 1928 and 1949, for example, complained that local poorhouses continued to house the aged, the crippled, the senile, the incurable, unwed mothers, dependent families, and children, 'separated only by one broad classification of sex.'[7] Even where the institutions concentrated on an elderly population, the character of the residents remained quite mixed, including the bed-ridden, the senile or severely depressed, the disabled, the alcoholic, the frail and the indigent – so mixed that any coherent institutional aims other than shelter were almost impossible.

Of particular importance for the argument of this study is the fact that such institutional support voided whatever electoral 'rights' the recipient held. For several decades after 1888, Ontario explicitly deprived residents of refuges the right to vote, underlining such persons' loss of the full privileges of citizenship and the perceived indignity of entry into the homes; a similar rule applied to the men in the Kamloops provincial home.[8] Institutional support was incompatible with political citizenship. Though few inmates would have qualified for the property-based franchise, the attitude behind the legislation was fundamentally important. For the elderly to accept state aid was to concede that they were not full or equal members of the host society.

By the turn of the century there were increasingly common manifestations of changing standards of care. Public care of the needy elderly ought to be formally institutionalized and associated with existing recognized organizations – such as the state or a church – felt to be representative of the broader community. The care should be more than custodial, involving a concern for the health, hygiene, moral character, and daily behaviour of the elderly recipients.

The late nineteenth-century expansion of institutions dramatically increased the number of houses aimed at the dependent elderly. Ontario had an extensive network of public and private homes for the aged by the early twentieth century. In 1900 there were thirty-six city homes in Ontario alone for the dependent poor, most of which specialized in caring for the elderly and all of which contained at least some elderly residents. Altogether these homes provided a residence for 2250 persons. There were twice as many female as male residents in these urban institutions, a surprising contrast to the reported reversed ratio in American institutions.[9]

A network of county institutions gradually developed over the last three decades of the nineteenth century in Ontario, expanding quickly after the turn of the century. In 1903 the Ontario legislature passed legislation requiring every county or union of counties to establish a house of refuge by 1906 (later extended to 1912). Though not quickly complied with in all cases, there were twenty-five such homes serving twenty-seven counties by 1906, with three more under construction – only three counties had failed to respond. As required, all the houses had at least forty-five acres of farm land, with associated barns and equipment; some had considerably more land, such as the Waterloo home with 140 acres, and the median acreage was 60. The average number of residents ranged from a high of eighty-six (Waterloo) to a low of six (Prince Edward), with a median of fifty-three; on an average day, the county refuges provided residence for almost 1300 dependent persons. At least as important as the direct government aid to these homes was the acknowledgment of government responsibility for their general supervision through a provincial inspector.[10]

A group of less formal institutions was established around the turn of the century. The Salvation Army, for example, did not begin to establish homes explicitly for the elderly until the late 1920s. But its rescue homes, which are often assumed to have catered only to single mothers, in fact took in needy persons covering a spectrum of social characteristics. In Newfoundland, for example, where the Army was quite active, it operated two St John's institutions under a variety of names, receiving modest government grants for each. At the time of the 1911 census, the Rescue Home had in residence nine men and twelve women of undetermined age. By the 1921 census, however, the various Army institutions had become sex specific.[11]

Elsewhere, the early twentieth-century institutional response to the elderly was less extensive than in Ontario, but followed much the same pattern. By 1912 New Brunswick had an incomplete network of almshouses and municipal homes for the indigent. State-supported institutions were in operation in three counties and three cities. These were supplemented by the provincial hospital in Saint John, which held seventy-two patients (13 per cent of the total patients) aged sixty-five or older.[12] In Nova Scotia there were institutions, referred to provincially as asylums and poor farms, in ten counties, as well as on Cape Breton Island and in four cities, including Halifax, where there was both a city poorhouse and a Masonic home. Most of these institutions housed small numbers of elderly; likely only the Halifax City Asylum had an elderly population of more than twenty-one persons. In contrast to the trend towards a predominantly elderly population in New Brunswick and Ontario institutions, the Nova Scotia homes were closer to the nineteenth-century pattern of a broad spectrum of ages. Approximately 50 per cent of the residents in most homes were sixty-five years old or more; in Halifax County, just nineteen out of fifty-seven residents were of that age.[13] In Prince Edward Island the only state-supported institution for the elderly was the Falconwood Hospital in Charlottetown, one-sixth of whose 252 residents in 1910 were sixty-five years old or more.[14]

In Quebec, there were a number of institutions for the elderly. The Grey Nuns operated homes for the aged and infirm in seven communities. Other Roman Catholic orders administered similar homes in five locales. The Montreal Protestant community funded three institutions in Montreal and Longe Pointe for the long-term care of the elderly. All these Quebec institutions received some state aid, usually from both the provincial and the local governments. A 1912 parliamentary committee estimated that of 111 charitable institutions in Quebec receiving government grants, 23 were 'hospices' for the aged poor.[15]

The western provinces had fewer facilities for the needy elderly. In Manitoba, there was an Old Folks' Home in St Boniface, administered by Roman Catholic nuns, and a second home in Middlechurch, formally founded in 1908 and run by the Christian Women's Union. In 1916, after several years' consideration, the provincial government moved beyond merely assisting these private institutions to establish the provincial Old Folks' Home at Portage la Prairie.[16] While Alberta and Saskatchewan continued to rely on hospitals and local relief to administer state aid to the elderly, British Columbia had moved beyond that. In 1894 the provincial government opened a provincial home for 'aged, indigent and infirm persons' in Kamloops, which, despite its title, was exclusively for men. Privately, a group of middle-class women organized a home for elderly women in Victoria in 1898 to match the existing city-operated home for elderly men; the city provided support for both homes, though a higher proportion of the female residents brought funds with them for their support. The Victoria Aged and Infirm Women's Home was the only institution, beyond the hospitals, which would take in elderly women from anywhere in the province.

In all jurisdictions, local jails continued to offer temporary shelter for the indigent elderly, who would often be charged with vagrancy as a way of giving the homeless aged a meal and a roof over their heads for a few nights. Jails in Ontario usually kept a small amount of civilian clothing on hand for the use of old people committed as vagrants, so as to distinguish between them and the common criminals, and they tried to serve such elderly nourishing meals. In most jails the number of these elderly prisoners was steady rather than large – in 1895, seven old men in the Goderich jail and six old men and two old women in l'Orignal jail, and in 1897 twenty-four old men and two old women in the Toronto jail, all incarcerated as vagrants. But their length of stay was remarkable in some cases, one Goderich elderly 'habitué' having lived in the jail for eleven years.[17]

As state-supported old age homes proliferated, the use of jails as other than very temporary refuges for the needy elderly declined. In a 1906 Vancouver case, a destitute and infirm sixty-five-year-old labourer had for several months been in the habit of applying at the police station for shelter and food, often being given a night's shelter in a cell. Finally, in mid-December, the chief of police ordered that a charge of vagrancy be laid 'so as to shelter him during the severe winter months,' but the magistrate refused to convict him, ordering instead that the necessary steps be taken to send him to the old men's home in Kamloops. Nevertheless, despite the new attitudes about the appropriate forms of care for the elderly, some such use of the jails continued for several decades.[18]

The elderly themselves did not always take well to these new institutional options. For many, particularly men, simple shelter and the occasional meal was all they wanted, whatever anyone else thought they needed. One old man in 1906 was so incapacitated that he was able to move himself around only by crawling on his hands and knees. Nevertheless, despite his dependent condition, he found the various institutions quite constricting. His solution was to move repeatedly among the different institutions available to him in Toronto. The governor of the jail reported that the man 'has been in jail very often, as also in nearly all the charitable institutions in Toronto, including the House of Providence, Home for Incurables, Hospital, House of Industry & elsewhere.' A Salvation Army officer confirmed this history, and included the Army's shelter in the list of institutions used. He explained this transience by the man's character 'deficits': the man 'was very hard to get along with. He would drink if he could get out and get it. I have heard a good deal of the trouble he caused while at the Home for Incurables. He used the vilest language, so much so that any Institution he had ever occupied would never take him back. In fact the jail seemed the only institution for him.'[19] The officer's bias against such 'intolerable' behaviour was likely matched by the old man's resentment against his own infirmities and against his loss of freedom in the institutions. The insistence by the elderly on maintaining their independence, at least to the extent of choosing for themselves among the options available, is a constant theme across the period under study. So, too, is the attempt by various formal and informal processes to shape their behaviour.

Some elderly, as is still the case, were unwilling to accept the loss of freedom or choice. It is unknown just how many chose suicide as a way of coping with the infirmities and destitution of old age. But there is no doubt that it was an option that was adopted by some. A seventy-year-old man living with two adult sons had been suffering from melancholy and insomnia for several months in 1903 when he swallowed a half ounce of laudanum and cut his throat with a razor to have, as his suicide note put it, 'a good long sleep.' In another instance a fifty-seven-year-old man shot himself after seven years of 'spastic paraplegia,' including the last five years in a wheelchair and with a catheter for urinary incontinence. His suicide note in 1902 was addressed to his wife and seven children:

Excuse me for the last act I commit my case is in the state that will not get better between any time.

You don't know what I suffer and I am tired of it. I do not see what to live [for] any longer. Let people enjoy themselves who are in good health. I was thinking about this [a] long time and at last I came to the conclusion to do it at once. My paper money you find in my coat pocket; give it to them. My funeral money you get from Canada Lodge in Yonge Street. I have a little Tin Cash Box in my Table; there is my Insurance Paper for $1,000.00 ... Say good-bye to ... Don't carry nothing bad after me what I done was only mischief.

You know Fritz [the oldest son] gets my watch, Willie [the third oldest son] gets all religious pictures. Good-bye to all of you, and I hope you come not in the trouble I am in and be compelled to do this one act I did.

Don't forget Helena, my dear wife, gets the Insurance. Good-bye to all.[20]

Both of these examples – whether representative or not is unknown – opted for suicide rather than accept any institutional solution to their problems, an option that was certainly available for at least the latter man. Both also had the support of a family situation that was important – the second man was clearly concerned about his family, and the first man signed his note 'Father' – but was no longer enough.

Though family was the preferred solution to all problems of the elderly throughout the period under study, there were situations where the community approved of families handing over responsibilities for an elderly relative to an institution. In such cases the family nevertheless retained some liability for the old person's well-being. A sixty-five-year-old man, just released from the hospital for chronic bronchitis, was found wandering by police on a cold January night in 1904; he was taken to the police station and thence to jail for food and shelter. He died in the jail within two days, and the coroner's jury censured the old man's family for their behaviour. Having had a meal at his married daughter's house, he was sent by her and her brother to the House of Industry, there being scarlet fever and no room in her house. The jurors were not critical of the decision to turn to the House of Industry for help; this was the sort of situation that these institutions were designed to meet. Instead, the jury was upset by the family's decision to send the old man, rather than take him; they censured them for abandoning the old man on the street.[21] Indeed, such censure was publicized because families were usually so open to providing extensive support for the elderly.[22]

By the turn of the century the transition of the various poorhouses to homes for the aged was well under way. The directors of the Kingston Home for Aged, Friendless and Infirm commented in 1914: 'As the years go by The Home is gradually losing its identity as a poor house and – becoming what it is intended to be – a place where the friendless and infirm [elderly] will receive care and attention in accordance with their condition and the sympathy and kindness due them as dependents.' More specialized welfare and institutional responses to various elements within the poorhouse population tended to leave the dependent elderly as the dominant group within such institutions. In 1897, Ontario banned children between the ages of two and sixteen from the population of the houses of refuge. The Toronto House of Industry had 256 men and 54 women by 1912. Of these men, just 4 were under fifty years of age, 24 were between fifty and fifty-nine, 80 between sixty and sixty-nine, 121 between seventy and seventy-nine, and 27 eighty years or older. Of the women 3 were under fifty, all of whom were 'crippled,' 5 were fifty to fifty-nine, 13 sixty to sixty-nine, 25 seventy to seventy-nine, and 8 eighty or older. The Catholic House of Providence in that city had 376 persons aged sixty or older, making up 64 per cent of the residents.[23] The average age of inmates at one Ontario county house of refuge rose from 38.5 in 1880 to 68.4 in 1906.[24] What is just as striking as the overall rise in average age is the disappearance of a sex-specific difference in age. The departure of children and of young mothers from the halls of these institutions turned them *de facto* from poorhouses into nascent old age homes, with little direct intervention by way of policy or legislation.

Yet even at this stage of the residential institution's evolution the population was not stable. Increasingly, elderly workers were members of the reserve labour force, and some used urban and rural poorhouses as a temporary means of coping with their marginalization. Though a minority of the elderly remained in the homes for a number of years, for many their stay was temporary – merely a matter of months rather than years – before they moved on or died.[25] In other institutions the transition to an overwhelmingly elderly resident population was quite slow in coming. Children and younger adults were residents of the Peel House of Refuge throughout the period under study. Children usually came with an unwed or widowed mother; young adults used the home when they were injured and unable to work or when they were severely disabled, mentally or physically. It was not until the 1940s that unwed mothers or young women with children stopped turning to the Peel home for help. Similarly, there were still children in the Saint John Municipal Home as late as 1948, and a school for such young residents operated in the home as late as 1940.[26]

The growth of residential institutions specifically for the elderly around the turn of the century occurred in both rural and urban locales. The romantic, pastoral view of the rural environment made that an attractive site from the point of view of many, but the reality of the presence of so many needy elderly in the cities meant that many institutions had to be located there as well. Both rural and urban societies shared new views about appropriate ways of caring for the needy elderly, in the absence of family. More formal and more specialized services were now regarded as fitting for the elderly. Though the local community, particularly in rural areas, recognized and accepted traditional obligations for care, sometimes it was felt that that care could be better provided in more 'modern,' meaning more formal, ways.

This transition of the poorhouses into old age homes was more than matched by popular perception. There were some incentives even in the early years of the institutions to describe the population as merely elderly. As the traditional subjects of respect and sympathy, an elderly group of residents could be more easily depicted as 'worthy' or 'deserving,' and as appropriate recipients of public and private charity. Appealing to increasingly authoritative images of the elderly as weak, ill, helpless, and incapable of paid labour, administrators of poorhouses deliberately exaggerated the elderly character of their inmates to stimulate and sustain support.[27] Such depictions were readily accepted, even more so when the degree of exaggeration declined. When a parliamentary committee considered old age pensions in 1912, it accepted information about poorhouses as largely synonymous with old age homes. Other government bodies made similar assumptions.[28] In common parlance, institutional titles emphasizing the elderly character of the residents – aged men's and aged women's homes, old folk's homes, old age homes – rapidly and easily replaced terms such as poorhouse and house of industry. The term 'home' began to be prominent, though its meaning was restricted in practice and certainly did not entail any of the romantic elements associated with a family residence.

By the early twentieth century the residents of these institutions were supported through a variety of sources. Many paid for themselves at least in part, and others were maintained by family or relatives. Local charitable and religious organizations often made significant contributions, and individual philanthropy was a source of a relatively small amount of support, usually in the form of specific contributions – books, a Christmas dinner, fruit or candy – though general bequests were not uncommon, particularly for the homes operated by charitable organizations. Few ethnic groups were yet showing signs of support for their own elderly, a phenomenon that would not become particularly noticeable until the 1940s. One exception was the Icelandic community around Gimli, Manitoba, which in 1901 began to collect funds for the building of its own home for the elderly. By 1915 the project had reached fruition, in collaboration with the Icelandic Lutheran Synod, and a home opened in Winnipeg, moving to Gimli permanently that same year.[29] But most local efforts aimed at the elderly did not discriminate among the needy elderly, except on the basis of sex. Otherwise, all needy elderly were the objects of local charitable endeavour.

The Moral Environment of 'Total Institutions'

The institutionalized elderly were the most disadvantaged element among the turn-of-the-century elderly in Canada. They were largely the objects of charity and were subjected to an environment emphasizing control and loss of independence. It was not that officials and citizens in general were unfeeling; indeed, many sought to be quite generous. But accompanying the impulse to provide for the needy elderly was a striking insensitivity to the feelings of the elderly recipients themselves. The physician to the Kingston Home for the Aged reported in 1915: 'I happened to be in the Home at noon hour and inspected the meals served. I found the quality good and the quantity sufficient. I asked the inmates if there were any complaints but received none.'[30] The comment was typical. The doctor cared about the residents' welfare, but was completely oblivious to their vulnerability and to the dependent character of their residency – so he offered the residents an opportunity for public, non-confidential criticism before the same officials who wielded considerable power over their daily lives and over their primary survival strategy. The environment and treatment were characteristic of what Erving Goffman called 'total institutions,' in which the regulations, the daily regimen, the staff's knowledge and power, and the inmates' vulnerability and loss of freedom combined to create a distinct and comprehensive culture that reshaped the elderly inmates' understanding of old age and their own identity.[31]

The most difficult task is trying to uncover just what these early old age homes were like. For most institutions the records are quite sparse, and almost always a product of the administration of the home. The residents themselves have left almost no record of their attitudes, perceptions, or treatment. Yet it is important to try to understand the environment of these institutions, the initial wave of old age homes in Canada.

The environment within these poorhouses, and in many instances the names of the institutions themselves, retained what to the late twentieth-century eye appears to be some of the pejorative flavour of the older English poor law. Names such as the Home for Friendless Women or House of Refuge implied that the homes were a last resort for residents and that they had been rejected and isolated by the rest of society. When officials of the Kingston House of Industry chose in 1909–10 to change the institution's name to reflect more accurately its new functions, the name selected was the Home for Aged, Friendless and Infirm.

Every such institution had a printed set of rules for residents, attempting to enforce a rigid discipline. The relevant Ontario legislation instructed houses of refuge to keep every able 'inmate' (the common term in the period) at work, and made anyone who refused to work 'or is stubborn, disobedient or disorderly' liable to punishment in accordance with the house rules. Usually the times of rising and going to bed were prescribed, and residents were always forbidden to leave the grounds without the permission of the matron or superintendent; standards of cleanliness were articulated, usually requiring inmates to bathe at least once a week and/or to wash before each meal. Unless ill, residents were not allowed to lie down on their beds during the day time. Instead, gender-specific work crucial to support the running of the institution and to reduce operating costs was expected from all who were able. To enforce such rules, some institutions constructed basement cells and used solitary confinement there as a possible punishment; in some cases, the recalcitrant and disobedient were punished through fines, eviction, or denial of readmission. Authorities generally felt strongly that order was essential and that the rules were there to be used actively. These institutions were 'homes' only in the sense that they were residences.

The dominant trait was the homes' institutional character – a natural product of the philosophy behind the homes. They were not planned as homes of the aged but as institutions for the needy elderly, who were receiving a favour – usually charitable – from the state and society at large. Years later an Ontario woman recalled her winter visit as a young girl to an old couple in the Peterborough house of refuge around 1914:

We were very happy to finally reach the County Home as we were anxious to get warm hopefully. How wrong we were, as we were ushered to the room for men only, across the hall [from the room] for lady inmates only. There were no furniture only chairs in both rooms for the inmates.

There was nothing for entertainment, even books to read, they just sat listlessly in this chilly room. Mother and I visited the ladies' quarters which was just like the men's room. These people were just left alone for hours.

My father always took a treat to Mr and Mrs Hughes, who shared it with the inmates who shyly thanked my father.[32]

The pervasive rules emphasized the institutional environment and the absence of inmates' formal control or even influence over conditions in their place of residence. Indeed, the authority of the senior staff in many old age institutions is quite striking. The complaints of one British Columbia old man stand out as an example: '[The superintendent] is most cruel to the inmates, I have seen him take hold of old men, 75 or 80 years old and give them a good shaking ... After being ordered out of the home I went to the mayor who told me the Superintendent had no right to send me away, but I was afraid to go back as he would have plagued me out of my life.'[33] Those in charge of these institutions did not easily tolerate challenges of any sort to their authority.

The early poorhouses/old age homes were judged by limited qualitative standards. There was humanitarian concern for the residents themselves, but it was restricted largely to an impersonal desire to provide shelter and food to persons who might well otherwise starve to death on the public thoroughfares. In 1905 the directors of the Kingston Home for Aged, Friendless and Infirm singled out the matron and superintendent, a married couple, for special praise: 'The Directors desire to make special mention of the general improvements which have taken place under the direction of Mr and Mrs Countryman. The house internally and externally has been renovated and made sweet and clean. Much of the bedding and other equipment has been replaced or renewed. The grounds have been cleared of much of their stone, and the fences have been repaired.' And more land was being brought under cultivation.[34] What is striking about the standards and criteria used to judge the effectiveness of their work is that they involved only the physical environment. A well-developed concern for the social life and mental health of the institutionalized elderly would not become generalized for several decades, though there is evidence of attention to the social environment in some women's institutions.[35]

Adjustment to life in an old age home could be difficult for some. A minority of men coped with this by moving in and out of the home, sometimes repeatedly, a phenomenon much less common for women, who lacked similar access to seasonal employment and who were socialized to reject some of the alternative living arrangements used by men. Many men had a seasonal pattern, living in the institution during the harsh winter months and then moving out during the better weather, either living off the land in unsettled districts or finding enough odd jobs to maintain themselves.[36] Others moved to the home for a year or two, leaving when their health had recovered and economic conditions were favourable. The options available to these men varied considerably, depending on individual circumstance and on the geographical location of the institution. A sixty-one-year-old farmer with no immediate family entered the Kamloops home in 1932 with a broken left leg and a broken right ankle. In 1941 he moved out, living in rooms at Revelstoke with the help of an Old Age Pension. Finally, by 1948 at the age of seventy-seven, the man had become frail and unable to care for himself; living temporarily with friends, he 'insisted' on returning to the Provincial Home.[37] Others left temporarily, to do a little prospecting in the wilderness or when they received funds, perhaps through a legacy, and they moved away until the funds had been exhausted.[38]

Once the homes were established, there was no movement for several decades to rethink the philosophy behind them. It is true that in Ontario the managers of these institutions came together in 1920 to form the first professional organization associated with them, but the Ontario Association of Managers and Matrons of the Homes for Aged and Infirm had little immediate impact in many of the homes, particularly in eastern Canada. In the Atlantic provinces the earliest poorhouses had been built in the first half of the nineteenth century, and by the early twentieth century many were old and had been designed to house a different group of residents. Some of the Atlantic provinces' poorhouses represent the worst examples of what had happened to these early institutions.

A Case Study of the St John's Poorhouse

A good example of an institution sharing many of the problems and philosophies common at this time is the St John's, Newfoundland, Poor Asylum, founded in 1861 to replace relief sheds built in 1846. The St John's poorhouse is used here as a case study of the changing characteristics and public expectations of old age homes across Canada. For many years the Poor Asylum was the only state-operated institution providing residential care to the indigent elderly in all of Newfoundland and Labrador. Located on Sudbury Street in the working-class district of the city, the T-shaped three-storey wooden structure bordered on a large public park with a small stream running through it close to the home. Nearby was the Bennett Brewing Company and another institution, the Methodist orphanage.

It was not long after the turn of the century before public challenges to the quality of life at the Poor Asylum began. In 1908 a grand jury's comment that the home was 'the saddest place in all of Newfoundland' resonated with popular currents so much that it was quoted in almost every report on the Poor Asylum for the next four decades. By 1911 the Poor Asylum, commonly known as 'the poorhouse,' was acknowledged to be so inadequate for its purposes that the government announced plans to abandon the existing institution; it was unfit for refurbishing or for conversion to any other purpose. Instead, in what the superintendent termed 'a progressive step,' the Poor Asylum was to move to the existing Lunatic Asylum, which was to be relocated in a completely new structure.[39] This is suggestive of the relative importance of the two institutions.

The existing Poor Asylum, despite its severe limitations and unfulfilled plans to erect an entirely new building, continued to serve the Newfoundland community until the 1960s. In 1911 the addition of electricity did away with the dangerous use of kerosene lighting, reducing the threat of fire and the labour-intensive lamps. The installation of water pipes for the upper floors of the home and the addition of new equipment from time to time enhanced residential life. New staff helped to improve conditions, overcoming the 'inefficiency' of elderly employees who were pensioned off.[40] But before long the depressing conditions in the old building took their toll. In 1922 the superintendent reported that because a new building had been expected and government funds had recently been reduced, the Poor Asylum had been 'allowed to go to almost utter ruin.' Three years later he was still pleading for more support from the state because of 'the absolute necessity of having this Institution renovated from the ground floor to the top.'[41] However, once established, such institutions received low priority in the spending plans of the state.

The St John's Poor Asylum had a large population. At the time of the 1911 census it held seventy-two men and forty-seven women; one hundred and sixty-eight persons had been residents at some point during the year. Ten years later, the numbers had not changed much – seventy-three men and fifty-four women. Sixty per cent of the residents were Roman Catholics, up to 30 per cent were Anglicans, and the remainder were Methodists, proportions reflecting their numbers and position in the society at large. In 1911 the institution had a male superintendent and a female matron, along with two men and eleven women employees. Ten years later, with a slightly larger resident population, there was one less woman worker. Salary and wage levels were low, particularly for women, although the inclusion of room and board raised the total level of compensation to workers at all levels of responsibility.[42] Both the number of staff and their level of wages are suggestive of the quality and level of care provided.

The home's registers provide a more detailed picture of the population (see tables 2.1 and 2.2). For the purposes of comparison over time, the registers were examined at twenty-year periods. The results reveal that some important changes were occurring at the St John's Poor Asylum and in the more broadly based perceptions of the elderly. The gradual aging of the resident population is striking. Though the elderly predominated throughout the period, the median age at admission rose from the low sixties at the turn of the century to the high sixties and low seventies by 1920; this was true for both sexes. The number of residents under forty years of age slowly decreased, so that by 1940 there were no admissions for either sex in the younger age brackets. Just as suggestive are the reasons for admission entered in the registers by staff. At the turn of the century there was considerable impulse to identify the specific ground on which the new admission was being made. Old age itself was not yet adequate ground; rather, one had to be perceived to be incapable of caring for oneself – thus, 'demented,' 'debilitated,' and various specific forms of physical disability were the most important labels being applied. This changed dramatically in the following

TABLE 2.1 Age at admission to St John's Poor Asylum, 1900, 1920–1, 1940–2

Age	1900		1920–1		1940–2	
	Women	Men	Women	Men	Women	Men
	per cent					
<30	10.6	5.7	10.4	2.2	0.0	0.0
30–39	9.1	14.6	0.0	2.2	0.0	0.0
40–49	10.6	8.1	0.0	13.0	17.9	6.3
50–59	15.2	19.5	10.4	8.7	14.3	21.9
60–69	18.2	22.0	31.0	17.4	21.4	18.8
70–79	27.3	22.8	31.0	43.5	25.0	28.1
80–89	9.1	6.5	17.2	6.5	21.4	25.0
>89	0.0	0.8	0.0	6.5	0.0	0.0
median age	63	62	68	70.5	69	71.5
n*	66	123	29	46	28	32

* Where age was unstated, the resident was omitted.

Source: PANL, Registers of St John's Poor Asylum

decades, as old age in itself became a criterion for admission. With incoming residents being more consistently elderly, it became less necessary to identify any ground for admission. Where grounds were identified, those associated more directly with old age fell into disuse, and social grounds – no home or no friends – began to be used with considerable frequency.

The residents were not simply old. They were old and unable to maintain themselves for physical, economic, and social reasons. On one inspection in December 1933, sixty-seven women lived at the asylum, ranging in age from sixteen to ninety. Fifteen to twenty of the women were estimated to be permanently bed-ridden, some for many years, and 'a number' of the women were 'mentally deficient and physically deformed.' At the same time, there were ninety-eight men residents, representing 'young people afflicted with epilepsy; mentally deficient and deaf and dumb of various ages; and fishermen and labourers who, through ill fortune and ill health, have been compelled to seek shelter in the institution.' There were also 'some [men] crippled and some are simple minded in various degrees.'[43] The population of the home was thus quite heterogeneous, most sharing only old age, and there was as yet relatively little distinction among the elderly institutional population.

In 1929 significant changes began for the Poor Asylum, some of which

TABLE 2.2 Reasons for admission to St John's Poor Asylum, 1900,1920–1, 1940–2

Reason	1900		1920–1		1940–2	
	Women	Men	Women	Men	Women	Men
Demented	51.5	35.5	0.0	5.5	0.0	0.0
Debilitated	30.3	39.5	0.0	0.0	0.0	0.0
Old age	0.0	0.0	6.3	9.1	0.0	0.0
No friends/ no home	0.0	0.0	25.0	20.0	31.0	28.1
Disabled (physically)	12.1	17.7	6.3	9.1	0.0	0.0
Disabled (mentally)	1.5	3.2	6.3	14.6	0.0	3.1
Vagrant	0.0	1.6	0.0	0.0	0.0	0.0
Medical	4.6	1.6	3.1	12.7	0.0	0.0
Unstated	0.0	0.8	50.0	29.1	69.0	68.8
n	66	124	32	55	29	32

Source: PANL, Registers of St John's Poor Asylum

were clearly detrimental to the home. On the positive side, major renovations were made to the physical structure. After two decades of pleading for a separate hospital wing, an infirmary was constructed on the ground floor of the home. With a capacity of forty-two beds, four lavatories for the patients, and separate nursing quarters, as well as a treatment clinic, ill residents of the home and the elderly elsewhere could now be transferred to proper facilities. On the upper floors of the home, the women's and men's quarters were 'thoroughly renovated,' though accommodations were still sparse. On the top floor of the home, for example, a separate 'dark room' served the incontinent. The one washroom, shared by approximately ninety men, contained two baths, five toilets, and six wash basins, 'all in one open room of no great size and it is not unusual for them all to be in use at the same time.' The washroom on the second floor was even smaller, with two baths, one toilet, and two wash basins for approximately sixty women. On both the second floor reserved for women and the third floor reserved for men, a large corridor ran the full length of the building, and benches lined both sides of the hall. This was the only area where the residents could rest or enjoy recreation. They spent most of each day there, 'the women, on their part, looking very neat and comfortable in their white aprons; the men smoking or chewing tobacco and looking very unkempt, unclean and uncared for.' In total, the government spent over twenty thousand dollars to improve the home.44 Unfortunately, new staff and administrators soon brought the Poor Asylum into disrepute.

In 1931, following the recommendations of the royal commission on health and public charities, the Newfoundland legislature fundamentally revamped the administrative and legal structure of public welfare. As part of this reform, the St John's Poor Asylum came under formal government control. The new legislation set out the aims of the institution, yet while the reforms were important structurally, the earlier custodial philosophy of the home had not altered. The purpose of the home was 'the maintenance and care of ... persons who are incapable through old age of supporting and caring for themselves,' as well as of the incurably ill and those seriously disabled mentally or physically. Symbolic of this recognition of the home's clientele was the change in the home's name to the Home for the Aged and Infirm. Henceforth, applicants to the home required a medical examination, establishing pseudo-scientific evidence of each applicant's claim to admission. Any change in a resident's financial or social circumstances that would have provided them with support elsewhere was sufficient reason for the superintendent to discharge the person; in its philosophy, the home remained a last resort for the needy elderly. The emphasis on rules and order continued to be so strong that the superintendent and the employees now acquired police powers to enforce the rules and regulations against residents and visitors alike.45

If some politicians and administrators had trouble conceiving of the home in different terms – whatever the change in name – this was less true of other elements in society. The residents, for one, were active in pushing the institution to change. One of the traditional characteristics of the nineteenth-century home, that of work by the residents, was still in place. But for some time it was challenged by the residents. As long as the resident population had included significant numbers of younger adults, the rule that residents had to work for their board had been useful in helping to control operating costs. However, as the resident population grew older on average, productive work was less feasible. Furthermore, many elderly residents felt that they now had a 'right' to support from such a state institution and that their labour was no longer necessary as partial repayment. In institution after institution the work philosophy met direct challenges from residents, particularly from men, and most of the farms attached to the homes became increasingly unprofitable. The Saint John (New Brunswick) Municipal Home, for example, began to question seriously the cost effectiveness of maintaining its farm in the 1930s; the farm remained – old traditions die hard – but implicitly a new philosophy of old age homes was being considered. Inmates themselves avoided the work expected of them. Administrators called this insubordination, as it was, but there was something more basic involved in such confrontations.[46] Insubordination had long been a minor problem in such institutions. In the past, recorded incidents had involved only individuals, rather than a group, and work had not been as common a source of friction as had the general environment of control or the rules against alcohol and swearing.

New standards began to be articulated for these residential institutions, particularly among the public. In St John's the grand jury played a prominent role in giving public legitimation to these standards. In the spring of 1932 the grand jury was sharply critical, commenting that the home was 'an absolute disgrace to our country and should not be tolerated a moment longer than necessary.' Twenty months later the grand jury's report was devastatingly critical of physical conditions at the home. 'Not much can be said in favour of such a dilapidated structure with its lack of convenience and accommodation such as are required in a public institution of this nature,' commented the twenty-three men making up the grand jury. The real solution was a new building, but in the meantime immediate repairs were necessary to prevent the collapse of floors and ceilings. The building was 'a veritable fire trap' and the hygiene was below standard, judging from the large number of flies in the kitchen and the sleeping quarters. The food, in contrast, was reported to be quite adequate. The justice receiving the report castigated both the government and the public at large for paying insufficient attention to the needs of the home's residents.[47] If the Newfoundland government was not in a position to spend additional funds for the home, new standards were nevertheless being set.

This process was furthered in the winter of 1933–4 when a major scandal concerning the St John's Home for the Aged and Infirm exposed some of the results of the old standards. In the fall a minor investigation into charges against one of the male attendants had revealed unexpected hints of much more basic problems in the administration of the home. To its credit the government moved quickly to get to the bottom of the problem, appointing a commission of inquiry conducted by Andrew Vatcher, stipendiary magistrate at Corner Brook. When Vatcher reported three months later, the findings were nothing less than 'shocking.'[48]

'A Horrifying State of Affairs,' read the newspaper headline. The atmosphere in the overcrowded home disturbed Magistrate Vatcher considerably. While the women's rooms appeared clean and neat, the men's rooms matched his depiction of their occupants. The men's beds were 'very badly made' and the bedspreads were 'very dirty looking,' often having 'large holes and rents in them.' When Vatcher conducted a surprise visit, several of the men were in bed with clothes and boots on and the bedclothes pulled over their heads. Many of the men spent the day roaming around St John's, but there is no indication that this was true for the women. Though there were a number of residents who were disabled or 'mentally deficient,' 'a large number impress me as being sensible, with a respectable history, and of clear intelligence, fully alive to all that transpires in the institution.' The storeroom had little food in it, and the air circulation around the kitchen was so poor that Vatcher found the odours 'almost nauseating.' But it was not the physical problems of the institution that most attracted the attention of the inquiry. Rather, it was the staff and the quality of care.

The size of the staff was minimal considering the number of residents and the level of care required by those in the infirmary. Ten men worked at the home, ranging from Superintendent L.J. White to six men employed as attendants, watchman, or furnaceman, and two residents paid token amounts for their work as orderly and laundryman. Eighteen women worked as nurses, cooks, or attendants. Though the various members were aware of their approximate duties, the staff was typical for institutions across Canada in that they had received little or no training in their specific work. The superintendent, for example, whose duties were set out in the pertinent legislation, had first seen a copy of the statute only three months earlier. Nor had the superintendent and the officials of the health and welfare department ever been in contact with one another, despite the supervisory responsibilities of the latter. The physician appointed to the home had never visited there, nor had any of the government ministers responsible for the home. Supplies were ordered haphazardly, and there were few controls over medicines (particularly brandy and heroin). What was new about this inquiry was that these standards of work and care were depicted as inadequate.

If the overall impression was one of carelessness and lack of responsibility to the detriment of residents, it was the behaviour of specific staff members that shocked the public into attention. Not only did the staff, particularly its senior members, demonstrate little concern for hygiene or care of the residents, but they also indulged in unacceptable behaviour that clearly suggested immorality. The superintendent did not inspect the residents' wards more than once a week and, according to Vatcher, did not take 'the slightest interest in the treatment of the inmates,' neglecting to notice the failure of employees to perform various duties. Many of the other staff were derelict in their duties, leaving residents ignored or uncared for – unwashed, using the same bed linen for several weeks at a time, eating meals low in nutritional quality and with little variety, bathing in the same water as several others, left alone when dying. Staff stole or misused institutional supplies, and no distinctions were made among the needs of various types of residents. What is unclear is to what extent these levels of care differed from those over the past several decades.

It is of fundamental importance that Vatcher found this situation totally unacceptable. The elderly residents of the home had a right to an absolute quality of care. 'I am convinced that the lot of these unfortunates has been made miserable, unhappy, intolerable and death looked upon as a lucky escape because the staff treat them like wild animals,' reported Vatcher, who appealed to the public for support. 'The character of the inmates is largely misunderstood by the public. Their conduct has been most commendable and forebearing under the circumstances. The men particularly ... have been grossly neglected and mistreated.' Such persons did not deserve to be looked down on, but rather warranted a quality of care and lifestyle that met the standards of the everyday world. Old age institutions were no longer judged by different (and lower) standards but by those of society at large. This was perhaps best captured by Vatcher's concluding recommendation: 'Some attempt should be made to make the place more homelike.'

Following the public exposure of the home's problems, new senior and junior staff were appointed in 1934. Even relatively unskilled employees in old age homes were now expected to acquire training specific to the needs of such an institution. The new superintendent reported that the new attendants, as well as some of the existing attendants, had been 'instructed in their duties and especially in the correct attitude that they must take in the treatment and care of the inmates under their respective charges.' Staff duties were organized and explicitly articulated. Enforcement of standards of propriety became more rigorous. Standards of hygiene and cleanliness were also raised. The lavatories were judged to be 'unpainted and looked dirty'; the kitchen and adjoining rooms appeared unclean 'and unnecessary rubbish was found lying about.' All received scrubbing and new paint, and food was stored in a more efficient and hygienic manner.49

The residents also received direct attention. Staff made distinctions among the residents as to their various capacities and needs: 'The patients were divided into very old or very weak who kept mostly to their beds, a middle group who mentally and physically cannot take care of themselves and a third group who are physically fit enough to support themselves but whose inclinations have been and are to make no attempt whatsoever to do so.' The new superintendent was disturbed that in the various wards 'both male and female inmates were found to be sitting aimlessly on benches in the corridors, or lying on beds without occupation or without anything to interest them.' Seeking to create 'a better atmosphere,' he organized 'light work' for the residents, particularly the men. A variety of tasks was arranged – gardening, raking, care and repair of the grounds and fences – all from a desire to give the residents 'a happier outlook and improve their conditions both physically and mentally.' This heightened concern for the residents beyond simple maintenance was important, but its expression through a work program was imposed by the administrators, and it completely failed to take into account the views of the residents themselves.

An organized residents' revolt was the result, persisting over several weeks.[50] At first there was simply a great deal of discontent, with the result that the very old and the sick 'were given the benefit of any doubt, and resumed the more slothful condition until some form of indoor work could be found to take its place,' in the words of the superintendent. But those left to work continued to complain. 'A combined refusal to work' was met with interviews and explanations of the personal benefits of a work regime.

This did good for a short while only, and on the 30th of May [two weeks later] a few malcontents started holding little group meetings which resulted in those who worked being cajoled into refusing. They decided that they would not make up their own beds, as formerly, and many that were made were undone; encouragement to come in late at night; and continuously grumble about the quality and quantity of the food; get in the way of attendants proceeding on their rounds; not hearing instructions that were given and many other small aggravating instances of subversive discipline were communicated to me by the whole staff of day attendants.

The superintendent sought to crush the revolt by dismissing the 'ringleaders' from the home. They were sent off to the homes of relatives, none of whom would take the men in.

They sought sympathy in their plight amongst members of the community, and finally sought refuge in the Police Station, and later gravitated back to the Institution. The deserved punishment that these men received had not been beneficial in teaching them a lesson, and the apparent strength in their position has made them less timorous as the memory of it recedes from their minds, and has further created a sense of injustice done them.

The superintendent then tried a new tactic. Men who agreed to wash and wax floors in a government building received rewards – street car tickets, additional food at teatime, and extra tobacco. But those men capable of the work met a request for more such workers with 'an unequivocal "no"'; when cautioned that the work was for the same department that operated the home, the answer remained the same. The superintendent took this as a direct challenge to his authority, unable to see that there was also a fundamental challenge to the basic philosophy of the home. 'The actual refusal represents a condition in the Institution which is intolerable, and which cannot be allowed to gather strength,' he wrote. He demanded that the government authorize permanent removal of the rebellious men 'who are physically fit enough to refuse the emasculating stigma of state support.'[51]

Both the men and the superintendent had implicitly raised fundamental issues regarding the nature of old age homes, without explicitly addressing them. The mixture of problems of gender, age, authority, hygiene, health, and staff necessarily created more confusion than benefits. But these would begin to be worked out over the succeeding decades. There is no evidence, however, that the residents' opinions or actions had the slightest impact on these public developments. In the 1930s no public voices demanded that the elderly be consulted about what they themselves wanted. A paternalistic process simply presumed to know what was best for the recipients.[52]

In part, the 1934 inquiry and subsequent confrontation were a product of a changing set of attitudes towards old age homes and the elderly. In this sense many of the criticisms were simply products of new standards, but they do help to reveal the older attitudes and standards regarding the institutionalization of the elderly. The first-wave institutions for the elderly were designed as 'fall-back' residences, as a place for the homeless, needy, and indigent elderly who had no other place to go. They were not designed to be attractive to the residents, nor were they intended to solicit a clientele. These early 'total institutions' provided minimal care for a small sector of the population who were desperate for shelter. The state, on behalf of society at large, generally accepted its obligation to assist these elderly, but there was a strong, if unstated element of 'less eligibility' in the kind of shelter provided. In the same way that nineteenth-century poor laws sought to discourage all but the desperate by providing lower financial support than one could receive from the poorest paid jobs, so too the institutions made available a level and quality of care that would appeal only to those who truly could no longer cope on their own and had no family capable of taking them in. With this philosophy, and with considerable pressure to keep costs down and to limit state involvement, it is not surprising that the institutions received relatively little public attention or encouragement to move beyond the minimal care offered in the first decades of the twentieth century.

In the years following 1934, grand juries kept up the pressure for significant changes in the St John's Home for the Aged and Infirm. There were no further signs of scandals or serious revolts. While the physical condition of the building remained distressing, the new staff had created a hygienic and healthy environment within the limits of the physical environment.[53] By 1944 replacement of the badly warped and worn floors began; a completely repainted interior in 'pleasing, restful colours' had improved the environment considerably – 'instead of the usual drab effect, there is now a feeling of cheerfulness – if such is possible – as far as decorating is concerned.'

The home now met the standards of the day in many respects. The new standards involved both a broader range of concerns and a better quality of life, and the Home for the Aged and Infirm was meeting the test in both areas, though concerns regarding the physical condition of the building and the need for more space remained.[54] Innovative new housing projects and old age homes in the 1940s gave full expression to these new standards (see chapter 7).

The Role of the Community

It is important to set the early wave of elderly institutions in the context of the more traditional forms of community support. These first old age homes met a real need among a small proportion of the elderly, and their proliferation across the country reflected both their place in state policy and the demand for such facilities among a limited portion of society. The records of a number of state programs reveal the circumstances of the elderly at the point at which they sought state aid, suggesting the balance that existed among family, community, and state support.[55] For the elderly themselves, and for their community of friends, relatives, and neighbours, an old age home was the appropriate answer to these old person's circumstances only after most or all other options had been exhausted.

Because of the nature of the often informal application process to the all-male Provincial Home for the Aged in Kamloops, British Columbia, community forms of support are particularly apparent in the records. Applications for places in the home came not just from the elderly themselves, but also from friends, neighbours, relatives, and local officials. A man in the provincial interior wrote on behalf of a relative, aged seventy-two and an ex-house painter: 'Since the death of his wife 8 years ago he has made his home with me, and for several years I have given him a home free, though I could ill afford to do so, But as he had no children or [other] relatives to go to, I took him in. But he is now getting to an age when I feel he should be where he can be looked after better than I can do as I am a bachelor and am away from home much of my time working.' The man offered to help pay for the old man's maintenance in the home 'as far as I am able.' Within a year the old man was living in another house in the community, from which entrance to the Kamloops Home was still sought.[56] But such support and concern were not limited to relatives.

Community support was commonly available to many needy elderly and was relied on by them as one element in their survival strategies. Several jurisdictions, including British Columbia, took advantage of such community support by offering small monthly payments to neighbours or lateral kin willing to take in elderly who would otherwise have to go to an institution. Communities aided the elderly in other ways as well. A logging contractor in the interior described how a seventy-three-year-old man 'has got so he cannot do any work to speak of ... altho I keep him at my camp all the time.'[57] Early industrial paternalism among employers was certainly not yet dead.

A different form of support was described by a concerned citizen in midwinter in Lumby, seeking admission to the Kamloops Home for a local seventy-five-year-old who

was living here in a shack adjoining Lumby in a very unfit state [so] I thought it my duty to bring the matter before the proper authorities. The Man is too old and feeble to earn a living or indeed to do any manual work other than chopping a little wood etc and of late he has failed so much that he is unable apparently to do this. He has been in this country some 15 years and here in Lumby some 3 years, during which time I have known him. During the last year the Hotel Proprietors here have been allowing him to get meals at their Hotel[s] continually and without charge, and he has been living in a shack adjoining the School house, this shack I visited today and found same in a terrible condition, there is nothing but a very small cook-stove which gives practically no heat, and he has a small mattress on the floor with very scant covering and so far as I could see no clothing or food of any description, and the man was asleep under the blankets, and when awakened he was hardly able to stand up.

Fearing that the man would soon freeze to death in the mid-winter cold, the writer – an apparently otherwise disinterested local insurance agent – arranged for the man to get his meals regularly at the hotel, but the man would not leave his shack unless assured of accommodation elsewhere. The local hotel operators did not begrudge the old man what support they had been giving him, but were not willing to take any additional responsibility.[58] The amount of informal support and the extent to which the insurance agent went to check on the old man's circumstances and to gain him more formal and effective aid is a striking example of the willingness of local communities to take care of their own to a very considerable extent.

Time and again these old men found support within the local community, and other records suggest that similar aid was available to elderly women and couples.[59] At times regular and at other times irregular, such support took various forms – shelter, food, prepared meals, firewood, occasional housekeeping or tidying up of a shack, or something as intangible as a general watchfulness over their health and well-being or an appeal to others who had a more explicit obligation to help. This support could last for years, falling on the shoulders of just one individual or a large number of neighbours. All such support reflected a powerful sense of community, which did not isolate the needy elderly but sought to aid them and to help them within their own community setting. On the other hand the informal, charitable character of this support cast the recipients in a very vulnerable and dependent position.

Elsewhere in Canada, similar stories can be found. Neighbours and friends rallied around the needy elderly, providing required support usually in services or in kind, but sometimes extending to full room and board for extended periods. A widow, aged seventy-six and living in rural central Ontario, relied on a neighbour woman (who had 'been helping this woman to live for years') to apply for a pension.[60] A farmer in eastern Ontario had provided a home for a seventy-three-year-old widower who had no relatives:

He has been living with us on the farm for 5 yrs. for his room and board. He does light chores (no wages) around the farm but cannot do much.

We would like to be free of him. I have two small children and he is a burden on me. He has no place to go other than the House of Refuge and I could never be the one to force him there. He was married to a friend of my mother's otherwise he had no claim on us. He could readily find a home if he had his [Old Age] Pension.[61]

The obligations of community and friendship were not easily escaped in this culture.

This community obligation was not limited to rural or small town life. Toronto coroner's inquest reports, for example, provide evidence of an urban community's caring and protection for the local elderly. Neighbours watched over and were concerned about the health and circumstances of one another, and where necessary took appropriate action to provide help. This sort of support was vital to many elderly. For example, a sixty-year-old man, whose wife was in hospital, had not been seen by neighbours for three days; concerned for his well-being, three married women neighbours checked on him by looking in his window, discovering him dead. The bodies of elderly who died while living in boarding houses were almost always discovered within a matter of hours, or by the next morning after the other boarders and landlady awoke.[62] Private, individual giving also occurred.[63] A Toronto woman interviewed in 1948 emphasized the centrality of the local community in her pensioner father's life. Unable to live alone, he had persuaded his daughter and son-in-law to move into his house, despite its being very old, damp, and inconvenient. His daughter acknowledged her father's dependence on her and her ultimate power to sell the house and force him to move in with her, but she rejected any such action because she was sure it would kill him: 'Dad has lived in this district for forty years and all the neighbors know him. If he has a weak spell when he is out for a walk I know someone will bring him home. I could not expect that in a strange neighborhood where no one knows him.' So they remained in the old house, supported by the local community.[64]

As this example suggests, the elderly played their own part in calculating the potential support accruing from various sources and in behaving in such a way as to maximize that support within the context of their own lifestyle. When a sixty-eight-year-old woman was widowed by her pensioner husband in 1940 in southeastern Newfoundland, she was left with no income but with ownership of her home. She immediately applied for a continuation of her husband's OAP (as was possible under the distinct Newfoundland program) and arranged to share her home with her sister-in-law, who was in receipt of a widow's allowance from the state. The woman also used her home to produce income from a boarder. By the mid-1950s she still lived with the boarder in the same house, but by that time the boarder had acquired title to the home, probably in exchange for an agreement to look after the old woman.[65] Family, state, community, and private property combined to sustain the old woman through her old age.

Other elderly, particularly men, maintained a lifestyle apart from community and family. What at the time was often referred to as vagrancy was a serious alternative, particularly given the vast expanses of unoccupied land in Canada on the fringe of settlement or beyond. In the Canadian wilderness an unknown number of men occupied a simple shack or lean-to, living off the land and enjoying a solitary lifestyle where the behavioural demands of the state or the community made little impact. Their few material needs were satisfied by exchange of the fruits of their efforts at prospecting or trapping, or by 'scrounging' among the used goods of nearby communities.

In 1945, for example, one John Perry came to the attention of state officials at Whitbourne on Newfoundland's Avalon Peninsula. Perry was a sixty-six-year-old bachelor without property or assets who lived in what was variously called a 'tilt' or a shack 'several miles in the woods from any settlement or neighbour.' During his adult life he had lived in a variety of places on the island, having spent the last two years in his present location. Unwell, Perry asked for help from the local welfare officer who, learning that Perry had two siblings, 'asked him if his brother or sister could look after him. He told me they could not, and if they could he would not live with them, stating if it came to that he had a gun and [would] look after himself, meaning he would take his own life.' As Perry's health deteriorated he wanted help, but only on his own terms. He would not seek family help, nor would he conform to community behavioural standards – Perry was 'not the type which peaceful people want in their homes,' commented one official. Attempts to provide him with state-supported boarding were generally unsuccessful, as Perry either left or was evicted after only short stays in a number of homes. Down to his death in 1959, each spring when the weather improved, Perry would take off for the wilderness, and each fall he would seek shelter in a boarding house, usually at state expense, as he adjusted his independent lifestyle to meet his changing physical capacity in old age.[66]

This independent lifestyle did not always readily mesh with various forms of community or state support. Measures of support, whether from family, friends, or neighbours, often acted as means by which the community's version of appropriate construction of old age might be imposed on the elderly themselves. State officials and, to a lesser extent, neighbours were often appalled at the living conditions of these independent elderly. The health and behavioural standards of these elderly were such that family and community found it difficult to accommodate them or others like them. Others in the community sometimes saw admission to an institution as a way of ridding the community of a socially deviant individual, at the same time that the individual was brought within community control.[67]

A welfare officer offered a detailed example of these conflicts in his description of a seventy-two-year-old Newfoundland widower, Ed Bunt, in 1949:

The applicant is dirty, & careless. This man was found living in the woods in a cave last winter. The matter was reported to the Ranger (Relieving Officer) and arrangements were made for pay[ing his daughter-in-law] ... the sum of $20 per month for his board and lodging. The applicant says he eats in the home, but lives and sleeps in a shack about 10 ft by 7 ft. [Daughter-in-law] says she won't allow him to sleep in the house, and she'd rather not receive the $20 to care for him. When I asked the applicant what he would do if he received the [OA] pension of $30 monthly he replied 'I'd shack myself.'

Once he was given direct state support, in the form of an OAP, Bunt moved into a small 'hovel' near Paradise, enabling the welfare officer to write headquarters with the ironic comment, 'There has been more trouble in Paradise.' The old man was certainly not using his funds the way that the social worker would have liked:

[Of his $40 monthly OAP cheque, he claimed to be spending $20 a month on clothing] but judging by his appearance I would say that he has not put on a new article for years. He lives in a Little House 5 1/2 ft. by 8 ft. He has a part of this house partitioned off to keep sawdust ... His stove is the oven of an old wood stove ... He has a bunk built up on one side where he lies most of the time. He has two salt fish hanging from the ceiling and the smell from these permeates the building. The day I called his clothes were filthy. He has no socks on his feet and I could see his legs hadn't been washed for so long that it looked like he had the scurvy. His face was covered with long hair where he hadn't shaved for weeks, and underneath his beard his face was as dirty as his legs.

Another official commented in similar terms: 'He is a pitiful looking creature, he is so dirty and the only description that I can [give] you of him is he is like a pig in a Sty.' Like John Perry, Ed Bunt was at first unwilling to accept any boarding house, but later adjusted to a seasonal pattern of winter support and summer independence.[68] The clash of lifestyles and varying expectations and standards of the different parties to Bunt's old age produced a constant atmosphere of tension, as Bunt struggled to maintain control over his own life, and others, usually with good intentions, sought to impose their own standards. New state processes redefined old age with varying degrees of success.

There were limits to community support. Usually some measure of self-help by the elderly was required. Where the old persons needed total support, it tended to be available only on a temporary basis, until their health or financial circumstances recovered or until more permanent and broader-based assistance became available. Where recovery did not occur or when the individual elderly lacked family or friends on whom they could call for support, the community support tended eventually to dissolve, and responsibility for the old person was transferred to the state. The available records suggest that both the elderly and the communities generally accepted this eventual resort to a state institution. All involved – the elderly, neighbours, the community, and state officials – realized that there was a limit to informal sources of support, unless the individual elderly had a strong claim, almost always through kinship or friendship, to continuing informal assistance. Such claims could be more easily made if the old person could contribute in some way to the household economy. Without funds, old men could contribute their labour on odd jobs and maintenance until ill health prevented; beyond this, there was little old men could do in a gender-based household economy. Old women were more likely to have the domestic skills to allow continuing contributions to such an economy in return for support. Once old age pensions were available, the recipients became an important source of funds in often cash-starved households.

Community understandings of the limits of responsibility for the needy elderly were never clearly articulated, emphasizing the vulnerability of individual elderly. Local state officials found the Kamloops home attractive because it shifted responsibility for the elderly to others and allowed various institutions and programs to specialize in 'target populations' in a bureaucratically tidy way. Thus, throughout the five decades under study here, hospital officials sought to move chronically ill or disabled elderly to an old age home or to a chronic care hospital.[69] Local health or welfare officials often sought to protect single elderly from the results of their own deteriorating skills and behaviour. As social workers became more prominent, they too reflected this attitude. Both neighbours and the elderly dependent upon them were usually able to sense when the old person's needs exceeded the capacity or the willingness of neighbours to share resources, and both could be found taking the initiative in applying for admission to the Kamloops home. In one case, for example, a seventy-four-year-old labourer in ill health lived in a one-room shack near Kamloops: 'Applicant is a very poor cook and his neighbours feel that he does not get an adequate diet while living by himself.' The old man allegedly agreed that his domestic skills were so limited that admission to the Provincial Home would be best.[70] There were generally shared community standards regarding care and responsibility for the needy elderly.

Some elderly were attracted by the security offered in institutional care. A social worker in Chilliwack described the circumstances of a seventy-five-year-old former bookstore clerk who was single, had no relatives, and was suffering from gastritis and malnutrition. Up to that point he had spent winters at the home of a friend in Vancouver and the other seasons camping in the interior.

Patient is becoming very nervous as a result of his present condition and is most anxious to be somewhere where he can obtain regular meals and a certain amount of care. He is at present sleeping in a small tent and living on the banks of the Coquihalla River. Conditions are most unsatisfactory considering the man's health is failing. He is most anxious to go to the Kamloops Provincial Home as he feels that the climate there would be of benefit to him.[71]

Yet even for this old man, resort to institutional care occurred only after his own health had deteriorated and he had exhausted any claims on the local community.

Community support for the elderly was pervasive in early twentieth-century society. It was based on both a feeling of generosity and a sense of individual and group obligation to the elderly.

Institutions by 1930

Generally, the pace of institutional expansion for the elderly slowed, but continued across the 1910s and into the 1920s. The regional distribution of the institutionalized elderly was very much a reflection of the facilities available.[72] The early provision of residential old age institutions in Canada was overwhelmingly the task of state and quasi-state agencies.[73] Where no old age institutions yet existed for any particular geographical or social group, the dependent elderly were forced to rely on community or family support, if they were to survive.

The proliferation of old age homes in the early decades of the twentieth century is witness to their new importance in the state's response to the needs of the elderly. On the verge of implementing an old age pensions program in the late 1920s for the dependent elderly, civil servants in several jurisdictions undertook a survey of existing facilities for the elderly. While the results of those surveys varied considerably in the quality of the information collected, they nevertheless provide a useful sense of the level of care provided by state and other institutions for the elderly. Another sign of the same concern was that, for the first time, the Dominion Bureau of Statistics included a study of the institutionalized elderly in its analysis of Canadian society in 1931.

By 1931 there were 118 'homes for adults' in Canada, most of which specialized in meeting the needs of the elderly. Few of these were exclusively old age homes, however, and there was no consensus as to the definition of elderly. A further seventy-nine institutions considered their mandate to cover both adults and children. Many of these were homes for unwed mothers and their infants, but a good many were willing to take in other adults, including the elderly. In some, such as the Salvation Army rescue homes, the elderly could expect only temporary shelter, but often this was all that was needed or wanted. Some institutions specialising in children or in single women were willing to take only women among the elderly. In others, the home deliberately catered to both adults and children in need, no matter what the age. While not offering specialized attention focused on the elderly, institutions with diversified populations perhaps had a more interesting environment because of this variety.

Gender very much affected the ways in which individual elderly experienced these early old age homes. The segregation of the sexes and the sex-specific work reflected the importance of gender within society at large. Old men's wider options among survival strategies has already been discussed, and state and quasi-state agencies tended to direct their initial concern and resources disproportionately towards the care of elderly men. Men, too, had been socialized to articulate their own needs and demands more assertively, and to struggle at least more directly to maintain a semblance of independence.

Gender was just as important for women, though its impact was different. The disproportionate numbers of women among those labelled 'insane,' 'feeble-minded,' or 'epileptic' in state institutions is a reminder of the socially constructed character of such labels.74 The elderly, especially women, were particularly vulnerable to such authoritative, constructive processes. There is also some interesting evidence regarding residency in old age homes. Older women were almost twice as likely to be paying their full cost of maintenance, despite the fact that men tended strongly to control a disproportionate share of the wealth, relative to women; women were more used to handing money over to others and were likely more concerned to gain the physical security offered by an institution. It is much less surprising that older women were well represented among those unable to pay any of their institutional costs. Where women received the Old Age Pension, they were more than twice less likely than men to resort to institutional support. Women pensioners tended to use the OAP to maintain themselves in a household setting more than men, probably because men usually lacked the domestic skills to do so.

Officials' genuine concern for the unfortunate condition of such older persons is unquestioned. But, at the same time, the care provided continued to be shaped by an authoritative paternalism. When the OAP was instituted in Ontario in the fall of 1929, some residents of the county homes wanted to use the financial independence offered by a pension to move out, usually moving in with family or friends now that the elderly could contribute to the household income. Officials in charge of the homes, however, worried that the pensioners might suffer if they left their protected environment. Various solutions were proposed – requiring relatives or friends to sign a contract for the pensioner now in their care, placing all OAP funds in individual trust accounts controlled by officials – and some were implemented.[75] This protective impulse was a common phenomenon among public and private authorities dealing with the dependent elderly, but it was a product of genuine concern and a sense of responsibility for and obligation to the needy elderly.

That concern resulted in the continuing presence of another form of state aid – outdoor relief. In 1924 the House of Commons Special Committee on an old age pension system asked 135 Canadian municipalities for information on the elderly receiving municipal support. Forty-one responded with incomplete reports, thirty-seven of which commented on the number of elderly aged sixty-five or more on municipal relief at that time. A total of 1887 elderly persons had received welfare support, of whom 61 per cent were male (where sex was recorded). The level of support varied considerably, even within a municipality, and presumably reflected an assessment of the needs of the recipients – ranging from a low of $3.50 a month in Ottawa to $30 a month in several centres. Thirty-five of the municipalities reported supporting a total of 2044 elderly in hospitals, institutions, and private homes, 58 per cent of the recipients being male.[76] In Ottawa almost exactly 10 per cent of the city's elderly population received state support in formal institutions or private residences.[77] Outdoor relief was a source of support for a significant proportion of the needy elderly in Canada.

Other needy elderly received support from private charity. Mutual aid societies were an important response to the early stages of industrialization, but tended to collapse against the demands resulting from monopoly capitalism. For the most part the membership in so-called friendly societies consisted of artisans and skilled workers seeking to protect themselves against financial problems such as funerals or accidents, rather than as protection in old age. Such societies were male-dominated, exclusive, and defensive, and in all cases and descriptions uncovered they provided assistance exclusively to men and their dependants.[78] The male bias of this process was paralleled in the municipal relief systems themselves. In the early 1910s and the mid-1920s when asked to provide statistics regarding the number of men and women receiving support, several municipalities – Brantford and Peterborough, Ontario, St Stephen, New Brunswick – could provide the information for men but not for women.79

Even within these traditional welfare processes, family remained of central importance. Relatives provided emotional support and contact with the non-institutional world. Relatives could supplement support received from welfare sources, offering clothes or food occasionally. While many families could not afford the costs of institutional care and relied on private or public charity, they could supplement this support by slipping the occasional dollar or two to the older person. One sixty-four-year-old woman in a Hamilton, Ontario, old age home, for example, lived in the same room as her ninety-six-year-old mother. The daughter had 'so far stood all expenses of extras' for her mother, who was unable to pay the maintenance costs. Now the daughter hoped that her mother would be awarded an old age pension so that she would receive $1 a week in pocket money, relieving the pressure on the daughter's tight budget.80 The new state programs promised supplemental support for these family processes. The institutional aid, however, was an alternative source of support for those lacking family resources. That institutional support expanded across the early decades of the twentieth century and was gradually reshaped in response to new standards and attitudes. Old age institutions were constructed and reconstructed within the changing language and perceptions of the elderly and their needs in the early twentieth century, a process in which the elderly themselves had an appreciable role.

Many of these processes for the support of the dependent elderly – but particularly those associated with the state or with charity – retained considerable stigma in the late 1920s. Poorhouses had always had a negative image, usually cultivated so as to discourage individual indigents from easy resort to state support. As poorhouses evolved into nascent old age homes they did not entirely lose that image, though certainly they offered a welcome and often much-sought-after haven from the vicissitudes of survival in the world outside these institutions. A private citizen writing from Ridgetown, Ontario, in 1912 commented, with possibly some exaggeration as to the final result: 'The dread of the disgrace and eternal onus which attaches to those compelled to take refuge in those institutions cause a vast multitude to commit suicide.'81 This disgrace had been associated with the poorhouse for generations, but what was new was a growing sense that the elderly deserved better treatment, at least because aging was beyond individual control and because the negative perceptions of the physical characteristics of aging particularly evoked sympathy and paternalistic responses.

This belief that singled out the elderly as deserving better treatment was increasingly articulated. As early as 1912 a Dartmouth, Nova Scotia, Salvation Army officer commented that his organization was caring for an elderly man and that it would 'not let him go to the poorhouse.' The 1930 New Brunswick royal commission on old age pensions referred to that province's 'de-humanized poorhouses,' emphasizing the institutions' links to earlier methods of dealing with the poor and destitute of any age.[82] Apart from the traditional stigma associated with such institutions, another negative factor was their location. Elderly 'sent' to these homes were often removed from their own community, neighbourhood, and family, leaving the old people isolated from essential support mechanisms. While counties in eastern and central Canada each tended to have a state-supported home, in the more sparsely populated west and in Newfoundland province-wide institutions had been established. The isolation of these homes in such centres as Wolseley, Saskatchewan, or Kamloops, British Columbia, meant an even more wrenching experience for the elderly involved and for their friends and family.

These institutions were also felt to undermine social status and to attack personal independence. A Quebec official complained in 1912 that not only were married couples separated on entry, but that the average elderly man was forced to live side-by-side with his social unequals.

There being no selection in these [Roman Catholic] institutions, this good, sound workman, who has toiled all his life, is made a neighbour at the table with an idiot or a man with some loathsome disease ... This man is made to feel that he is dependent on this institution; and, whether he has been a saint all his life, or a very moderate man in religion, he has got to pray all the time, and this, of course, you can quite understand, a man in this position feels it very hard. Of course, the separation [from his wife] is a bad feature of dependency, and also the fact that he is almost deprived of seeing his family; because, as soon as he is incapacitated, he cannot secure permission to go out anywhere.[83]

A new standard of care and concern for the elderly was emerging in reaction to the public perception of the 'problems' facing the dependent elderly.

When such problems combined with the frequent attempts at rigid discipline in the homes, the institutions fell well short of meeting the needs of many elderly. This failure, together with the stigma of the homes, inhibited them from effectively aiding all but the most desperate elderly, causing considerable tension within the institutions and preventing needy elderly from taking advantage of the support offered. When a Calgary relief official stated in 1924 that 'to see old age suffering through want is not tolerated to-day,' he was expressing more an important new attitude than an accurate reflection of the economic or social position of the elderly at that time. He was much more accurate when he went on to describe the current methods of support for the elderly as 'not uniform, but very haphazard.'[84] These new attitudes combined with a rising discontent with the current formal methods of aid and support to sustain a major legislative initiative in the late 1920s, establishing a non-contributory old age pension.

The Family and Intergenerational Support

Family was central not only to the survival strategies of the elderly themselves, but to the policies with which legislators and social commentators responded to the needs of the dependent elderly. Underlying both the old age pensions debates and the filial responsibility legislation of the 1920s and 1930s was a desire to entrench the traditional values and attitudes to the elderly within contemporary responses. A succession of statutes, regulations, and rhetoric underlined the primary obligation of family members to care for the dependent elderly, and provided means by which such obligations might be enforced. While the legislation itself was seldom employed to prosecute adult sons and daughters, it did become the basis of a powerful regulatory process attempting to coerce more extensive support for elderly parents from their children. This legislation reveals a number of features of state old age policy. The early twentieth-century state was decidedly ambivalent about its direct role in support for the dependent elderly, and it employed seemingly contradictory policies. This characteristic, which remains a feature of old age policy, emphasizes the extent to which continuities exist in the treatment of the elderly.

Another continuity in the 1920s and 1930s was the state's insistence on maintaining the fundamental centrality of the family among the support mechanisms of the dependent elderly. Embodying as it did most of the key social concepts and values of the time – such as domesticity, deference, gender, age – the idea of the family was basic to the ways in which the politically and socially articulate responded to various social problems and groups. In the case of the elderly, there was widespread concern that no new policies should impair the family's ability or responsibility to care for its own dependent members. Any sense of undermining the family as an institution implicitly threatened fundamental beliefs which, while often unarticulated, were none the less vital.

State policies across the Western world reflected such attitudes and values. The Victorian debate of the English poor law had explicitly warned against endangering family relationships through liberalization of poor relief. An early consideration of state pensions in 1907 in the United States rejected any such scheme as likely to discourage individual thrift and to destroy family solidarity by ending filial obligations to support parents. Even after state pension schemes had been adopted, they often remained secondary to familial support mechanisms. Twenty-five of the first forty American states to establish approved old age pension schemes under the 1935 Social Security Act required an investigation of the ability of family members to support the applicant; only where such family members were found unable to provide financial support was the applicant eligible for this new form of state support. In a sample of 1935–9 Missouri applications for an old age pension, almost 20 per cent of the rejections were based on the ground of having relatives capable of providing the support.[1] In the Western world, family support was consistently central to any new policies for the elderly, as the state shied away from any assertion of the primacy of the elderly's claim on the state for a citizen's wage.

Filial Responsibility Laws

Existing and new legislation gave direct expression to this emphasis on the primary character of family obligations in support for the elderly. Filial responsibility laws were based on a belief in a long-standing, homogeneous tradition about family behaviour and duties. A 1601 English statute had named children, where capable, responsible for the maintenance and support of their poor or disabled parents; in Scotland this law explicitly included grandchildren and married daughters. Nineteenth-century English policy concerning the poor consistently pointed to the duties of family members for their less fortunate kin – specifically children for their parents. This was strengthened in new poor law legislation in 1895, designed to encourage 'thrift and family affection.' In the United States this expression grew more insistent and more common as the nineteenth century passed into the twentieth and as concern for 'the decline' of the family increased. While just eighteen states (of thirty-three) had adopted statutes affirming family responsibility for dependent members by 1860, thirty-two (of forty-eight) had done so by 1914. In the 1920s five more states passed such legislation, and eleven others criminalized failure to provide for dependent parents.[2] Such legislation merely gave statutory expression to what was already a vital source of aid for the elderly.

The family was of utmost importance to the elderly. Nevertheless, it is possible to exaggerate the amount of support for the elderly provided by their families in previous centuries. For example, often less than 40 per cent of the elderly lived with their families in nineteenth-century England. In many instances, as people approached and advanced into old age, the movement away from living with children was at least as strong as the movement towards shared residences. The elderly of nineteenth-century England, David Thomson argued, had already found substantial support from sources outside the family.[3] Canadian insurance companies in the early 1930s estimated with self-serving bias that 63 per cent of the elderly population were destitute (though their definition of destitution is unknown); adult children and relatives cared for 23 per cent of those elderly, leaving 40 per cent to be looked after by charity or the state.[4] Though reliance on family members remained a traditional and prominent source of support, there were signs that it was not an attractive alternative to many, at least in comparison with independent living arrangements. Insurance advertisements in the 1930s underlined the unwelcome and constricting dependency inherent in such support. The Mutual Insurance Company, for example, threatened the unprepared with 'the narrow routine of a dependent relative,' and women in particular were regularly portrayed as clashing with children and in-laws. In her study of older Canadian women in the 1920s and 1930s, Veronica Strong-Boag detected a strong popular aversion to three-generation households as fraught with considerable danger.[5]

This suggests that the qualitative relations of the elderly with family members must not be romanticized. Support was certainly given, but its impact on intergenerational relationships was problematic. Nineteenth-century wills indicate that many elderly, particularly in rural areas, used property and potential inheritance to gain support from children, based on the fear that such support would not otherwise be forthcoming. Nor was the promise of inheritance always enough to lure adult children into accepting such responsibilities for their aged parents.[6] While reciprocity helps to explain some forms of intergenerational support, the negative elements associated with the elderly and their care suggest that, by the early twentieth century at least, some of the family support provided for the elderly was reluctantly or grudgingly given (as it no doubt had always been).[7] There nevertheless remained an authoritative family culture that insisted on family members' responsibility to aid one another throughout the lifecourse.[8] As already discussed in chapter 1, most elderly with families could count on those families to provide support.

However, such support, particularly where it was fundamental to survival or where it involved co-residence, ran counter to several influential ideas in the modern industrial world. Privacy was increasingly valued in Western society, and there is no reason to believe that by the early twentieth century this was less true for the elderly or their children. A survey of the elderly poor in England in the 1890s argued that 'old people as a rule are averse to living with their children and it seldom answers'; adult children were held to be just as reluctant to take in their parents. The elderly valued their independence, and sought to avoid reduction to a dependent position. When forced to choose between dependence on children or dependence on the state (in the form of the deliberately unattractive local poorhouse), some chose the latter. However, where the elderly could offer some form of reciprocal aid – perhaps in the form of baby-sitting or assistance in cottage work or light labouring duties around a farm – outright dependence could be avoided by both elderly parents and their children.9

Modern research has isolated a number of ways in which kinship support was manifested. Residence patterns (both shared households and proximity); daily, weekly, or frequent interaction and visiting or shared tasks; economic interdependence and mutual aid; and affective support have all been isolated as important means by which family members offered support to one another. Unfortunately, the new forms of state regulation tended to emphasize just one kind of support – direct financial aid. As Jill Quadagno has argued, this narrow definition placed great strain on intergenerational relations among the working class, where financial resources were often inadequate, but where other forms of significant support could still be offered. The tension caused by government-coerced financial support often led to an overall deterioration in intergenerational relations within the families involved, suggesting the very real possibility of a loss or a reduction in the non-monetary forms of support.10

Such coercion had another, perhaps minor, side to it. One English study found that in many families adult children could accept the idea of being responsible for supporting their needy parents. What was difficult was working out the form of support and allocating the amount of responsibility among the various siblings. In England, children sometimes solved this problem by putting their parents on poor relief in order to make the state agents determine a fair division of responsibility. At the same time, this reaction points to another form of stress caused by the principle of filial responsibility; not only was there parent-child tension but also sibling conflict.11 Canadian officials consistently declined to take on any role mediating among siblings, though in practice some OAP offficials did make such decisions.

Paralleling legislative initiatives in England and the United States and in response to some of the same pressures, several Canadian provinces followed the lead of American jurisdictions in enacting filial responsibility laws in the 1920s and 1930s. Such legislation already existed in Quebec and Newfoundland. The 1866 Quebec civil code (articles 166, 167, 171) required support for both parents and parents-in-law, while nineteenth-century Newfoundland legislation made liable 'any child [who] has left destitute, abandoned or deserted his aged or infirm parent ... being destitute of the means of support and likely to become a burden on the colony.' While other provinces had not yet adopted such legislation at the turn of the century, there is no doubt that public and private welfare was distributed with an eye to the family circumstances of the poor. Where the family was capable of supporting potential recipients, welfare was not granted. Local governments and officials felt strongly that state aid should be available only where family members were judged unable to provide a minimal level of assistance.[12]

This primacy assigned to family responsibilities for the care of the elderly was long-standing. Public welfare officials in the early twentieth century enforced a policy of family responsibility for care of the needy elderly even before explicit legislation was adopted. The case of Donald Boston in London, Ontario, offers a fine example of the questions asked and the techniques used to press families to accept their moral obligations to support elderly members. Boston was seventy-five years old when his case came to the attention of the city welfare officers. He had lived in London for forty years, prior to going to Australia in 1910, returning early in 1915, and applying for admission to a local old age home as a city charge in the fall of that year. Boston was married, but had not lived with his wife for nineteen years, and she was now a resident of another local old age home. They had six sons living in 1915, and Boston well understood the 'rules' regarding becoming a city charge, for his application was accompanied by 'an inventory of his family and the positions they hold.' Though the location, occupation, and weekly income of each son were provided, details of their family responsibilities were sparse, noting that every son was married and that there were nine grandchildren, two of whom were married, and five great-grandchildren. At the time of Boston's application he was living 'on the bounty' of one his grandsons, who was himself married with three children.

The first step of the city welfare department was to write each of Boston's sons, pointing out that their father had applied for city aid and had supplied information about the sons; 'it appears to the [City] Council that if each member would contribute probably three dollars per month he would not need to be a charity patient. The City Council feel that six sons all earning good money would prefer to contribute a small amount per month instead of their father living on charity, and what publicity it might bring forth.' But this appeal to the social stigma of welfare did not produce the desired result, at least in the case of the son who was in northern Ontario. 'Before I am condemned for not doing my part,' he wanted to explain his past relationship with his father, who had a history of abusive behaviour, of extensive non-support, and of bigamy. As the oldest son, the writer had supported his mother and younger brothers, and continued to pay his elderly mother $4 a month. Nevertheless, the writer was willing to consider helping his father, 'although I don't think he deserves it after the way he has acted so if when you hear from my other Brothers let me know what they will do and then I will let you know what I will do. But for the publicity of the matter I don't care as I have always done my duty and am not afraid of the public.' One of the London sons also replied, stating that his existing family obligations were as much as he could meet, but he considered himself in a position to give his approval of the disposition of his father's case – 'a home is the best place for my father, knowing the kind of man he is who requires looking after, and I feel sure he will have all the attention and care given him there.'13

The idea of family obligation was already firmly implanted in individual state and family expectations regarding the care of the elderly well before the passage of explicit state legislation articulating this policy. Family responsibility was fundamental to many of the participants in this case: to Donald Boston, who returned to London to be near relatives and a community on which he had some claim and who carefully supplied the welfare officers with details of his family; to his grandson who supported him; to the welfare officers and to city councillors, who viewed state charity as a last resort; and to Boston's son who had continued to support his mother, was willing to consider helping a father he did not respect, and, while denying the power of public opinion in the matter, sought to defend himself against it.14

In a renewed spate of concern, other provinces enacted filial responsibility legislation, beginning with Ontario in 1921 and followed by Alberta and British Columbia (1922), Saskatchewan (1923), Manitoba, Nova Scotia and Prince Edward Island (1933), New Brunswick (1936), and the Northwest Territories (1938). The legislation took a fairly standard form. Adult children of both sexes who were capable of doing so were required to support parents who, because of age, disease, or infirmity, were unable to maintain themselves. Any such dependent parent could, with the written consent of the crown attorney, summon the child or children before a magistrate, who could order support payments of up to $20 weekly, depending on the means and circumstances of the children. Proceedings under the act could be taken on the parents' behalf by a designated public official, the governing body of any government or charitable institution where the dependent parent resided, or (after 1927) by any local authority paying an Old Age Pension to a dependent parent. The sporadic amendment of the legislation in the various jurisdictions indicates that enactment was not a transitory fancy; nor was the legislation intended to be a 'dead letter.' This was a serious attempt to bolster family structures and values and to assist the elderly, while the state avoided primary economic responsibility.

Nevertheless, the legislation was seldom used as a basis for prosecution. Five local courts were examined for the frequency of parents' maintenance acts prosecutions. In Carleton County, Ontario, there were thirty-two cases before the courts prior to 1951, twenty-six of which occurred during the 1930s Depression. In Ontario County, Ontario, there were nine cases, all but one of which occurred prior to 1941.[15] In New Westminster, British Columbia, just one case was heard during the years 1928–40, while not one was heard in Vancouver district court for 1930–51 or in Penticton, British Columbia, for 1932–6.[16] The legislation was seldom employed on a judicial basis to coerce support from adult children for their parents.[17]

Coercion of familial support through judicial processes was doomed to failure. The adversarial system at the heart of the judicial process was quite unsuited to the needs of the elderly. Family remained a central source of assistance and potential aid for the elderly, including emotional support. The overwhelming majority of the needy elderly could ill afford to take their children to court, jeopardizing existing forms of assistance in the probably forlorn hope of regular monetary support. The potential benefits from court action seldom promised to outweigh the costs in lost support and in financial and emotional costs. But among the general public the idea behind the legislation was so appealing that the flaws in the legislation were ignored.

An examination of the various state processes aimed at assisting the elderly reveals a quite different picture from that of judicial inactivity. On a regulatory basis, rather than through formal prosecutions, the state was strikingly active. State and quasi-state officials already carried out this mandate. As discussed in chapter 2, almost no residents of state-operated old age homes had living relatives who could look after them; where family existed, they were expected to and usually did look after their elderly members. When municipal authorities assessed an individual old person's eligibility for state aid, they always inquired into the person's family status: Where were the children? What were their financial circumstances and familial status? How much aid could they and did they give to the parent involved? Where family were felt to be capable of providing sufficient support, welfare was denied.[18]

The regulatory use of the parents' maintenance legislation simply legitimated existing, informal state practices and gave officials greater authority in wielding their regulatory powers. At no time did government officials turn regularly to the legal processes made available in the legislation. Instead, officials simply employed the legislation to render more successful their attempted coercion of families. In a 1925 case, for example, the deputy provincial secretary of British Columbia instructed a local government agent to write to all the adult children, informing them of the parents' maintenance legislation and warning them 'that they will not be permitted to avoid their responsibilities; further that unless they take prompt action to support their parents you will have to consider the necessity of proceeding against them under the Act.'[19] Officials felt strongly enough about this obligation that they were willing to lecture elected politicians on the principle.[20]

OAP Regulatory Processes

With the OAP program the insistence on the primacy of family responsibility continued, but a new enforcement technique was available. Now the regulatory use of parents' maintenance legislation became much more systematic and pervasive. At first glance, state pensions and family maintenance appear to be contradictory programs for the elderly; the first recognized a government responsibility for care, and the second articulated a primary familial responsibility. Yet the two policies were not seen to be contradictory at the time among legislators or bureaucrats.[21] In the same legislative session in which the parents' maintenance legislation was adopted, Ontario passed a motion supporting the initiation of an old age pension plan; more than a decade later, the New Brunswick legislature enacted Old Age Pension and parents' maintenance legislation in the same session. The two programs for support of the needy elderly were compatible not because of any explicit statutory stipulation as to how the two meshed, but because of the well understood primacy attributed to the role of the family.[22]

At the outset of the program, all agreed that the dependent elderly must be helped and that the traditional and primary source of that help was the family of the elderly. Only where the family was unable to provide care for its needy elderly members was the state expected to give assistance through the Old Age Pension. Officials lacked a statutory basis for refusing (or reducing) an OAP on the ground that the children could support the applicant. This sufficiently disturbed the federal Department of Justice for it to suggest that any such policy required an amendment to the act. The belief in the primacy of filial responsibility was so firmly entrenched, however, that administrators proceeded without any legislative ratification.[23] In practical terms, the parents' maintenance laws and policies facilitated an attempt to employ a household or extended family means test to the OAP, rather than an individual or couple-centred test.

Neither political leaders nor senior civil servants had any intention of allowing the Old Age Pension to interfere in traditional family processes of support for needy members. Nor would families be allowed to devolve upon the state responsibilities that the family had traditionally shouldered. While acknowledging the plight of the elderly in modern society, the nation's leaders sought to assist the elderly through the most traditional and least innovative means possible. Support for the role of the family was central to both the parents' maintenance legislation and the Old Age Pension. The OAP became a second and more powerful weapon in reinforcing the family's role in assisting the elderly.

OAP administrators, politicians, and social leaders repeatedly bemoaned what they perceived as the decline of traditional family values and behaviour. For such spokespersons this was a source of very real anxiety, for the state must never help the elderly in such a way as to undermine the family's primary support functions. Youth came increasingly to be blamed for their alleged failure to support their aged parents. At the 1937 meeting of the Interprovincial OAP Board, 'it was unanimously agreed that the provincial governments should be requested to cooperate in an effort to check the growing tendency on the part of younger persons well able to support their parents to shift their responsibilities onto the State.'[24] In a memo concerning the future costs of the OAP program, an official in the Dominion Bureau of Statistics in 1939 emphasized the primacy of the family:

It is also important for us to keep in mind that the natural unit of human society is not the individual, but the family. In the cases of widows and widowers, the aged Canadian should probably be living with sons or daughters, who, if in a position to do so, should properly contribute to the support of their parents, in return for their own maintenance during childhood and youth. In former times, it was considered that a poor man's main reliance for support in his declining years should consist in the possession of a numerous family. Unquestionably thousands of aged parents are being so supported to-day, though it is probably one of the worst features of the great depression that young married people, themselves with little or no employment, find it impossible to contribute toward the support of their aged parents.[25]

The frequent appeals to tradition and to natural law throughout the period under study suggest the centrality of the values involved.

There was a fear on the part of some that the OAP itself was playing a negative role in contemporary family culture. In aiding the elderly the state was discouraging help in many forms from the children, it was claimed. 'You would be struck,' wrote the chairman of the British Columbia board, 'to find at times how little interest in the way of practical efforts is shown by some of the children. If an aged person is drawing the Old Age Pension then the tendency is for all of those socially inclined to leave them out of any helpful efforts being made to assist those in distress.'[26] Nothing the state did should add to this fundamental undermining of the traditional family. Indeed, the regulatory process of the OAP, using the philosophy of the parents' maintenance legislation and the legal power that that legislation provided, could be employed to halt that decline and to reinforce traditional family values.

Where the family structure was strong, the OAP was expected to play a more reduced role. For both English- and French-speaking Canadians, the family culture of Quebec was perceived to be particularly authoritative, and traditional values to be fully functioning. In 1932 a federal civil servant estimated the possible impact of adoption of the OAP in Quebec: 'The situation in Quebec does not lend itself to comparison with other provinces, due to filial reasons. The young people of Quebec, particularly among the French-speaking, consider it not only a duty but a privilege to care for the aged. This characteristic is perhaps more pronounced in the Province of Quebec than in any other province.'[27] In this regard, Québecois culture served as a foil for broadly based fears about the family elsewhere. When Quebec joined the OAP program, the province proved itself to be more generous to its elderly and certainly no more demanding of family support mechanisms than several English-speaking provinces, but this did nothing to alter the ethnic stereotype.

As with the requirements about pensioners' property (discussed in chapter 4), federal authorities took the lead in pushing provincial officials to be more aggressive in inducing families to aid their elderly members. It was a federal regulation that required provincial OAP authorities, in applying the means test, to consider as income contributions received from children 'or contributions reasonably expected to be made by children ... in money or in kind.'[28] What was crucial was that potential income – contributions that local officials decided could reasonably be expected, given the children's income and circumstances – would thus be assumed to be real income for the purposes of calculating the pensioner's payment level. This notion of fictive income placed a powerful weapon in the hands of pension administrators, if they could be persuaded to use it.

In preparation for the 1937 meeting of the Interprovincial OAP Board, a senior federal civil servant in a lengthy memorandum singled out family support as an issue demanding attention. The federal minister of finance took up the issue, arguing at the 1937 meeting for more effective provincial policies and actions. Such measures would not only save costs for the OAP program (and this was decisive, given the financial exigencies of the 1930s), but would also strengthen the moral order of the nation, he suggested: 'There is a moral element in the responsibility of children for the care of their parents ... I am inclined to think that there would be a considerable measure of public support behind the enforcement of these acts compelling children, where they are able to do so, to support their parents. And most acts are reasonable in that regard.' He urged all provincial governments to provide for the 'efficient enforcement' of parents' maintenance legislation.[29] But the 'reasonable' character of such legislation was in the eye of the beholder.

The Quebec board was one that responded positively to these suggestions, looking for ways to enforce the philosophy more effectively. Knowing that the federal income tax process allowed an exemption for income used to support a dependent elderly relative, the board requested some sons and daughters to submit copies of their returns, uncovering a number of cases in which the support claimed rendered existing pensioners eligible for a reduced payment or even no pension at all. The Quebec board pushed Ottawa to make available for systematic surveillance all such income tax returns.[30] Though the idea was not new, it reached Ottawa at the right time. The powerful deputy minister of finance immediately adopted the suggestion and followed up on it. Federal officials saw the proposal as meshing nicely with their push to force more support from adult children:

We are insisting that the provinces enforce their own legislation with reference to the maintenance of parents by children. In a number of provinces a serious attempt is being made to put a stop to children neglecting their duties to their aged parents and, if at all possible, the Dominion should assist by furnishing any information which will be of assistance to the provinces in checking the present tendency among children to shift their responsibilities onto the State.[31]

Children who claimed to one agency to be providing support and who denied it to another agency would now be caught out; officials would accept their claim of support as valid and would lower or discontinue the pension to the parents. The potential savings were considerable. And those savings were important. Officials knew that any investigations and repercussions had to be designed in such a way that the children were not simply penalized for supporting their parents. 'Where children are making this effort to support their parents I think we should encourage them to do so' by continuing to allow them a considerable tax exemption. The savings should come through reducing the payments to pensioners, those who were most vulnerable to such administrative action.[32]

Support for a more prominent role for the family certainly existed in some quarters, particularly if combined with more general rhetoric appealing to traditional ideas about the family. The Canadian Manufacturers' Association, for example, advised the 1937–8 Royal Commission on Dominion-Provincial Relations that near relatives should be required to support the elderly as a means of reducing the cost of the OAP program. A hard-hitting speech of the Ontario minister of welfare in 1932 received considerable newspaper coverage for its attack on what the *Windsor Star* called 'prosperous children who force aged parents to exist upon Old Age Pensions.'[33] The articulate public seemed to favour policies and values that sustained what was believed to be traditional family culture. But it must be emphasized that this support for the so-called traditional family owed much of its motivation to the fact that it promised a way to cut costs. In the desperate economic times of the 1930s, political leaders latched onto a comforting, familist rhetoric to meet their primary financial concerns.

Several provinces followed this lead by strengthening the parents' maintenance legislation. In 1938 Saskatchewan took control of prosecution out of the hands of the parents, by allowing charges to be laid by the commissioner of Old Age Pensions or by the municipality where the parents resided; permission of the parents to charge their children was no longer necessary. British Columbia adopted a similar amendment in 1940. In 1941 Alberta amended its statute to render an adult child liable to remove a dependent parent from hospital, and the following year prosecution by public officials became possible.

Yet provincial and local authorities still hesitated – indeed, declined – to commence actual prosecution of individual sons and daughters. In a letter bragging that the legislation had been amended and strengthened, the Saskatchewan premier commented: 'With this amendment the [Parents' Maintenance] Act would appear to be sufficient to meet the situation but under present conditions in this Province it is not practicable to utilize it to the extent it might be done under other circumstances.'[34] The British Columbia board did not support the amendment giving it authority to institute legal proceedings, and did not want to be singled out as having particular responsibility for such proceedings; the board was even more appalled when the amendment was altered so as to require the board to lay charges.[35] Every level of government favoured the enforcement of the parents' maintenance legislation, but each government shifted responsibility to another. The unwillingness to institute legal proceedings, however, was not widely known, and the amendments served to draw public attention to the legislation and to strengthen the regulatory use of the legislation by making the threat of prosecution seem more potent. So too did the not-infrequent press reports, particularly in British Columbia, that the provincial board required parents to sue the children for support before being allowed to apply for a pension.[36]

While direct, legal action against adult children was avoided in every jurisdiction, other forms of coercion were readily employed. An informal regulatory process best suited the needs of the OAP administrators. Provincial boards put considerable direct pressure on individual families to provide support. If the needy elderly were left the losers, caught between the board and their children, the board could fall back on the pious hope that the children would feel the moral pressure of the state and the immediate pressure of their parents' circumstances, and would respond positively to their parents' needs.

Officials in all provinces employed the approach that had long been acceptable – informal coercion of support from adult children. Some officials talked directly with the children or the parents, maintaining the tactics seen in the Donald Boston case two decades earlier. Alberta authorities, for example, explained that in cases where adult children appeared to have sufficient means, officials would 'discuss with them' the legislation 'and point out their responsibility,' at which point the adult children had the opportunity to furnish a statement or provide an explanation of their financial obligations that prevented their giving parental support.[37] The burden was on the children to persuade officials that support could not be provided, and this reverse onus was an authoritative weapon in the hands of civil servants. In British Columbia, when a pension was refused because of the children's ability to support the parents, pressure was placed on the children through the parents: 'We do not ask the parent to sue the son or daughter but we do point out to the parent that the responsibility is first on the son or daughter to support before the support comes from the public treasury.'[38] The problem with this approach was that the message would not necessarily reach the children whose behaviour the policy was designed to change.

A less direct form of administrative pressure used bureaucratic processes. The OAP application form in every province required the elderly to provide details about their living children. Age, sex, residence, marital and family status, occupation, income, and amount of aid given in the past year were all requested. This demand for information about children became more and more detailed over time in Ontario. The 1929 application form demanded the children's name, sex, address, marital status, and occupation. Another question asked how much support the applicant's sons and daughters had given in the past year, and, if there was nothing to report, the form pressed this point, too: 'If any of your sons and daughters have failed to contribute, give names and reasons for such failure.'[39] In 1934 these questions were consolidated; the revised form requested information regarding the number of children born to each adult child, annual income, and amount of support contributed to the parent. The 1943 form retained all these categories of information and asked for each child's age and whether they were living with the parent. By 1935 standard forms had been prepared provincially for each adult child to complete and to attach to the parent's OAP application; the forms quoted several clauses of the parents' maintenance act and required the children to acknowledge their legal responsibility to support their parents and to declare how much they were able to contribute on a weekly basis to the parent; any inability to meet this obligation required an explanation. In addition, the municipal clerk's report required him to express an opinion as to the children's ability to support the applicant parent. The cumulative information about the adult children was considerable, and the message inherent in requesting such information was at least as important as the data themselves.

That message was one of intimidation. For example, when a seventy-three-year-old labourer, a widower living in Lambton County, applied for a pension in 1945, he listed all seven of his children. All were married, and all but one, a daughter in Detroit, had children. One of his three daughters lived in the same community as her father, as did one of his sons, a janitor with two children with whom the old man lived. His other sons' occupations were listed as mechanic, welder, and baker, but he claimed to have no idea of any of his children's income except that of his janitor son, who earned $1000 approximately. Every child filled out a parents' maintenance act declaration, including the son and daughter living in Detroit and the wife of the welder son. His oldest daughter, in Toronto with three children, claimed to have ill-health. His second daughter, who had two children, declared: 'our income isn't large enough to properly raise my own children.' The Detroit son with two children asserted that he was 'not in a position to support.' The Detroit daughter with no children gave a slightly more expansive explanation, as though she had a weaker case than her siblings: 'I am unable to contribute to the support of my father as I have no income other than my husband's earnings and that is consumed in living expenses.' The welder son with five children explained that he was ill and not working, and his wife confirmed that declaration. The baker son with one child pleaded the costs of supporting his own family. Finally, the janitor son affirmed: 'My father owns the place where I live and I have been keeping him, paying taxes and keeping him supplied with food, clothing and fuel and my total income for the year is only $1,000 and I find that this is not enough to keep my wife and child as well as my father.'[40] In total, the declarations must have been somewhat humiliating for the man's children, having to expose private characteristics of their own families and to admit their inability to support their father. Nevertheless, they did so, to help their father gain a pension and to ease the financial straits of their janitor brother.

The provinces varied in their willingness to enforce parents' maintenance legislation indirectly through the OAP. In the 1930s, Manitoba tended to disregard any family obligations in calculating OAP eligibility. In 1940 the provincial board followed the lead of federal officials and several other boards by sending out to every pensioner a new form designed to reveal the incomes of adult children. The procedure sparked vigorous attacks in the legislature on the grounds that the board was exceeding its authority, and the attorney general advised the board to discontinue the new practice. By 1945 provincial authorities had adopted a general rule for fixing the income proportion of board and lodging paid by adult children living with their parents – 20 per cent – but they did not apply the rule rigorously, preferring not to place the family in a position where the parent might benefit (receive a higher pension) if the children left home.[41]

Nova Scotia, too, was reluctant to adopt any position that would tend to place obstacles or tension in the path of supportive intergenerational relations. For this reason, explained that province's OAP director, the board favoured paying the OAP even when the recipients visited children in the United States; to do otherwise would be 'cruel and wholly unnecessary,' he argued. The provincial minister responsible for the OAP later set out his understanding of local policy: the OAP was not intended to provide full maintenance, but rather to be supplementary to other income, and its payment should not alter (or discourage) the children's responsibility to provide for their parents.[42] While agreeing on the dual ends of supporting the needy elderly and strengthening intergenerational relations, authorities could adopt diametrically opposed means to achieve those ends.

Saskatchewan, with perhaps the highest proportion of agricultural population in the country, had a special problem with family farming and the particular family culture it engendered. Traditionally farm families shared labour and property, each generation contributing to maintain and enhance the total holdings for the benefit of all family members. As property was transferred to succeeding generations, the elderly would be cared for by the family. The devastating drought and crop failures of the 1930s combined with harsh economic conditions to render it increasingly difficult for the farm property to support the extended family. The 1936–7 annual report of the Saskatchewan OAP board commented: 'Quite a number of sons who are farmers had been keeping their aged parents but owing to complete failure of their crop this year they were obliged to see that their parents made application for an Old Age Pension.'[43] The children were not turning their parents out. Rather, application for the OAP was part of a family strategy for coping with severe economic hardship – this was one financial contribution that the elderly could make to the continuing family economy. Though Saskatchewan began to consider contributions from children as income at the very beginning of the program, this quickly came under attack in the provincial cabinet; the result was a less rigorous procedure.[44] Saskatchewan was the only province by 1940 that still had no set rule for the amount of income to be charged against parents through the presence of a fully employed child in the home.[45]

By 1950 all provincial boards had a reasonably clear understanding of amounts that would be systematically charged against the elderly in common circumstances of family support. But the amounts charged varied considerably, generally being lowest on the prairies and the west coast, highest in central Canada, and slightly less high in the Atlantic provinces.[46]

The province of Ontario talked seriously about family responsibility for the elderly, but officials were somewhat lax in carrying through and enforcement was quite sporadic. A few local boards, such as Toronto's, tended to ignore filial responsibility regulations entirely. When the OAP first started in Ontario in the fall of 1929, the provincial board informed local authorities that pensions were being awarded 'in the great majority' of cases where applicants had married children with large families. While a fixed rule was judged an impossibility, the board did not intend to be 'too harsh' in this area.[47] A 1930 St Thomas newspaper report suggested that where some local boards were discontinuing OAP payments because children were judged capable of providing support, the cases were turned over to the local courts, where the relatives were required to testify as to their income and behaviour. Unfortunately from the officials' point of view, magistrates refused to enforce the legislation in almost every case brought before them.[48] Part of the problem was the provincial board's refusal to give unambiguous guidelines to local officials. When one son wrote on behalf of his parents, inquiring as to the definition of 'sufficient means' as applied to an adult child's capacity to support, the board refused to offer any general definition.[49] Several local boards made similar requests. In response to one such question, the provincial board declined to offer any guidelines, but made explicit its policy of regulatory coercion: 'We think the real test in cases where the applicants have a number of children is whether if an application is made to a Police Magistrate under the Parents' Maintenance Act an order could be obtained against these children to support their parents. We do not mean that these applications should be made.'[50]

In 1932 the federal deputy minister felt that the Ontario board was using the parents' maintenance legislation 'to very good effect.'[51] Years later grandchildren could still recall inspectors visiting families in the 1930s in the hope of persuading them to support elderly parents more fully.[52] Field investigators by 1938 'had definite instructions to make a complete report as to the ability of children of applicants to contribute toward their parents' support.' They carried with them forms that pensioners and applicants were instructed to give to their children, if the children were single and living in Ontario. By 1940 these reports requiring the self-reporting of income were supplemented with forms sent to these children's employers.[53] Single children of either sex were particularly the targets of officials' attention. In the early 1940s 'scores' of pensions were reduced or suspended as a result of more rigorous standards.[54] But by mid-war the provincial board had eased its aggressive stance. The effect, in the view of one federal official, was to 'practically eliminate compulsory contributions from children' and to tend to ignore any voluntary contributions, much to the displeasure of Ottawa officials.[55]

British Columbia, in contrast, had a reputation for strict regulatory enforcement of its parents' maintenance legislation among OAP applicants. In 1932 a local member of parliament complained that the legislation was being used 'in scores of cases.' 'I am satisfied,' commented one knowledgeable federal civil servant, 'that many persons are prevented from applying for [the] pension knowing the pension authority will investigate their children's incomes as well as their own.'[56] Others who applied were rejected on the basis of their children's ability to provide support. In 1934 and 1935, for example, 111 applications had been turned down on this basis, representing approximately 3 per cent of the total applications received; the following year, a further 78 were rejected (4 per cent of applications).[57] In 1937 the board claimed that of 1868 OAP applications rejected for ineligibility since 1927, 44 per cent had been on the basis that the applicants could reasonably expect adequate support from their children; no estimate was given for those whose pensions had been reduced on similar grounds.[58]

At least as early as 1934 the British Columbia board had established explicit criteria to be applied systematically against adult children, criteria revised in 1938 and 1942.[59] In June 1942 a different provincial department suggested that the parents' maintenance act be rescinded and the coercion of adult children be stopped, underlining the policy confusion within the bureaucracy. The provincial OAP board denied that the act had ever been used to threaten people, but pointed out that federal regulations required the board to consider as income contributions or potential contributions from children. The parents' maintenance legislation was the only machinery available to enforce payment from children whose parents were without support.[60] But this was mere sophistry, and was quite disingenuous. The *threat* of the parents' maintenance act was central to the operation of the OAP in most provinces, but in none more than in British Columbia.

In contrast to some other areas of OAP policy and administration, the provincial politicians were noticeably reluctant to support any coercive actions aimed at families. Both the British Columbia premier and the minister responsible categorically rejected any general policy of coercion.[61] Legislative motions in 1938 and 1939 attacked the regulatory use of the parents' maintenance legislation and defended the OAP as 'an inalienable right.'[62] The Old Age Pensioners' Organization of British Columbia was particularly outspoken in its attacks on these regulatory policies, and further spurred the judgmental language of the local press. The *Vancouver Sun* led the way with editorials such as 'Our Gestapo for the Aged,' which described the investigative policies of the provincial board. Such wartime rhetoric was particularly powerful, as when one ninety-year-old Vancouver pensioner attacked the niggardly attitudes of officials: 'Even Hitler would be more humane than that, for he would have us all lined up and shot and put out of our misery, as he would think it a sin to grow old and useless.'[63] It was the seemingly arbitrary character of the application of these policies and the considerable amount of discretion available to the board in their application that particularly opened the provincial boards to attack.

The administrative judgment of family capabilities for parental support was highly discretionary, and the enforcement of such responsibilities was, in practical terms, quite difficult. First, the ability of the individual children to support their parents was a matter of opinion. While the children's income was usually determinable, the cost of their own upkeep was arguable, as was the cost of the upkeep of their spouse and young children. How much of their income could be considered excess and available for aid to their parents? Such decisions on the part of pension authorities were by their nature largely discretionary and often inconsistent. Second, even where adult children were held to have excess income, how could they be forced to give a portion of it to their parents? The authorities were decidedly reluctant to take individual children to court; in the parents' maintenance court cases uncovered prior to 1951, not one case was initiated by state officials, despite their statutory authority to do so. The idea of taking adult children to court was politically sensitive, and no provincial government was willing to adopt such activity. Third, if the adult children could not be forced to support their parents, was it fair to penalize the parents by refusing them a pension or reducing the payment level?[64]

Despite its many dubious characteristics, however, this regulatory process was potent. Both the elderly and the individual sons and daughters lacked the normal protection available to 'defendants' in judicial or quasi-judicial proceedings: counsel, trained judges, procedural rules and controls, evidentiary rules, formal appeal procedures. Bureaucrats and their field inspectors now defined family responsibilities and appropriate behaviour, covering a wide spectrum of conduct – ongoing maintenance, gift-giving, extent and frequency of contact, responsibility for the eventual funeral, inheritance, payment of life and property insurance premiums. Both family members and the elderly had only limited ability to interact with this process.

The Application of Parental Maintenance

British Columbia records[65] offer the most detailed glimpse at the case-level application of state expectations of family support for the elderly. But the policies and attitudes reflected there are also apparent in less detail in the Saskatchewan records.[66] The records of the Lambton County OAP applications allow a glimpse at the response and attitudes of the elderly and their families.

Time and again elderly were denied a pension or had their payment level reduced through the board's judgment that the family was capable of providing more support than it was doing. In 1933 a widow in Alberni occupied five acres of farm land (assessed at $1575) – there was a dispute as to whether she owned the land or merely had a life interest in it. The farm was operated by her son, and produced sufficient vegetables, fruit, eggs, and chickens to maintain the residents, including the widow. With the widow and her one unmarried son lived a daughter and her two young children; the unmarried son did occasional relief work, but the daughter was apparently fully occupied as a single mother, receiving a mother's allowance at times. Nearby, another unmarried son operated a second farm in partnership with the widow's son-in-law, producing food that could be used to supplement the widow's fare. 'In view of the foregoing it may be readily seen,' wrote the secretary of the provincial board, explaining the rejection of her application, 'that this applicant, with her single sons, is considerably better off than a large number of tax-payers in the province.'

The widow was fortunate enough to have a member of parliament take an interest in her case; he corresponded with the board, allegedly being informed by the board that it would not alter its decision until the woman had taken her children to court under the parents' maintenance act. In response to the board's summary, he offered several additional facts and commented: 'The woman is not applying for a pension on the ground that she is worse off than a number of other people, but on the ground that she qualifies under the Old Age Pension Act, and I submit that she is entitled to it and the Board has no alternative than to grant it.'[67] Here is a clear example of both the discretionary nature of judging family capacity to offer support and the strong tendency in the 1930s to apply a needs test to prospective pensioners.[68]

The British Columbia board was struck by the developing culture of entitlement among the elderly and their families. From the board's point of view there was a growing inclination among the elderly to prefer state support to family support – the alleged tendency among the elderly was to see this as an 'either/or' proposition. Large numbers of workers throughout the province maintained the dependent members of their family, commented the board chairman in 1938; 'I do not think that any particular credit should be given to a son or daughter who maintains a parent or parents, or assists to make the parents' last few years a little more pleasant. I have noticed, however, that in the past few years an effort is being made by some of the old people to choose to live on support from the public treasury, that is, the tax payers, in preference to receiving maintenance from their own children.'[69] The board adopted a variety of techniques to discourage any inclination to replace family support with state support.

The board consistently challenged adult children who still lived in their parents' home but contributed nothing to the parents' income. The board insisted that where earnings were available, it was reasonable to expect payment for room and board.[70] Whether the presence of an adult child meant the taking of free board or the contribution of vital support depended, of course, on the point of view of the observer. Though adult daughters were less likely to have significant incomes, where they did they were as vulnerable as their brothers to the board's expectations of unmarried children. In a 1939 case, for example, there were no brothers present. A widowed daughter with no dependent children earned $145 monthly as a telegraph operator; she lived with her sister, who as a beautician was a partner in a small business and 'admitted' to earning $85 a month. Their combined monthly income was greater than 85 per cent of British Columbia workers, the board pointed out, many of whom maintained families on much less. With no other special expenses or obligations, the daughters 'could well afford to set up a modest establishment and the three of them live very comfortably on that income,' held the board.[71] Here daughters were expected to change their lifestyle significantly so as to meet the needs of their mother. Sons tended not to face such formidable expectations.

Financially, those elderly with married daughters were left much more vulnerable by the OAP process. While spouses, unmarried daughters, and sons, especially unmarried sons, were consistently pressed to help an elderly relative, married daughters could not often be required to provide financial support, since most income and assets were in their husband's name and control.[72] In one example this problem dramatically shaped the outlook of a northern Ontario widow. Her frustrations were apparent, if somewhat incoherently articulated: 'soninlaws dont want old people around when they have children of their own to raise ... Young people cannot live to raise their children on account of old people they die with nervus Breakdown as the Soninlaws dont want their Mothers around anymore so there will have to be something done or no children raised. they will be mostly all put into Homes.'[73] Such a structure and process emphasized the powers of husbands and the vulnerability of both dependent elderly parents and married daughters who sought to help their parents.

Gender crucially shaped the experience of old age and each family's strategies for dealing with the elderly. Among adult children it was not the children's sex but their marital and financial status that determined the application of parental maintenance regulations. Adult daughters were likely to have lower incomes than sons, but both were liable to support their parents up to the limit of their financial capacity to do so. Marriage altered filial responsibility fundamentally. A married son had primary responsibility for his wife and children; his parents took a secondary position, but he continued to have a legal obligation and often the financial ability to assist them. Sons could dispose of their filial obligations through the simple transfer of funds to their parents. Most daughters, immediately at marriage, lost any financial capacity (and thus legal obligation) to support their parents. Married daughters, if they wished to fulfil their socialized obligations to aid their parents, had to persuade their husbands to allocate the needed resources, further entrenching the power of the husbands within the family. Without financial resources to offer direct monetary aid, married daughters tended to provide non-monetary forms of support.

Both the legal and the political process accepted and condoned this uneven division of power through the gendered construction of marriage on which it ultimately rested. Despite the explicit desire to support needy elderly and to force adult children to accept full responsibility for such support whenever possible, no serious consideration was given to redefining marital obligations and power so as to facilitate such support. The maintenance of unequal gender relations through marriage was far more important than assisting the elderly or supporting more fully the idea of intergenerational family support.

With the presence of parents' maintenance legislation, state tactics in pressuring children to assist their parents could be much more elaborate than the simple letters sent out in the earlier Donald Boston case. In August 1933 a seventy-four-year-old Cranbrook-area widower had applied for a pension. On investigation the British Columbia board found that his unmarried son had earned $1427.13 from the Canadian Pacific Railway for the past year, and on this ground the father's application was rejected. It was standard practice in such cases for the board to contact such adult children, making 'a demand' on them to maintain their parents and indicating the legal obligation to do so.74 In October 1933 the board wrote to the son pointing out that on the basis of his earnings, 'the Board was without jurisdiction to grant his father's Old Age Pension application.' Within a few weeks the son reportedly gave his father $100, but did not follow this up with any regular support. In May and June 1934 the board again contacted the son, 'pointing out his obligation under the Parents' Maintenance Act,' but received no reply. Twice in July the board wrote to the son, unsuccessfully asking for a response.

When the board's direct tactics proved ineffective, a more authoritative arm of the state entered the case. The board went to the commissioner of the provincial police and, after one of his officers had interviewed the son, the son agreed to pay his father $20 monthly support. At the time, the young man impressed the police 'as being most willing to help his father.'

Payments were made for only three months, before the son reneged on his commitment. Pressure was exerted on the board by local authorities who were responsible for assisting the father out of local relief funds, and the board again turned to the police. When the police interviewed the son again in March 1935, another month's support was paid, but then payments stopped again. The elderly father had now been without regular support for at least eighteen months, but there is no evidence that the OAP board gave any consideration to granting the man a pension – to do so would have been to accept and thus tacitly condone the son's behaviour and values. Instead, the board turned finally to the attorney general, asking that charges be laid against the son.[75] While the board's patience in harassing the son seemed almost endless, such tactics did not solve the father's problems, which seemed lost from sight.

Board investigations of family members could be extensive. In a 1938 case, when the father had applied for a pension, he had tried to protect his unmarried son with whom he lived, reporting the son's annual income as only $600. The board followed up on this, seeking confirmation; the son refused to cooperate until several letters had been exchanged. Finally, he disclosed that he had earned $1423 in the past year, making it unnecessary for the board to approach his employers as the board did in instances of complete lack of cooperation.[76] Although single children with income tended to be targeted for the board's attention, detailed investigation nevertheless tended to be carried out for all married children and their spouses, except for those living outside the jurisdiction.[77]

Investigation of families could go even further, and the results could reveal fundamental gender bias. An elderly Vancouver resident already received a full pension in 1940, when his wife applied as well. The couple had two married sons, each with one child. Both sons were clerks, one earning $1949 and the other, $2405. Both claimed they were unable to help their parents because of their wives' illness; medical reports were acquired regarding the condition of the two daughters-in-law. When all the facts were in, the board concluded that the sons had sufficient funds to provide for their mother. Her application was denied.[78] The sons had not been expected to support their father; that would have left the couple with no pension at all. But with the father receiving state support, the sons could be expected to supplement their father's income so as to look after their mother. The gender bias of the economic system was replicated in the OAP; while the elderly male received a pension from an independent source and his breadwinner role was confirmed, his wife was required to remain dependent on her male providers.

Many elderly resisted as strongly as possible any state pressure to coerce support from their adult children, and this resistance was heightened by the economic distress of the 1930s. Gordon Everett of London, for example, was a retired officer of the Huron County children's aid society. He lived with his wife, Ellen, and an unmarried, adult daughter in his own home, which was mortgaged at 50 per cent of its value. His three sons were all married with children and lived away from London; his daughter worked sporadically as a clerk. Mr and Mrs Everett had no income when they both applied for a pension in 1931 at the age of seventy-two. In return for the pension, he and his wife were willing to transfer ownership of their home to the OAP Commission, but they resolutely refused to beg their sons for help. Their sons had their own responsibilities, and would contribute what they could voluntarily. If the OAP authorities insisted on an appeal to their sons, the couple preferred to withdraw their pension applications.[79] The maintenance of existing family relationships was more important to them than the partial alleviation of financial hardships, reflecting the central importance of family as a source of assistance and support.

Some elderly refused to cooperate with the board's intrusion into the family. Both elderly and adult children could decline to provide the necessary information, particularly regarding the adult children's earnings. The elderly could claim lack of knowledge, though not always credibly; sons and daughters, particularly the former, sometimes failed to answer inquiries and at other times bluntly refused to cooperate. In the absence of information, the board usually declined to proceed with consideration of the file, so that the individual elderly were forced to pay the price for any insistence on individual privacy.[80] Again, the prime losers in such conflict were usually the elderly parents.

Yet few elderly, if they were truly dependent, could afford to adopt such a confrontational stance, however much they might wish to do so. The needy elderly were extremely vulnerable to the board's authority and power, and were often forced into the position of suppliants, begging for the favourable exercise of the board's discretion.[81] As often as not, the pleadings came from family members, sometimes on behalf of the elderly applicant and sometimes on behalf of their own interest in the applicant's receiving a pension. A daughter provided a home for her invalid, pensioner mother; when the pension was discontinued, the daughter begged for its reinstatement: 'Mr. Huey if she doesn't get that pension I don't know what we are going to do as my health is failing again lately, my nerves are going to break also. She has been a great care in bed most of the time for over two years and not capable of doing anything. I had a serious illness two years ago caused by overwork and worry and now I feel as though I cannot stand the strain much longer.'[82]

The resistance of some families to accepting financial responsibility for their elderly members and the devolution of that responsibility onto the state was seemingly becoming more common in the 1940s. This was a reflection of many developments – a growing sense of the wide-ranging functions of the state, a diminution of family resources, a limitation of extended family obligations to affective functions, a willingness to supplement family support with state support. Having deflected some responsibility for the elderly onto the state during the economic problems of the 1930s, most families were reluctant to take back that responsibility once war and economic recovery replaced the Depression. A culture of entitlement to state support for the elderly now complemented the continuing familial culture of support.

A London, Ontario, welfare case offers an excellent example of these new attitudes. Mrs Margaret Hull was a seventy-four-year-old widow, owning her own unencumbered home on Queen's Avenue in June 1948. She rented three rooms at the back of her house and a garage, producing $24 a month; this rent reflected a reduced rate, in exchange for which the renting couple looked after Mrs Hull and provided her meals. She also received $18.78 a month from an insurance policy on her late husband's life, though the payments were to cease in 1950. Recently, however, Mrs Hull had developed acute nephritis. She was now incapable of administering her own affairs and was seeking admission to a local private nursing home. Mrs Hull had arranged to bequeath her house to her husband's nephew, Ralph Hull, and he had now agreed to take over administration of his aunt's affairs. He refused, however, to contribute anything to the cost of Mrs Hull's care in the nursing home, and rejected the city welfare officers' suggestion that he arrange to sell Mrs Hull's house and use the proceeds to pay for her maintenance. Instead, he formally asked the city to pay for Mrs Hull's maintenance, retaining the potential proceeds from the house for himself.[83] City officials refused, but the attitude of the family is a useful indication of the extent to which they at least believed that the responsibilities of the state had expanded and those of the family had diminished.

Families and individual elderly were not the only ones to rethink the state's enforcement of filial responsibilities. Across the 1940s, OAP officials were increasingly reluctant to use the coercive powers of the state to compel particular forms of family behaviour, and they were equally persuaded that potential Pensioners should not be denied support because of their children's conduct. As discussed further in chapter 7, officials applied OAP regulations with greater selectivity and discretion, and more and more elderly began to receive the citizen's wage.

Filial responsibility laws and regulations were inefficient and ineffective instruments in the spectrum of policies assisting the elderly. The regulations themselves were applied arbitrarily and without any semblance of due process. The definition of support employed was based on narrow assumptions regarding proximity and types of assistance.[84] In its continuing attempts to avoid or at least to limit responsibility for the elderly, the state sought to use coercion to enforce certain types of family behaviour. While the familial ideal on which these laws relied resonated with genuinely held beliefs in Canadian society, there is no evidence that the laws actually increased the level of support for the elderly from their adult children; indeed, there is some evidence to suggest that both intragenerational and intergenerational support, broadly defined, was reduced.[85] Instead, coercive tactics and officious regulations sent messages of increased state rigidity and inflexibility about family behaviour and strategies. This could result in tension and conflict (both within the extended family and between the elderly and the pension bureaucracy) from which the elderly seldom benefited.

By insisting on the primary responsibility of adult children, these state processes helped to undermine traditional extended family and community support for the needy elderly. Increasingly, it was adult children alone who bore the brunt of these expectations of support. By holding adult children strictly accountable, the state processes by implication began to rewrite the more broadly based support ethic of the past.[86]

But despite these ineffective and sometimes harmful intrusions by the state, family remained a vital source of succour and support for the elderly. The records used here emphasize the instances where families failed or resisted supporting elderly relatives, rather than the majority of families where support was provided. In the changing economic and social conditions of the twentieth century, there is no evidence that family culture altered in the traditional importance placed on intergenerational support and relations. What altered was the substance and character of that support. The elderly's ability to sustain an independent mode of living tended to increase, and their reliance on accommodation with their adult children decreased. A social worker in 1951 offered what he found to be a typical example in an older woman from Toronto: 'My family think I can't manage by myself any more and insist on me living with them ... I'd like to be near them all right but in my own place. I still think it isn't good for three generations to be living in the same house.'[87] What had changed was that regular OAP cheques permitted greater independence and flexibility for both generations.

Family continued to play a significant role in the lives of the elderly, but many families were no longer capable of operating as the primary source of financial support. Nor were many families willing to do so, having accepted the role of the state in this regard. At the same time, most elderly had no wish to be dependent on their adult children or relatives. The rise of individualism affected the expectations of both the elderly and their children, and the increasing standard of living allowed both generations to insist on their independence. Cooperative, intergenerational, intrafamilial exchange of assistance and resources continued to be important in the lives of the elderly. Affective support tends not to be reflected in the historical records, though there is no reason to believe that it was not of primary importance. Substantial support can be readily uncovered, however, in the property relations of the elderly.

The traditional values and attitudes of the past sustained the OAP program established in 1927, which at the same time was genuinely innovative in its provision of regular monetary support for the needy elderly of both sexes. The family had long been primarily responsible for its elderly members, and the OAP program and filial responsibility laws simply reinforced that primacy. However, the changing economic circumstances of working-class families and developing attitudes regarding the state and individualism placed the OAP program in a position unintended by legislators or social workers. The capacity of many families to offer financial support or even shelter to the elderly shrank, particularly during the 1930s Depression. Individual elderly and family members saw the pension as a welcome and attractive solution to the problems of the needy elderly. Despite the persistent efforts of bureaucrats, many elderly and their families reshaped the OAP program to better meet their needs. As a result, families lost their primary responsibility for the economic support of the elderly, shifting their duties to other areas of support. Both the traditional character of the OAP program and its reshaping by the elderly are manifested in an examination of the property relations of the elderly.

4

Property and the Culture of Entitlement

As with all generations, property was central to the social and economic position of the elderly. The elderly had long employed control over property to structure the character of their social and physical environment. Property was an essential element in family reproduction, in the maintenance of the material conditions of the family over succeeding generations.[1] Though the details varied, the elderly had traditionally used family property rights acquired over a lifetime to support themselves in old age while at the same time maintaining the family.

The elderly were particularly important to the structures of the family economy because control of family property tended to rest in their hands. There can be no doubt that the elderly exercised that control in decisive ways to protect their own interests, though all such behaviour reflected an authoritative family culture. Family tended to be the most important resource available to most persons, including the elderly, and family members helped one another make their way, sharing assets and labour continually so as to sustain the individual and the group. Most of the property had been acquired through family-based processes – inheritance, marriage, communal family labour. It was family labour that had drawn out the sustaining benefits from the property and had kept it within the family on a productive basis. Gender, birth order, and age continually determined the labour contributed and the benefits derived in each family and household, but this did not alter the fundamental reality of the sharing of the property among family members, however inequitably. Whatever the law stipulated and whatever the extent of the elderly's formal control, the property was in many ways the family's as a whole – to be employed by the family and by individual members in their individual and common interests. This necessitated a delicate balancing act among competing and not always compatible interests. While historically the elderly had a disproportionate influence in establishing this 'balance,' it is clear that all family members were involved in such processes.[2]

By the early twentieth century the elderly had adapted customary property-based tactics for survival to fit changing circumstances and conditions. Property remained a central instrument in the hands of the elderly for protecting themselves and for defending their position as heads of the family. The OAP introduced a new form of property that both threatened existing practices and offered new opportunities.

The OAP program aimed to help only those elderly with too little property or income to meet the meagre poverty line of one dollar a day. Those with greater amounts of property were excluded from the program, and the state sought to recover its costs by claiming its expenses against the estates of pensioners with property. But the elderly themselves and their families increasingly thwarted the state's intentions and expanded the boundaries of the program. A growing culture of entitlement to state support regardless of the elderly's property position eventually reshaped the OAP program.

Maintenance Agreements

Historically, the most common form of property transfer that promised security for the elderly was the maintenance agreement.[3] Early twentieth-century North Americans continued to use this age-old practice, adapting it to local circumstances and reflecting the cultural variations of different ethnic groups. Adult children were expected to, and usually did, work in the family economy for many years, drawing little or no income. The children slowly acquired a vested interest in the communal family property that, it was expected, was expanding in value with all the additional labour. Eventually the children drew on the family property when they were prepared to establish their own household; daughters gained a marriage settlement, and sons took land, equipment, or funds necessary for their independent start. One adult child, often the youngest son because he tended to reach the age of majority closest to the time of the parents' old age, took over the main property – for example, the family fishing vessel or farm – in exchange for a commitment to support his parents throughout their old age. This commitment or maintenance agreement could be formal or informal, detailed or vague, written or spoken, but it was founded in a family culture of intergenerational support.

German Canadians offer a useful example of the practice of maintenance agreements and of the ways that one ethnic group adapted and perpetuated the custom.4 It was common for elderly German-Canadian farmers to turn over their farm to a son, often with a written agreement as to the son's responsibilities during his parents' remaining years. A written agreement was particularly likely where the farmer had remarried and his wife was the step-mother of the inheriting son. The son would be required to build an extension to the current farmhouse. Usually small and known as a doddy-house (a corruption from 'gross-dawdy' or grandfather), the extension would be somewhat more flimsy than the main building, intended to last only for the remaining few years of the parents' lives. The agreement typically promised to maintain the parent in the doddy-house in a warm, clean environment, providing food, clothing, and sometimes a small amount of money annually. The parents received the freedom of the house, the well, and the grounds for themselves and their guests, and at times the children promised such things as transporting the parents regularly to church. The elderly received security in old age, while the adult child gained a firm financial position for his own wife and future children.

Maintenance agreements were also common in rural Quebec.5 An elderly couple there in 1929 offers a good example of such agreements. The couple transferred their property (valued at $3000–5000) to their son, who in turn agreed to assume all his father's debts ($3200). The couple retained a life-time right to continue living on the property, during which time the son would provide them with lodging, clothing, food, medical care, and a decent burial. In the fashion of the partially impartible inheritance processes discovered by David Gagan in mid-nineteenth century Peel County, the son also promised to provide similar support for his only sister.6 Such agreements had been fundamental to the family culture of rural society and its economy for many generations, employing the productive capacity of the property to serve the various members of the family in different and highly gendered but vital ways.

Though historians link maintenance agreements with rural society, where they were probably more common, some elderly had, by the early twentieth century, adapted the custom to an urban setting. Urban property tended to fit this strategy less effectively, since the elderly could usually fully exploit the economic potential of urban property right up to their death. Nevertheless, the adaptation of the custom to a different environment and new circumstances demonstrates the continuing interdependence of family and elderly and the continuing centrality of property in survival strategies.

Two examples illustrate this trend. John McAlton of London, Ontario, a widower, transferred his two residential properties in the city to his adopted son on the understanding that his son would thereafter care for him. Soon after moving in with his son, the elderly McAlton became dissatisfied and left, moving in with a nephew. The courts rejected an attempt to recover the properties from his son, although the elderly McAlton was awarded a life interest in the properties. His son continued to be willing to take in his father and objected to the granting of an Old Age Pension, but the elderly McAlton insisted on his relative independence and refused to return to his son.[7] A more traditional agreement occurred in another London family. A male pensioner remarried late in life and transferred ownership of his house to his new wife, who put some of her own funds into the home; when she died two years later, she willed the home to her daughter, on condition that the daughter provide a home for her step-father. The pensioner clearly felt that his room and board were properly coming to him in return for the property, because instead of helping his step-daughter with his OAP cheque he preferred to give his grandson assistance.[8]

In the early twentieth century, property continued to serve the needs of the elderly in traditional ways, but new mechanisms had also been added in meeting the same ends. Demographic change dictated some of the impulse to alter these traditional processes. The declining fertility rate and the compacting spacing between births could result in a lack of 'fit' in timing between the parents' willingness to turn over primary control of the property and the son's readiness to take over, particularly when adult sons were aware of the opportunities for social and economic independence in rapidly growing urban communities. The changing character of the economy was also vital in encouraging these new tactics. Adult children increasingly had viable opportunities elsewhere and were no longer as dependent on their parents. Urban property, while valuable, did not have the same economic potential in a wage-labour economy as a farm had in an agricultural economy. The tactics of the elderly and of their adult children necessarily adapted to these changing conditions.

In the past, in the absence of available relatives, the elderly had turned to others – friends, neighbours, fictive kin – who might accept the elderly's property in exchange for a promise of support. Some of these alternatives continued to be used, as with an elderly New Brunswick widow who, in 1939, transferred her property to her parish priest on the understanding that she could continue to live there and that he would supply fuel and pay for taxes and any repairs. The Nova Scotia royal commission on old age pensions reported in 1930 that where elderly were forced to rely on friends for support, 'many had assigned their property in consideration of their being looked after for the rest of their lives.'[9] Others adopted more innovative alternatives.

The most striking of these new mechanisms was evident in the actions of those elderly who turned over their assets to state authorities in exchange for lifetime support. Where parents lacked adult children willing to take over the family property and, with it, responsibility for supporting the elderly parents, the elderly looked elsewhere. There are several examples in the welfare case files and in the old age home records of elderly approaching local authorities with a firm offer: in return for a promise of full maintenance for the rest of their lives, the elderly would transfer their property to the local authorities. Applicants to old age homes offered to turn over all their assets to the institution, hoping to make their application more attractive to the authorities. Though sometimes consisting of cash, more often the property consisted of real estate, often of little or no market value.[10]

The London, Ontario, welfare records reveal a number of instances in which individual elderly transferred their property (cash and/or real estate) to the city in exchange for lifetime support, while either remaining in their home or moving to a local old age home. In one example the city entered into a 1932 agreement with Mr and Mrs Len Golden (ages sixty-four and fifty-nine, respectively): the couple turned over their house and land, assessed at $1500, in return for 'the usual terms' – lifetime support at $30 monthly (less any funds received through the OAP), continued use of the house (on which the city would pay the property taxes), two tons of fuel annually, and reasonable funeral expenses.[11] Within a few years the city became less generous in the agreements it was willing to consider, as the financial problems of the 1930s forced a reconsideration of such practices. City council placed limits on the extent of its financial obligations – though it failed to keep a regular accounting of its expenditures in such matters – and city officials pursued family members who had accepted property from an elderly relative, but were not living up to their maintenance commitments.[12] Finally, in the fall of 1941, London city council adopted a resolution discontinuing the practice of accepting property from individuals in exchange for maintenance, suggesting that such agreements were relatively frequent and that the city too often experienced financial losses in such arrangements. Henceforth, the city resolved to force the elderly to manage their own property and assets to generate sufficient funds for support. Nevertheless, when individual elderly were too incapacitated to do so, the city continued to accept their property in exchange for support.[13]

It is important that the initiative for transfer in these cases came as often from the elderly as from local authorities. The English poor law had required the transfer of any property by the poor when they entered a local poorhouse. In Canada, provincial legislation continued this practice.[14] Charitable institutions had long accepted property transfers from those receiving the protection of the institution. The practice had been basic to municipal welfare processes for at least as long, and was acknowledged and legitimized in a number of contemporary provincial statutes. This transfer of property by the elderly to the state could thus be regarded as no more than the meeting of a legal requirement to gain state assistance. But the variety of terms, the elderly's frequent continued occupation of the home now transferred to the state, and most of all the enterprise of the elderly in often initiating these maintenance agreements with the state suggests that control of this survival tactic was at least as often exercised by the elderly as it was by state officials.

The elderly had a long tradition of employing whatever property they had to provide physical security in old age. They adapted existing property-based customs to meet the new circumstances of family and property in the twentieth century. These practices meshed in well-established ways with state and quasi-state institutions. The OAP program, in its initial form, simply perpetuated this system, while extending the benefits of the program to include the needy elderly without property.

OAP Regulations and the Culture of Entitlement

Legislators adapted many of these traditional practices and attitudes to the Old Age Pension legislation. The state had the explicit right to consider a potential pensioner's property in two ways. First, property was an essential element in perpetuating the means test philosophy. Each item of real property and some items of other property that had potential income-producing value (such as livestock or machinery) were given a value, often a very subjective process. Officials then calculated the fictive annual income of the property if it were sold and the total amount used to purchase a lifetime annuity through the government annuities scheme. This fictive income was charged against the applicant as real income in the calculation of OAP eligibility and payment level. Second, the legislation gave the state the right to claim recovery of the total individual OAP payments (plus 5 per cent annual interest) from every pensioner's estate. Such claims could not be made until after the death of both the pensioner and the pensioner's spouse, and in practice were not made in preference to any heirs who had contributed directly to the care of the pensioner during old age. This latter condition fitted nicely with the state's other tactics for coercing family members to help their elderly relatives.

In allowing state pension authorities to make claims against pensioners' estates, legislators simply maintained long-standing practices. What changed was the timing of the transfer and the relative strength of the parties involved; the state had at its disposal so many more powerful resources that a balance of power was completely lacking and there was no possibility of continuing, overt renegotiation of positions as could occur on an intergenerational basis within families. While the procedure was founded on traditional practices and values, it also violated fundamental ideas of even longer standing. Property was a family-based asset, owned in some ways by the family rather than just the individual (whatever the law said formally); the elderly had a strong sense of their own family-based status and of their responsibility to other family members, particularly of the next generation, and property transfer was a central mechanism by which that status and responsibility were recognized and reinforced. Family remained a vital resource for the elderly, and any development that threatened the elderly's relationship with their extended family was ominous. This had important implications not just for the perceptions of family and property, but also for attitudes towards the state. For if the state pension was not received in exchange for property, then the pension had to be thought of in new ways – as a 'right,' as part of a citizen's claim on the state.

The OAP was not initially a normal pension. The OAP created a debt that could be collected at the death of each pensioner, and in the eyes of many elderly this considerably reduced the value and status of the pension. The early OAP process gave immediate warning of this element in the program. Ontario application forms, for example, asked the elderly to identify and list the value of all their property, and then asked if they were willing to transfer their property to the OAP Commission. Though there was no requirement for this sort of transfer, the question left the strong impression that the applicant ought to reply 'yes' if the application was to be successful. Even local officials were confused, inferring that an application ought to be rejected when applicants refused to transfer their property.[15] Though this question was dropped when the Ontario form was redrafted in 1936, the reputation of the program was already well established by then.[16]

In accepting the OAP, pensioners lost some control over their property and assets. Desperate for immediate support, many of the elderly poor were forced to accept the OAP under the conditions set out by the state, but there was a continual contest among individual elderly, their family members, and the authorities at various levels over the future claim by the state against the estate. Other elderly had enough financial flexibility that they could debate whether or not to accept a pension. The questions of a farmer near Owen Sound, Ontario, for example, suggested the various considerations that were important to him in 1929. Once a pension had started, could it be stopped whenever he wanted and the money repaid with interest? He wanted to have the freedom to sell his five-acre property if he so chose. Was it correct that the property was automatically transferred once the pension started, if he had answered positively on the application regarding transfer to the state? If he answered this negatively on the application, did the pension payments simply become a debt against his estate? Did being a pensioner interfere with his right to conduct business or to sell any of his personal property or farm produce? Did his wife also have to apply for an OAP 'to receive enough for maintance [sic] of us both?'[17] For this man, and for many elderly like him, the pension involved vital considerations involving personal freedom and control over their own property. If the elderly were fortunate enough, these were considerations they could afford to take into account; other elderly, desperate for any support, could not afford such choices.

For many, acceptance of the pension did not mean acceptance of the accompanying terms. Many of the elderly and their family members already believed that the OAP ought to be a real pension, rather than just a loan. They articulated this belief in their dealings with state officials and politicians,[18] and they put the belief into practice as they manoeuvred over the following years to remove the pensioners' assets beyond the reach of the state. In doing so they were generally unaware that the state had from the beginning softened the application of the regulation by deferring recovery from an inheriting spouse during the spouse's lifetime; recovery was also precluded from the portions of estates willed to persons who had materially supported the pensioner regularly over the years immediately preceding death. Yet even in these instances, individuals were forced to rely on state officials in the interpretation and application of such regulations. There was some justification for pensioners' and their families' reluctance to trust officials fully.[19]

The federal government held that recovery from pensioners' estates was mandatory for provincial authorities, while privately admitting that the constitutionality of the requirement was doubtful at best.[20] The provinces hesitated to enforce recovery from the estates of pensioners, much to the frustration of Ottawa. At the 1937 meeting of the Interprovincial Board, the federal minister of finance pointed out that the courts had upheld the crown's claim against such estates. He badgered the provincial representatives regarding the mandatory character of the regulation: 'You must proceed. You have not, as some of you think, any discretion in the matter; you have to recover from the estate if recovery is possible.' But it was an issue on which provincial and local authorities were deliberately obtuse.[21]

Indeed, Nova Scotia and New Brunswick led the way in disagreeing with such controls on pensioners' property and in declining to enforce claims against estates in most instances. The Nova Scotia board, for example, consciously decided not to adopt a policy of placing liens on property. As the board saw it, there were two fundamental options. First, a high level of payment could be adopted, liens placed against property, and claims made against estates to offset the costs of the high payment level. Or, payments could be made at a substantially lower level, 'taking into account the value of the property held by the pensioner *as a means of livelihood*' and permitting the pensioner to transfer the property as he or she saw fit; in this policy, few claims would be made against estates. It was the latter policy that the board put in place. What is more, that policy was defended as both financially attractive and more responsive to local values and attitudes. Nova Scotians, it was alleged, were more attached to their land or cottage than most persons.

Many of these little homes have been for generations in one family. There are hundreds of records which show that the pensioner would rather suffer the most dire poverty than to give up his little property, which is perhaps assessed for only two or three hundred dollars, if he must do so in order to obtain a pension.

There are hundreds of records which show that boys and girls living away have made considerable sacrifice in order to retain the title to the old homestead which has a very small market value but a sentimental value untold.

Beyond that, in many cases a daughter or son had remained at home to care for the parents and the property. Though the property had not formally been transferred to the adult child, it was theirs by the parents' intention and by tradition.[22] The Nova Scotia policy was thus designed best to reflect local attitudes and to meet the needs of the elderly and their families. New Brunswick officials similarly declined to place liens against pensioners' property, and pensioners were noted for their tendency to transfer their property to an adult child while continuing to live on the property. New Brunswick authorities consistently refused to pursue claims against pensioners' estates there.[23]

Ontario was one province where recovery from estates was often carried out. One reason why the provincial board from the beginning of the program discouraged local boards from administering pensioners' properties was that recovery from estates already protected the state's interest. At first the Ontario board anticipated that where a pensioner's estate was quite small, which would be true in 'the great majority of cases,' a claim would probably not be made.[24] But before long finances became somewhat tighter, and the application of regulations shifted accordingly. Without strict guidelines, however, estate claims devolved into highly discretionary practices, featuring marked inconsistency. In such circumstances it was difficult for either the elderly or their families to calculate effectively the place of a pension within their personal or family strategies.

Many estate claims occurred, as might be expected, particularly in the 1930s. At first, regardless of the size of the estate, the state pressed its claims. Where heirs had made no direct, substantial contributions to the support of the elderly person, the state insisted on reclaiming the costs of its support.[25] This policy underlines the state's narrow definition of support; officials required evidence of relatives' co-residence and/or regular financial aid before allowing their claims to take precedence over those of the state.

But even this definition was not applied consistently. A few examples demonstrate the pettiness, harshness, and inconsistency that at times shaped the Ontario board's policies regarding estate claims. A 1933 example indicates just how strict and rigid the board could be. A seventy-one-year-old labourer in the village of Courtwright lived with three unmarried sons, one of whom was an invalid; the old man had no income and his only asset was a second mortgage for $600, on which no payments were being made. He applied for a pension in February 1933 and was awarded a monthly payment of $15. After just three months he died, and the board made a claim against his estate for $46.25 ($45 in payments plus $1.25 interest).[26] In another case, a seventy-eight-year-old widow lived alone in her home, valued at $1320 and mortgaged for $500. She received a $10 monthly pension for a little over fourteen months, totalling $145.40 when she died in 1932. The board claimed $133.90 from her estate (the basis of this calculation is unclear), and her daughter sold the house and paid off the claim within the next three years as payments for the house were received.[27]

As this example demonstrates, some relatives accepted without challenge the state's right to claim against the deceased pensioner's estate. There was nothing new about such payments to the state, and the pension was often vital in easing the last years of the pensioners and the burdens of their families. A seventy-year-old labourer lived in Sombra, Ontario, with his daughter, who received $61 a year in interest earned by money left by his wife; he himself received $50 yearly in rental income from property left by his wife. In addition, this widower had $600 in the bank. He was awarded a pension of $8 a month, which he received for twenty-four months before dying. The board claimed $200, including $8 in interest, from his estate, and all but thirty cents had been repaid within three months.[28] By contrast, in another case the OAP board recognized the financial and other contributions made by an adopted daughter to her elderly mother's support. The woman had been receiving the pension since 1929 when she died in 1940; she willed her home to her daughter on condition that the daughter pay for the funeral expenses. The house's estimated market value was $300 and the funeral expenses were just over $200, and the board waived its claim to any portion of the remainder of the estate.[29] Why one daughter's contributions were acknowledged in this way and another's not is unknown, though it suggests a discretionary and inconsistent process.

Local officials felt confident enough about the appropriateness of the claims policy that they were quite open about it. Certainly the Lambton County board was candid regarding its potential claims. When one pensioner inquired about property taxes and insurance, the board advised her to continue paying both because the state would have 'nothing to do with your property until after you are dead and gone. The facts are, that you can sell or dispose of your property at any time you wish providing you notify me and explain what you have done with the money you receive from the sale of it.'[30]

Unfortunately, for most elderly and their families the situation seemed much less straightforward. Some read the application question about willingness to transfer property to the state as implying a precondition for receipt of the OAP; others assumed that a positive answer would increase their chances of gaining a pension. In fact, neither was the case, though it is difficult to be certain about the second point. Where applicants responded positively and began to receive a pension cheque, they were confused as to the status of their property. Some assumed that the state had automatically acquired title. In fact, the pension board took no action until after the pensioner's death, regardless of how the applicant had answered the question about transfer. It is unclear what purpose the question served – as a reminder of the state's eventual claim on pensioners' property it was quite misleading. There were ample examples of the state's willingness to assert its claims, and the discretionary character of the enforcement could have done little to mitigate what, for the elderly and their families, was a threatening prospect.

In the late 1930s British Columbia authorities compiled a list of recent claims made against pensioners' estates: in nine instances, periodic payments were being received, and in eight cases payment had been made in full; in ten instances the claim was pending or no payment had yet been received, and in six cases the claim had been dropped.[31] There is no evidence about how representative this list is, but it does underline that in practice claims were made against only a small proportion of estates; it also suggests that as much as half the time the claims resulted in no substantial gain to the state. From the point of view of the pensioners and their heirs, however, the issue was not the small number of claims actually made, but the continuing threat to what were strongly regarded as family-based assets.

In the early years of the program most provincial and local authorities supported the philosophy behind the regulation. A local official in Rossland, British Columbia, complained in 1932 of the developing culture of entitlement among the elderly: 'a number of applicants claim benefits simply because they have attained the age of seventy, regardless of the fact that they can carry on in comfortable surroundings.' The government should respond by providing for the conveying of a pensioner's property to the state, thus ensuring that only the truly needy would apply and that the state would be reimbursed wherever possible. The Middlesex County clerk in Ontario pointed out in 1932 that pensioners could frustrate the regulation by disposing of their assets before death, citing a local case where this had happened. The solution he recommended was to amend the legislation so that a lien was filed against such property.[32] Manitoba was one of the provinces where claims against estates were vigorously pursued. In 1936 a federal official on a visit to Winnipeg described the provincial board as 'very persistent' in its claims policy. A young lawyer was employed in this work five mornings a week, and even the federal official was surprised by the harshness of the provincial policy: 'From a number of cases which came to our attention, it appeared to me that the Board's decisions are, if anything, too severe but this is only my opinion.'[33] Ontario continued to support the policy of recovering from estates. As late as 1943 the Ontario board asked that the legislation be amended to strengthen the state's power in this area.[34] Until the late 1940s many civil servants at both the federal and provincial levels shared a traditional view that, where possible, the state should be compensated for any form of welfare support within the ability of the recipient to pay.

The federal government maintained its support of the regulation and of the philosophy behind it throughout the 1930s and early 1940s. Federal auditors pushed provincial authorities to make claims wherever funds seemed likely to be recoverable. The courts also upheld the regulation in the early years. In a 1935 case, the British Columbia Supreme Court decided that an OAP claim against a pensioner's estate was proper and took precedence over other debts. But later courts were less certain. A 1937 Manitoba decision restricted the provincial board's power to make claims against estates, giving priority to the needs of the pensioners involved, while an Ontario court made a similar finding in 1946. But the Nova Scotia Supreme Court articulated no restrictions on the board's right to make a claim against a pensioner's estate, although in practice few claims were made in that province.[35]

Some provinces responded to federal pressure by stepping up their collection efforts. In Prince Edward Island in 1937, for example, some two hundred cases of deceased pensioners' estates were handed over to two lawyers with instructions to proceed with any collectible claims; but most of the estates consisted of only small properties, and there were few positive results.[36] The administrative costs of maintaining such files and of carrying out the necessary bureaucratic and legal procedures raise serious questions about the cost effectiveness of these regulations, and underline the philosophic importance of these regulations in an otherwise cost-conscious environment.

Though these policies undermining the pensioners' claims to property ownership faced opposition throughout the duration of the OAP program, that opposition grew in support, tactics, and rationale across the period. A culture of entitlement took firm hold of many of the elderly. State support often lost its stigma and became preferable to other sources of assistance. Where the elderly were unable to support themselves through work or existing assets, and required support from some outside source, growing numbers preferred to turn to an impersonal source, such as the state, rather than or in addition to family members. Inherent in this development was a new attitude towards the state and its responsibilities, and a sense that the state had an obligation to assist those who had served the nation and had paid taxes over their prime working years.

The expansion of state support during the 1930s fundamentally altered Canadians' expectations of and claims to state assistance, fostering a culture of entitlement. Mothers' allowances, various support measures for farmers, and veterans' pensions were among the major programs now supporting various sectors of society in need. The relief programs of the 1930s, both in their extent and in their prominence, brought the state's role of support constantly before the public. This was also the first generation of income tax payers to reach old age, and the idea of direct, personal contributions to the state likely drew attention to the range of direct and indirect taxes paid to the state.[37] At the same time, many felt that their contributions to society in general and to the growth and expansion of the economy entitled them in some vague way to the benefits of that growth. The OAP application question regarding willingness to transfer property to the state offers one measurement of this latter factor. In just 5 per cent of the pension applications coded for Lambton County and London did the pensioners indicate their willingness to turn over their property to the state in return for an OAP.[38] Three-quarters of these positive responses occurred during the first five years of the OAP program in Ontario; after the fall of 1934, few applicants volunteered to surrender their property. By the middle of the Depression many elderly were acquiring a new view of their position in society and of their claims on the state.

These new views developed across a class spectrum. A middle-class Toronto spinster had squandered her funds on foolish investments and found herself by the end of the 1930s in reduced circumstances. She appealed to Prime Minister Mackenzie King for aid when the OAP officials rejected her application:

I went some time ago to see about the old age pension, thought it would keep me in clothes, car fares, one does not like to take such things from a relative, and I felt I had served Canada well, spent freely here when I had it and that I would have no difficulty in getting it. Never thought I would get up the courage to ask for it, but I had heard of others who have families & property getting it. Well no one will ever know what it took out of *me* to go, never thinking it would come to this, however, I went, and after putting me through so many questions, being very rude to me, they refused it because I had a few hundred dollars in the bank, which they said I must spend before I could get it ... After two years I went back, having no money destroyed Bank Books not having any use for Blanks, they say I have to go through all the same questions again, show Bank Books, which I have not got, tell them what I did with the $400 how I spent it in two years (Imagine).

The application experience must have been humiliating for such a woman, but she was also very manipulative. She played effectively on the alleged helplessness of an elderly female; she deliberately destroyed evidence of her financial activities; she misrepresented the amount of funds that she had had when she first applied ($771.60 in stocks and $235.85 in cash).39 Her apparent humiliation was certainly not nearly as strong as her determination to gain support from the state.

The needy elderly's struggle for survival was constant throughout the period studied. What was new was the growing sense that the state, as well as family members, ought to be a primary source of support once complete independence could not be sustained. This view was apparent early on and among all adult generations. 'It would appear that the men and women of this generation are forgetting their filial responsibilities and are without any desire to even take care of the parent,' wrote the provincial treasurer of Saskatchewan in 1932, 'but on the other hand there is a desire to get as much money as possible out of the State.' As early as 1925, one ex-soldier wrote in support of an OAP program as a 'measure of social justice,' and showed that men too could play on a romanticized image of old age: 'I have 6 of a Family myself & I know what the struggle is. life is a very hard battle at the present but it would be nice if God spares us to 65 or 70 years to know that in the evening of life we shall not be the creatures of Charity or dependent on relatives.'[40] Increasingly, the elderly came to view the OAP as a means to independence, rather than as a mechanism leading to reliance on the state. This empowering attitude is vitally important to the developing culture of entitlement.

One Lambton County couple offers a good example. Conrad and Ema Kessler lived in a rented home in Oil Springs, where he worked for his son doing odd jobs at a creamery and egg grading station for $23 a week. An unmarried daughter lived with them, contributing from her part-time work to the household expenses. The couple had almost no assets, relying entirely on the income from Conrad's work, until he suffered a severe, incapacitating stroke in 1946. Within three weeks of the stroke, the couple turned to the OAP for support (Conrad was seventy-six, Ema was seventy-one). They had fully supported themselves in a family setting until their health failed, whereupon they immediately opted to seek state support. At the time, apart from the single daughter living with them, they had three married sons (the local creamery operator, a local egg grader, and a Toronto dairy worker) and one married daughter.[41] As long as they could give their son some value for money, they accepted the job from him and the independence that it offered. But once Conrad could no longer work, the state rather than family became the most desirable source of support.

The OAP participation rates rose with the broadening culture of entitlement. The proportion of elderly on the OAP rolls increased steadily through the 1930s depression, reflecting individual financial difficulties, straitened family circumstances, and a stronger sense of the elderly's claim to state support. Participation rates dropped considerably during the war as employment opportunities opened up for many elderly, but after 1945 the rates returned to and often surpassed those of the 1930s, as once again the elderly were forced to the employment sidelines (see figure 4.1).

This culture of entitlement could be found across Canadian society – among the elderly, their adult children, and even state officials. A township clerk in rural central Ontario commented in 1928: 'We have old people who have lived their lifetime on farms, which are not very good farms and who deserve something in their old age.' Any old age pension legislation should ensure that these elderly gained a pension, rather than being forced to rely on their adult children.[42] Such statements are particularly impressive because they articulate claims without self-interest.

FIGURE 4.1 Proportion of elderly as pensioners, 1931–51*

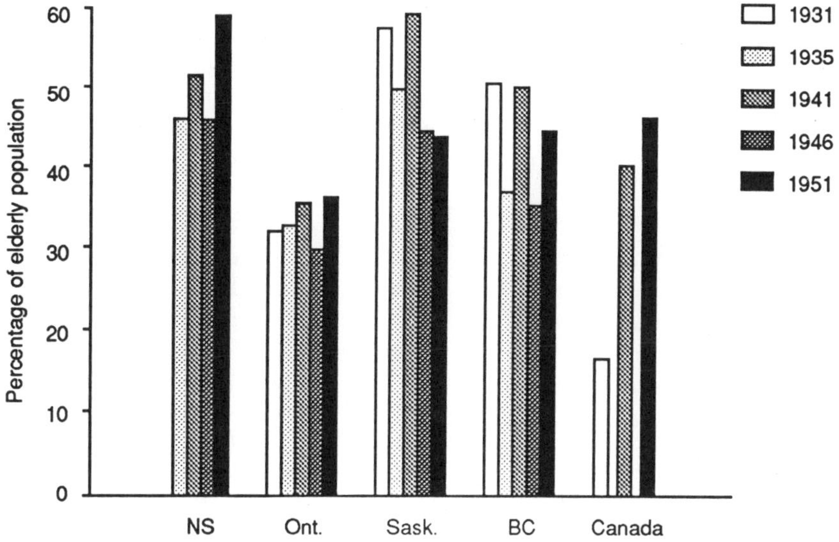

Source: Annual reports of the administration of the Old Age Pensions (Ottawa, 1931–51); *Census of Canada, 1941* (Ottawa, 1946), III, table 1; *Census of Canada, 1951* (Ottawa, 1953), II, table 1

More often, the culture of entitlement served personal needs directly, and, if paid work itself was a key source of entitlement, it would privilege men disproportionately.[43] A seventy-five-year-old Toronto man pointed out that he had worked all his life in Canada, contributing to the national economy and to the national revenue as a farmer and a fisherman. In 1948 he was employed as a caretaker, earning $18.35 weekly after taxes (giving him an annual take-home pay of $954.20). His only son had been killed in the war, and the veteran's pension was being paid to the son's wife and child, both of whom lived in England and had never contributed anything to this country. The man asserted a right to a pension from his son's death, to an OAP, and to keep his job.[44] For this man the state's obligation to the elderly had clearly gone well beyond mere welfare for dependent people.

By the middle of the Second World War the developing culture of entitlement was strong enough to push officials to reshape the application of estate claims regulations. Federal officials conceded that if the provincial authorities had the sole constitutional authority to put forward such a claim, then provincial procedures alone must govern when such claims were made.[45] The placing of liens was under attack publicly, as was the broader issue of reclaiming from pensioners' estates. In 1944 the minister of finance announced in the House of Commons that provincial pension authorities could use their discretion on collecting claims from estates valued at less than $2000. This was followed in March 1945 by a motion in the Manitoba legislature to end the placing of liens on property valued at less than $2000.[46] The problem with this 'solution' was that it drew an arbitrary line at $2000, and estates of only slightly higher value ended up with considerably fewer assets than those just under $2000. Furthermore, as some provincial officials were quick to point out, not only was there no legislative authority for adoption of the $2000 figure, but the federal 'backdown' admitted that that section of the OAP Act was permissive for estates of all value. Officials at both federal and provincial levels agreed that OAP applications were likely to rise once the public learned that claims against estates were being relaxed. In spite of the 1947 federal-provincial agreements for the passage of provincial legislation facilitating recovery from pensioners' estates, provincial governments were reluctant to take the required action because public opposition was so strong.[47]

The new federal position on claims against estates merely condoned what was already practice in several jurisdictions: every provincial authority developed its own response to this issue, as did every family touched by a potential claim. By the 1940s the issue had become particularly sensitive politically for the vast portion of estates that were under $2000 in value. An Ontario official described the 1946 popular sentiment on the issue: 'The recovery from estates is another point on which there is tremendous public criticism, at least in our province. There is no getting away from the fact that the old person has an idea that if he applies for an old age pension the pension authority is taking his property from him. We know that is not so, but he does not know, and that attitude has spread across the whole group of old people.'[48] By 1946 only Quebec had a policy of claiming from every such estate. Five provinces – British Columbia, Alberta, Saskatchewan, Ontario, and Prince Edward Island – made no claim on the first $2000 of any estate unless there were no relatives or 'reasonable' heirs; over $2000, discretion was exercised. New Brunswick made no claim against estates unless they were over $2000 and would otherwise be inherited by someone who had not contributed to the pensioner's support. Manitoba waived its claims on estates under $500, but used its discretion in claims against larger estates. Nova Scotia claimed against any estate where such a claim was deemed just, which in practice meant that almost no claims were made.[49]

This changing attitude towards claims against pensioners' estates was reflected in the statistics of actual recoveries. Given that such a claim against estates accumulated with time, a considerable increase in amounts claimed each year would be predictable, all else remaining stable. But, instead, the amounts being recovered began to decline markedly in 1945, particularly in proportion to the funds being disbursed to pensioners.[50] New attitudes about the state's role in social programs and about old age pensions combined with the continuing pressure from the elderly themselves and their families – pressure that was manifested through their behaviour and their political organizations – to force a major change in government pension policy.

Family Culture and Financial Independence

The OAP represented a new form of property for the elderly. Old men and old women – many of the latter for the first time in decades, if not in their lifetime – could now count on a secure, regular income. Although the OAP payments were themselves not enough to bring all needy elderly above the poverty line, they were nevertheless significant sums that gave many elderly some useful leverage or perhaps even financial independence. The OAP was property that could be employed by the elderly to meet their own needs and those of their families, and yet it was a transitory form of property, one which could not be transmitted to future generations and which undermined the property claims of inheriting relatives. In competition with state claims against their property, both pensioners and their families struggled to find the most effective system for meeting their various interests, though these interests were not always compatible.

State claims against the property of the elderly, or even the threat of such claims, raised some fundamental issues for the elderly themselves and for their families. Though the relative weight of ownership varied in every case, the elderly's formal ownership at law was balanced by the traditional, informal claims of the various family members, particularly those of children who as young adults had worked to sustain the property and to increase its value. The existence of the OAP program further complicated this picture of competing interests. On the one hand there was a potential new claimant to the property; on the other hand a pension could enhance the family assets, bringing new income into the family and slowing any drain on the assets caused by the necessitous circumstances of the elderly.

There was not much doubt in the minds of many pensioners or their families that the philosophy behind claims against pensioners' estates was wrong. Early in 1928, while the program was still only a few months old, British Columbia officials reported that children of deceased pensioners were 'inclined to insist upon their claim' to their parents' estates, even where the children had not helped to support their parents in the final years. An old man in central Ontario complained in 1930 that there was 'quite a lot of talk around here' that pensioners had to hand over their property to the government: 'Now Gentlemen do you think it is a proper thing for the Government to expect a man that has worked hard and been saveing and built a nice Comefortuble home for himself and Family and than if he wants the old age pension to sign his property over to the Government. And than at his Death for the Government to take and Sell that Property and turn his Wife & Family out on the road.'[51] This opposition to the state's claims against pensioners' property was already well developed at the start of the Depression.

The culture of entitlement was shared among all adult generations because all might benefit both directly and indirectly. Certainly some families and some elderly took action to prevent recovery of the state's claim. In some families, potential heirs were concerned to protect their own claims, beyond those of their elderly relatives. They had often vested years of labour in the acquisition, maintenance, or expansion of the family property, and the assets played a role in their own long-term strategy for survival. A married daughter in Indianapolis, for example, wanted to protect her own interest in the family property, while gaining the OAP for her seventy-six-year-old widowed mother. The mother was deaf and ill, and she supported herself through $150 in rental income as well as funds and goods from her daughter. The rental income came from pasture land surrounding the father's birthplace, allegedly endowing the property with great sentimental value (according to the daughter). Adding to that, 'since my grandfather cut the virgin timbers of this Crown land, I am foolish and sentimental I know, but when I grow old I want to live there just like my father did.' How could the property be retained for the family and the OAP acquired for her mother, 'because I would like to feel that she would always be cared for?' Other relatives implied that their continued interest in helping the elderly was dependent on the fate of their inheritance.[52]

Though family members exhibited considerable concern that their potential claim in a parent's estate was being jeopardized by acceptance of an OAP, this was just as apparent among the pensioners themselves. One means of maintaining a sense of independence while accepting various forms of physical and emotional support from family members was the pensioners' real or potential ability to reciprocate. Most elderly could provide only limited immediate reciprocity, but they could rest somewhat more content with the thought of past aid and that their estates, however small, would reward immediate family members for their past support and would be a final reflection of shared affection and ties. Inheritance – whether during the elderly's lifetime or after their death – was a means by which individual elderly ensured their memory and status within the family and helped to maintain the continuity of the family as a whole, something that many elderly value highly.[53] Estates thus represented potent emotional forces in addition to having more obvious economic importance.

The elderly and their families cooperated in a range of measures designed to keep property within the family and out of the hands of the state. A British Columbia official reported that in 1936–8, seventy-four claims against estates had been frustrated by prior property transfer, sixty-eight pensions had been cancelled because of such transfers, and seventy-seven applications had been rejected on the basis of prior property conveyances. 'Easily one-half' of the board's time, he claimed, was taken up with cases of allegedly improper property transfer.[54]

The OAP Act specifically declared ineligible those who had transferred property so as to qualify for a pension, and every provincial application form asked for detailed information about property transfers within the past five years. Such transfers were not uncommon among the elderly, and officials sought to put an end to such activity by prospective pensioners.[55] Though a number of potential pensioners took such action and often paid the penalty for it, their motivation was more complex than a simple desire to gain the OAP. An equally powerful impulse was to hand over property to family members so that the assets remained in the family rather than reverting to the state.[56] This transfer was a process that empowered the elderly. They were deciding the timing and the character of the property transfer; in their continuing role as parents, they were giving to their children; they were helping to sustain the economic power and status of the family, from which they could continue to draw support of various kinds.

Both the elderly and their family members cooperated in various forms of property transfer that sought to retain ownership and control within the family. Five weeks before a Nanaimo, British Columbia, widow applied for a pension in 1932, she transferred her property to her son. When this was challenged by state authorities, she explained that she could no longer afford the annual taxes (totalling $32.34), though the officials were doubtful since she had more than four hundred dollars in a savings account. Six years later the woman, now living with her married daughter, again applied for a pension. She claimed to have no money in the bank, but was discovered to have $313.61 in a joint account with her daughter. In each case she had sought to hide her assets and keep them within her family, in cooperation with her adult children.[57] The behaviour in another British Columbia case was somewhat more open. By means of an unregistered conveyance, a Langley area farmer transferred his home to his daughters for one dollar, nine months before applying for a pension in 1936. When officials refused a pension and advised that the property be reconveyed to the farmer, his agent commented: 'Mr Ellery desires so much to make sure that his daughters will have a home that he would rather, he said, proceed with the conveyance to his daughters and try to go on earning his living on the farm if the government would not give him his pension.' Shortly thereafter the land sale was registered, and the government stood by its refusal. In 1940, five years after the original transfer, he reapplied for a pension, but again officials refused, pointing out that there was no time limit on taking property transfers into account.[58]

The description of another west coast case unwittingly emphasized the status and empowerment gained by the elderly through such manipulation of property. A man had received a pension for several years before officials recalculated his assets and ruled him ineligible; his pension was discontinued. In the words of one official, 'the weak old man proceeded to stage a potlatch and on the 25th of the month [just three weeks after receiving notice of discontinuance] he deeded his property to his daughter and later, I believe, flattened out his bank account by backing his son's note for a thousand dollars. Having dispossessed himself,' he then reapplied for a pension, with the help of a solicitor.[59] Others were simply intent on helping their children, rather than defrauding the state.[60] Such activity was designed to retain property within the extended family, while gaining a pension for the applicant.

The state's use of liens aimed to close a loophole of which many pensioners were taking advantage.[61] Prevented from transferring property within five years or more of pension application in order to qualify for a pension, some elderly chose to keep their property from falling to a state claim by shifting the property to a relative once the OAP had been granted. Pensioners' organizations actively counselled such action, as allegedly did solicitors. Pensioners were advised to transfer ownership to their children, but to leave the conveyance unregistered until after death so it could not be detected by authorities; at that point the state was left with little or no estate against which claims could be made. For the elderly, the disadvantage of this procedure was that they lost any substantial leverage that the ownership had given them, and they were literally dependent on the goodwill of their children to whom they had transferred the property. For many elderly the pressures of family obligation overcame any doubts, but the requirements of the state procedures forced them into a vulnerable position.

Another tactic was used, particularly on the west coast. Elderly owners, on the indisputable basis of their straitened financial circumstances, simply stopped paying the taxes on their property and eventually allowed the property to be sold by the local municipality in a tax sale. Powerful, informal community controls prevented the general public from bidding on the property and directed the property to be sold to family members for a small amount, usually sufficient to meet the back taxes.[62] Family and community thus collaborated to maintain family property and to frustrate the aims of the state treasury.[63]

Though the OAP regulations barred the transfer of 'property' in order to qualify for a pension, in practice this came to be applied only to real property, ignoring such property as cash or securities.[64] But those without real estate displayed many of the same attitudes and took comparable steps to protect their assets, their family, and their OAP qualifications. Officials noted the tendency of some elderly on their death-beds to transfer their savings to their children so that the state would not be able to claim the funds. Where lump sums were received through inheritance or otherwise, pensioners allegedly often squandered the money or quickly transferred it to family members so as not to alter their OAP payment level.[65] Such reports served to convince officials of the appropriateness of the regulations.

For their part, many elderly readily adapted the custom of maintenance agreements to the new circumstances of state support for the elderly. Timing of the transfer of the property was now affected by an additional factor – the age of eligibility for the OAP. An account of property transfer to the next generation in 1930s Ireland emphasized this adaptability, and the common character of this phenomenon across the Western world:

The introduction of the old-age pension has facilitated this transfer. Originally designed for the support of the aged in an industrial population in England, it has speedily woven itself into the fabric of Irish rural life. Nowadays, the farmer can turn over his land at the age of seventy. In doing so, he divests himself of his property which stands in the way of his receiving the pension. One countryman ... sang the praises of the pension in no uncertain terms. His words show clearly that, even with this new source of income at his disposal, the old, abdicating farm father forms part of the family economic unit. 'To have old people in the house,' he said, 'is a great blessing in these times, because if you have one it means ten bob a week and if you have two it means a pound a week coming into the house.'[66]

What was true for Ireland was equally true for Canada, though state officials did what they could to frustrate such blatant attempts to manipulate the elderly's property so as to qualify for the means-tested OAP.[67]

Some elderly adapted traditional maintenance agreements so much that they were no longer recognizable as mechanisms for the support of the elderly. In these cases, state officials could and did step in to redress the balance. In 1938, for example, Francois Lebrun of Cookshire, Quebec, had transferred his property (valued at $3500) to one of his sons, providing that the son met certain obligations to Lebrun's other sons and daughters. Struck by the fact that there was no provision for support of Lebrun himself, the Quebec board decided that the property transfer had been carried out in order to qualify for a pension and that the adult children could be expected to contribute $240 annually to their father's upkeep. A monthly pension of $10.41 was awarded, though the chair of the board protested that this was too high.[68] In a Saskatchewan case an elderly farmer had turned over a half section of land valued at more than $7000, livestock, and a full line of machinery to his son. In return, the son, who had worked on the farm all his life, promised to pay his father $200 annually for the rest of the old man's life. The father was receiving only a small return on the property's total value, and he tried to supplement this income with a pension. But it is impossible to say to what extent the father was influenced by a desire to take advantage of state support systems or by a desire to repay his son for years of work.[69] The availability of the OAP was manifestly reshaping the ways in which families distributed property and responsibilities among members.

Nor was this phenomenon merely a rural one. Families in urban centres experienced similar frustrations at a new state process interfering with family assets. An elderly Toronto couple, for example, complained in 1950 that they could not accept an OAP without jeopardizing ownership of their home. That home was not merely theirs but also their children's, paid for in part through the contributions made by the children deliberately boarding at home to help their parents pay for the house. In such circumstances, the couple refused to apply for an OAP, giving clear priority to the culture of the family; instead, they retained title to their home and argued for changes in the OAP legislation.[70] Such dilemmas help to explain the appeal of the culture of entitlement.

The OAP boards were aware of only some of the intent behind these various attempts to protect property. For example, the board (reflecting perhaps a middle-class bias) seemed quite unable to appreciate that adult children might have earned a share of the property through their own labour. Officials turned down a Vernon, British Columbia, man for a pension in

1937 because he had transferred his property to his son; the board ruled that the son should in turn support his father. Throughout his adult life the son, married with no dependent children, had lived with his father on the family ranch. In 1921 a one-third interest in the ranch had been transferred to the son; this was followed by a transfer of the remaining two-thirds in 1937, along with title to another property. The son had soon sold both properties for a total of $4500. The father appealed to a cabinet minister: his son was only a working man and had his own family to support, 'and had I paid him the wages coming to him the property would have had to have been sold ten or fifteen years ago to pay him off.'[71] The board was not wrong in asserting that the father had a considerable claim on his son, but it seemed incapable of appreciating that the property transferred had, in a moral and family sense, been at least partly the son's already, earned through his labour. For the board, the property was legally the father's and the transfer absolved the board of any obligation to the old man. In such cases, argued the board, it had 'no course open but to consider that whatever maintenance was provided by the son ... did not obligate the father to transfer his property to the son, nor does it now excuse the son from maintaining his father if financially able to do so.'[72]

Provincial administrators, however, were cognizant of the emotional bonds behind such property transfers. 'If these poor old chaps would not attempt to take the law into their own hands, all of us would have a great deal easier time in the administration of this type of social legislation,' wrote the chair of the British Columbia board. 'I am convinced that Mr. Watson was quite sincere in what he did. He wanted the children to have the property rather than have any claim against it through the granting of the Old Age Pension.' The children could acquire the property through inheritance, but only if they continued to contribute to the elderly parent's support, as judged by the board.[73] The board was quite comfortable controlling family behaviour through such levers, but many families were not.

Most elderly bitterly resented what they saw as state interference with their property. For pensioners, claims or liens with a view to claiming the property after death made the OAP not a pension but a loan. Rumours of state procedures became distorted as they spread, so that one common belief among the elderly was that homes would have to be sold in order to qualify for an OAP.[74] One elderly man, who was deaf and worked part-time as a gardener while trying to support a wife who was blind and diabetic, argued strongly for a lower OAP age limit, 'but I do not want assistance if it means losing the house.'[75] In the 1930s Manitoba officials placed a lien against all pensioners' real estate, and in Saskatchewan a caveat was filed, giving the provincial authorities some influence over any sale or transfer. Similar procedures were followed in Prince Edward Island, Ontario, and Quebec, but other provinces had no mechanisms for preventing such activity.

It is a sign of the financial straits of the needy elderly that the meagre OAP payments raised a further complicating issue – the potential for some financial independence. Many of the elderly sought to maintain their independence as long as possible. In Canada one of the most obvious means to maintain independence was to avoid heavy reliance on family members. Some elderly equally sought to resist accepting aid from the state. An Alberta official described the circumstances of a seventy-three-year-old woman who defined her independence in terms of her relationship with the OAP program. In poor health, she was living in a farm house owned by her son-in-law; 'The place is not fit to live in as it is too cold and far away from medical aid. She has nothing except two old chairs, a bed and dresser.' Although she qualified for a pension at the age of seventy, 'she preferred to keep going [on her own] as long as she could' until now she had totally exhausted her resources. She was now willing to accept an Old Age Pension, but would not apply for local relief.[76] Her reluctance to accept aid was based on a sense of self-worth and independence, and her distinction between the OAP and relief is suggestive of an increasingly common attitude.

For many elderly, especially women, the OAP program represented an opportunity to improve their standard of living or to reduce their total dependence on family or friends. Indeed, for many women the OAP represented their first source of regular, significant income independent of husbands or family. Women, whose wages were consistently far lower than men's and who were more usually involved in unpaid labour, were now eligible for pensions fully equal to those of men. In Newfoundland the contrast offered by the Canadian OAP was even greater. Not previously eligible for the OAP, many elderly Newfoundland women in late 1949 or early 1950 received cheques for up to $200 or more in retroactive payment – probably the largest sums of money they had ever received and quite possibly the largest sums anyone in their families had ever handled. Among couples, this windfall offered an interesting challenge to the balance of economic power, though the records reveal little of such marital dynamics or of the impact on the local economies. OAP officials, however, took substantial steps to ensure that the OAP disturbed male economic power within marriages as little as possible.[77]

Others who experienced systemic discrimination in employment and income discovered new-found equality in the OAP program. Immigrants and visible minorities, provided that they met the British citizenship and twenty-year residency requirements or were not Indians (within the meaning of the Indian Act), had access to an important new source of income. Within distinct limits, the OAP program and regulations challenged existing structures of ethnic/racial inequality. One group whose standard of living ironically improved under the OAP was elderly, interned Japanese Canadians during the Second World War. While younger internees on relief received $11 a month plus shelter and fuel from the British Columbia Security Commission, older Japanese Canadians received $20 a month from the OAP plus shelter and fuel from the Security Commission.[78] While the amounts of monthly payment through the OAP often seem pathetically low when compared with the contemporary cost of living, the payments offered substantial improvement in the standard of living and in the psychological position of many elderly.

But, at the same time, the OAP also made the individual pensioners dependent on the state for support. Their vulnerability to bureaucratic decisions is brought home by the case of one farmer in Lambton County. Adam Kielly lived with his wife in a small home, which he had severed from his 100-acre farm. In his mid-sixties, Mr Kielly found he was unable to continue to work the farm and turned it over to his son, who was able to make only enough profit to pay the interest payments on the $3100 mortgage. On the advice of the mortgagee, Mr Kielly then deeded the farm to his son on the basis of the mortgagee's opinion that the farm was now worth only the value of the mortgage. A year later, Mr Kielly turned seventy and applied for an OAP, but this was refused on the grounds of the land transfer and his son's presumed ability to support him. Only after several months had passed and the mortgagee had explained the circumstances did the board reverse its stance and grant a full $20 pension. Less than a year later an inspector decided that the son was capable of supporting Mr Kielly and the pension was cancelled, but on appeal it was restored to the reduced payment level of $10. Over the next three years Mr Kielly and local persons of influence appealed for a higher pension, which was finally raised to $15 in 1935. Two years later he remarried in London and moved in with his new wife; as a result, his pension was cancelled. However, in traditional patriarchal fashion, his wife's home and income had been left to her by her late first husband on condition that she not remarry, so her home and income were lost. Mr Kielly was forced to return to his family for a home, and once again began his appeals for reinstatement of his OAP.[79] His vulnerability to the decisions of the OAP bureaucracy and his dependence on their judgments are striking. It is little wonder that the elderly sought to maintain their economic claims on the family, which offered an alternative source of support and reduced reliance on the state.

Where the elderly individual relied heavily on family support, the OAP offered a welcome prospect of some limited independence. The economic power that flowed from the availability of a regular pension cheque should not be underestimated, particularly among extended families that were near or below the poverty line. For some elderly the ability to share in household expenses gave them an important sense of self-worth and reduced their vulnerability. For others, even the meagre monthly OAP cheque gave them a modicum of financial independence. A Vancouver woman was adequately supported by a husband (on full OAP), two daughters, and a granddaughter, all of whom lived with the woman; the daughters insisted on their ability to support their mother, but the woman applied for a pension because she 'thought that she would like to have some money of her own.' Some pensioners contributed their cheques to pay for household expenses. Others retained at least portions to be able to offer occasional treats, particularly to grandchildren.[80] For elderly in such circumstances, the OAP represented perhaps their only prospect of gaining even a small measure of financial leverage, and thus some important influence over their own lives.

For other pensioners, the OAP provided an opportunity to escape uncomfortable or unwanted situations. A seventy-six-year-old widow in northern Ontario envisioned the advantages an OAP would bring her:

I have some children but are all married and all have family of their own and are all working out by the day to earn their livings for their familys and they also have to support me. And I cannot live very happy with large familys they can not give me any money and dress me up neatly. So I would like to know if you would take the matter up and let me know what you can do for me to help me out to live. I am pretty old and must still work for my living. And with that my eyesight is very poor I can hardly see anything. Therefore it makes it kind of hard for me to work.[81]

In Galt, Ontario, a seventy-five-year-old widow found herself unhappily dependent on her son: 'I am living with my son now but he cant give me anything I am unable to do th [house]work he has to pay a woman & she dont make life as pleasant for me as might be am thinking of taking rooms again ... altho my son dont give me anything i'm afraid he would think it [a] disgrace for me to get th pension.' The prospect of moving to a rooming house was attractive to her: 'if I had rooms I could take care of myself & have a good time I would use my money enuf to make me comfortable.' The pension would offer the woman a welcome means of leaving such an uncomfortable and possibly abusive environment.[82]

The culture of the family was central to understanding the lives of the elderly in the first half of the twentieth century. Adult children, and other relatives to a lesser extent, played an active and continuing role in the lives of most of the elderly examined in this study. Those children provided continuing support and assistance to their parents,[83] and that support tended to increase as the parents aged (as discussed in chapter 5). The details of this support are limited by the nature of the sources used here; OAP records tend to emphasis substantial assistance, such as accommodation, food, or money, providing no opportunity for the recording of emotional support. Nevertheless, the support of adult children is best understood as a reflection of reciprocity and attachment across the lifespan. Emotional attachment has been found to enhance intergenerational exchange of support; mere obligation is unlikely to evoke much assistance. Furthermore, reciprocated helping is more likely to occur when both generations feel emotionally close.[84] It is notable that the records suggest that familial support flowed both to and from the elderly. The elderly themselves continued to give considerable support to their children. Both generations tended to share a family culture of support and attachment across the lifespan.[85]

The OAP offered those elderly dependent on their family one means of offering some return for that support. Increasingly, both the elderly and family members felt that this was reasonable and justifiable. Such attitudes were not limited to interested parties. In 1947 a town clerk commented on the OAP application of a retired, widowed farmer, now aged seventy-three, who for seven years had been living with his married daughter in Forest, Ontario: 'pension should be granted so that this man can help pay his way, I believe that his daughter is getting a little fed up with keeping him and receiving very little for her work.'[86] The old man's situation had not changed over the past seven years, but his daughter was now exerting pressure to gain some return from the state as recompense for her work. The developing culture of entitlement had determined the timing of the OAP application. The British Columbia minister responsible for the OAP supported the 1937 application of 'one of the finest of our old time working men.' Several years earlier the man had moved to Nelson to live with his married daughter; his son-in-law was trying to establish himself in the plumbing business, and the old man wanted to make some contribution to the family income, rather than being a drain.[87] The positive status implications for individual elderly were considerable.

Elderly who were dependent on their family for support were vulnerable, helping to explain further the attractiveness of the independence offered by a pension. Martha Elice, a seventy-four-year-old widow in the Petrolia area, had two married daughters and no assets or income. One daughter was married to a labourer with eight children and could offer no support whatsoever; the other daughter was married to a farmer with two children; both daughters lived in rural Lambton County. Mrs Elice lived with the farming daughter, but in unhappy circumstances. In response to the question as to who contributed to her support and how much, Mrs Elice replied: 'I am stopping with my daughter.... a bite to eat.' The town clerk commented that both sons-in-law were 'engaged in a life or death struggle to exist'; as a result, there was 'little care given her; much unpleasantness with son-in-law; living conditions most undesirable.'[88] A pension would give Martha Elice some real power: she would be able to offer her daughter and son-in-law some tangible and vital return for her support, making her presence economically valuable, or she could take a room somewhere else. Either way an OAP would empower her decisively.

For families on the edge of poverty, having an elderly member with a steady pension income could often be quite valuable. The daughter of a London widow was particularly anxious to find some way that she could take her mother into her home and thus take advantage of her pension. The mother had been living with a second daughter in London, but that daughter had recently died. Now the first daughter admitted that she was not in a financial position to care for her mother: her husband earned only $30 a week, they had four children to care for, and they owned no property. For such a family, an additional regular income would be attractive. Unfortunately, the first daughter lived in Detroit and the Canadian pension could not be paid to a non-resident, so the mother could not move there. Nevertheless, until local OAP inspectors caught up with them, the mother was living in Detroit and a London nephew was forwarding the pension cheques to her there.[89] Families had long tried to incorporate state and community support mechanisms into their survival strategies.[90] The OAP simply provided a new opportunity, one to which many felt increasingly entitled.

At times, family members were somewhat assertive in their attempts to gain access to the pension income. A Toronto daughter, who claimed to have been supporting her eighty-year-old mother for eighteen years, calculated the lost income resulting from the old woman's occupation of the best bedroom in the house; a portion of that continuing lost income ought to be deducted from the OAP cheque and paid directly to the daughter, 'as if she [the mother] gets it I will never see a cent & I understand when she is gone I get nothing whatever of what belongs to her.'[91] This interest of family members in the pensions of their parents and relatives was realized early. In 1926 a Conservative Party supporter advised the federal party leader to endorse the OAP: 'I believe this plank alone would turn the tide, as it is not only the pensioners, but the army of relatives and adherents who are interested.'[92] For a number of families among the working poor, the presence of an elderly family member receiving a pension could have significant, substantial impact, particularly during the 1930s.[93]

One of the primary manifestations of their impulse to independence was an intense desire among many dependent elderly to retain in their own control sufficient funds to pay the costs of their own funeral. 'I am astonished at the sacrifice many of our poorer members, existing on a mere pittance of $15 a month, would make to get a respectable funeral,' wrote a member of a pensioners' organization in Calgary. 'It seems to become an obsession with some of them.'[94] For some needy elderly, such funds represented their only cash savings. Many feared that the state's claims against their estate would wipe out these savings and deprive them of the final dignity of a proper funeral; they often went to unusual lengths to hide these funds from the state. Others maintained small insurance policies for the purpose of paying funeral expenses.[95] In some instances, state officials collaborated in protecting money designated for funeral expenses.[96] This reflected a developing sensitivity to the feelings and needs of the elderly themselves.

The elderly receiving the OAP were among the dependent poor in Canada. Receipt of the pension both alleviated their economic condition and complicated their social and familial position. By intruding into family relationships and processes with an inherently 'heavy hand,' state officials disrupted or at least threatened family values and traditions that were central to the predominant family culture and to the continuing emotional and physical support that the elderly needed from their adult children and relatives. At the same time, for many the OAP program offered the means to perpetuate the same family culture and values. The elderly and their families were not without their own influence, developing a number of ultimately effective strategies for asserting their own needs and interests. Nor was the picture one-dimensional. The pension represented a new form of property that the elderly could use in the continuing renegotiation of relationships with their family. The result was a complex, interactive process among the mixture of competing and cooperative interests of the state, the family, and the elderly.

5

Agency among Old Age Pensioners

The first and most important challenge to the predominant philosophy behind the early OAP program came from the elderly themselves. The organized elderly were the most articulate in this regard (as discussed in chapter 6), but the unorganized elderly acting individually also played an impressive and at least as influential role. The conduct of many elderly and of family members sought to reshape the state program to meet their own needs more effectively. They tried to present themselves in ways designed to appeal to the informal standards that redefined old age in the twentieth century. In the face of a paternalistic and increasingly authoritative environment shaping their lives, the elderly responded as active agents in shaping their own behaviour. This interactive process has already been seen in the discussion of family and property as they affected the various mechanisms for supporting the dependent elderly.

Popular attitudes among the unorganized elderly were an important force behind the initiation of the OAP program.[1] The New Brunswick royal commission on old age pensions found that when it distributed questionnaires early in 1930, the elderly demonstrated a strong desire to have their voices heard. Press notices informed elderly provincial residents where copies of the questionnaire could be obtained, and the New Brunswick elderly, both inside and outside the province, responded with enthusiasm. Almost eleven thousand elderly residents, representing two-thirds of the total provincial elderly, filled out the forms, providing the commission with detailed information about their economic circumstances.[2]

A response rate of this magnitude for a mailed questionnaire is truly astounding. Since participation in the survey was not controlled, it is fair to assume that large numbers of potential pensioners younger than the age of seventy also filled out the form to encourage action by the provincial government. Yet the survey participation was spontaneous and individual; New Brunswick is one of the provinces where there is no evidence of organizational activity among the elderly in the 1930s or 1940s. Individual elderly were insistent on claiming support from the state and on helping to shape the form of that support. This articulation of the elderly's views and of their claims on the state is central to understanding the changes in the OAP program and the development of cohesive seniors' organizations across Canada. Even more important, the behaviour of individual elderly demonstrates the changes taking place in the position of the elderly and in the definitions of old age.

It is not that there was anything new about elderly pensioners actively shaping their own destiny. Historically, the elderly had long been doing just that. They had used inheritance strategies to control the behaviour of children and kin. They had used residential strategies, such as households or stem families, to optimize labour and support. They had employed property to coerce adult children to contribute labour and support for extended periods. They had operated a family-based economy to sustain their own interests and ends, 'stepping down' from labour gradually while children maintained the productive levels of the family economy. In doing so, the elderly had often sought to assist other family members as well, but their own interests were never far from sight.

The medicalization of old age in the nineteenth and twentieth centuries has blinded us to some of the activities of the elderly.[3] It is time to recover our awareness of their scope.

Social Characteristics

To understand the pensioners' behaviour it is first essential to establish their demographic characteristics. Two groups of OAP applicants, one in the rural districts of Lambton County in southwestern Ontario and the other in the city of London, were randomly sampled.[4] This information permits an analysis of those applying for a pension, but not of the total population of pensioners. There is no consistent information base that would allow a systematic study of the evolving population of pensioners. The applicants are therefore employed here as representative of that total population.[5]

The social characteristics of the pensioners reflected the demography of the elderly in general. There were slightly more men than women among the applicants, and the proportion of the sexes among the London and Lambton applicants reflected the skewed rural-urban distribution among the elderly. Of the Lambton applicants, 55 per cent were men, while in London men made up 40 per cent.

Family status was a crucial element in determining the social and economic position of the elderly. There are no statistics that allow measurement of the qualitative character of family relationships, but some insight into potential and actual support can nevertheless be gained. The marital status of the pensioners varied predictably between the sexes, but less predictably spatially. Widows made up a much greater proportion of female applicants than did widowers among the males; men were two times more likely to be married. But rural male applicants were almost twice as likely to be single as urban males, and the reverse was true for females. Rural married women made up a significantly greater proportion of the pensioners than did urban married women, and the reverse was true for males. For those applicants that were married, just 17 per cent of their spouses already received an OAP.

Next to the presence of a spouse, support from children was of utmost importance to the elderly. Lambton and London OAP applicants, however, were likely to have surviving children. Just over a quarter of the applicants had no surviving children,[6] women being slightly more likely than men to find themselves in this position. Almost as many applicants had five or more children to call on for assistance, with the number of applicants having one, two, three, or four children being relatively evenly distributed.[7] The differences between the rural and urban samples with respect to surviving children were insignificant.

The location of these children was important in determining the character and extent of the support they were able to provide for their elderly parents. Of those applicants with children, fully three-quarters had at least one child residing within the same municipality. Older OAP applicants were somewhat more likely to have children nearby; although the needs of the parents would seem to influence propinquity, it is unclear whether children chose to be near their parents or vice versa.[8] Gender was certainly a factor influencing the presence of children. Women applicants were significantly more likely than men to have at least one child living in the same municipality as themselves, and again this tendency increased noticeably with the age of the elderly women.[9] Gender also influenced the children's behaviour, daughters being more likely than sons to live nearby. The marital status of the children was even more influential; where children lived in the same municipality, they were more likely to be single than married. For both sexes (children and parents), the likelihood of propinquity declined with the marriage of the child. But here, too, gender was a significant factor, elderly mothers being more likely to have an unmarried child nearby than were elderly fathers; with marriage, the gender difference was considerably reduced.[10] Marriage altered the obligations of adult children, but until then the culture of the family prescribed that unmarried children and parents should reside near each other so they could continue to exchange support. Even with the children's own marital obligations, more than half the elderly with married children had at least one married child in their community. This is suggestive of the place of intergenerational support in the family culture of the period.

Social class and community culture were undoubtedly also factors in influencing the presence of children. Urban pensioners were less likely than their rural counterparts to live near their unmarried children, but somewhat more likely to live near married daughters.[11] This evidence does not reveal the timing of this proximity, but Wilmott and Young's research in a London, England, suburb in the 1950s suggests that for working-class families propinquity was a characteristic of family relationships across the adult life-course, not just a phenomenon that developed once the parents approached old age.[12] Nevertheless, its role in old age was significant.

At the point of application, most pensioners had limited resources. Judging from the case files, this was a reflection of the elderly's already limited assets as well as their conscious decision in many instances to expend most of their existing assets before applying for a pension. In a 1948 Toronto survey, three-fifths of the men applicants were self-supporting, relying on a combination of wages, savings, and private pensions. The women tended to be much more dependent – on spouses, on relatives, on public assistance – and only half as likely to be self-supporting. A study of pensioners in Montreal found that a majority had been dependent on some private agency or government aid in the ten years pervious to gaining an OAP, though this dependency likely reflects the urban character of the sample.[13]

Of all the information provided by applicants to OAP officials, that regarding resources and sources of income and support is most suspect. Applicants had good reason to hide assets and did so; underreporting income and aid could help to enhance eligibility and to increase the size of the pension payment. The income and assistance most likely to be underreported was informal, coming from family or neighbours, and would not otherwise be recorded. Nevertheless, this information was analysed. Although the total support was likely to have been considerably underreported, it is less likely that the types of help or the distribution of support among the applicants' children were distorted.

As expected, applicants reported that most children provided no support. Of the 2075 children listed on the applications from London and Lambton, almost three-quarters allegedly gave their parents no substantial assistance.

Where aid was given, it was most likely to take the form of cash.[14] Elderly women were significantly more likely to receive (or at least to report) children's assistance, and that support increased with the age of the parents.[15] The marital status of the children affected reported aid in the same way that it affected propinquity. Single children were much more likely to be giving substantial support than married children, and elderly mothers were much more likely to be the recipients than fathers.[16] Gender had an equally striking impact on the children. Sons, with greater access to wages and control of property, might be expected to give more help than daughters, but this was not the case. Daughters, particularly when single, gave substantial support to their parents, and significantly more frequently.[17] For both sexes and regardless of marital status, the reported aid consistently increased with the age of the parents.

Many persons had an understanding of the order in which family members should be called on by the elderly for support, but the understanding varied considerably. Gender was frequently a major criterion, but often in different ways. One London anecdote is suggestive of the varied ways that gender influenced the participants' views of familial obligations. The old woman involved had two married sons and two married daughters; all her sons and sons-in-law were farmers living in the region. Her sons felt themselves unable to take their mother in, so she moved to her sister's home in London; she admitted to OAP inspectors that her daughters were willing to have her live with them, 'but she does not like to have a son-in-law keep her, when she has sons of her own.'[18] Claims on one's family of orientation thus for some took precedence over claims on one's own children, and the impact of gender also varied. Although children had the strongest obligation to aid their elderly parents, for some the claims on children could be superseded by those on siblings or other family members.

Although the impact of gender was multifaceted and not always consistent, it was nevertheless profound. Both sons and daughters had been socialized to believe that their mothers needed more support than their fathers in old age, and there were sound reasons for this belief. Elderly men tended to own more assets and to have better access to paid work (and presumably better paid work); men were disproportionately the beneficiaries of the few private pensions that existed. It is likely, as well, that the mother as the primary parent and nurturer had built up significantly greater bonds of affection and a stronger sense of obligation with her children. That sense of attachment and obligation, while strong for children of both sexes, was particularly well developed among daughters – partly because of their socialized role as care-giver, partly because of their personal identification with their parents' vulnerability and needs. Old age was not only more difficult for elderly women, but it was more onerous for their daughters. There is nothing new in the late twentieth century about the phenomenon of the 'sandwich generation'; it is just that with rising life expectancy, the obligations of adult children to elderly parents may now be extended over a longer period.[19]

Surprisingly, the median age of pension applicants rose slowly across the time period, particularly in rural society. The median age in the first few years of the OAP program was distorted because the elderly of all ages were applying for the first time. Thus, the initial spate (1929–34) of applications from all ages of elderly produced a median application age of 73.8 and 73.5 in the countryside and in the city, respectively. Thereafter, the median age fell to 71 for the later 1930s, reflecting the continuing economic difficulties of the period. During the war years, 1940–4, the median age rose to 71.8 and 71.3, followed by 73.8 and 72.2 for 1945–51, in the countryside and the city, respectively.[20] It is likely that improved economic conditions encouraged many elderly to delay application for a pension, as they preferred to retain the opportunity to earn unlimited income rather than accept the severe restrictions imposed by the OAP program. Where possible, many elderly chose to rely on traditional means of support rather than turn to the state with its associated stigma. Those traditions were stronger in rural areas, where the opportunities in farming and other occupations were less constrained by the increasingly authoritative views about the elderly worker. The meagre OAP was a last resort. Only when available work contracted or ill-health made paid work too difficult, did individual elderly turn to the OAP program.

[The impact of general economic conditions on the elderly's OAP behaviour is further suggested by statistics for the 1940s. For the years 1940–4, the proportion of men applicants fell in both rural and urban districts, reflecting their increased income opportunities; for those years women made up 60 per cent of all applicants. By the postwar years, however, elderly men were being pushed out of many jobs and, in numbers more closely reflecting their application patterns of the 1930s, older men again turned to the OAP for support.]

An analysis of the Lambton County and London pension applicants suggests a small but perhaps significant difference between the two sexes in the timing of their applications. Across the two decades and in both locales, but particularly in the city, men tended to apply for the OAP earlier than did women. While almost 56 per cent of the sampled men applied between the ages of seventy and seventy-four, this was true for just 53 per cent of the women. The median age for men applicants was consistently six to nine months younger than for women in each quarter of the period studied, except for the second half of the 1930s when the median age was the same for both sexes. Men had been socialized to take on responsibility for bringing in income, and thus found it easier to seek a pension. Women, who undoubtedly made up more than half the elderly poor, delayed asserting their claims to a pension.[21]

Though the explanation is not completely clear, the gendered timing of applications does suggest that women may have been more intimidated by the pension bureaucracy and rules, more deferential to their spouses' breadwinning role. Women were also perhaps more accepting of the minimal support available from their children and extended families, being content to supplement this support with their own domestic work in the household economy. Older men, in contrast, had less opportunity to contribute to the household economy through unpaid labour, particularly in the city, and so resorted more readily to the OAP. The OAP was gendered not only in its rules and structures by the pension bureaucracy, but also in the behaviour of the pensioners themselves.

The evidence regarding the applicants' accommodation status is suggestive of the conditions experienced by the elderly. A large minority of OAP applicants owned their own homes. In Lambton County more than a third of the applicants lived in their own home, and in London fully a quarter did so. Furthermore, only a third of the homes were mortgaged, though women were somewhat more likely to be living in a mortgaged home than were men; given their reduced income opportunity compared with men, women exploited the economic potential of their available assets in whatever manner assured the women's survival – whether that meant taking in boarders or mortgaging the home. Rural elderly women were somewhat more likely than men to live in their own home, and the reverse was true among urban applicants. Until the 1945–51 application cohort, London applicants were consistently less likely than their rural Lambton counterparts to own their own home, and consistently less likely to rent their accommodation. Elderly men were consistently almost twice as likely as women to live in some form of rented housing. The rural-urban dichotomy was also significant in other types of accommodation. A majority (almost 60 per cent) of urban elderly of both sexes were living with family or in an institution, whereas just 40 per cent of the rural elderly in the sample were doing so.

This breakdown suggests the greater flexibility retained by the elderly in rural society. The continuing opportunities for self-employment and for paid employment were wider in rural districts. The rural elderly could use their economic assets more variously, and were subject to fewer constraints in the marketplace. Perhaps rural society placed a more authoritative value on independence, persuading the elderly to be as self-reliant as possible for as long as possible. The urban elderly, in contrast, found that their assets were less capable of producing sufficient income for survival, and, certainly in the case of London, they had greater access to institutional support, which must have made that option easier to adopt.

The urban elderly likely had increased access to employment opportunities in the 1940s. For the application cohort of 1940–4, the percentage owning their own home was reduced by fully half, and the percentage for those renting accommodation fell even more, suggesting that the non-applicant elderly at this time – particularly women – had disproportionately found at least partial employment. For them the OAP was no longer financially attractive. No such decline could be detected among the rural elderly.

Most pensioners lived with others. A 1948 Toronto sample found that 19 per cent lived alone, while 35 per cent lived with a spouse and 37 per cent resided with relatives. Given the demographic and familial characteristics of the elderly, it is not surprising that old men were much more likely to live with a spouse or alone, and old women were significantly more likely to reside with relatives. Of the twenty-seven pensioners living alone, two-thirds (disproportionately men) were in a boarding or rooming house. While older couples living together found rooming houses an important option, most (over 60 per cent) lived in their own house (whether rented or owned); this enabled the couple to supplement their income by renting rooms to others, or to share expenses by turning over a portion of the house to a married child. Of those pensioners living with relatives, most were dependent on familial charity.[22]

The London and Lambton case files detail the human element in such behaviour. Boarding, for example, could lead to the creation of strong bonds within the household. Frank Aspen began boarding with a widow and her mother in Chatham, Ontario, in 1934; when the two women moved to nearby London in 1936, he moved with them, continuing to rely on his OAP cheque to cover the cost of his room and board ($4.50 weekly).[23] That he was willing to undergo the social and physical disruption of such a move is suggestive of the kind of dependency that elderly boarders could develop.

For many dependent elderly their home represented their only significant asset, and they used it to help gain the support they needed. The home could be mortgaged or sold to gain access to funds; family members or strangers could be brought into the home to share expenses or housework.[24]

When the elderly manipulated their assets and potential sources of support so as to qualify for an OAP, they were simply doing what they had always done to survive. They employed all the assets and resources available to them to gain the most effective support possible. When the OAP became available as a possible resource, it was subject to the same behaviour – nothing more and nothing less.

If at the same time the pensioners could help others – especially family members – many elderly were anxious to do so. In London an ex–street-railway employee had retired in 1939 at the age of sixty-seven, receiving a lump-sum pension payment of $600, most of which had been spent one year later. He shared his home with his married daughter and her seven children (ages fifteen to two), whose husband lived apart but sent her $20 a week. In return for his board, the father shared his home and paid half the water, electricity, and fuel costs.[25] In this way the father aided his daughter with the only asset he had, while gaining her domestic services and support. While this arrangement suited his own survival strategies, the old man gained intangible benefits as well that were probably vital to his psychological well-being. He confirmed his status as father/grandfather in a positive manner, and his reliance on his daughter was matched by her's on him. When he applied for an OAP, it was with the prospect that his status would be further enhanced through his increased financial power. By such behaviour, pensioners empowered themselves in significant ways.

The paternalism that so powerfully characterized the mechanisms of support available to the dependent elderly served as a vital motivating factor in such behaviour. Nowhere was this paternalism more evident than in the OAP program, but it was also a characteristic of more informal processes. It was a paternalism that sought to define the nature of 'acceptable' old age, and to shape the behaviour of the elderly to conform to the norms articulated by the various mechanisms of support.

Many persons in the community distinguished between the elderly who conformed to normative standards and those who did not. Only the former deserved an OAP, it was generally felt. The criteria used by officials and by those commenting on an OAP applicant's merits are particularly instructive as to the norms associated with being elderly. These standards applied to both the elderly themselves and to their families. Reasonably poor health was important for the applicant, frailty and advanced old age appealing to the paternalistic impulses among officials and the locally influential. Past life-style was now recalled as a present-day test; in particular, the person's economic and moral standards were assessed on the basis of past behaviour. Industriousness, frugality, honesty, reliability, and previous self-support were all frequently cited characteristics in an applicant's favour. Linked to these criteria was an earlier manifested desire to avoid welfare; if applicants had demonstrated a lack of reliance on the state in previous times, they were considered to be more deserving now. Both sexes, but particularly women, were found worthy on the basis of having a clean, well-kept home. Such norms gained considerable authority when they became conditions for support.

Several examples show how such criteria were applied. In 1938 the municipal clerk of Bothwell recommended that a local woman's payment level be raised to the maximum $20 (from the present $15). The pensioner lived with her son, who was unable to leave his farm for outside employment because his eighty-one-year-old mother required considerable care. Neither the pensioner nor her son had ever had a car, radio, or telephone, the clerk pointed out:

The Pensioner's ability, and habits are such, that the pension money that has been granted her in the past has been carefully, and intelligently expended.

It would appear to me within the meaning of the act, this poor old pensioner would not be asking for more than she is really in need of, at a ripe old age, in a weakened, run down physical condition, and finances at a low ebb.[26]

When a seventy-three-year-old woman applied in Lambton County, the municipal clerk quoted the local reeve: she 'has worked hard all her life and now is entitled to some assistance. she never spent her money foolishly.' To this the clerk added his own assessment: 'Applicant and husband have been day labourers all their lives. by careful living have bought and paid for their own small home and accumulated a few dollars in the Bank for their old age. This sum is very small and they want to keep it intact, if possible, for sickness and funeral expenses ... Their manner of living is excellent. home conditions are clean and bright.'[27] Others deserved support because they had avoided turning to state support for as long as possible or had lengthy roots in the community.[28] Nineteenth-century traditions distinguishing between deserving and undeserving poor thus took on only slightly new forms in the twentieth century.

Failure to meet the criteria meant that the individual was deemed to be undeserving of a pension. Older men were particularly vulnerable to such negative judgments, being assumed to be more capable to help themselves. Failure to have worked recently, dependence on a wife's labours, marital misconduct, and past dissolute conduct were common grounds for denying men an OAP.[29] Among many in the community there were limits to the developing sense of entitlement.

To be in receipt of a pension cheque was to be labelled by some as being not fully competent. It became much easier to adopt paternalistic practices. In the case of one London pensioner, the city welfare administrator commented: his wife 'complained that pensioner does not spend his money wisely, making it harder for her to manage the house on what they receive, and after hearing how he spends his pension money, we are of the opinion if he gave the money to his wife she would shop to better advantage.' But when a welfare officer suggested that the pension cheque could be sent to the wife, she rejected the notion; her husband 'would make living more miserable for all,' so it would be better if some official could be named to supervise the funds.[30] If others were manoeuvring to deprive him of some of his power, the pensioner certainly was still able to intimidate and assert some authority.

This general tendency to paternalism was particularly striking among the institutionalized elderly. Here some authorities tried to insist that residents appoint a local official as trustee. Where the resident refused to co-operate, the board could be quite cavalier about the resident's rights. In a Hamilton state-operated institution, for example, one woman refused to sign the form assigning her pension to the home, causing much dissatisfaction among all the other residents who had agreed to sign under the officials' pressure. The provincial board suggested that her refusal could be overridden and the head of the institution be named trustee; such trustees 'may then, if they desire,' give the pensioners involved a small sum from the pension as an allowance.[31]

Much of this paternalism was the result of genuine community and official concern for the individuals involved. Nevertheless, support for the elderly was frequently highly conditional – dependent not simply on meeting the formal criteria of the program involved, but also in conforming to the informal standards of what it was to be a member of the dependent elderly. As potential support for the needy elderly grew across the first half of the twentieth century, these informal standards became increasingly authoritative. It is not surprising that many elderly responded by presenting their behaviour and characteristics in ways designed to meet those standards, while seeking to reshape both the formal criteria and the informal standards to suit their own needs better.

'Reshaping' the OAP

The severe limitations on access to the OAP program were repeatedly challenged and avoided by individual elderly in need of support – a situation

that eventually led to the adoption of universality. In all provinces the elderly sought to make the OAP program operate to their best advantage. Where
possible they did so within the regulatory environment, but where necessary individual elderly instinctively manoeuvred among the regulations to
best meet each applicant's own ends. The 1936–7 Ontario OAP application
figures suggest the relative importance of the ways in which some elderly
sought to manipulate the program to their own advantage. In that province,
whose OAP Commission was considered by federal officials to be one of
the most efficient, almost 11 per cent of the 9019 new applicants had been
rejected as ineligible because of assets (20%), failure to disclose assets
(0.2%), age (25%), Parents' Maintenance Act (15%), residence (10%), earnings (4%), property (6%), transfer of property (13%), and other reasons
(6%).[32] These figures reflected only those applicants whose inelgibility or
false information had been detected. Potential pensioners and their families
constantly challenged the barriers to the OAP program, testing the criteria
and shaping the information provided to authorities.

The contest with state authorities to improve the potential pensioners'
financial position and economic security empowered the individual elderly,
often in collusion with their families. Individual cases reveal considerable
manipulation of information by the elderly and their family so as to strength-
en eligibility. At times community members colluded in this behaviour,
often offering supportive false information. The somewhat cavalier attitude to accuracy, particularly among the applicants themselves, suggests
that their dishonest behaviour was justified, at least in their own minds, by
a 'higher truth' – the culture of entitlement.

One way of manipulating the OAP program and its officials was to appeal to age-based stereotypes. Some of the elderly were quite astute in playing on the stereotype of the aged as a basis for engendering sympathy. This
was true not only of the dependent elderly but of the wealthy and powerful as well. When Prime Minister R.B. Bennett spoke to the Canadian people over the radio prior to the 1935 general election, he described himself in
stereotypic terms: 'I am 65 years of age. When one reaches my time of life,
ambitions dim, the love of power dies, the plaudits of the multitude can
scarce be heard, its condemnation is just as meaningless.'[33] But for the dependent elderly this was a 'game' with often vital stakes. One widow lived
alone in her unencumbered home in Shetland, Ontario; she had transferred
her 50-acre farm to her only son, and had less than $400 in the bank. She
was turned down for a pension in 1934, so when she reapplied in 1937 she
was careful to play on the elements of the stereotype that applied to her.
According to the town clerk, 'she informs me that she very much regrets to

have to appeal for help, and never thought it would come to asking for help, and is one that will be very grateful for assistance.' She also emphasized her ill-health (weak heart and high blood pressure) and her medical bills, and this time she was awarded a pension of $10 a month.[34]

This sort of playing to a stereotype was not new, of course. Nor was it unique to the elderly. It was a typical device of the disadvantaged in appealing for some benefit, and in confirming their status as suppliants such an approach was particularly unthreatening. Many of the applications for admission to the state old age homes had for many years carefully emphasized the applicant's frailty and decrepitude. A 1924 letter seeking admission to the McCormick Home in London, for example, stated that the application was based on the fact that 'i am 73 years old and nearly Blind and lame with Reuhmatic and unables to do for myself.' The inspector who looked into the old man's situation found him working as a gardener (the half-acre garden was in 'splendid shape') in return for his board; the old man was in fact simply 'sick of work' and did not intend to help in the McCormick garden if admitted, saying he no longer wanted to do anything for anybody. But his own description of himself painted a quite different picture.[35] Like many other elderly, his portrayal of ill-health and dependence was designed to gain maximum benefits for himself within the prevailing stereotype.

[Given the centrality of the means test to the OAP program, manipulation of financial information was another common tactic among OAP applicants.] Failure to disclose income or assets was a fairly common phenomenon and could crucially affect eligibility or payment level. The records disclose many instances where applicants 'forgot' to list all their bank accounts or to mention a bond or a small piece of property they owned. Others applied for an OAP without mentioning that they already received state support through the veterans' pension program or that their spouse was a pensioner. For example, a married woman applied for the OAP in 1937 when she was seventy-four, stating that she had no children; she was awarded a full pension. In 1943 an investigator discovered that she in fact had a son and that her husband had been working for almost a year, earning more than a thousand dollars. Such fraud was allegedly so frequent that popular periodicals presented generic examples.[36]

The residency requirements were quite precise, but it was difficult to prove that an applicant had not lived within the jurisdiction during the period stipulated. Most of the evidence for residential ineligibility came from applicants themselves. It was not difficult for those more knowledgeable about the OAP process (or with a more flexible definition of the truth) simply to avoid giving residential information that would have been damaging. In the absence of systematic state records regarding residency, affidavits from neighbours or local authorities were generally acceptable.

When one man applied in Saskatchewan in 1928, he failed to mention that he had resided in the United States for some time; appearing to be eligible when in fact he did not meet the residency requirements, he was awarded an OAP. Six years later his wife applied for her pension, but this time the residency in the United States was disclosed and she was ruled ineligible. Provincial authorities caught the discrepancy in her husband's information six years earlier, suggesting a reasonably thorough bureaucratic sifting of the evidence. Nevertheless, the Saskatchewan officials expressed their willingness to continue paying his pension provided the husband did not discuss their error in awarding a pension initially. A few months later his wife asked for the return of her original application; she then reapplied on a new form, this time not mentioning her American residency, and was awarded a pension. In the meantime her lawyer had written for a copy of the OAP regulations, and he swore to the accuracy of her new claim that she had been absent from Canada only for a permissable period. When the federal auditors arrived in December 1935, however, both pensions were cancelled.[37] In other cases, individual elderly suppressed evidence of naturalization in the United States or falsely claimed naturalization in Canada.[38]

In contrast to residency, age was at the heart of the OAP program and was something about which the state had become strikingly precise and bureaucratic. For many applicants, age was one of the most difficult things to prove. Registration of births and recording of ages had been haphazard or non-existent in the past. Even where present, government or private records were often inaccurate, sometimes because people's sense of age was imprecise and sometimes because they had recorded their age incorrectly (deliberately or otherwise) on earlier occasions. Little did they know in responding to the 1871 or 1881 census that, sixty or seventy years later, those records would be checked to help certify an individual's age. Officials thought carefully about which informal records would be less likely to have been subject to misrepresentation. Inherent in all such discussions was the understanding that individuals tended to misrepresent evidence in their own self-interest.[39] Birth certificates, infant baptismal certificates, and census records from the individual's early years were all considered particularly accurate – more recent 'evidence' was felt to be vulnerable to distortion.

State officials were particularly vigilant for pension applications by those who were not yet seventy years old. For example, in the 1938 audit of New Brunswick cases, federal officials found eighteen cases in which pensions had been granted on the basis of inaccurate information about age. Most of these cases simply involved inadequate evidence, but at least five entailed deliberate misrepresentation. In three instances, applicants had used the birth certificates of an older sibling; in one case, the applicant and an adult child had sworn false affidavits, as had an applicant and a sibling in another case.[40] The OAP program demanded a precision about the dating of birth that was anachronistic, and some applicants saw the opportunity to take advantage of the resulting confusion.

Inaccurate information about age did not always involve deliberate misrepresentation or fraud. It was often the result of applying a later era's newfound precision about time and age to an earlier period's relative vagueness on the same matters.[41] By the late nineteenth century, records were more readily being kept, but the people giving information for the records did not necessarily share the developing sense of precision or accuracy about time. The case of a Saskatchewan farmer offers a good example. In 1905 he took out land patents, giving his age as forty-two; three years later, he still recorded his age as forty-two. In 1910, when taking out naturalization papers, he stated that he was forty-four years old. Finally, in his OAP application in 1938, the farmer alleged that he had been born on 18 November 1861 and was now seventy-six. As one official commented, 'it is obvious the applicant does not know his age.'[42] While it is not so obvious that there was intentional fraud here, in many cases the new accuracy of the state regarding time was not shared by individuals; their vagueness about age allowed them to agree that they were whatever age seemed appropriate to the circumstances.

Not all the applicants' misrepresentation of information was fraudulent in intent. Some elderly had, to their own minds, good reason for not making full disclosure of information to the state. A sense of privacy provoked resentment of repeated state probings into their personal financial dealings and a few ultimately refused to cooperate further.[43] One old woman in northern Ontario wrote in 1929 retracting her OAP application:

i must of been Craby and out of my head to answer so many questions i did not realize at the time what i had done or i would of never done such a thing, my boys would be mad if i done such a thing as to answer so many questions ... i do not want to have anything to do with the old age pension all i want is them papers for them papers are not lawful papers for i did not know what i was answering them questions for that morning i have felt out of my head ever since i done that foolish thing [44]

Different attitudes regarding privacy and a strong sense of the boundary between private and public were but further manifestations of the clash of cultures that the new state program made apparent.

This clash of cultures was inherent in the modernizing world. Rural collided with urban, industrial with pre-industrial, foreign with domestic. For some, especially immigrants, this also involved an inherent distrust of the state. A Russian immigrant in Manitoba, for example, appeared to be almost eighty years old, but was unable to produce any proof of age. Immigration records failed to record her entry into Canada. Eventually inspectors persuaded her to reveal her story. Imprisoned with her family at the age of seventeen, she had been exiled to Siberia; from there she escaped, leaving Russia with a man whom she eventually married. The woman had entered Canada under an assumed name (by 'the secret way') and ended up in Manitoba. Ultimately she was persuaded to produce her Russian passport from a secure hiding place, though she still feared being sent back to Siberia.[45] For such people, the OAP application and inspection process must have been particularly difficult. This example points to the added difficulties experienced by immigrants generally. Distance from their place of birth, and frequent language problems at the time of immigration and perhaps naturalization made it difficult to produce records that accurately reflected the applicants' age.[46] In such instances the intent behind the fraud had an entirely different meaning.

The OAP program was a frustrating one in many ways, particularly for the elderly. It enforced a particular, even narrow view of the state and society and, at least formally, demonstrated no flexibility. The OAP program represented a view of the individual and society that was biased in favour of an urban, industrial, masculine world.[47] Designed to assist the dependent elderly in need of support, the program nevertheless had a number of regulations that inhibited the achievement of this major end. Its flaws almost invited challenge from those disadvantaged by the program. Given their relative political impotence in formal terms, it is not surprising that the individuals involved challenged the OAP program in informal ways designed to best achieve success for them personally.

State policy, for example, encouraged the dependent elderly to call on family resources for as much assistance as possible, promising a pension where family resources fell short of the minimum level of support. Many adult children and relatives had migrated to the United States over the years. If the elderly turned to these family members for support and left Canada to do so, their eligibility for a pension was seriously undermined, because of the residency requirement.[48] Surely the state programs did not intend to discourage such rational and appropriate family support, and yet that is just what the OAP did. Little wonder that some elderly sought to suppress information in order to qualify for a pension.

Much of the inaccurate or missing information was intentional. Some of the information demanded could not be provided with the accuracy demanded by bureaucratic processes. In other instances the OAP simply offered too valuable an opportunity to make much needed financial gains for the elderly to be worried about full disclosure. Individual elderly felt justified in 'bending the rules' because of their own culture of family and of entitlement.

What is more, as many of the cases demonstrate, family members were equally capable of fraudulent behaviour. Many families adopted their own parameters for acceptable deviation from the state program, seeking merely to facilitate access to the pension. At what point their facilitation crossed over into the area of fraud is impossible to determine so many years later. The head of the Ontario board expressed concern to bank officials that pension cheques were being accepted with dubious endorsations: the signature changed from month to month; a signature in one month was followed by a mark in the next. While some of this could be explained by relatives assisting enfeebled pensioners, the board had 'positive evidence that there are members of families who have no hesitancy in forging the names of the pensioner and receiving the cash.'[49] Family receipt of the cash did not mean that it was not being used for the general support of the pensioner, but certainly the program was quite vulnerable to the sort of distortion feared by the Ontario board and others.

Community members too cooperated in some forms of misrepresentation. A widower, residing with his daughter in Nanaimo, British Columbia, was granted an OAP in 1929. His annual declaration forms failed to record his permanent residence in England since mid-1933; his daughter signed the annual declarations, endorsed his pension cheques, and allegedly sent the funds overseas to her father. At various times local justices of the peace, notaries, and a postmaster attested to the accuracy of her annual declarations. The daughter claimed not to be aware that she had done anything wrong, but the fact that her husband was on relief underlined her otherwise straitened circumstances and made provincial officials sceptical of her innocence.[50] In 1937 a woman from Doe River, British Columbia, was having difficulty meeting the residence requirements for a pension. A doctor in Grand Forks was able to affirm that she had been in British Columbia from 1905 to 1924; when it was pointed out to him that it was still unclear where the woman had resided between 1924 and 1926, the doctor quickly amended his declaration to cover the missing years.[51] Authoritative members of the local community thus colluded in individual cases defrauding the state.

Such collusion and connivance pointed to a broad community acceptance of the expanding role of the state in supporting the local dependent and needy. Beyond the elderly themselves there was growing support for the culture of entitlement. Both family members and the elderly at times were quite willing to take advantage of these attitudes and to commit fraud in order to enhance the resources under the elderly's or the family's immediate control. Community and family members gained at least indirectly by deflecting potential demands for support from their own resources onto the OAP program.

This depiction of OAP applicants is not meant to imply that the elderly behave in any remarkably different manner from other groups. Authoritative processes controlled access to many desirable ends. The officials in charge of those processes enforced the prescribed criteria by which individuals gained access to the desired ends. The individuals shared the respect for authoritative process, but did not necessarily accept the prescribed criteria. In the case of marriage, for example, individuals were often willing to attest falsely regarding age, residency, parental consent, or marital status in order to meet the authoritative criteria and to become married in a manner that best met their needs.[52] Individual agency contested with officials for control of authoritative processes, with all parties usually winning some form of 'victory.' Many elderly were sustained by a culture of entitlement that justified in their own minds the presentation of information in such a shape and form as to qualify them for a pension.

There is considerable anecdotal evidence to support this growing sense among the elderly that the OAP was theirs as a right. In 1946 a British Columbia politician jokingly recounted the views of his ninety-three-year-old mother, for whom he had been providing complete support for the past twenty-three years. Every time the politician went to Ottawa his mother commented: 'Now, I want you to take up with Mr. Mackenzie King the fact that he owes me a lot of money; that I have not been getting old age pension for twenty-three years.'[53] The underlying message here, though her son seemed to have missed it, was that she had been doing the state a favour by not claiming the pension that was hers for the asking.

This sense of pension rights was manifested in a public 'tempest in a teapot' at the end of the period. By this time free hospitalization was available to pensioners in several provinces; there was considerable concern among bureaucrats and in the press that pensioners would be able to reap inordinate benefits from the state. While receiving free room and board from the hospital plan, the dependent elderly continued to receive their pensions. The plans were seen to be providing overlapping benefits to the great advantage of some elderly. The *Vancouver Sun* carried an editorial cartoon depicting an elderly man leaving hospital in a chauffered limousine, with a nurse explaining: 'They say he saved up a fortune in pension cheques during the weeks he was in here.'[54] This was the justification offered by the provincial governments of both Saskatchewan and British Columbia in suspending the pensions (except for a small amount of spending money) of anyone hospitalized. But this interference set off a powerful public response among the elderly. It was not merely state support that the elderly claimed. Pensions were theirs and could not be taken away; other support should be forthcoming from the state as needed, but the Old Age Pension had by now been placed in a special category.

The pensioners' campaign was a particularly public one. Although lobbying on the issue did occur, the debate they led was conducted largely in the public press. One pensioner, in a letter to the editor, challenged the head of the British Columbia Hospital Insurance Commission to try to live on the $5 pension payment available to the pensioner after she had left the hospital. More directly she described the pension as hers: 'If the cheque is made on my name nobody is going to get it without a fight. Old age pensioners take notice.' Other writers described the state actions as 'despicable' and 'heartless.'[55]

Overall participation in the OAP rose across the period, reflecting the culture of entitlement. In 1940 a senior federal civil servant pointed out that Canadian participation rates were steadily rising and were higher than for anywhere in the United States, being similar to those in Australia: 'Apparently people now regard old age pensions as a right and are not at all backward about applying for such assistance. Each year the per centage of pensioners to population 70 years of age and over is higher than in the previous year in all nine provinces.'[56] OAP numbers declined during the war. But with the return of peacetime labour norms and the increasingly strong tendency for employers to adopt mandatory retirement policies, the OAP rolls soon began to fill out again, especially after 1947 (see figure 4.1, on page 115).

For the vast majority of the elderly, once they had become pensioners the security of their OAP cheque was uppermost in their minds. The OAP was after all a stable source of income and ought not to be casually jeopardized. Some elderly resented the dependency created by such support, and the discretionary power of bureaucrats irked and intimidated others. Others sought reassurance or permission from local officials, who articulated different and varied values and interests and who gave contradictory advice. During the Second World War, the Department of National War Services was interested in encouraging all able-bodied persons to contribute their labour to the national cause, but local OAP officials held that such paid labour would affect OAP eligibility and payment levels. A janitor in Calgary, for example, left his job because he feared the loss of his OAP. Another elderly man about to take work in 1943 went to officials with his fears that once the work stopped there would be a lengthy delay in re-examining his OAP eligibility, and that he risked being rejected on reapplication.[57] Clearly there was a fine balancing act to be carried out by the elderly among the competing sources of potential income and support.

Many elderly were willing to take on occasional or part-time work, but only if it did not risk loss of the OAP. Some simply failed to report their work and income. Some employers were willing to take advantage of the situation, offering work at reduced wages combined with the promise of secrecy. Farmers were alleged to be particularly prone to such practices, partly out of sympathy for the pensioner and partly because the lower wage structure of a 'hidden economy' was beneficial to themselves as well.[58] Such employers used the state program to subsidize their own businesses, and the processes further entrenched the marginalization of elderly workers, who increasingly found themselves among the reserve labour force. Other pensioners took on at least part-time employment regardless of the impact on their pension, and their payment levels were adjusted accordingly.

But not all wanted to work. Increasingly the elderly accepted the authoritative new norms regarding retirement. By the age of seventy, elderly persons, if they could afford it, had left paid employment and expected to live off a combination of their savings and assets and their private and public pension payments. One provincial board reported a common comment among OAP applicants:

'Oh no, I won't be working any more. You know I'm 70.' This idea is so often repeated in one form or another that one cannot fail to see the reflection of a society which, more and more, tend[s] to determine ability to participate in normal activities by a date on the calendar rather than individual capacity.[59]

While provincial officials were not yet fully comfortable with the idea that employable persons were leaving work and drawing public assistance simply because of their calendar age, large numbers of the elderly had certainly come to accept this standard.

Pensioners, it must be remembered, represented the physically and economically most vulnerable among the elderly – those with few or no assets and without much ability to secure significant income. For them the centrality and importance of the OAP program is difficult to exaggerate. For many the regular pension cheque simply sustained them through their final years. But for others the OAP gave them new power to control the shape and character of those final years. Some pensioners gained new-found economic leverage with their families. A small minority of institutionalized pensioners were able to move out to independent accommodation. Other pensioners took even greater advantage of their increased agency.

Some elderly took advantage of retirement and the potential mobility provided by a national OAP program to move to more desirable locations. Particularly from the Prairie provinces, but also from Ontario, many moved west to the warmer climate of British Columbia. Not only was the physical climate attractive, so too was the level of state support for the elderly. British Columbia had been the first province to adopt the OAP program and, in the 1940s, had led the way in providing supplementary payments to raise pensioners' incomes. The province introduced free hospital and medical care for pensioners in the second half of the 1940s. No wonder that many elderly were 'voting with their feet' and making British Columbia their new home.

This relocation to the west coast was underway before the OAP program commenced. The city of Victoria on Vancouver Island, so well known in recent years as a retirement destination, gained a disproportionate number of elderly during the first three decades of the twentieth century.[60] But the OAP gave pensioners a noticeably increased level of mobility. Once they had gained steady access to a regular pension income, pensioners could move anywhere within the country (whether or not the province participated yet in the OAP program) without jeopardizing their pension. Only residence outside Canada threatened their pension. The potential mobility allowed pensioners to move to a location that best suited their needs, taking into account support networks, climate, and other criteria. The movement of elderly to Victoria, for example, picked up speed after the OAP became available, and Vancouver became another centre experiencing a disproportionately high rate of growth in its elderly population. In 1946 British Columbia reported that an apparent peak of 296 pensioners had moved east to live in other provinces, but 2131 had migrated from other provinces to the west coast. In succeeding years the net influx continued, but was much lower.[61] While the primary costs of each pension continued to be paid by the original host provinces, British Columbia still had to carry the secondary costs of this growing number of pensioners.[62]

The OAP program could not have made any pensioner well-to-do. It did, however, give them fundamentally important benefits that many others in society sought for themselves. The pension was a secure source of income that arrived steadily each month. It gave them increased – if not new-found – independence: a new freedom to relocate, for example, or the ability to contribute substantially to family or household income. Social stigma there was, especially with the continuing means test, but receipt of the OAP was not quite so simple a matter as the acceptance of stigma in exchange for physical survival. For many elderly the OAP was a genuine source of strength, and its acquisition was certainly worth bending a few minor rules. More than that, the process of collusion and fraud itself was empowering; the all-intrusive state was not quite so omnipotent as some of its bureaucrats felt or as its popular image portrayed.

State Responses

The regulatory inconsistencies within the OAP program and among the various bureaucratic levels confused many elderly and others and invited challenges to the program. Pressure for labour, for example, was so severe in some sectors and regions during the war that provincial officials appealed to Ottawa to allow pensioners' additional income to be exempt in eligibility calculations. Ontario and British Columbia officials were particularly desperate for farm and industrial labourers in 1943 and sought such an exemption. The fact that American authorities had recently adopted such a policy was used as an additional justification. Federal officials rightly pointed out that any such exemptions breached an enormous hole in the fundamental philosophy of the OAP. Any suggestions that the OAP be paid regardless of income levels attacked the welfare character of the existing scheme and pointed to the idea of universality. Such debates implicitly encouraged challenges to the program's regulatory parameters.

Authorities showed a great deal of concern regarding the tendency of some elderly to misrepresent their circumstances in order to qualify for the OAP. When the chair of the Ontario board addressed a convention in Hamilton in 1930, he claimed that there were hundreds of cases in which applicants misrepresented their assets in order to qualify for a pension; a local newspaper headlined 'Many Fakes.' In 1932 a federal official commented that in the first few years of the OAP program there had been 'numerous' cases in which 'deceit was practiced, children repudiated all filial duty towards parents, property was transferred, bank accounts dissipated, and able-bodied men refused work.'[63] Though he felt that these behaviours were being stopped by tighter administration, he was overly sanguine. The federal finance department was particularly anxious to stop such cheating when it assumed responsibility for the OAP in 1935. When the minister proposed a penalty of $50 or three months in jail for false declarations, six provincial authorities agreed, but Nova Scotia, British Columbia, and Quebec did not. The finance department was anxious to raise the quality of investigations made of OAP applications, urging all authorities to employ their own investigators. This was unrealistic, because trained personnel were often not available in some areas and because the costs of such a system would be too heavy for some provinces.

A much cheaper system was to rely on the honesty of the elderly, allowing them to swear affidavits. All OAP application forms required applicants to make a declaration as to the veracity of the information provided, and several provinces asked neighbours to make declarations about the elderly involved. Beginning in the late 1930s all provincial authorities were required to carry out an annual examination of every pensioner's continuing circumstances, and a number of provinces simply asked the pensioners to fill out a form and swear to its accuracy. But there was general agreement that such declarations were not much use, except perhaps as a reminder that one ought to be truthful. Provincial officials were quite open about the dubious character of affidavits and declarations. The senior Nova Scotia official, for example, commented:

In rural areas where we require statutory declarations, I have personally experienced that these declarations are very little good unless we examine [the applicants]. They do not know what they are signing. These declarations are almost worthless unless the inspector examines the witness ... We have been taught to be canny about accepting declarations. We want our inspectors to examine very carefully. A declaration made by a neighbour would not be worth a 'hoot.'[64]

Yet the reliance on such forms persisted throughout the period, giving the elderly ample opportunity to make the program operate to their best advantage. Federal officials were disturbed by this manipulation wherever it occurred, but particularly in Manitoba, where officials consistently refused to undertake any direct inspection of applicants or pensioners outside the city of Winnipeg.[65]

Indeed, the 'forgetfulness' or plain dishonesty and fraudulent behaviour of many individuals encouraged state officials to distrust the accuracy of individual attestations and to respond to cases of fraud with considerable vigour. In Ontario, for example, Margaret Crown was receiving a full pension when she was found to own a $1000 bond and to have cash assets that had not been reported; her pension was cancelled in 1936. Helen Brady's pension of $20 monthly was cancelled in Windsor, Ontario, when she was discovered to be receiving a veteran's pension of $30 a month. Gordon Lynch of Toronto failed to report his spouse's pension, and subsequently had his pension reduced from $20 a month to $10.42. Minnie Pickford of Oxford County did not disclose $2325 in bank deposits; she lost her $12.50 a month pension, which she had been receiving for three years, and was required to pay back all the pension payments made to her, a total of $450. Muriel Brown of Alberta deliberately suppressed information about assets she owned so as to qualify for a full pension; when this was discovered, her pension was cancelled and the authorities recovered $1311.61 in improper payments.[66]

The variety of techniques employed by the elderly to facilitate the award of as large a pension cheque as possible posed multiple problems for state authorities intent on frustrating any 'distortion' of the OAP program. A New Brunswick woman qualified for a pension in 1937, when she reported sharing $1100 with her husband in a bank account. Within two years there were no reported bank funds, and for two further years she reported no cash assets. When provincial inspectors finally carried out a thorough examination, they discovered that she had had at least $3500 in the bank when she first applied; what was more, her husband had left her $1289 when he died in 1939. But this situation was not simply a matter of failure to disclose assets or of mis-spending declared assets. The husband's will had deliberately left his wife a relatively small portion of his estate, compared with that left his son, presumably to avoid any reduction in her pension cheque. Not only were officials intent on recouping the overpayments on her recalculated payment level back to 1937, but legal questions were raised as to whether her husband could appropriately leave a larger sum to his son than to his wife in these circumstances.[67] This new form of 'patriarchy from the grave' showed the potential for families to employ state support programs to enhance overall assets.

The state's response to individual cases of fraud was remarkably inconsistent. Usually authorities sought to recover improper amounts of payments only where there was particularly flagrant fraud or when pushed strongly by federal officials. Suppression of minor assets or income simply resulted in alteration of the payment level. But where the suppression involved significant amounts, federal officials could be decidedly aggressive. Some pensions were simply suspended until the overpayments had been recouped, but others were cancelled outright.[68]

The organized elderly themselves frankly admitted the tendency towards fraud by prospective and existing pensioners. But for the organized elderly the fault lay not with the pensioners, but with the OAP system. One OAPO official complained in 1950: 'The indignity that the means test now implies is very unnecessary. It makes people untruthful and should be abolished.'[69] The culture of the state and of the elderly had outstripped the OAP existing program, and the behaviour of the elderly themselves was forcing a reconsideration of the program's basic philosophy.

Yet the determination with which some elderly pursued a pension and the rising OAP participation rates ought not to be allowed to obscure a continuing sense of stigma attached to the OAP. Not only was receipt of a pension a clear sign of negative age status, but it was also associated with charity and welfare. While attitudes were certainly changing, there remained authoritative echoes of earlier orthodoxies. When the OAP first began in British Columbia in 1927, cheques were mailed out in envelopes with the message: 'If not called for within ten days, return to Old Age Pensions Department.' The board also used postcards for acknowledgments. Both tended to disclose that the recipient was an Old Age Pensioner, and the board reported that it was 'immediately swamped with protests' and strong complaints.[70] This attitude helps to explain the hesitancy of some elderly or family members, particularly those with aspirations to a higher social status, to apply for a pension. A seventy-five-year-old Galt, Ontario, widow was tempted to apply for a pension but feared the reaction of her machinist son with whom she lived: 'altho my son dont give me anything i'm afraid he would think it [a] disgrace for me to get th pension.'[71] Another woman also feared her sons: 'my boys would be mad enough to do anything to me if they knew i had filled out them [OAP application] papers.'[72] The culture of entitlement was not yet strong enough to remove the stigma attached to state aid.

Some local officials tried to take advantage of this sense of stigma to induce families to support their older members. With the effect of the 1930s Depression and of changing attitudes towards the state, this stigma was probably declining for many elderly. The British Columbia minister responsible for the OAP commented in 1941: 'I think, too, that the attitude of the Old Age Pensioners has considerably changed of late for the majority of them belong to the Old Age Pensions Associations, and there is ample evidence that they are not at all backward at the present time about indicating that they are in receipt of pensions.'[73]

Some elderly could be philosophical when officials detected undeclared income and the government chose to seek recovery. One old man in British Columbia had been earning extra cash through odd-jobbing in country woodlots and through occasional carpentry; when informed that his OAP payments would be suspended, his humourous 'confession' appealed to the traditions of the Christian church:

Dear Sirs:
The writer has received your letter of the 23rd. After reading the letter I find I have been doing many things I should not have done and left undone many things I should have done and for that reason you are holding back a cheque that the Government is obligated to pay on to me each month (until death do us part). I must admit that there is nothing I can do about it as I know you have the joker up your sleeves or in your sack.[74]

But that humour did not entirely cover the old man's claim to the OAP as a matter of right, or his frustration at his relative powerlessness.

Several factors prompted some individuals to respond in a more concerted manner: frustration with their relative powerlessness, the frequency and public character of some individual challenges to the OAP regulations, the emerging culture of entitlement, and the state's inconsistency, as well as its persistence, in enforcing its powers. Arising from the challenges exerted by individual elderly and their families were the challenges issued by the first organizations of the elderly that fought publicly, throughout the 1930s and 1940s, for an end to the program's harsh regulations, the adoption of universality, and the expansion of a universal program to include younger elderly.

6

Organizing Politically:
The First Grey Lobby

To many elderly, the OAP provided a new focus and a new identity. The needy elderly were now pensioners, with an apparently secure, if small, source of income. This income, and the sense of self-worth and independence that came with it, were vital new characteristics of the elderly as a group. Although many elderly still viewed any form of state support as equivalent to the dole – and, thus, as carrying a considerable stigma – many elderly poor were able to distinguish the OAP from relief or welfare payments and to consider it to be theirs as a right. As shown in chapter 5, this attitude justified in many pensioners' minds the 'shaping' of personal information and the 'bending' of rules so as to qualify for as large a pension as possible. A much smaller contingent of this group used the culture of entitlement and the OAP as active organizing issues. Not only was the OAP rightfully theirs, but the state and its minions had no business placing various obstacles in the way of those elderly poor who desperately needed a regular pension at an adequate level. This was something worth fighting for, and there were some elderly who were prepared to do so. More than that, they would fight not just for a better pension, but for recognition of the elderly as senior citizens, legitimizing their rising status and their claims to the citizen's wage.

With the help of a small number of supporters from the general adult population, a few needy elderly in the early 1930s began to organize themselves and other elderly into politically active associations. What was significant about these organizations was that they gave voice and substance to a new sense of identity among the elderly in general: the elderly were coming to think of themselves as a distinct social group. In the words of gerontologist A.M. Rose, the elderly began the process of changing 'from a category into a group.' A minority among the needy elderly began to

demonstrate an awareness not merely of being old, but also of being subject to social and economic deprivation *because* they were old, and they reacted to these deprivations with resentment and with a sense that positive
change was possible.[1] The various political achievements of the organizations founded by the elderly were secondary to this fundamental manifestation of social meaning.

The individual awareness of their new position manifested by individual
pensioners paralleled a more limited group awareness. Relatively small
numbers of elderly formed their own organizations to serve the interests of
the needy elderly as perceived by those people themselves. These organizations must be distinguished from the various recreational groups, such as
Toronto's Second Mile Club, Victoria's Sixty-Up Club, or Edmonton's
Friendship Clubs, established in the late 1930s and throughout the 1940s
by social workers, reformers, and other non-elderly.[2] Organizations to deal
with the elderly poor had long existed, though those focusing on recreational and social needs were relatively recent. What was distinctive about
the organizations discussed here is that they were founded and operated by
the elderly, and that they focused on the needs of the elderly as determined
by elderly themselves.

The new seniors' organizations established in the 1930s and 1940s were
advocacy groups, seeking to put pressure on politicians and state officials
to alter government policies, or at least the application of those policies.
They challenged the OAP payment levels, the means test, the parents'
maintenance legislation, the minimum pensionable age, and other particular elements of the OAP program. The focus provided by the inadequacies
of the OAP program and the unfairness of the OAP regulations combined
with shared age to facilitate viable political organizations among the elderly. These organizations were fundamentally weakened by an acute and
constant shortage of funds, which inhibited interprovincial and national
activity; but the groups enjoyed the leadership of a number of remarkably
committed and able individuals who achieved a good deal, given the problems under which they laboured.[3] What is more, these groups rarely de-
scended into self-aggrandizement, a characteristic of some later elderly
associations,[4] but instead consistently sought better conditions for the elderly as a group. The old age political organizations played a central role in
making the elderly politically visible, thus building on a process already
begun with the OAP program.

In Canada the political organization of the elderly shared a number of
the characteristics of developments elsewhere,[5] shaped by the special character of the Canadian environment. Beginning in British Columbia in the

early 1930s, the Old Age Pensioners Organization (OAPO) spread at a modest rate throughout that province before moving eastward. In Canada, political activism was facilitated by the central role played by provincial governments in the OAP; a national organization was unnecessary for effective political action. At the same time, however, the provincial focus of much of the political activity inhibited the development of the OAPO nationally. Indeed, the organization was largely unable to spread east of the Great Lakes throughout the 1930s and 1940s. Nevertheless, the OAPO can be credited with reasonably effective political actions that played, particularly at the provincial level and especially in British Columbia, a significant role in bringing about changes in government policy, most notably but not exclusively related to the OAP. Led by seniors often with previous experience in trade unions or farmers' organizations, the western elderly acquired a public voice and a new-found sense of self-worth and political significance.

The character and tactics of the Canadian organizations of the elderly stand in some contrast to their American counterparts.[6] The Canadian groups did not rely on the personal or charismatic leadership of one or two individuals, but rather had a broad leadership base. In direct terms, both the Canadian and the American groups were peripheral actors on the national political scene, but the Canadian groups, particularly the Old Age Pensioners of British Columbia (OAPOBC), became a significant element in the political history of the OAP on the west coast; the Canadian OAP was structured in such a way as to facilitate a regional focus to the organized elderly. The Canadian movement showed itself to be pragmatic, to be able to adapt to changing political circumstances, and to be effective in establishing connections with government officials and politicians at all levels. In short, if 'political activity' is defined more broadly than the studies of the organized elderly in the 1930s and 1940s have previously done – so as to include not just legislation but also the ways in which the legislation was applied and the attitudes and behaviour of other political actors such as the courts, the press, and other organizations – the western elderly were successful at influencing the political process. The organized elderly demonstrated weakness, however, in their attempt to expand nationally, in providing for leadership succession, and in their ability to survive the OAP reforms of 1947–51. Like their American counterparts, the Canadian organizations entered a state of 'near dormancy' for several years after mid-century.[7]

The OAPO in British Columbia

Pushed by the arbitrary decisions of the provincial OAP board regarding income determination and parents' maintenance, a small number of Vancouver pensioners organized the OAPOBC in 1932. The OAP was a public phenomenon that large numbers of needy elderly had, or hoped to have, in common. The other major developments associated with the elderly at this time – mandatory retirement and the founding of residential institutions – were perceived as largely negative developments, not the sort of thing that offered the group a positive self-image. The Old Age Pension was different; it was, for many, positive, and its central place within the first seniors' organizations was a reflection of its special role. The OAP was also a public program that an organized interest group could reasonably aspire to shape. The OAPOBC aimed

to protect the rights and interests of Old Age Pensioners or prospective pensioners over 60; to prevent discrimination, avoid technicalities and undue delay in the consideration of applications for pensions; to endeavor to secure and maintain fair and just legislation and executive action at all times in the best interests of Old Age Pensioners; to preserve their status as citizens, entitled to pensions, as [a] social and legal right, and not by way of relief or charity; and enable them to maintain their dignity and self-respect as pioneer citizens of Canada.[8]

The language of rights was present from the start, and was a manifestation of these elderly's sense of injury and injustice.

One of the OAPOBC's first steps was to petition successfully for provincial incorporation, under the title Old Age Pensioners' Organization – a sign of their search for status and of their strength of purpose. In its applied character, the OAP program provided many, even daily, examples of the discrimination suffered by the aged poor, yet that same OAP was the vehicle by which the needy elderly sought to redress their grievances and to achieve a new status.

The political agenda of the non-partisan OAPO was made prominent from the beginning. During the 1930s it quickly elaborated its political agenda, exclusively focusing on the OAP. First, the OAP regulations should be applied in such a way as to include the largest number of elderly possible under its benefits. Here the OAPOBC found itself to be in direct conflict with the provincial bureaucracy, whose philosophy and responsibility were to apply the OAP restrictions rigorously so as to limit the program costs and to direct the pension benefits only to those qualified elderly truly in 'need.' Thus the OAPOBC attacked such restrictions as the most-recent-twenty-year residency qualification, inflexible income determination, and the application of the parents' maintenance legislation. On these issues the OAPOBC sought to redefine the existing OAP regulations so that the program could operate more effectively for the elderly.

Second, the OAPOBC fought to improve the OAP Act itself. The age of eligibility should be reduced to sixty-five, so as to align better the timing of the pension and of involuntary retirement. The value of the pension should be raised so that the OAP itself met the subsistence needs of the elderly, rather than the earlier intention to meet merely a portion of those needs. In the 1930s the convenient measure for the desirable pension level was one dollar a day;[9] in the 1940s the OAPO pushed for a higher level – $40 or $50 a month. Finally, the OAPOBC argued for a national OAP. British Columbia was home to a disproportionate number of elderly from other provinces, and local residents frequently witnessed the even greater problems suffered by needy elderly from elsewhere in Canada. Since the provincial costs for each pensioner were allocated proportionally to the pensioner's years of residence in each province over the twenty-year residency period, those elderly who had spent all or some portion of those years in a province as yet without the OAP found themselves with a much reduced payment level or without a pension altogether. The basis of OAP qualification, argued the OAPOBC, should be Canadian citizenship and residence in Canada. If the OAPOBC's early interests were narrowly focused on the OAP, its view of pension problems was not narrow. The OAPOBC fought from the beginning for non-pensioners and would-be pensioners, as well as for existing pensioners, and its agenda always included a national perspective.

At the same time, the elderly began to form other organizations as well, some with political aims, and more with social or recreational goals.[10] The latter groups in particular brought together not just many of the needy elderly, but also older Canadians who did not qualify for the OAP but who experienced the increasingly pervasive construction of old age. For many elderly the shared characteristic of being 'old' had come to reduce the relative importance of class, gender, and ethnic or racial differences in their daily lives. What all these organizations had in common was that they were founded and operated by the elderly themselves. The elderly were developing a sense of group consciousness sufficient to sustain their own institutions. While that group consciousness was not monolithic, it was shared by a number of elderly with diverse interests and needs, with varied class backgrounds, and concentrated in urban communities.

Groups such as the OAPO tended to be dominated by a small number of individuals with a common set of skills and outlook, but never by the one or two dominant personalities characteristic of similar organizations in

the United States. In their earlier years the Canadian leaders tended to
have been active in political (though not necessarily partisan) organizations
such as farmers groups or labour unions.[11] These individuals shared a particular outlook, having the requisite skills and knowledge to operate in
such groups, and believing that by working in these organizations meaningful change could be effected. This essentially positive outlook, along
with the personal self-esteem gained through their work, sustained the leaders through the long periods when no headway seemed to be made; it imbued the organization with the sort of optimism that was essential for
sustaining the movement and for its eventual success.

The work could be time consuming, but the personal rewards were considerable. J.J. Whiting of Vancouver confided that 'somehow I get quite a
kick out of it [the OAPO work]'; Agnes Nurse of Saskatoon recalled, 'I
certainly spent many many hours working for the Pensioners myself – but
I don't know, I always enjoyed it.' When Ethel Baker of Calgary saw her
letter to Violet McNaughton reprinted in the 1941 *Western Producer*, she
wrote: 'I was so surprised to see my own letter in your Paper, I just gasped,
but appreciate it that you thought it good enough for print ... I am very
proud of my first letter in print for I have never asked for any publicity
personally just a cog in a machine behind the scenes, & so I am very grateful that you thought it good enough. Would you send me 2 or 3 copies of
that date as I want to send it to three homes in England, just to let my Sisters & Brother know that I am not altogether wasting my time here.'[12]
The leaders had been political activists in their earlier adult years, and
tended to continue this activity as they acquired elderly status.

Some scholars have found that status anxiety is a major preoccupation of
those elderly who join elderly advocacy groups. With the attenuation of
family relationships and the loss of status through the cessation of employment, members feel 'a need to be "respected" by society at large.' The ever-
present stigma of a means-tested OAP would have accentuated this status
anxiety. A study of American pensioners at mid-century found that receipt
of Social Security had changed the attitudes about the old age pension of
only a small proportion of pensioners; a majority found receipt of Social
Security to be a mixed blessing.[13] But this status anxiety could be manifested positively. One response to status anxiety was status assertion. The
OAPO appealed to those elderly with status anxiety, but it also gave those
same persons an opportunity to assert their claims to higher status and to
do something positive about those assertions and their anxiety. And there
is good reason to believe that OAPO members were successful in using the
organization for such purposes. Recent studies of voluntary associations

have found that members (compared with non-members) have more favourable self-images, and are less likely to feel powerless or alienated.[14] The culture of entitlement was personal as well as political.

There was a militancy to the pensioners that found expression in the movement to organize. There was not merely a sense of injury or ill-treatment, but a claim that injustice was being done and that right was on the side of the elderly 'victims.' The organized elderly developed their own songs and wrote motivational poetry about their cause. The OAPO, for example, adopted a recruiting song, written by an English pensioner to the militant tune of 'Onward Christian Soldiers,' that was regularly sung at meetings, legitimating their cause and inspiring the participants.

> Onward, Old Age Pensioners, Stand up for your Right;
> Rally round our banner – Membership is Might.
> We will fight for Justice, We have waited long.
> Lift your hearts and voices In the triumph song.
>
> Chorus
> Onward Old Age Pensioners, Fighting for the right;
> Swell the ranks and join us – Membership is might!
>
> Onward Old Age Pensioners – Raise your standard high;
> For a better pension Sound the battle cry.
> Higher prices meet us, Make us strive the more;
> Forward then with millions calling We are sure to score.
>
> On then all ye people Onward every one;
> We will never waver Till the fight be won.
> Swell the ranks and join us – Come, both young and old;
> For our fight is YOUR fight Answer then the call.[15]

The use of a popular Christian hymn as the central music of the OAPO was not, however, just a simple device to capture support. The religious motivation or philosophy of many of the leaders of the organized elderly stands out repeatedly in their comments. The treasurer of the OAPOBC sent new year's greetings to everyone in 1951 by pointing to the fundamentally Christian ethic of the movement. If everyone joined hands across the country, he wrote, there would be a great flow of 'Brotherly Love and Friendship' that would inspire the participants to live 'above the sordid things of life, and give grateful thanks to the Giver of all GOOD things for the blessings bestowed upon us ... So, let our universal wish to each other be: Heavenly Father, Lead us all the way.'[16] For many of the activist elderly, they were doing not only their own work but God's work as well.

This blending of political and religious motivation imbued the movement of the organized elderly with considerable strength. An early Old Age Pensioners of Saskatchewan (OAPOS) call for membership regretted 'that the pension is considered a dole, and [the OAPO] maintains that it is a due, and just reward for services rendered during a lifetime of work as good citizens.' It continued: 'Fellow citizens: this is your movement, working for your benefit. The more members and branches we have the greater will be our power and influence, and the sooner will our objective be attained. Union is strength. Join the organization and help a worthy cause ... No one is too young or too old to become a member.'[17] The theme of empowerment consistently runs through the rhetoric of the organized elderly. 'The Pensioner's Resolve,' for example, was published by the *Pensioner* and the *Western Producer*: 'That I shall do all in my power to assist the effort being put forth on my behalf to secure a better deal, knowing that, if all others do likewise, ultimate victory will come the sooner for all concerned.'[18] The practices and the participatory behaviour of the organized elderly were fundamental in sustaining the groups through two decades of political struggle.

The OAPO adopted a variety of political tactics. In the early years, petitions were important, not only for drawing political attention to the organized elderly's views, but also for stimulating the public at large and the elderly in particular. The forwarding of resolutions was a constant technique for keeping their views and problems before their elected representatives. Direct electoral activity was also tried. Pressure was placed on elected politicians, directly or at all-candidates meetings, to adopt a public position in favour of the OAPO's proposals, but with only limited success in terms of substantial results. The most immediately effective political tactic directly tied to the organized elderly was their use of the courts, particularly in British Columbia. Through a succession of cases, the provincial boards' application of OAP regulations was challenged by the OAPO and was altered significantly in favour of pensioners, frustrating some boards' calculation of fictive income from adult children and thwarting some forms of control over pensioners' real property.[19] In the end the organized elderly formed close ties of cooperation with the provincial bureaucracies, especially in British Columbia, working to make the OAP program operate more effectively in the interests of the dependent elderly.

Public confrontation was another common tactic. Fundraising events, such as tag days,[20] and the distribution of food hampers brought the problems of the dependent elderly before the public, raising the general consciousness by dramatizing the needy elderly's economic problems. Letters to the editors of local newspapers were a persistent tactic, because they used none of the organizations' meagre financial resources and had the appearance of gaining immediate public prominence. What was important about this tactic was that the local press in several cities was quite willing to publish many of these letters, and eventually adopted much of the viewpoint of the organized elderly in editorials and articles on the plight of the elderly and the weaknesses of the OAP.[21]

Yet there remained a significant element of paternalism in the public response to the organized elderly, encouraged by the pathos of popular descriptions of the plights of pensioners, and partially fostered by the organized elderly with their 'tag days' and their Christmas hampers. Local notables began in the 1940s to sponsor recreational events among the organized elderly in much the same way that various forms of charity had been sporadically distributed to residential institutions at the turn of the century. A description of the 1942 annual picnic of the New Westminster OAPOBC branch, for example, pointed to the various types of charitable support that the elderly still received, albeit in different guises more appropriate to the 1940s. Area 20 of the Fraternal Order of Eagles had lent their hall and their kitchen equipment to the OAPOBC branch; members of the local Red Cross branch, the Burnaby League, and the Household League had helped serve, and others had furnished transportation; the mayor had donated ice cream for all. Elsewhere, local service clubs and businesses lent their buildings or equipment to the organized elderly for meetings, sponsored banquets, or donated funds, goods, or services.[22] For all that had changed, the elderly were still objects of charity and paternalism, emphasizing and entrenching their dependent character.

The tactics of the organized elderly themselves encouraged this treatment. Their appeal to the public and to the politicians focused on the needs of the elderly. An image of the elderly that engendered the greatest sympathy was that of the pathetic old woman or old man with a kind heart who, after a lifetime of hard work, was now incapacitated for earning any income. The OAPO frequently manipulated stereotypes of the elderly, just as individual elderly did, to advance their cause. The use of such pathos undermined the culture of entitlement and invited public paternalism.

Implicit in the presentation of the elderly's economic plight was support for a minimum standard of living, judged not only in economic but also in social terms. This is best captured by the concept of the elderly's right to dignity, a concept that is inherent in much of the 1940s public discussion of the problems faced by the dependent elderly. The bureaucratic procedures and the state investigations to which OAP applicants and pensioners were subjected came under increasing attack during the war years as inappropriate, wasteful, and demeaning. The elderly found it 'cruelly embarrassing' to have to provide detailed explanations of why their children would not or could not support them, complained the *Vancouver Sun*. According to the press, the state's 'snooping' and 'spying into family lives' should stop, and the elderly should be 'entitled to their pensions by virtue of having grown old.'[23] An important element of the culture of entitlement was the freeing of the needy elderly from the 'moral gaze' of the state.

The culture of entitlement entailed state support as well as societal recognition. The citizen's wage was important not just as income. It also endorsed the status of the needy elderly as full-fledged citizens of the country – as senior citizens.

Western Expansion

The OAPO had more than provincial aspirations. Hoping to help the elderly across the entire country and realizing that reform of the federal legislation would be much more likely if the elderly exerted pressure nationally, the British Columbia organization sought to use its meagre resources to encourage the development of branches in other provinces. Early in 1941 discussions were held about the dispatch of two organizers out of province. Other individuals carried out various initiatives to assist the development of the grey movement elsewhere. For example, Gerald Pelton, the OAPO solicitor, contacted the Alberta government seeking its support in mid-1941, and he began to accept speaking engagements in Alberta promoting the OAPO agenda.[24]

One of the most important instruments in this expansion program was the press. The *Western Producer* was the first journal to represent the OAPO position wholeheartedly, confirming the association's informal links to organized farmers. The weekly *Western Producer* offered the earliest consistent, public forum for communication among the elderly, informing many about the organizations now available to them and spreading some of the ideas and attitudes central to the movement. Published in Saskatoon as the organ of the Saskatchewan Grain Growers' Association, the paper's interest in the elderly derived entirely from Violet McNaughton, who placed the women's page that she edited at the service of the political movement of the elderly. While the paper's contribution to the movement cannot be underestimated, it was McNaughton's own tireless efforts, both personally and professionally, on behalf of Canadian pensioners that were most fundamental. One major figure among the organized elderly spoke for many when she complimented McNaughton:

I do not think that we can thank you enough for all that you have done in the past to help this Society to grow & to advertise our cause, I certainly know that you have a big corner in your heart for this same work, & I also know how much you have meant to me, by your many cheerful & encouraging letters & words of help & advice, you will never know how much this has meant to me, & now your offer to still give us space in your paper is just wonderful for we know how much the press means in publicizing any cause.[25]

As the first journal to demonstrate forthright and consistent support for old age pensioners and as a newspaper with an established circulation across the entire west (and on a limited basis into Ontario and the east coast provinces), the *Western Producer's* commitment to the cause of the organized elderly was crucial to its development.

It was members of the British Columbia OAPO who had migrated west from Saskatchewan who first stimulated Violet McNaughton's interest in pensioners. Though she herself turned sixty in 1939, she would not have been eligible for a means-tested pension. But she empathized with the plight of the needy elderly, particularly as it was brought home to her by individual OAPO spokespersons. J.J. Whiting, a leader of the OAPO in New Westminster and a former activist in the Saskatchewan farmers' movement, found personal motivation in seeking to stimulate broader concern for the cause of organized pensioners. He believed not only that the movement could be enhanced by development in other provinces, but that his own pension through the Saskatchewan board might be improved. Whiting's letters to the *Producer* first caught McNaughton's eye, and her link with Whiting was her most important contact with the organized elderly. Whiting's approach to the *Producer* on behalf of the organized pensioners made a particularly good fit. The *Producer* already opened its pages to readers more than most, sometimes devoting up to three printed pages to its 'Open Forum' for letters to the editor, as well as printing additional letters on the women's page and the Young Cooperators' page. A participatory movement meshed with a populist journal with very positive results.

McNaughton maintained personal ties with the OAPO in British Columbia and elsewhere. Her correspondence with west coast leaders such as

Whiting and J.W. Hope was extensive, and she made several visits to the area, meeting with local OAPO activists and occasionally speaking to OAPOBC meetings. Violet McNaughton played a crucial role in helping to link the various provincial groups. In Manitoba and Ontario, where there was little or no organized activity, she was constantly on the lookout for signs of a movement, and she tried to stimulate interest.[26] Where organizations already existed, she passed information back and forth and offered support in a number of ways. When the OAPO founded its own newspaper, for example, McNaughton did not see it as a competitor to the *Producer;* instead, she offered her support, printing subscription information in her column and promoting the paper in her public talks.[27] In Saskatoon itself she worked with the local elderly, helping them to found and maintain a viable organization; while she provided considerable information and knowledge about how successful branches operated elsewhere, McNaughton never pushed herself to the forefront locally, sensitive to the idea that the OAPO ought to be *of* the elderly, not simply *for* them.

After Whiting's first letter in March 1939 describing the beneficial results of the OAPO,[28] occasional letters and articles appeared in the *Western Producer* about the needs and conditions of the elderly, often written by pensioners themselves. The writers signed many of the letters with pseudonyms, suggesting that while pensioners felt increasingly assertive of their claims to support, they feared the stigma associated with receipt of the OAP and/or possible retribution from the OAP bureaucracy.[29] The letters in particular served to bolster the will of the elderly readers.[30]

By early 1940 McNaughton's support for the elderly was fully committed, and the newspaper placed no barriers in her use of its pages. McNaughton decided to promote OAP reform through adoption of the Vancouver OAPO's current campaign to mount a national petition, soliciting and consciously selecting letters to the editor that would lend momentum to the campaign and give it legitimacy through endorsement by individual elderly.[31] The timing of the *Western Producer's* coverage was carefully aimed to avoid the federal election, 'since we do not wish it [OAP reform] to be regarded as a political question but rather as a matter of social justice.'[32] By mid-March 1940 Old Age Pension Reform had become a regular column on the women's page of the paper, and up to seven or eight letters were being printed in each issue.

Although McNaughton's support was crucial, it is clear from the letters received from residents of the three most westerly provinces that she simply gave voice to a growing groundswell of resentment and affirmation among the pensioners and elderly themselves. Some elderly promoted the idea of a petition. Others offered to work in a petition campaign, spontaneously selecting their own tactics. One seventy-year-old woman, crippled with rheumatism, asked permission to make up posters of letters to the editor in the *Producer;* she would display the posters in the post office and take them around with her when she collected signatures.[33] McNaughton adopted the Vancouver OAPO's petition idea and facilitated its spread across the western provinces. Apart from printing the petition in the *Producer* and supporting it over several weeks in the press, she encouraged other populist and labour newspapers to do the same: the Edmonton *People's Weekly,* the Regina *Saskatchewan Commonwealth,* the Winnipeg *Manitoba Commonwealth.*[34] In total, 40,553 signatures to the petition were sent in to the *Producer* office for forwarding to the OAPO and to parliament, while other signatures were sent directly.[35] Over the following decade, McNaughton and the *Western Producer* were constant in their support of organized pensioners, but the amount of space allocated to the movement and the cause dwindled as the seniors found their own voice.

Even more important as an instrument of expansion, though its circulation was certainly lower than the *Western Producer's,* was the OAPO's official magazine, the *Pensioner.* First published in October 1941 under the name the *Old Age Pensioner,* the monthly *Pensioner* was thought of as a national vehicle for the views of the organized elderly. Initially centred in New Westminster, the paper soon moved to White Rock, well known as a retirement community south of Vancouver. The editor and publisher, Benjamin Stone Kennedy, who founded and supported the *Pensioner* out of his own funds, was not a pensioner, but he was fully committed to the cause of the elderly and was already an active figure in the OAPO. Five thousand copies of the first issue were distributed free among the elderly and among influential individuals; subscriptions, costing one dollar a year ($1.50 in 1948; less through a club rate), were concentrated in the three most westerly provinces, although they were sold in all sections of the country.[36] The *Pensioner* in the early years consisted of eight 8 1/2-by-11-inch pages.

Ben Kennedy died in 1944 and the initial reaction of his widow, Anna H. Kennedy, was to cease publication. However, she was persuaded to carry on with the help of her daughter. Three years later, Charles R. Bennetton of White Rock, who had worked in the OAPO for several years, took over responsibility for the paper. Under Bennetton the paper expanded to sixteen pages and received more support from advertisers. But the magazine's existence was always precarious. Subscription and advertising revenues did not cover its costs, and the *Pensioner* was forced to rely on unpaid labour and on occasional pleas for direct donations. Its pages were filled with reports received from local branches and with letters from individual elderly or interested persons, necessitating relatively little writing by the editors themselves.[37]

The *Pensioner* played an indispensable role in communicating with the elderly and their supporters and in creating a sense of community, commitment, and solidarity. It was a self-conscious role. The magazine's letterhead declared 'In Unity There Is Strength – Organize!' and the masthead throughout the paper's existence depicted a brilliant sun rising over the mountains with the label 'The Dawn of a New Era.' In 1947 Bennetton printed a card advertising the *Pensioner*. On the front it read: '*The Pensioner*, your national monthly ... Subscribe to-day and help carry on to Victory. The Objectives of Our O.A.P. Organization: Recognition of Senior Citizens' Rights. Adequate Pensions. Security and Comfort. Happier Old Age.' The reverse reproduced the OAPO's recruiting song.[38]

The editor's ambitions were not just for the magazine itself but for the organized elderly. After making initial gains in British Columbia, Alberta, and Saskatchewan, Ben Kennedy planned 'to turn our guns on Manitoba ... and then on to Eastern Canada for the final organization campaign. Final victory will only come if we keep up a persistent and consistent pressure on Ottawa and that pressure will have to come through the weight of public opinion.' The *Pensioner* would play an important role in forming that public opinion and in exerting political pressure, if Kennedy had his way.[39]

Bennetton was equally as vital to the *Pensioner* and to the organized elderly as Kennedy had been. Bennetton not only invested his own funds and enormous energy in the magazine itself, but was a tireless worker in the cause of the needy elderly. His wife, H.M. Bennetton, worked with him on the magazine as assistant editor, giving him more time to spend on the road. Bennetton visited most of the OAPOBC branches every year, offering support and encouragement and giving inspiring talks. He regularly attended the OAPOS annual conventions, becoming a major personal link between the Saskatchewan and British Columbia organizations. His positive role in this regard is suggested by the action of one branch following the 1950 OAPOS convention in Saskatoon; the Prince Albert branch unanimously voted to contribute $25 to Bennetton's convention expenses 'as we could not think of not having him present at our conventions.'[40] Bennetton also found time to be the long-time president of the White Rock branch of the OAPOBC. It was through the efforts of a small number of such truly devoted workers that the organized elderly forged a place for themselves in mid-century Canadian society.

The *Pensioner* also filled an important role in communicating with the governments and politicians. Constantly reminding them of the views and demands of the organized elderly, the paper gradually expanded its circulation to the politically powerful. In 1945 the British Columbia OAPO subsidised the monthly distribution of the *Pensioner* to fifty members of parliament, though it is unclear on what basis the fifty were selected. By the late 1940s copies of the paper were sent to every member of parliament while parliament was in session and to every provincial government; the costs of almost all this lobbying were absorbed by the paper itself, the OAPOBC paying the distribution costs of only one issue.[41]

Thanks in large part to the development of this public communication network, the organization of the elderly spread to neighbouring provinces. After a false start in the late 1930s, the Alberta elderly established two major associations. In Edmonton, led by a dominating figure, Edward Fisher, they founded the Alberta Pensioners' Society (APS) in 1940. Although the APS concentrated on the needs and concerns of the elderly, it deliberately articulated a broader mandate than other seniors' groups by not focusing exclusively on the OAP. Instead, the APS argued for a broad national system of social security for those of all age groups. The APS talked of founding branches elsewhere, but there is no evidence that this occurred on any firm basis, just as there is no sign that anyone other than Fisher ever spoke for the association. In Calgary a separate organization was founded as a result of local efforts to collect signatures for the OAPO's 1940 national petition. Here the major figure, Ethel Baker, readily shared power with others in the organization, and the result was an energetic local group that was able to communicate its enthusiasm for 'the cause' to neighbouring communities in southern Alberta and elsewhere. The Calgary group came to be known as the Alberta Old Age Pensioners' Society and was firmly linked to the OAPO through the *Pensioner* and the *Western Producer*. Following the founding of the Calgary group in 1941, branches were established at several other southern Alberta towns and cities, though there is evidence suggesting a higher failure rate than for local branches elsewhere.

In Saskatchewan the pattern of elderly organizations followed that of British Columbia more closely, though the timing was similar to that in Alberta. Stimulated significantly by retired members of the farmers movement, such as Whiting, and by McNaughton and the *Western Producer*, the elderly first organized themselves in Saskatoon. Following some shaky beginnings in 1941–2, marred by internal conflict over the major goals of the organization, this first branch of the Old Age Pensioners' Organization of Saskatchewan (OAPOS) quickly became the dominant branch in the province, in much the same way that the Vancouver area branches dominated the OAPOBC. Branches spread to other cities and smaller towns, eventually covering much of the settled portions of the province. Again following the pattern of the OAPOBC, the OAPOS relied on a large group of leaders, such as Anne Douglas, Agnes Nurse, Samuel Lovell, E.W. Sager, and Marcie Reid. The OAPOS established a close relationship with the Cooperative Commonwealth government elected in 1944, finding particularly useful Anne Douglas's position as mother to the new premier. Although its meetings did not rely on political speakers to the extent of the OAPOBC or the AOAPS, the OAPOS had easy access to the Regina government and bureaucracy, and made good use of this connection.

The elderly organized much less effectively in Manitoba than in any of the other western provinces. By 1942 there was an organization of the elderly in Winnipeg. By mid-1943 the Manitoba Pensioners' Society (MPS) was active in Winnipeg and was loosely affiliated with the OAPO, though there is no evidence that this occurred with any direct assistance from British Columbia or Saskatchewan. The MPS, having organized the support of nearby municipal officials, soon began to petition the provincial government for increased OAP payments. Direct political action took several forms – arranging for the radio broadcast of the 1944 OAPOS agenda and circularizing local candidates in the 1945 federal election and union locals regarding OAP reform.[42] Outside Winnipeg, a branch of the OAPO was briefly reported in Portage la Prairie in 1942,[43] but otherwise there is no evidence throughout the 1940s that the Winnipeg-based organizations were able to move beyond that city. The Manitoba groups played no significant role nationally.

Extending the Political Horizon

With communication well established among the various sections of the organized elderly and with at least the beginnings of organizations in all four western provinces, the stage was set for the move to pan-provincial organization. The British Columbia OAPO took the initiative in the fall of 1943, issuing a call for a meeting of all pensioners' associations to 'draft a plan of campaign' regarding the government overhaul of the social welfare system that was clearly coming as a result of the Marsh and Beveridge reports. The convention was projected for Saskatchewan, because the pensioners in British Columbia and Alberta were the only ones so far receiving an OAP supplement and thus could more readily afford to travel. Collections to pay the expenses of delegates were enthusiastically supported by the membership. The meeting itself was delayed by difficulties in coordinating the various groups sending delegates, particularly those in Alberta, where the Calgary and Edmonton organizations resisted pressure to form a provincial body parallel to those in other provinces.[44]

The British Columbia OAPO had great expectations for the first 'national' convention. It was the next substantial step on the road to full social status and a financially adequate pension. Given the relative maturity and experience of the west coast branches, it is not surprising that they took considerable initiative in structuring the convention. The provincial council printed and distributed in advance its recommendations for the delegates. The convention should establish a central, national organization, to be known as the Canadian Pensioners' Congress, to which all local and provincial pensioners' groups would affiliate. The congress would act as a central coordinating body, facilitating communication among affiliates, meshing objectives and resolutions, and organizing expansion into eastern Canada. The general objectives of the congress and its affiliates should be:

To promote the welfare of the Senior Citizens of Canada, that they may enjoy their remaining years in peaceful security as a rightful reward of their life of service;
That all men and women of Canada 60 years of age be granted Dominion Pension of $50.00 per month, without *Means Test* or charge against estate;
For provision where and when needed [of] hospital, medical, dental and optical services, food, clothing, shelter and funeral expenses;
Simplification of Pension Application Forms.[45]

Responding to this pressure from the west coast and from its own provincial mandate, the OAPOS in June 1945 issued a call for a fall convention of all pensioners' societies.[46]

On 16–17 October 1945 representatives from the organized elderly in the three most western provinces met in convention for the first time in Saskatoon. Attendance was modest, being constrained by the relatively heavy costs for those with limited financial resources. There were twenty-four delegates, representing Saskatoon, Prince Albert, Robsart, Lloydminster, Regina, and Moose Jaw (eighteen Saskatchewan delegates), Pincher Creek (a member of the Alberta legislature), Dawson Creek, White Rock, Vancouver, and New Westminster (five British Columbia delegates), in addition to forty-six visitors. Using the British Columbia proposal as the basis for discussion, the convention – after what one local newspaper reported as 'considerable and at times heated discussion' – drew up a national constitution for the Canadian Pensioners' Congress and elected an executive.[47] The convention was publicly judged to be 'a great success and charged with hope for those old age pensioners and pioneers of Canada.'[48]

As the political aims of the congress indicated, by the mid-1940s the OAPO was prepared to broaden its political agenda. The organized elderly showed self-confidence in their cause and an expanding sense of their claim on the state. The movement went beyond OAP reform to include demands for other types of services and support from the state. In advance of state action regarding medical aid, the OAPOS began in 1943 to agitate for free medical care for pensioners. Concern expanded to greater provision for housing, especially for the disabled elderly.[49] Vancouver area branches took an active interest in promoting housing proposals designed exclusively for the dependent elderly. Municipal finance committees were approached in 1945 to provide free land for a low-cost housing project; the OAPOBC wanted to arrange the construction itself and planned to conduct fundraising sufficient to qualify for the 90 per cent state support available under the National Housing Act. In keeping with the character and philosophy of the OAPO, the elderly initiated the project and intended to run it. At a public meeting organized by the local OAPOBC branch to discuss the project, two hundred members turned out and sixty-six immediately indicated their willingness to take shares in the proposed housing corporation.[50]

Support for such projects was stimulated by suggestions and accounts relating elderly suicides to the poor living conditions of the dependent elderly in postwar cities.[51] The flexibility evident in the proposal's adoption by the OAPO was a sign of the organization's growing maturity. Other interests and concerns were also brought within the purview of the OAPO in the postwar world. Earlier concern for free medical, optical, and dental care expanded to include demands for state support for hearing aids required by pensioners and for inclusion of chiropractic care within the new health plans being developed for pensioners. The OAPO's support for the relaxation of restrictions on margarine addressed the need to keep food costs down. 'Unemployables' who did not qualify for a pension were brought within the purview of the movement.[52]

In this broadening agenda, the OAPO credited itself with repeated success. Although it is unclear just how many of the gains for the elderly in the 1940s can be attributed to the various seniors' groups, the organizations repeatedly found confirmation of their own role and influence in the various new benefits and programs 'won.' In the winter of 1949–50, for example, one local OAPOBC official lobbied the provincial and city welfare departments regarding the treatment of institutionalized pensioners and spoke out publicly on the issue at an OAPOBC meeting in Victoria. As a result of the newspaper coverage generated by his remarks, the provincial department sent the deputy minister to meet with the OAPOBC official and to share some 'confidential' information with him. 'During this interview he [the deputy minister] told me that he had noticed a great improvement in some of the [nursing] homes since I had stirred them up. Such a remark from the Administrator of Welfare justifies my agitation on behalf of our members.'[53] The account clearly suggests that provincial officials could be adept at co-opting leaders of the organized elderly, but at the same time relations between the provincial government and the OAPOBC had developed to the stage that those leaders were able to generate a quick response from state authorities.

The provincial governments, particularly in British Columbia, had learned to work with the organized elderly to the general benefit of all seniors in the province. The OAPO's role and purpose were at the same time confirmed. More broadly, such activities legitimated both the political status of the senior citizens and the increasingly broad definitions of the citizen's wage.

Yet despite this broadening perspective of the needs of the elderly, the OAP program never lost its position of primacy in the OAPO agenda. In the 1946 British Columbia convention, for example, resolutions were adopted calling for a series of reforms: commencement at the age of sixty without a means test for all those who had resided for a total of twenty years in Canada since the age of twenty-one; fifty dollars a month; no charges against pensioners' estates or liens against their property; greater liberality regarding proof of eligibility and movement outside the country; and reciprocity with the old age pension programs of other countries. The savings accruing from the consequent reduction in OAP bureaucracy would help to pay for the increased program costs. In addition, the OAPO argued for a tax free pension and spousal benefits extending below the OAP minimum age. Most fundamentally, the structure of the OAP should change to a contributory program so as to place it on a more adequate fiscal foundation.[54]

Taking the national initiative from the congress, in 1946 the OAPOBC drew up a brief on OAP reform, demanding an increase in maximum payment levels and a lowering of the minimum age. The brief was circulated to all members of federal and provincial legislatures, and was allegedly used by a number of trade unions and service organizations as a basis for their own submissions to the federal government. This was followed later in the year with a letter to selected members of parliament attacking the means test.[55] As a single-issue political organization, the OAPO fought for pension reform with only partial success, never adopting a strategy or tactics that would enable the organized elderly to penetrate the barrier of partisan politics. But the organized elderly never stopped trying to use the logic of their electoral strength to make political gains. As one writer commented in 1946: 'OA Pensioners can do much if they will stand together and refuse to give a vote to any politician of any party who will not give a definite and binding pledge on this matter. Make your slogan "Pension Before Party" and stick to it through thick and thin,' forcing legislators to hold a free vote on OAP reform.[56]

In this constant fight for pension reform, there was a perseverance and tenacity on the part of the articulate among the elderly that is impressive. In the face of limited reforms so far, Anna Kennedy could still write a strikingly aggressive and assertive editorial at the start of 1947:

You must work and fight as never before if you want a bigger and better pension. This is how the first pension was won. FIGHT! FIGHT! FIGHT! ...

The call goes out to each and every pensioner, from the vigorous western provinces, where the battle proves that old age pensioners CAN do things, to the far east, where it appears too many pensioners are asleep! ...

No government, or group of men who seemingly control that government, can ignore the cries and demands of Canada's Old Age Pensioners IF EACH PENSIONER WILL DO HIS AND HER SHARE IN MAKING THIS A REAL FIGHT.[57]

What is more, the activities of the organized elderly had played a role in persuading the general public that all elderly deserved a basic minimum of support from the state. The language of rights that had been part of the movement's rhetoric from the early 1930s was adopted by members of the general public.[58]

Just how far the organized elderly had developed in their sense of community and common demands is suggested by their response to the federal government's five dollar increase in the maximum OAP monthly payment in 1947. Such a 'meagre' sum was dismissed as mere tokenism and as proof that the elderly were the 'forgotten people' of Canada. That a 20 per cent increase could be rejected as 'parsimonious' and worthy of defeat in parliament suggests just how much strength and 'justice' was felt to be behind the elderly's demands. The *Pensioner* attacked the legislators for approving the statute, alleging that the large number who, when the vote was about to be taken, left the House 'with the speed of jet propelled rockets' were 'headed for the washroom to emulate Pontius Pilate and wash their hands of the whole shameful measure.'

The explanation for such a weak bill was the failure of the organized elderly to come together in an effective national body, decided the paper: 'At present we are in the position of a general commanding a number of army units, who, instead of using them in one organized attack, sends them to exhaust themselves in individual attacks on the enemy, thus inviting defeat.' When the first payment of the increase finally arrived, the *Pensioner* emphasized the elderly's disappointment, for at the same time price controls were removed and prices jumped even higher than the pensioners' incomes: 'The feeling of nausea and disappointment felt by these aged citizens can be more easily imagined than described. Whether this action of the powers that be was intentional or accidental is not known, but, it contains the essence of cruelty.'[59] The organized elderly were no longer content with mere dollar increases; they wanted – demanded – a substantially new form of pension and would settle for nothing less. They sought a citizen's wage.

Much of that confidence and assertiveness came from the sense of accomplishment in creating their own organizations and in fighting for and achieving significant OAP reform. Arguing on behalf of the Canadian Pensioners' Congress in 1947, J.W. Hope underlined the status assertion gained by membership in any such organization:

To be in an organization today is to be a somebody. A member with rights and representation to all authorities, Civic, Provincial and Dominion ... A member of the Canadian Pensioners' Congress is a person of dignity and responsibility far beyond his own backyard. In organization there is found dignity, self-respect, a confidence in ourselves and in one another.[60]

For the *Pensioner,* the key to seniors winning the sort of environment they wanted was to use the instruments already at hand – faith, courage, and determination: 'Armed with these weapons and bearing the shield of Christian brotherhood and friendly co-operation, Senior Citizens can march on to an assured victory in this year of 1949. RIGHT AND JUSTICE WILL PREVAIL.'[61] The rise in maximum federal OAP payment to $40 monthly, passed just two months before the 1949 election, was recognized for the electoral ploy that it was, but it was also a sign that the federal politicians recognized the elderly's needs and the support behind their demands.

Elsewhere, organization of the elderly was slow or non-existent. There is no evidence of organizations formed by the elderly themselves in Newfoundland, Prince Edward Island, New Brunswick, or Quebec.

In Nova Scotia the organized elderly reflected an important element of the local class structure. In August 1947, in the aftermath of the strike at the Dominion Coal Company, twenty-five pensioners met in New Aberdeen and founded the Nova Scotia Pensioners' Union (NSPU), also known as the Industrial Pensioners' Union. Branches were soon established in several other communities. The NSPU was different from the organized elderly elsewhere in that the branches tended to be occupationally specific, underlining the association's close links with organized labour: the Sydney branch consisted of steelworkers and the Halifax branch of retired Canadian National Railway workers, the others being for former coal miners. The NSPU's first provincial convention was held at Glace Bay in June 1948. The United Mine Workers offered considerable support, both substantial and emotional, and the local press and radio provided sympathetic coverage; the Sydney local of the Steelworkers of America donated funds. Prior to the 1949 federal and provincial elections, the Glace Bay branch had all candidates address members at meetings. The NSPU held its second convention in 1949 at Sydney, and by mid-1949 the provincial group was firmly enough established to make contact with the OAPO, to begin to make frequent reports of activities in the *Pensioner*, and to petition the provincial and federal governments.[62]

In Ontario the elderly were slow to organize despite the relatively harsh characteristics of the OAP program there.[63] Simply because of population size, that province had more pensioners than any other Canadian jurisdiction, and the province consistently had the lowest proportion of elderly on the OAP rolls, but beyond the twin cities at the head of Lake Superior the elderly did not organize around the OAP program to make their voices heard. In April 1943 Violet McNaughton visited Toronto, but could find no evidence of any pensioners' organization in the province. The OAPO was limited to the Lakehead where, at least since 1947, a group of some two hundred members (in 1948) met together monthly, alternating the regular meeting between the twin communities of Fort William and Port Arthur. Though this branch was well supported locally and was in contact with the western movement, joining the congress and even attending the Saskatchewan conventions in 1948 and 1950, the OAPO was unable to expand elsewhere within the province.[64]

It is difficult to account fully for this varied regional response to organizing politically. At least part of the explanation lies with the nature of the local political culture. Wherever the pensioners organized to further their cause, there was a local tradition of labour or farmer activism; the cooperative movement tended to be well established. Members of the working class and farmers had gained experience in organizing, and accepted the idea of articulating and fighting for their views and needs publicly. Among the socially and economically non-dominant groups there was a local political culture of challenge and of establishing organizations designed to compete with dominant processes and institutions. Along with the past experience of several individual pensioners' leaders, the links of the elderly organizations to union locals, farmers' groups, and the *Western Producer* help to confirm the importance of activist traditions. Where such local traditions were weaker, as in most of central and eastern Canada, no grey lobby arose. It is possible that the occupational diversity among the elderly also inhibited organizing pensioners in many sectors of eastern and central Canada.

Where organizations operated, gender played a significant role in limiting their agenda and in shaping the use of the available human resources. Some of the associations had ladies' auxiliaries – Saskatoon, for example, had both an old boys' club and a ladies' auxiliary, with which the Regina branch was so impressed that it copied the practice.[65] Several branches, for example the Vancouver OAPOBC, had an active visiting committee to drop in on those elderly who were shut-ins, and the committee was invariably chaired by a woman. Women were also expected to do the work of providing food and drink at various meetings and events. In the entertainment that made up such an important part of most meetings, women tended to be as well represented as men among the pianists, singers, and performers.

But when it came to wielding power, gender restricted women's role and enhanced men's. Women were prominent among the workers for the movement; for example, when the OAPOS set up an information booth at the Saskatoon Exhibition, the treasurer, S.A. Lovell, was credited with being 'in charge,' but the nine others who 'manned' the booth were all women.[66] When it came to positions of influence or power, women were strikingly underrepresented. A few women, such as Anne Douglas, Ethel Baker, Anna Kennedy, or Agnes Nurse, played significant roles within the executives of the various organizations, but most of the executive positions were held by men. For example, when the OAPOBC held its annual convention in the summer of 1951, sixty officers and delegates attended. One of five executive officers was a woman, and there was one woman among the four other members of the executive. One-third of the fifty-one delegates were women, but this is somewhat misleading; where branches sent more than one delegate, there was a strong tendency (seven of ten branches) to send both men and women, and this is how most women became delegates. But where branches were represented by just one person, there was a strong tendency for those branches (fifteen out of twenty) to choose a man.[67]

Women who made up a majority of the elderly were more important among the organized elderly than in other political groups shared by both sexes, but gender remained a subordinating factor.

Nor was it easy for the dominant men to share their new-found influence. The Nova Scotia Pensioners' Union, probably because of the occupational character of the branches, excluded women as members. After a visit to OAPOBC branches in 1951, one NSPU official reported that he was impressed by the active part taken by women at meetings; 'the women he said showed keen interest and understanding in the work of the Pensioners and in their further demands for better security for pensioners.' As a result, the New Waterford branch of the NSPU voted to invite the wives of members and women pensioners to attend the next regular meeting.[68] The men likely found themselves in positions of influence for one of the few times in their lives, and had considerable difficulty in sharing power equitably with 'the weaker sex.'

Not surprisingly, gender was seldom a factor in the organizations' analysis of the problems of pensioners or the elderly. The particular problems facing women or men were not discussed, and probably were not even perceived. When the *Pensioner* published the life stories of several 'typical' pensioners in 1947, all were men.[69] At the 1951 annual convention of the OAPOBC, Elsie Buckley, the first vice-president, drew attention to the fact that she had finally been joined on the nine-person provincial executive by another woman: 'One of the nicest things in the whole year has been the fact of having another woman on the Board, after all, a woman's viewpoint is often very different to that of a man and Mrs. Price-Needles and I have been able to confer with and lend a hand to the Women's Auxiliaries and social committees of other branches.' An exception to this tendency to ignore the special problems of older women was a resolution adopted at the 1950 OAPOBC convention regarding the particular problems of pensioners' widows under the age of seventy.[70]

The limited expectations and the constraints placed on their interests are telling comments on the continuing power of gender, even in old age, to shape the lives of the individuals and the agendas of organizations. While the organized elderly challenged ageist structures and policies, they were noticeably silent on such limiting factors as gender or race. In this regard the first grey lobby was quite conservative.

The Congress Fails

By 1948 the elderly had successfully organized on a significant scale in the three most westerly provinces, and there was some slight organization in Manitoba, Nova Scotia, and at the Lakehead. However, the attempt to meld these organizations into a truly coordinated effort had failed. Reporting to the 1946 OAPOS and the 1947 OAPOBC conventions, the secretary of the Canadian Pensioners' Congress laid the blame entirely at the feet of the president, Mr McWhinney of Regina, who 'had failed in what might have been expected of him and no progress had been made.' McWhinney, with little or no previous experience in the OAPOS, had been a surprising choice as president, and had failed to work with other members of the executive or to take any action to further the cause of the congress; indeed, he quickly disappeared from the records of those active in Regina or Saskatchewan, much less in the congress.

The OAPOS responded late in 1946 by naming Nathan Medd as the congress's new president. A four-person committee was assigned the task of developing and implementing plans for a national membership campaign. While both British Columbia and Saskatchewan named delegates to the congress, neither the Alberta nor Manitoba provincial organizations did so, frustrating any claims to national status or any attempts at effective coordination.[71] When the congress held its second 'convention' in 1946 at Moose Jaw, only four delegates showed up, two each from British Columbia and Saskatchewan; no constitution and no financial structure had been approved.

Meaningful support for a national congress soon crumbled. At its 1948 convention the OAPOS discussed the congress and generally agreed, without any formal motion, that province-level organization was adequate for the needs of the movement, since the OAP program was administered separately within each province. When the heart of the movement, the British Columbia OAPO, held its annual meeting in the summer of 1948, there was a 'battle' over whether the Canadian Pensioners' Congress had truly been brought into existence. In the end there was agreement that the proposed national organization had failed, despite three years of struggle to sustain it.[72] Though some problems had been caused by the lack of support and recognition of the congress in some areas, much more important in its eventual failure was the weak leadership in the congress and the lack of funds to facilitate meaningful national coordination.

The result is not particularly surprising, given the scant resources of the organized elderly. But it is a sign of the limits of the various provincial movements, and it was a particularly difficult result for those provinces where little or no organization had yet been accomplished. Essentially the movements in the three western provinces found themselves in a position where they were forced to ignore further aid to the elderly in the other seven provinces, except for the continuing role of the *Pensioner* and for the pressure indirectly placed on provincial boards by gains made in the west.

The OAPO did not rest content after the failure of the national congress. With the raising of the OAP federal maximum payment level to $40 in the spring of 1949, the OAPO felt a great sense of accomplishment, particularly in British Columbia. On the west coast, the provincial supplement of $10 continued after the federal increase, so that the maximum OAP payment had finally reached the target figure of $50 a month. The OAPOBC took much of the credit for this, and for good reason. Pointing out that west coast pensioners received the highest payments in the country, C.R. Bennetton claimed: 'This is due to the fact that we are organized better than in any other province.'[73]

With this sort of success immediately in mind, and knowing that the OAP program was being fundamentally reconsidered in Ottawa, the OAPO was determined to carry its fight forward. The November 1949 annual meeting of the OAPOS established a committee to negotiate with the executives of groups in other provinces with a view to setting up a national body of pensioners.[74] Early in 1950 the British Columbia executive council announced new plans for the organization of Canadian senior citizens into a 'compact, co-ordinated association.' The new national body would aim to press for improved pension legislation and to facilitate social contact among the elderly nationally. But action within the OAPOBC was slow. The summer convention referred any action to the provincial executive, which at its next meeting agreed to set aside 'thirty minutes or more if required' at the following meeting to discuss the value of forming a national association. Little action ensued. In the second half of 1950 the OAPOBC attempted to bring all the various seniors' organizations in British Columbia and Alberta under one umbrella association. With one exception, none of the groups in Alberta bothered to reply, and, although many of the British Columbia groups responded, no substantial result occurred.[75]

It was the branches without strong province-wide associations that felt the greatest need of a national organization. Support certainly emanated from such relatively weak centres as the Lakehead and Winnipeg, which had no provincial organizations to work with, share ideas, or call on for support. But the active provincial bodies did not have the requisite resources to commit to a meaningful national organization. The development of a meaningful national body was an idea 'whose time had not yet come.'[76]

Yet the organized elderly themselves felt that the absence of a national association significantly weakened their position as a political force. The

OAPO had forwarded a petition to the joint parliamentary committee investigating the OAP in 1950. In presenting the brief to the committee, 'the weakness of our position as an Organization was brought out very strongly at this hearing; the question being asked, had we a national organization and the reply was no; there were a number of scattered groups throughout the Dominion.'[77] Indeed, the joint committee gave little weight to the organized pensioners. At the first meeting, one member explicitly raised the issue of hearing from the OAPO, but in practice significance was attributed to the views only of those groups with recognized status, such as the Canadian Manufacturers' Association or the Canadian Association of Welfare Workers. No elderly organizations were invited to testify before the committee, and only two, the OAPOBC and the OAPOS, presented briefs. In submitting their briefs, those two organizations gave evidence of their limited political sophistication and their lack of lobbying experience. The documents were both extremely short – less than a printed page each – and simply listed in point form the organization's principal demands in a reformed OAP, making no case as to the organization's credibility, the proposed overall philosophy of the new OAP program, or the potential effectiveness of the proposed reforms.[78]

The perception that the federal politicians did not attribute significant representational status to the OAPO is undoubtedly correct. In the parliamentary committee's final report, the testimony and proposals of several groups and individuals were discussed, but there was no mention of the views of the organized elderly. During the later stages of the proceedings, Stanley Knowles drew the committee's attention to letters several members had received from the Calgary branch of the AOAPS:

they feel a bit badly because of the fact they had not submitted a brief. The reason they did not do so was due to the fact they were caught by shortness of time and then felt it was not necessary to submit a brief ... I would judge from the comments in Miss Baker's letter that their only concern is that some people may think they have not been on the job. They recognize all the points they would want to make have been presented.[79]

In this statement, Knowles captures the fundamental problems of the organized elderly. Operating with limited resources and experience, they were unable to put together quickly a persuasive brief. At the same time, even their most sympathetic supporter saw no need to hear the voice of the pensioners themselves, when others could just as easily speak for them. Paternalism continued to be a characteristic of the public response to the elderly.

In the midst of these mixed indications of success and failure, there are signs that enthusiasm for the OAPO was beginning to wane among the elderly. The treasurer of the Victoria branch, for example, complained in 1950 that the rate of increase in membership had slowed noticeably. This was the result 'to a great extent [of] the idea among a great number of old age pensioners that the pension and certain benefits have reached the limit and feel there is no use in carrying on.' Subscriptions to the *Pensioner* began to decline shortly after the 1949 federal OAP increase, when the maximum payment in British Columbia (including the provincial supplement) reached the target of $50 monthly. OAPO leaders complained of the waning enthusiasm of members in the established branches. In 1951 OAPOBC branches folded in four communities. In Saskatchewan, attendance at the provincial convention of the OAPOS peaked in 1947 at thirty-nine delegates, before falling off to between twenty-three and twenty-five in the following three years. Individual branches suffered a similar problem.[80] As well, the first generation of leaders was beginning to step down from office or die, leaving a new group of leaders with different personalities and agendas.

The ending of the means test above the age of seventy and the extension of means-tested pensions to those aged sixty-five to sixty-nine also marked the achievement in 1951 of a considerable portion of the original OAPO agenda. The resulting sense of victory encouraged many elderly to 'rest on their laurels.'[81] The *Pensioner,* which had been in financial difficulty for some time, shrank to just eight pages in January 1952 and then to four pages in its final issue of January 1953. With the adoption of universality at the age of seventy, the OAP was lost as a focus for the movement; new concerns tended to be broader and vaguer, with a consequent loss of focus and shared concern among the various branches and individuals. The achievement of much of the OAPO's legislative program undermined and defused the movement for some time. Study of more recent organizations suggests that old age political activism is isolated, sporadic, and without major impact in most local jurisdictions, and that people are more responsive to threatened losses than to calls for new and extended benefits.[82] In contrast, the positive program of the OAPO had surprising appeal and endurance, but the rapid decline in interest at mid-century is even more understandable, in spite of and in part because of its successes at the local level. The organizations continued on and many of the branches maintained a lively existence, but the years of growth and expansion had ended for a time.

The organized elderly were significant in the 1930s and 1940s for several reasons. Their direct political impact was felt primarily in two ways. They repeatedly manipulated the local media to portray the elderly's needs in a sympathetic light, and they pushed local politicians and civil servants to listen to the elderly's complaints and to adjust the application of state policies to best meet the elderly's needs within the overall boundaries of state policy. In British Columbia they were successful in using the courts to channel the application of state resources in directions supported by the elderly. Their ability to lobby the federal government or national political parties was quite limited, though the organized elderly were able to build on the experience of the 1930s and 1940s to exert greater influence by the late 1950s and in the 1960s. The organized elderly's influence over the articulation of general government policy was indirect and meagre, but their capacity to influence the local definition and application of policies related to the elderly was increasingly significant. This was to become characteristic of Canadian seniors' groups in the decades to come.[83]

More important, the various elderly organizations – from the politically oriented OAPO to the socially and recreationally oriented Friendship Clubs – were evidence of a new and largely shared sense of identity and status among Canada's aged population. These organizations brought together both the needy and non-needy elderly as they faced their common problems. Canada's elderly perceived themselves to be different from other social groups, and those differences were cumulatively significant enough to result in a sense of group identity for the first time. The elderly were coming to see themselves as socially valuable, and as worthy of the respect and of the assistance of society at large. These groups were all established by the elderly for the elderly. While the focus on the OAP indicated a dependence on the state for many, at the same time that this dependence was underlined the elderly gave voice to their own sense of self-worth and independence. They came to the state not as suppliants, but as people demanding fair treatment through the citizen's wage. The organized elderly certainly made use of stereotypes of the elderly to gain whatever advantages for themselves were possible, but there is a sense of group strength and of a positive identity in their work and activities that suggests that the elderly had 'come of age' as a group. They now thought of themselves as senior citizens, with all the rights and privileges inherent in that phrase.

But the change suggested by that phrase should not be exaggerated. Only a small portion of the elderly joined seniors' organizations as yet. The organizational movement was limited to a minority of the country spatially; vast numbers of the elderly in rural areas and in most of the provinces of Manitoba, Ontario, Quebec, New Brunswick, Prince Edward Island, and Newfoundland did not create their own associations. The sense of group identity had by no means yet fully developed. There was also a fundamental conservatism in much of the movement.

Organizations of the elderly are exposed to particular problems in sustaining themselves. The leadership is inevitably confined to the well elderly, and loss of personnel to death and illness is higher than for organizations of most other social groups. Since physical mobility can become a problem for some elderly, attendance at meetings can be troublesome. Because of the turnover among leaders and members, it is difficult to maintain continuity and to sustain long-range goals. Finally, it is difficult to persuade some elderly activists to vest time and effort in long-range goals from which they themselves may not be alive to benefit. This inevitably narrows the political agenda of some elderly organizations, and fosters a conservatism by discouraging fundamental, long-term challenges.

Many of the organized elderly accepted the basic parameters of old age dictated by state, economic, and social processes, seeking merely to alter their impact to the benefit of the elderly. A 1938 motto emphasized this idea: 'We may be too old to work, but NOT too old to vote!'[84] Letters to the editors of various newspapers manifested this mixture of conservative acceptance of some of the economic parameters of old age and aggressive claim to better treatment. The elderly letter writers often selected apt pseudonyms: 'One of the Haunted,' 'Nil desperandum auspice Deo,' 'Disgusted,' 'Also Hopeful,' 'Still Hopeful.'[85] The limited aims of most of the organized elderly made their impact more concerted; they also made it easier for officials to adjust state policies to these goals, and so were undoubtedly a factor in attracting public support for the citizen's wage.

7

Shifting Policies of Old Age Pensions

In its original form, the 1927 Canadian OAP program adopted many of the traditional approaches to support for the needy elderly. A means test restricted the number of eligible elderly; the state insisted that family remain the primary source of support; and those elderly that took advantage of the program had, in effect, to mortgage their own scant property to the state. Legislators and officials constructed this penurious approach with little or no input from potential recipients or from the general public. Though the OAP program accurately reflected long-standing views of the role of the state and of the treatment of the needy, there are signs that many elderly poor and their families and elements of the general public had already moved well beyond these older views. The impact of the culture of entitlement that they manifested was tempered and reshaped by the financial and social exigencies of the 1930s and 1940s.

Both the bureaucrats and the legislators changed their views only gradually, and often with considerable reluctance. They reacted negatively and often harshly to the demands of the organized elderly and to individual behaviour that officials usually regarded as fraudulent in intent. Any formal program changes were slow in coming, and entailed no fundamental rethinking of the character of the OAP program at the legislative level until the end of the 1940s. But at the administrative level, both provincially and federally, there was an almost constant, albeit usually implicit, reconsideration of the program's basic principles throughout its twenty-four-year history. It was at the administrative level, particularly locally, that the results of the often harsh limitations of the program were witnessed in individual human terms.

The conjunction of at least four developments forced a continuing reconsideration of the OAP program. First, popular attitudes and perceptions of the elderly and aging sustained a growing acceptance of the need for a broader program. Second, the difficult circumstances of individual elderly generated considerable sympathy for the elderly as a group, particularly in urban areas. This concern was driven by a widespread awareness in the 1930s of poverty among the elderly, and in the 1940s of the rapid rise in the cost of living and, more generally, by the increasingly common mandatory retirement.[1] Third, a growing sense of the potential role of the state and of the appropriateness of such a role emboldened both the bureaucrats and the public supporters of an expanded OAP program. Finally, the organized elderly pressured both administrators and the press, and helped to keep the deficiencies of the program on the political agenda. The force of these factors pushed bureaucrats, urban officials, influential individuals, and the elderly themselves to reconsider the terms of the program and to 'nibble at the edges,' in order to adjust the Old Age Pension program more effectively to meet the needs of the elderly and the expectations of an increasing proportion of society. More than anything else, it was this interactive process throughout the 1930s and 1940s that led to the fundamental changes of 1951 when universality was adopted.

Yet the policy changes went beyond the fundamental revamping of the OAP program. The broad acceptance of the culture of entitlement by the public led to the expansion of support for the elderly. The state was no longer responsible merely for minimal monetary support. Claims to health care, to reduced-cost services, and to new forms of institutional care reflected an expanding culture of entitlement. The citizen's wage now entailed a broad range of state-supported services due to all the elderly.

Administrative Structures

The local administration of the OAP was central to its history. Although by 1931 Ottawa paid 75 per cent of the pension itself, and its inspectors and auditors were increasingly careful in examining provincial accounts, files and regulations, the federal government had little real power in forcing local authorities to adopt practices or policies favoured in Ottawa. Apart from appeals to the authority of the actual legislation, or to practices in other provinces and the bureaucratic ideal of uniformity, federal officials could simply cajole, prod, and plead for their beliefs. The real power lay closer to the actual pensioners. Every province designated a board or commission to administer the OAP program. Several provinces initially required municipalities to share in the provincial portion of the OAP program's costs, and made use of existing municipal officials to administer

parts of the program. Local officials were particularly useful for interview-
ing applicants and for checking on pensioners' continuing eligibility, but,
as far as the relatively rigid federal observers were concerned, this system
tended not to work well.[2] In the mid-1930s Ontario exemplified the pattern of change when it abandoned its scheme of local committees and centralized the assessment of applications for all but a handful of large cities.
Nevertheless, local officials continued to play a role, so that the multiple
levels of administration – federal, provincial, and local – all continued to be
important.

Manitoba offers a useful example of the administrative structure. The
province assigned the existing Workmen's Compensation Board responsibility for the Old Age Pension. Individual cases were investigated at application in two different ways. In Winnipeg the municipal social welfare
officers inspected the circumstances of the applicant and recommended
whether a pension should be granted and at what level. Elsewhere in the
province, the board used largely untrained agents of the Retail Credit Association, on a contract basis, to perform the same task. The board examined each individual case before a decision was reached, relying heavily on
the accuracy of the information submitted on the forms and on the inspector's report. Manitoba was one of the provinces that charged a portion of the
OAP costs against the local municipality, and, as a result, municipal councils could make recommendations regarding the applicants and the program.[3] 'Fortunately,' commented one federal official, 'the Board pays little
attention to the recommendations of the municipal councils which are, as
a general rule, contrary to the terms of the Act and the Regulations.'[4]

Several pension boards prided themselves on their approachability. The
head of the British Columbia board, for example, bragged of the extent to
which his staff aided applicants in completing their claims. The most important cog in dealing with the individual west coast elderly was Mrs Philippa
Reid, a clerk whose job it was to interview prospective pensioners who
came to the Vancouver office and to help them fill out their applications.
Later Mrs Reid added some field work to her job. Though untrained, she
was particularly adept at handling the personal relations inherent in her
tasks.[5] Within the constraints and limitations of the bureaucratic environment and of the statutory boundaries, the provincial pension boards and
their staff generally adopted a sympathetic attitude to the plight of the elderly in general and to the individual problems that daily passed across their
desks.

In Ontario the application process emphasized the influence of local individuals.[6] City boards operated under the direct control of local city coun-

cils. In all local boards, county or municipal clerks filled out their own report on each applicant, a form that consistently called for a subjective appraisal of the applicant's merits. The form asked clerks whether they were
'satisfied' regarding much of the information provided by the applicant.
After describing the support, care, health, and living conditions of the applicant, the clerks were to report on their investigation of the applicant's
children and their ability to provide support. At another point the clerk
was invited to comment on the 'manner of living' of the applicants or their
children. The results of the clerk's 'careful and full investigation' of the applicant's property and assets were followed in the report by the clerk's comments on the applicant's 'habits and ability' regarding the 'proper' spending
of a pension. Finally, the form asked clerks not only to provide their own
reasons why a pension should be granted or refused, but also to pass on the
second-hand comments of 'disinterested persons' in this regard. The entire
form gave the local clerk a potent authority, even after the handling of
pensions had become highly centralized.

The application process was not only judgmental but also intrusive. Ontario applicants were asked to sign Form C 'Access to [Bank] Account of
Pensioner,' allowing the provincial board or its representatives to have access to any bank accounts or any assets held in trust for them. This permission applied from the time of application through to the end of the receipt
of the pension. Before the assessment of applications was centralized, a variety of individuals inspected potential pensioners. In one Lambton County
township, for example, a local real estate agent supplemented his income
by carrying out investigations for the county board.[7] Bank officials in all
provinces seemed ready to cooperate with such investigations, whether or
not the OAP applicant had granted permission.

In 1933, 1935, and 1937 the Ontario government introduced changes aim-
ing to centralize control, increase efficiency, and standardize decision-mak-
ing. With this centralization, the provincial bureaucracy grew considerably.
In 1936 there was an office staff of just twenty-one clerks, and no inspectors except in the five largest cities, although two years later there were
fifty-three trained women, operating as field investigators. By 1949 the
Ontario board had an office staff of 190; there were a further 150 full-time
investigators, though these handled all mothers' allowances cases, too.[8] A
confused local bureaucracy had gradually given way to an extensive provincial administrative structure.

Despite all the cumbersome rules and procedures for acquiring a pension, the setting of a payment level by the expanding bureaucracy could be
impressively arbitrary and imprecise. Provincial pension authorities had

their own well understood policies regarding standard sets of circumstances. There was a strong tendency among all authorities to establish payment levels at numerically convenient amounts. Every province centred on these basic levels of payment: $5, $10, $15, or $20.[9] For all the evidence of detailed examination of cases, assets, and incomes, the result tended strongly to be imprecise, at least as reflected in the actual payments made monthly.

Rural pensioners were treated differently from their urban counterparts. Most rural elderly had some farm land, and the usual assumption made by officials was that this land was important in maintaining the elderly. Pension staff believed that regardless of the surrounding economic conditions, such rural residents could count on their vegetable garden and whatever livestock they had to put food on the table on a regular basis. The views of the senior federal OAP official were paraphrased in support of this stance: '$20.00 in a city, especially in a large city, is not so good as $15.00 in the country districts ... A man in a city either has a job or he has not. A man on a farm always has a job and can provide himself with assistance that is not obtainable in the cities.' As a result, in New Brunswick, for example, a rural resident could expect a maximum payment level of $15, rather than $20. At least in part, this helped to explain the relatively low provincial average in a province such as New Brunswick, where the rural population was proportionately large. British Columbia, which had a relatively small rural population, was normally the province with the highest average payment.[10]

The application of this sort of policy is easily appreciated. A seventy-year-old unmarried woman in Lambton County, for example, had looked after her father until he died; now she lived free of charge in a house owned by her brother-in-law. From her garden she could keep herself in some foods, and annually earned $40 from vegetables sold. She was recommended for a pension, 'but [the clerk] did not think she should get the full amount as she has a large garden and can raise most of her living.'[11] Regardless of their actual income and of the terms of pension legislation, therefore, individual elderly could expect to receive a pension that reflected officials' judgment of each applicant's needs.

Some county boards reinforced this rural bias by being particularly 'tight' with funds in the early period, often reflecting a harsher rural view of the state's limited obligations. In 1930 a federal official reported that in nine Ontario counties and two districts, no pensioners were receiving more than $15 a month, as a result of the decision that this level of support was sufficient in these areas. In some cases where both husband and wife applied for a pension, one was accepted and the other rejected, or both were paid only $10.[12] That year the Dufferin County board explained that its decisions were based on its assessment of the applicants' actual needs, rather than on the provisions of the legislation, which were often more generous. Where applicants owned their own home or lived with friends and had more than $500 in available cash assets, 'they are in really no immediate want, and in all probability would not be applying had not some pressure been brought on them by others who might benefit thereby ... While our decisions are probably not according to the act we believe the applicants are getting justice.'[13] Rural officials had different standards and expectations from their urban counterparts, and they applied these to OAP applicants.

It is in rural communities that the OAP program's role in the spectrum of social relationships becomes most apparent. Pension applications required an initial inspection/report and, in theory, an annual re-examination. Applicants had to furnish the names of two referees, who were almost always influential local personages. For the Lambton County sample, these referees were analysed. Although 44 per cent of the applicants were women, fully 93 per cent of the referees named were men.[14] Occupations were listed for only sixty-five referees, but almost all of those had high status: eighteen clergy, fourteen doctors, five merchants; only six blue-collar workers were named, along with one housewife. This scrutinizing and judging of the dependent elderly by their social and economic 'superiors' was important in confirming and strengthening the status and influence of authoritative local individuals. New Brunswick's assessment of OAP applicants, for example, was described as follows:

We have throughout the Province a number of responsible citizens whom we use as what might be termed 'key men.' These persons serve without any remuneration whatever in their several localities and generally are acquainted with every pensioner and his circumstances. They are merchants, clergymen or other professional men who take a deep interest in this matter of old age pensions and, with their assistance, it is quite possible to reach a conclusion with reference to a very large proportion of our pensioners. Our investigators make a personal contact with these key men on their frequent trips through the different localities.[15]

The local character of the OAP process was thus of central importance, facilitating a reinforcement not simply of age hierarchies but also of gender, ethnic, and class hierarchies as fundamental to the structure of local society.[16]

Officials administered a restricted and narrow program of support for only the most needy elderly in the provinces joining the early OAP program.

Provincial and federal policies implemented an aggressive insistence on familial support and on the state's claims to pensioners' property. In the early years of the program and across the 1930s, there was little change in these policies, both because they accurately reflected the views of the bureaucrats and legislators and because the financial exigencies of the 1930s forced officials to insist even more on operating the least costly program possible.

Changing Popular Attitudes

Public pressure to extend the parameters and the benefits of the OAP program in the 1930s took place within a discourse of expanded state responsibilities for a considerable spectrum of society. Old people were simply one of the targets of new state initiatives. Arguments for greater state programs were based on a mixture of motives: genuine altruism and a sense of social justice, political and economic financial expediency, the gains to be made by others as a result of new programs, and a blunt desire to shift costs. Social insurance in its various forms, as Alvin Finkel has pointed out, 'was intended to stabilize a destablized economy and not necessarily to redistribute wealth.'[17]

This rising public interest in expanded state responsibilities began soon after the introduction of the OAP program, and could be found among diverse groups and individuals. The elderly were frequent targets of this discussion of the state's role. As common subjects of relief programs, removal of the elderly to the more regularlized OAP program would lessen the burden on municipal and provincial treasuries. What was more, such a shift would take the 'less deserving' elderly from the paid workforce, opening up opportunities for their younger counterparts, who were perceived more often to have familial burdens. The availability of an OAP allowed employers to feel much easier about releasing elderly workers where no private pension plans existed (as in most cases). Early in 1930, for example, the Canadian Patriotic Fund urged the Interprovincial Old Age Pensions Board to allow the fund to supplement the OAP payment without the supplement being taken into account in the calculation of pensioners' income eligibility. The Canadian Manufacturers' Association presented a similar argument on behalf of private pensions: the OAP should be paid to anyone eligible who was receiving an industrial pension, and the employer should be allowed to supplement the OAP payment to the amount of the industrial pension without the supplement being taken into account by OAP authorities.[18] Both groups shared some important attitudes. They sought ways to increase the level of support for the elderly, certainly implying that the OAP payments were less than adequate. They sought to make the OAP basic to all other forms of support, accepting the fundamental role of the state in this area. Finally, they challenged the basic concept of a maximum allowable income, replacing it with the idea of a minimum income, a key concept in social policy administration.

But in the early years of the OAP program such sentiments were not widespread among politically influential elements. Provincial and federal officials largely shared a similar viewpoint regarding the philosophy behind the OAP program, one that reflected the traditions of welfare discussed in chapter 2 – less eligibility and cost-consciousness. A federal official congratulated the Prince Edward Island staff on their early administration of the program: 'They seem determined to keep the total number [of pensioners] within 1200. I do not think that there will be much room for argument [between the two governments], as they are cutting very closely and none but indigents are receiving pensions.' The Island board was quite blunt about how it determined payment levels: officials decided the amount of each pension 'arbitrarily'; if they believed that any applicants could live 'comfortably' on a particular amount, that was what they received, even though they might be entitled to a higher sum under the regulations.[19] The early OAP program was based on a more discretionary needs test, rather than a simple means test, thereby increasing the power of local officials.

The early years of the 1930s Depression initially reinforced such traditional attitudes among most officials and politicians. The financial exigencies of the Depression pushed officials to even greater insistence on tight fiscal controls. The British Columbia minister of finance is a good example. When he received his officials' 1933–4 estimates for the pension program, he was appalled: 'It is altogether beyond the policy of this Province to meet this list and I must ask the Board to go into this matter very fully and endeavour to get the amounts reduced. I cannot believe that the requirements for Old Age Pensions reach an amount of this nature. The most rigid inspection and supervision will have to be exercised in checking up the list, and I sincerely hope that the investigators under the Old Age Pensions Department are carrying on a rigid inspection. It is beyond any Government to keep on meeting increasing costs of this kind.' As one means of cutting the number of pensioners, he urged the board to gain access to personal income tax reports to ascertain those claiming to support individual elderly.[20] In the early years, most officials of the provincial and federal governments shared a similar philosophy regarding the OAP program.

This common outlook eventually dissolved under the pressure of a number of forces. Encouraged by the elderly themselves, popular attitudes led the way in sustaining serious doubts about the levels of support offered by the OAP. The head of the Nova Scotia board reported in 1940 that 'there is a good deal of opinion in this Province, and I believe elsewhere in the Dominion, to the effect that there is altogether too much red tape, too much niggardliness, and too much of the "accounting" stamp on our system. It may be that in our zeal to comply with Mr. Dunning's urgent request for economy that we have gone a little too far.'[21] A federal official agreed about public opinion: on the west coast 'for years' there had been 'a deep rooted conviction by the general public' that the OAP benefits ought to be raised. By the early 1940s, west coast pensioners were especially effective in complaining 'of their plight to the heads of fraternal societies, service clubs, etc,' who were all too aware themselves of the rising cost of living. There the press, especially in Vancouver, played a particularly vocal role in persuading the public that the program was mean-spirited and that pensioners had a need and a right to more benefits.[22] Resolutions came forward from such organizations as the Union of Manitoba Municipalities in 1943, and the four western provincial legislatures in 1941–2.[23]

The elderly had been active enough in articulating their views that local and provincial officials began to be intimidated. When the maximum monthly payment level rose to $25 in 1943, Manitoba officials reported that while over 80 per cent of pensioners would qualify for the entire $5 increase, 19 per cent would not, and those pensioners 'will all nurse what is to them a substantial grievance.'[24] The idea of grievance implies the existence of a popular notion of pensioners' right individually to all increases; among pensioners the OAP was no longer regarded as a program to help differentially those with fewer assets or lower income, but rather as a program that ought to provide aid equally to all. The line between the needy elderly and other elderly was becoming blurred. The elderly believed they had a right to their 'citizen's wage,' and were increasingly prepared to fight for it.

This popular support for a much broader OAP program was shared by the majority of Canadians across the country. Stimulated further by the expansion of the state during the war – unemployment insurance, family allowances, rationing, wage and price controls, conscription – the same political and economic expediency as in the 1930s continued to push public support for a more generous OAP program that would move the elderly more fully to the economic 'sidelines' and into an increasingly well-understood social category.[25] In the 1940s the Canadian Institute of Public Opinion polled adults repeatedly for their views about the OAP. There was a consistent and rapid trend in the postwar years towards approval of universality by abolishing the means test and towards a higher payment level.

TABLE 7.1 Canadian views on the OAP payment level, 1943–51

Maximum amount	1943	1946	1949	1950	1951
		per cent			
$20 or less	7	1 }	5	1	1
$21–30	38	12 }			
$31–40	30	21	11	11	10
$41–50	13	27	29	29	27
$51 or more	10	34	47	52	53
Qualified answers }		2			
	2		8	7	9
No opinion }		3			
Total	100	100	100	100	100
Maximum paid at time of poll ($)	20	25	30	40	40

Source: Canadian Institute of Public Opinion, polls of 29 May 1943, 20 November 1946, 15 April 1950, 24 February 1951

Public opinion consistently supported an earlier age than the program itself adopted.

Throughout the decade there was widespread sympathy for the economic plight of the elderly poor. A late 1942 poll revealed strong support for a cost-of-living bonus for the pensioners; 84 per cent of respondents nationally approved of such a measure, with support being markedly lower in the Maritime provinces and in Quebec than in the rest of the country.[26] In the following years support for a more generous payment level for the basic pension grew rapidly, running consistently far ahead of government action (see table 7.1). It was among those most likely to feel the immediate impact of the rising cost of living – young adults and persons living in large cities – that support for a more generous pension level was strongest throughout the period. In keeping with the culture of entitlement, income tax payers were noticeably more likely to support a high level of payment.[27] Similarly, there was widespread and growing support for ending the means test and moving to universality, particularly in the years immediately preceding the enactment of the universal program (see table 7.2). Support was especially strong among organized labour, residents of Ontario and British Columbia, and supporters of the socialist CCF.[28] Public opinion was massively behind a more generous program for the elderly.

TABLE 7.2 Canadian views on abolishing the OAP means test, 1946–51

	Nov. 1946	April 1950	Oct. 1950	Oct. 1951*
		per cent		
Pension for everyone	34	38	55	81
Pension only for those with no other means of support	58	50	43	8†
Don't approve of OAP at all	n/a	‡	1	n/a
Qualified answers	6	‡	‡	9§
Undecided	2	‡	1	2
Total	100	‡	100	100

n/a: Category not asked
* While the questions for the other polls were consistent, for this poll respondents were simply asked whether they approved of the recently adopted universal pension program.
† 17 per cent of respondents disapproved of the new pension plan; without providing the figures, it was reported that 'nearly half' of those disapproving of the new pension plan did so because there was no means test.
‡ Information not provided
§ 17 per cent of respondents disapproved of the new pension plan; without providing the figures, it was reported that other than the 'nearly half' who disapproved of the removal of the means test, the remainder had a variety of criticisms, including that the age limit should be lower or the payment level should be higher.

Source: Canadian Institute of Public Opinion Polls, 23 November 1946, 15 April 1950, 14 October 1950, 24 October 1951

This support for a more expansive program extended to a broader definition of the elderly. While the polls demonstrated no significant change in the age at which the OAP ought to begin (see table 7.3), a large majority – around 85 per cent – consistently believed that the qualifying age should be lower than seventy. The OAP was a vehicle through which the public construction of old age could be extended in significant ways.

At least as striking was the extensive character of public opinion on the topic of the Old Age Pension program. The number of respondents reporting no opinion was remarkably low for a public opinion poll, particularly concerning the means test and the pensionable age. This was a subject of which almost all Canadians were well aware, and which they had thought about enough to have considered opinions. And although there remained important areas of disagreement, it is fundamentally important that fully 98 per cent of Canadians supported a state Old Age Pension system by October 1950. State programs for the elderly, and more generally the elderly

TABLE 7.3 Canadian views on qualification age for OAP, 1946, 1950

Pension age	1946	1950
	per cent	
50	2	2
55	4	3
60	39	34
65	41	45
70	6	6
Miscellaneous	5	5
No opinion	3	5
Total	100	100

Source: Canadian Institute of Public Opinion Polls, 23 November 1946, 15 April 1950

themselves, had moved to a central position in the social and political consciousness of the nation. As a result of such attitudes, in the later 1930s and across the 1940s the OAP program gradually inched back from a needs-tested to a means-tested basis, and informally began to move in the direction of universality in its application.

As the changing popular views regarding the means test suggest, the element of the OAP program subjected to the most fundamental and continuing challenge over the period was the question of who was to receive such a pension. The means test faced the most frequent public challenges, though the issue of eligibility was also fundamental to most discussions of the program. As table 7.2 suggests, there was a considerable shift among the general populace in favour of a universal OAP. That shift was driven in part by the proliferation of state support programs during the 1930s and 1940s and by the continuing insistence among families and the elderly that the state pension be considered separately from the property and possibly even the income of OAP applicants.

The 'Citizen's Wage'

The OAP had been the first great social welfare program when it was established, but by the mid-1940s a number of other programs had surpassed it in generosity and character. Unemployment insurance, war dependents' allowances, cost-of-living bonuses in war industries, and family allowances had played a fundamental role in reshaping Canadians' view of the state and of its social support programs. Citizens contributed much to the state in the form of high income taxes, and they relinquished considerable freedom, accepting rationing as well as wage and price controls. In return, a 'social safety net' of state assistance programs offered support to various groups. The extent and liberality of these other programs made the OAP program, legislatively unchanged since 1927, appear even more parsimonious and anachronistic.[29] It was not difficult for either the elderly or the general public to see that the OAP program required considerable reform to a number of its features – and implicitly to its basic philosophy – as the OAP program moved closer to becoming the 'citizen's wage.'

Some quite specific bureaucratic problems reflected the growing attack on both the payment level and on the means test. The proliferation of state benefits programs in the 1930s and 1940s frequently gave rise to the question of what should be considered eligible income in applying the means test to pensioners. In the early years the answer was straightforward: everything. With such programs as veterans' pensions, the response was clear and readily forthcoming, but soon more complicated benefits were being distributed. On the prairies in particular there were extended debates about which farm benefits should be considered personal income, and which support for an industry. Schemes such as the wheat acreage reduction bonus, the prairie farm income payments, and the prairie farm assistance payments caused endless headaches among officials at different levels.[30] Elderly veterans of the First World War were eligible for veterans' pensions, and so too were their dependent parents. Old people could not receive both the OAP and the veterans' pension, and the Canadian Pension Commission declared that it was willing to raise its payments to any eligible elderly to a level that would render the individual ineligible for the OAP.[31]

During the Second World War, dependents' allowances and assigned pay complicated the pension levels of many recipients. Many elderly lost important support from sons or daughters when they enlisted; some provincial OAP officials received 'extremely vicious' comments about such financial losses. If a member of the armed forces assigned a stipulated portion of his pay to his mother or his widowed father, the parent became eligible to receive a dependents' allowance if the parent qualified as dependent. Sons used this ploy as a means of gaining additional income for their parents and of accumulating savings for themselves after the war; though the pay was technically assigned to the parent, there was often an understanding within the family that these funds would be used for the son – savings for his future, payments on insurance policies, or purchase of goods to be sent off to the soldier. Others assigned the pay in order to qualify for the allowance, but expected their parents to send the pay to them overseas. This sort of cooperative, family financial manoeuvring at the expense of the state not only paralleled some of the individual actions to qualify for the OAP, but also left the authorities in a quandary on how to assess such income. In some cases the soldiers felt that they had a right to send funds to their parents without affecting their OAP payment levels – that is, that the parents' actual income ought not to affect the level of payment.[32]

But there was more to this than the problem of how to compute income. The state's obligation to assist the elderly was coming to be seen as distinct from internal family activities and support. Many soldiers and elderly parents were 'deeply offended,' reported a Nova Scotia official, by state intrusion into internal family affairs; 'in the minds of most people the money assigned by a soldier to his parents is not in a strict sense "pay" or "wages." It is so small in comparison with the earnings of civilians, and earned under such conditions, that to regard [it as] other than a gift from a soldier boy to his parents is considered the very epitome of heartlessness.'[33] Beneath the sentimentality of such a viewpoint lay a fundamental attitude of vital importance – small contributions from adult children to their elderly parents should be irrelevant in the provision of the 'citizen's wage.' The state should adopt no policy that might discourage closer contact and greater support among elderly parents and their children. Furthermore, while federal officials regarded the dependents' allowance and the OAP as programs to guarantee minimum social support where required, many recipients and their families saw such programs differently: the state had an obligation to distribute funds in these programs equitably, and everyone had a right to a share. Within the context of each program, public attitudes led increasingly to a belief in universality.

This was complemented by the increased value placed on privacy. A Saskatchewan woman wrote to her provincial premier describing a social call on a local pensioner. While the woman was visiting, the OAP inspector arrived and questioned the woman pensioner, after which the visitor described her own response:

I says to the beautiful aged lady is that democracy. *oh no* she says thats humiliation she cried & says you cant even have a few hundred dollars in case you are in your declining years a burden to some one. I never realized we lived in a country supposed to be Christian for aged people to have to be taken to task for every dollar they possessed after denying themselves all their younger days. I dont think there was anything that poor old soul possessed but she had to give an account for.

When she followed up on this 'frightening' experience, the visitor claimed that many pensioners told similar stories.

The way they are questioned about every dollar even how much they have in the house spells discord & unhappiness for them all and as he drove away in his big car well she says if I spent my few hundred dollars in a car like that where would I have anything to pay my funeral expenses.[34]

This emphasis on privacy and on not investigating too rigorously led naturally to support for more general regulations applied to groups rather than to individuals.

A number of provincial and local officials, particularly in urban centres, agreed at least as regards giving the maximum to those applying, and began to implement policies reflective of this attitude. Alberta authorities felt strongly enough about this to challenge the federal government to a direct, public confrontation on the issue. The provincial board refused to consider assigned pay from soldiers as pensioners' income. When federal officials in 1941 threatened to consider these pensions as overpayments and to deduct them from federal transfer payments, the Alberta officials conceded that they had foreseen this possibility and that they were willing to absorb the additional costs if Ottawa was willing to risk an open clash on this issue between the two governments. The board explicitly adopted the point of view of the elderly – since 'the old people do not consider A.P. & D.A. [Assigned Pay and Dependents' Allowance] as income' – and ignored such payments wherever possible, absolutely refusing to charge individual pensioners for overpayments.[35] By the end of the Second World War even federal officials argued that mothers' allowances and family allowances should be exempted from such income calculations.[36] For the means test the implications of these developments were fundamental.

Evidence of this developing trend towards more generous standards for granting an Old Age Pension is suggested by figure 4.1 (page 115). The proportion of the elderly population receiving an OAP varied considerably over time and place. Clearly provincial policies and criteria differed, New Brunswick elderly having consistently easier access to a pension than did members of the same cohort in either of the other Maritime provinces, for example. As each province entered the program in the 1930s, a higher percentage of the local elderly than in the other provinces tended to be included in the program. This trend reached its most notable point with Newfoundland's entry into Confederation and the program in 1949 – within a year more than three-quarters of all Newfoundland elderly had been ruled eligible and were receiving a monthly federal OAP cheque. Similar views arose among American OAP officials at the same time, pointing to the international character of these changing attitudes and policies.[37]

More stringent policies in some provinces such as British Columbia during the Depression brought about a noticeable shrinkage in the proportion of pensioned elderly locally, as did the increased availability of employment during the Second World War. But generally the trend towards greater numbers of pensioners is apparent. In 1930 there were just 42,553 pensioners across the country, but by the end of the decade, after all existing provinces had joined in, fully 186,035 elderly received a monthly OAP cheque. After a period of almost no growth during the war, a massive expansion occurred in the last five years of the 1940s, so that by 1951 more than 47 per cent of those aged seventy or older were Old Age Pensioners (see figure 4.1).[38] The number of pensioners and the generally rising proportion of the elderly involved suggest just how fundamental the OAP was becoming to the elderly.

Further evidence of changing attitudes among provincial and local authorities is available in the average monthly OAP payment (see figure 7.1). In the 1930s there were striking differences among the provinces, with the three Maritime provinces tending to pay well below the maximum. In 1937, for example, when all nine provinces had joined the program, the average provincial payments were quite disparate. By 1945 those differences had shrunk markedly, as all provinces but Prince Edward Island moved strongly towards the maximum level. In every province there had been movement towards the maximum possible payment, and in some provinces – Saskatchewan, Nova Scotia, New Brunswick, and Prince Edward Island – significant movement. This trend continued in the following years.

This same tendency to grant increasingly high levels of payment is also reflected in the average national OAP payment in the 1940s. While in the mid-1930s the average national payments had ranged between 86 and 87 per cent of the maximum, in the second half of the 1940s they ranged between 95 and 98 per cent of the maximum possible pension.[39] The elderly as a social group attracted not just considerable sympathy, but meaningful and substantial support.

The courts, too, expressed changing attitudes towards the OAP program. In the early years provincial superior courts showed no desire to supervise the provincial boards' determination of pensioners' eligibility. But by the 1940s the courts' stance had changed somewhat. A British Columbia decision decisively restricted that board's authority to limit pensioners' eligibility, and a Quebec court held that the provincial board had no legal standing in a case involving the distribution of the pension in a particular instance, while

FIGURE 7.1 Average monthly OAP payment, 1937, 1945, 1948

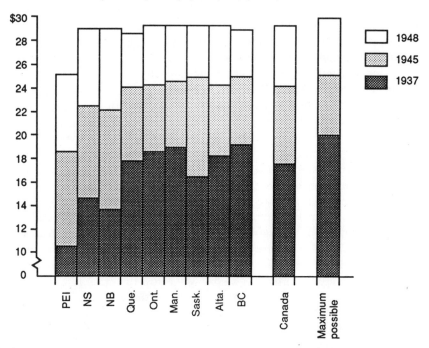

Source: Calculated from NA, RG 29, vol. 126, no. 208-1-4. These figures are for 31 March and do not include the provincial supplements, which by 1945 had increased the level of total monthly payments in all provinces except New Brunswick, Quebec, and Prince Edward Island.

other judgments upheld particular aspects of the boards' statutory authority.[40] Increasingly the bureaucratic authority of provincial boards was limited, particularly in British Columbia where popular pressure was strongest.

At least as important was the courts' growing tendency to find in favour of pensioners in legal contests with the provincial boards. Though the right of the dependent elderly to the OAP was never directly tested, those elderly already with a pension took provincial authorities to court several times to challenge the boards' power to interfere with the pension once granted. A 1932 British Columbia court had described the pension as a 'gift' from the state, part of a 'humane' program to which an individual had no claim as of right. But by the late 1930s new attitudes were apparent. The courts repeatedly insisted that the actual needs of the individual elderly took priority over any particular regulations. By 1942 the British Columbia courts had overruled their own precedent, holding that once granted the OAP was the pensioner's by right.[41] The changing rulings of Canadian courts thus reflected the attitudes found elsewhere in the country about the OAP.

Federal-Provincial Tensions

In the spring of 1935 the Conservative government in Ottawa made a significant change in the administration of the OAP, seeking to bring fiscal responsibility to the increasingly costly government program. The OAP program moved from the labour department to the powerful Department of Finance, where systematic financial analysis of such an expensive program could be assured. The finance department immediately instituted much more thorough federal audits of each provincial OAP board, and these continued in the following years. To understand the operation of the system better, the department assigned federal officials to accompany Nova Scotia inspectors on their visits to OAP applicants in 1935.

This departmental initiative received firm, influential leadership. The powerful deputy minister of finance, W.C. Clark, took a hands-on interest in the OAP program, corresponding actively with provincial administrators and challenging their practices repeatedly. He was, Clark informed the head of one provincial board, particularly concerned about 'abuses' in the administration of the program. He correctly perceived that the most vulnerable point in that administration was at the local level, where community leaders ('who have a particular object in view in securing a pension') could have undue influence; a system of 'qualified, independent inspectors' was essential to counteract the potentially irresponsible attitudes and conduct of such local individuals.[42] These views meshed nicely with a shift in the ideology about welfare, away from the paternalism of local notables and élites to what was seen as a more neutral and 'scientific' state-based assessment. Led by the influential and highly respected Clark, Ottawa civil servants sought to bring order and responsibility to the administration of the OAP program, but they would meet their match in a group of informed and generally able provincial administrators who brought to the OAP program a quite different set of attitudes and expectations.[43]

Nova Scotia administered the OAP reasonably efficiently by Ottawa's standards, but with the 'new broom' of the Department of Finance there were certainly clashes between the two levels of administration. Ottawa bureaucrats placed primary emphasis on uniformity of interpretation and bureaucratic efficiency; Nova Scotia officials came closer to placing the pensioner first, interpreting the rules and regulations flexibly 'in the spirit of the Act.' 'I cannot conceive of any Government wishing to impose what is clearly a hardship on worthy people [by a rigid interpretation] and I do not believe that you or any official of the Government would want that done,' wrote the senior provincial official. But the federal officials responded that the uniform interpretations of the regulations 'seem on the whole to be fair and reasonable and although hard cases may perhaps arise, this is almost inevitable in legislation of this kind.'[44] The provincial board based many of its individual decisions on rulings handed down by the deputy attorney general who, complained a federal official with unintentional irony, 'apparently is convinced that the Act was intended to assist those in need and that a strictly legal viewpoint cannot be taken in all cases.'[45] Federal officials in these years, in contrast, tended to see the OAP program as designed to help specifically identified dependent elderly, rather than the needy elderly in general.

Such conflicting perceptions of the OAP program occurred elsewhere. Federal officials complained in the early 1930s that the Alberta board had 'taken certain liberties and in many cases completely ignored the Dominion Act' and that provincial auditing of the files was inefficient.[46] Local officials appear to have aimed to use the program to help alleviate the terrible hardships of the Depression. By deflecting the elderly poor onto the OAP rolls, local relief funds were freed to assist other groups. But more than that, many local authorities felt great empathy for the plight of the individual elderly, whose problems were brought home to these officials every day and who traditionally deserved respect on the basis of their age alone. The chairman of the Alberta board defended his officials against federal criticisms: 'I feel that the administration of Old Age Pensions in this Province is not only efficient but courteous, and, what is more important, humane, every consideration and courtesy being extended to applicants in view not only of their circumstances, but of their age.'[47] If overpayments were made to individual elderly, Alberta officials were willing to adjust the current payment level, but they strongly resisted any federal pressure to recover overpayments from the elderly.[48] When the federal deputy minister of finance questioned the large number of increases awarded to existing west coast pensioners in 1938, the chief provincial official defended the increases as deserved in every individual case; pensioners had often received the higher payments several months after becoming entitled to the increase. 'Might I suggest that the attitude we have adopted ... is the fairer course to take,' he concluded. 'In adopting this course, I don't think we could be accused of generosity but rather that we were meting out justice.'[49]

The use of words such as 'justice' and concepts such as fairness is an indication of just how fully provincial authorities believed in their approach.

Indeed, provincial authorities found support for their position in the law. E.S.H. Winn, the head of the British Columbia authority, wrote to his Nova Scotia counterpart in 1938 that it was a well-established rule of law that all remedial legislation, dealing with such matters as welfare or pensions, should be construed 'as liberally as possible': 'The law is not to be interpreted in a technical but in a popular sense.'[50] This liberal attitude began to take the OAP program towards more generous practices.

Where the elderly had organized, this attitude of generosity was even more firmly entrenched. At the height of a vociferous press campaign, led by the *Vancouver Sun* and by the Old Age Pensioners' Organization, on behalf of more generous pensions, Ottawa officials questioned an individual award made by the British Columbia board. Provincial officials bluntly challenged Ottawa's initial response, refused to alter their ruling without specific orders from Ottawa, and threatened to 'go public' with the dispute: 'the Board had in the past taken the brunt of all condemnation, but if Ottawa turned down this action we would feel free to give the information to the press.' Whereas relations between the board and the OAPO had been competitive in the 1930s, by the mid-1940s the organized elderly 'have at all times been met with genial courtesy, and willing co-operation,' in the words of one OAPO official. Board members appeared occasionally at OAPO meetings, and were able to announce the sort of changes to OAP regulations that the OAPO had been fighting for: up to ninety days absence from the country each year, no insistence on calculating income from adult children, greater tolerance for outside income.[51] Pushed by community opinion and by the views of such influential welfare figures as Harry Cassidy and George Weir, provincial officials on the west coast repeatedly adopted more generous stances than did Ottawa.

Organized elderly were not a necessary condition for such attitudes among provincial bureaucracies, however. Quebec is a good example. When the province joined the OAP program in 1936, provincial policy included fundamental challenges to the earlier philosophy behind the program. From the beginning, Quebec officials insisted that a pension ought to be paid to an applicant's estate when the applicant had died before a pension had been granted. This was a critical policy issue, because it suggested that the pension was not simply there to help the elderly in need but rather was a payment as of right.[52] This belief was quickly made explicit. When the provincial OAP legislation was amended in 1936, a new clause made the payment of the pension obligatory to anyone entitled to it. This reduced the discretionary power of officials to lower payment levels on the basis of perceived need and undermined the legitimacy of current practice in several jurisdictions, including all three Maritime provinces. Federal officials were disturbed enough by this prospect to ask law officers for an opinion. When the law officers agreed with Quebec's position, there was no choice but to accept that province's policy, but federal officials did nothing to push for change in the conflicting discriminatory policies elsewhere. The extent of Quebec's commitment to this position can be questioned, however, since in 1940 the board began to reduce the payment levels for some groups of pensioners.[53]

The one province that was an exception to this federal-provincial tension was Ontario. It is suggestive of Ontario's influence in Ottawa and its position as the leading source of federal revenue that its officials generally shared the views of the federal finance department after that department had taken control of the OAP program. The Ontario board maintained its usually parsimonious attitude towards pensioners longer than any other province, and stands as an important exception to developments in the pension boards in other provinces.

One main problem area for the dependent elderly where local administrative attitudes manifested themselves involved the residency qualifications. Not only were there specific limits on how long one could have been out of the country during the twenty years prior to application, but once a pension was granted, pensioners could be absent from the country for only a month before the pension was supposed to be suspended. This was particularly hard on those elderly with family members outside the country, most often in the United States. Such regulations prevented the elderly drawing on the emotional and physical support that distant relatives might offer. But provincial authorities were not always strict in enforcing these rules. In New Brunswick, for example, the pension cheques continued to be issued to anyone who merely went to the United States on a visit, even for several months. Only when the pensioner changed residence permanently were the cheques stopped.[54] Provincial officials insisted on ignoring federal regulations that had been accepted by the provincial government.

The extent to which local officials sought to assist the dependent elderly is reflected in case files. In one British Columbia case the file revealed that the applicant had not resided in Canada sufficiently long, since she had travelled to England twice over the previous sixteen years. In order to help this woman meet the residency requirements, the provincial board included the time spent travelling back and forth across the ocean, despite federal complaints. The British Columbia board argued that, until she had been granted entry to another country, she was still resident in Canada. When the provincial authorities refused to consider federal suggestions regarding such cases, federal officials contemplated an ultimatum threatening refusal to pay the federal share.[55] In an Ontario case, London welfare officials argued with provincial authorities on behalf of a local man whose age was in dispute. According to the board in Toronto, the man had received his pension several years too early; although now entitled to receive the OAP, his payment would be cut in half to $10 monthly until the $1892.79 overpayment had been met. London officials argued that he was physically unable to supplement his pension through employment, that there was good reason to believe he was older than the board said, and requested that the case be reinvestigated and his pension raised at least to a level to pay his board.[56]

Urban local officials led the way in articulating and enforcing a more liberal interpretation of the OAP program. Their proximity to the elderly themselves gave them an understanding of the group's problems and needs. The needy urban elderly often had fewer resources than their rural counterparts, and had a higher proportion of women, who had even fewer resources. In addition, urban observers often had a more expansive view of the state's role. At the same time, it is important to point out that the distribution of the OAP program's costs encouraged the manifestation of the local officials' sympathies. London, Ontario, officials, for example, were anxious that welfare recipients apply for an OAP as soon as possible, and they facilitated the transfer of these persons from city rolls to the OAP program. Rural officials, who might be considered most closely in touch with pensioners, were often much less sympathetic than urban officials, reflecting some of the more traditional values of self-help, less-eligibility, and familial primacy.

The fundamental provincial philosophy of using the OAP to help the needy elderly as a group continued throughout the period. When Newfoundland was preparing to join Canada in 1949, for example, the provincial board adopted its own method of calculating the payment levels on the explicit ground that this was potentially more advantageous to pensioners.[57] The director of the Saskatchewan board challenged the basic philosophy of the OAP legislation and regulations in 1946. The rules required the board to penalize those elderly who had frugally managed to save, and to reward those who had been profligate, he argued; perhaps the time had come to standardize the pension amount regardless of assets.[58] This was but one of many indications of the growing support for a more generous OAP program, one that was beginning to treat all elderly the same regardless of their financial circumstances.

Finances were absolutely fundamental in driving this bureaucratic and governmental stance at the local and provincial level in favour of generous terms to the elderly. The federal government paid 75 per cent of the cost of the OAP program for most of its life, so it was in its fiscal interest to try to keep costs down. This was particularly so throughout the Depression years, during the Second World War, and in the early years of reconstruction, when cost-consciousness was pronounced. It was in the interest of local and provincial politicians, in contrast, to be generous, because this transferred dependent individuals who would otherwise rely entirely on relief payments from local and provincial governments.

Local officials were occasionally quite forthright about this factor. When a Lambton County man applied for a pension in 1935, the county clerk recommended the applicant on the grounds that he was a 'man of good habits and high character ... Pension should be granted so that he will not become a charge on the municipality.' A seventy-year-old married woman partially incapacitated by a stroke was recommended by the town clerk for a pension in 1941 because, 'if not granted [she] would have to be given relief from municipality.'[59] In another case an elderly wife and husband were both pensioners; they had no assets and no income other than their pensions, their five married children offering little support. Having been burnt out of their previous accommodation, they took a room with a woman in Petrolia 'who has been keeping them for their pension,' according to the town clerk. Nevertheless, the provincial board felt it had grounds for reducing their payment level to $8.67 each per month, to which the town clerk objected because the couple would then become a charge on the town.[60] Such financial motivations were strengthened when several provinces ended the responsibility of municipalities for a portion of OAP costs – Ontario on 1 April 1937.

Provincial officials had crucial leverage in their confrontations with the federal government; they could appeal to the growing public opinion in support of a more generous interpretation of OAP regulations. From the beginning of the program, the British Columbia board had distributed the 31 December pension cheques so that they were in pensioners' hands in time for Christmas. In 1936 the federal officials challenged this practice as unwise, arguing that some of the recipients might die before the end of the month and the funds could often not be recovered. Provincial officials defended the practice on the grounds that it allowed pensioners to enjoy Christmas celebrations and that actual losses were low. Provincial authorities did agree to cease the practice if the federal officials insisted, but warned that British Columbia pensioners would be informed that the change had been the result of an Ottawa ruling. Federal officials backed down at this point.[61] When pushed by provincial officials who saw the individual results of arbitrary rules, federal officials could give way and adjust rules to take fuller account of the actual circumstances of potential pensioners.[62]

Some members of the increasingly authoritative social work profession joined with provincial officials to push for a more generous OAP program. After serving as the director of social research at McGill University for a decade, Leonard Marsh became research adviser to the federal government's advisory committee on reconstruction in 1941. By early 1943 Marsh's *Report on Social Security for Canada* had been written and presented to the House of Commons. Often hailed as the Canadian equivalent to England's Beveridge report, the Marsh report recommended important changes to existing OAP provisions. Among all the various social security schemes discussed, only in the case of the OAP program, he correctly pointed out, was there 'a full acknowledgement of social responsibility' by all ten federal and provincial governments. Nevertheless, Marsh criticised the various governments for failing to develop a program designed to 'meet this responsibility in a socially satisfactory manner.' The current restrictive practices and philosophy, he recommended, should be altered by removing 'many of the unjustifiable restrictions as to eligibility' associated with fictive income, residency, and citizenship, and by increasing the maximum pension payment. There should also be flexibility as to the age at which the OAP commenced, allowing both an earlier starting age and a premium-induced deferred age. More fundamentally, Marsh pushed for a transition to a state-operated, contributory pension program to cover all Canadians in their old age.[63] The status of the report as a state document and as a blueprint for postwar reconstruction policy regarding social programs helped to legitimate the existing trend towards a new OAP scheme.

By the mid-1940s even federal officials had caught some of the new attitude regarding the elderly. The deputy minister of welfare complained about the 'almost impossibly complicated amount of information [required] from people who apply under our present old age pensions legislation'; the process should be simplified wherever possible, he recommended.[64] This new attitude was manifested in a number of ways at the federal level. The levels of payment and permissable income rose substantially in the years immediately following the end of the war, and a number of regulations were modified. After relaxing their insistence on making claims against all pensioners' estates, federal officials again followed the provincial lead in allowing pensioners to accept local relief where necessary, contrary to earlier regulations.

Yet federal officials continued to lag behind developing public and local attitudes, probably out of dissatisfaction with a costly program they could not administer effectively. At one point Ontario and Ottawa officials disagreed over policy on how to calculate one aspect of OAP applicants' assets, and the federal officials pushed to include all possible assets. The federal deputy minister himself described his position: 'This sounds even to myself like a very hardboiled stand to take and it is ... much less generous than that suggested by Mr. Green [the Ontario official]. At the same time, I think it is the only line which can be consistently taken.'[65] Federal officials were well aware of their differences with provincial authorities, and by the mid-1940s, were increasingly uncomfortable in the position in which they found themselves.

Nor were federal officials the only ones to adopt new views of the OAP program. Particularly in the years immediately following the end of the Second World War, employers increasingly demonstrated an interest in formalizing their retirement policies. Many, especially those with small numbers of employees, perceived the OAP as an alternative to the adoption of private pension plans and as facilitating the mandatory retirement of workers.[66]

Organized labour, too, changed its discussion of the OAP program. Where in the 1920s and early 1930s unions simply pushed for the adoption of a pension scheme for the elderly, by the 1940s union conventions and newspapers concentrated on the quality of the program, arguing that the age for eligibility should be reduced, the amount of the pension increased, and the means test ended. In cooperation with the lobbying efforts of the Old Age Pensioners' Organization, organized labour lobbied the government in support of these changes, began an advertising campaign, and distributed postcards and coupons to facilitate lobbying by individual workers.[67] Organized labour, which had played a significant role in gaining the OAP in the years before 1927, now contributed to the shift to universality.

Extending the Parameters of State Support

The late 1940s marked a new era for the elderly in many ways. It was not just that the value of the OAP began to increase markedly or that there was significant public support for a universal OAP. Nor was it simply that the elderly were no longer regarded as a 'problem' that could be solved merely by employing more public funds, though monetary support certainly grew both directly, through such programs as the OAP and grants for housing, and indirectly, through such means as the institution of an income tax deduction for the elderly beginning in 1947. Rather, there was a new respect for the elderly as a distinct group deserving special attention. That attention shifted officials to increasingly pro-active policies. In 1946 a motion in the British Columbia legislature proposed a new name for the elderly – no longer were they 'the old'; instead, they took their 'proper' place in society as 'senior citizens,' with all the rights and obligations inherent in citizenship.[68] This recognition of the elderly's new public and political position was vital to their history in the coming years, and was reflected in a variety of ways.

Popular attitudes about the elderly changed slowly, still perceiving this particular age group as weak, vulnerable, and in need of some protection. But now those popular attitudes had important, positive elements: senior citizens had a right to respect and to at least a minimum standard of living in the broadest sense of that phrase, and they were not so weak that they were unable to do much for themselves. What was more, those popular attitudes were meaningful because they were linked with the belief in an extensive new role for the state, which would provide much of the means by which these new attitudes could be given substance. Furthermore, the organized elderly displayed a new assertiveness which, combined with a developing sense of human rights, gave senior citizens an enhanced role in implementing and sustaining the new programs.

Provincial governments and boards applied new attitudes towards the state's obligations regarding the dependent elderly. Innovative policies and programs were built on attempts to guarantee a minimum quality of life and on a view of the elderly's fundamental financial and social (rather than physical) vulnerability. In the mid-1940s several provinces began to offer various forms of health support to pensioners, using the OAP as the sole test for eligibility. The governments of British Columbia and Ontario were the first to broach the subject of free medical service explicitly for the dependent elderly, followed shortly by the Saskatchewan government.[69] In 1943 the British Columbia government established a program under which pensioners acquired access to free medical service by general practitioners and free prescription drugs, provided the municipality in which they lived agreed to absorb 50 per cent of the costs. Most municipalities quickly joined the scheme, judging from the estimate that after just five months the program covered 80 per cent of British Columbia pensioners. Local branches of the OAPO put pressure on their municipal governments to join the program, but there was no way of forcing individual doctors or druggists to participate, and some refused on the ground that the government fees were inadequate. The scheme was administered through municipal relief departments, adding some stigma to the program.[70]

In Ontario the scheme was similarly limited among the elderly to Old Age Pensioners. In 1935 the provincial government reached an agreement with the Ontario Medical Association to provide limited medical services to relief recipients in all organized municipalities in the province, in return for direct payment by the state while relying on no local funds. Old Age Pensioners were added to the program in 1942. The care was to be equal in quality to that provided for private patients and was to be available to all family members; users could select any general practitioner, but the physician could refuse to accept anyone as a patient. Payment to the doctors was made by the state through the Ontario Medical Association at a set rate per pensioner, and the payment level was raised in 1950. A limited number of generic drugs and lotions were made available, at no charge, to pensioners; in Toronto, the city welfare department provided those drugs and appliances (such as glasses or dentures) not listed. The medical plan was closely integrated with the OAP program, being administered directly by the provincial board. Local officials began to adopt a much more comprehensive concern for the welfare of the dependent elderly, using government processes to achieve these ends. In response to the initiative taken by the provincial scheme, the chief welfare officer in London, Ontario, for example, developed new administrative techniques for ensuring that pensioners received medical attention when needed. That the plan met significant needs among the elderly is suggested by the fact that in the month of March 1949 alone an astounding 17,443 Ontario pensioners, representing just over 22 per cent of all provincial pensioners, received services under the program.[71]

By 1949 the concept of the 'citizen's wage' had expanded to the extent that access to medical care was coming to be recognized as a basic right. The five most easterly provinces had no special programs, the needy elderly having to rely on the general state provisions for the indigent. But the five most westerly provinces had developed reasonably extensive coverage for Old Age Pensioners. British Columbia, Alberta, Saskatchewan, and Ontario provided free medical services to pensioners and some dependents; Manitoba had a scheme giving free medical care to pensioners, but not their dependents; Alberta, Saskatchewan, and Manitoba offered free dental and optical services to pensioners; free hospital care was available to pensioners in British Columbia, Alberta, and Saskatchewan, and in some Ontario municipalities. The availability of free drugs varied. In British Columbia and Alberta the state provided free drugs only during a hospital stay; in Saskatchewan, pensioners were usually required to pay 20 per cent of the drugs' costs, while in Manitoba and Ontario free drugs were available on a limited basis.[72] This was just part of increasingly sophisticated attempts to understand and respond to the needs of the elderly in the years immediately following the end of the Second World War.

This extension of the 'citizen's wage' had a major impact on municipal governments. Not only were they drawn into the operation of provincial medical programs, but local authorities initiated their own schemes to assist the dependent elderly. In 1947, for example, Calgary began to provide free transit passes for pensioners.[73] What is more, seniors themselves pressed the powerful in all sectors to recognize seniors' particular rights by providing benefits and advantages on the basis of seniors' special needs and their financially disadvantaged position. Citing a British commercial precedent for charging reduced rates to seniors, a Toronto resident pushed for reduced prices for sports events. The Nova Scotia Pensioners' Union was able to persuade Nova Scotia coal companies to sell coal to seniors at a reduced price in the winter of 1950–1.[74] Such programs tended to rely on a more traditional perception of the elderly, combined with an enhanced awareness of their financial vulnerability.

Quasi-government agencies, too, accepted the elderly's expanded claims on the state. In the 1940s various social agencies established, often for the first time, special committees to examine the needs of the elderly. In Montreal the Family Welfare Association responded in 1936 to Quebec's imminent adoption of the OAP program by establishing a separate office to deal with the needs of the elderly. The Montreal Council of Social Agencies appointed a Committee on the Problems of the Aged, which in the spring of 1947 articulated the rights of the elderly in a 'Charter for the Aged':

1 The right to gainful employment so long as they can meet the normal requirements of the job.
2 The right to sheltered employment and a useful existence once they are no longer able to compete with their fellows in the open market.
3 The right to a minimum income sufficient to provide the basic necessities of life and to assure them independence in their declining years.
4 The right to health and medical services commensurate with their increased need for such services by virtue of the infirmities and disabilities which accompany old age.
5 The right to care and treatment in homes or institutions, operated in terms of desirable standards, in which respect for the aged as individual persons is assured them.
6 The right to individual consideration along physical and psychological lines which makes due allowance for what is customary behaviour in old people.
7 The right to life, liberty and pursuit of happiness to the end of their days.[75]

In an era when charters and declarations of the rights of various disadvantaged groups were spreading across the Western world, such a statement is indicative of the problems that the elderly continued to face and of the recognition that this situation ought no longer to be tolerated. Social workers helped to lead the fight for greater sensitivity to the needs of senior citizens. By articulating the struggle through the language of rights, social workers undermined some of their own authority and accepted the ideas implicit in the 'citizen's wage.'

In many instances these municipal committees took the lead in seeking new understandings of the elderly. They initiated the first social scientific studies of the Canadian elderly and their circumstances. In 1943 the Committee on the Care of the Aged, a subcommittee of the Family Division of the Welfare Council of Greater Vancouver, began meeting and, before long, determined that a survey of the local elderly was required before plans and policies could be intelligently formed; the survey was completed by 1945 and revised in 1948. Shortly after the first survey was finished, the city's social service department investigated the housing of a sample of 1500 local pensioners.[76] Schools of social work, where graduate programs began in the 1940s, found some interest among a minority of students in studying the elderly. One or two studies a year were written about the elderly in the second half of the decade at the University of British Columbia, the University of Toronto, and McGill University. A related sign of the new attitudes about the elderly was the attention given by universities. In the fall of 1950, for example, the University of Toronto brought together a number of experts in various related areas in an extension course aimed at bringing social workers up to date with current thinking and knowledge; 135 practitioners and students registered in the course.[77]

When the term gerontology began to be used in Canada in the late 1940s, it was in the context of a cry for greater knowledge of the elderly. At a 1947 western regional conference on social work, the chair of the British Columbia OAP Board criticized the social work profession for its relative lack of concern and the absence of constructive work regarding the elderly:

Case work principles which they apply to all other ages and categories for some reason seem to be dropped when they come to think of the aged. Just as the aged present a new frontier in medicine so they present a new frontier in case work. Case work with the chronically ill aged is a virtually unexplored field. There is a crying need first of all for interest in and then an understanding of the characteristics of old people and the possibilities for really constructive work. The volume of the work and the newness of the field are a challenge to the worker who takes pride in being 'up-and-coming.'[78]

The appeal to professionalism was a potent one, but the idea that the elderly required creative, positive attention, rather than mere palliative care, was of more fundamental importance.

Senior citizens as a whole were beginning to be perceived as a significant social group with their own varied characteristics and needs. The views of the elderly themselves, rather than simply the institutions' cleanliness or attractiveness, were now fundamental in the assessment of old age homes, as suggested in one headline regarding Dania, the Danish old age home in Burnaby: 'Places Where Old People Are Happy and Understood.' In the accompanying article, the assistant inspector of institutions for British Columbia attacked older homes whose names she parodied as the 'Home for Genteel, Indigent, and Aged Females,' suggesting that such titles indicated a relative lack of empathy for seniors and a consequent unhappiness among residents of such homes.[79] In the same way, the term 'inmate' for residents of old age homes fell into official disuse, as did any statutory connection between indigency and residence in the recently renamed 'Homes for the Aged' (dropping the title 'Houses of Refuge') in Ontario.[80] The impulse to politically correct language reflected a more fundamental recognition that the elderly were a distinct group that needed to be 'understood.'

While turn-of-the-century policies aimed at the elderly were concerned primarily that their physical condition met minimal standards, mid-century policies and programs were based on both an expanded and enhanced level of concern – a raised standard for seniors' physical environment and a new attention to their mental health and social condition. The elderly themselves called attention to the new characteristics of old age encouraged by mandatory retirement. Most jarring for those women and men forced out of the workplace was their sudden loss of the daily social contact with fellow workers. Other elderly were forced for health or economic reasons to uproot themselves from neighbours and friends of long-standing, moving to an entirely new district. 'In many instances,' commented the *Pensioner*, such circumstances led to

a sense of social isolation which, if not quickly remedied, leads to the adoption of an inferiority complex. This is perhaps the most regretable condition of all, and it affects aged married couples and single men and women alike, and very soon develops a tendency to withdraw from the social companionship of their fellowmen. The result of this withdrawal is that these fine old people begin to look through the wrong end of the telescope, and instead of seeing the broad fields of happiness and comradeship which is theirs for the asking, they contract their vision until the picture contains only loneliness and sad memories. The worst aspect of this condition is that it is unnecessary and [there is] not the slightest need for this unfortunate complex.[81]

Fortunately, these problems were coming to be recognized, and responses were developed.

A prominent new feature of these postwar responses to the needs of the elderly was recreational programming. Leisure was coming to be recognized as an important phenomenon for all age groups, but with the increasing prominence of mandatory retirement, no group but the very young tended to have more leisure time than the elderly. It was natural that the new attitudes to leisure would eventually mesh with the fresh perceptions about the elderly. The elderly were no longer to be merely 'warehoused' in institutions. The stereotype of the elderly as debilitated and infirm was weakening, as more varied perceptions of the elderly now encompassed the well elderly. 'We need to get the phrase and reality of the *well old person* firmly in our thinking and planning,' commented a lecturer at the University of Toronto. 'Old age need not be identified only with sickness and ailments ... [but rather with] living full-valued, productive, interesting lives in the later years, and not merely existing.'[82] These were people with legitimate social, physical, and mental needs, and one method of meeting those needs was with an increasingly varied recreational programming. 'The crucial question concerning old people today,' wrote one social work student in 1952, 'is how we can add life to their years, not merely years to their lives ... Recreation is one means by which we can make a real contribution to adding life to those years.'[83]

This programming was introduced in old age homes and in the new community centres that began to spring up in cities across the country. When a community centre opened in West Vancouver in the early 1940s, most of its adult members were over the age of sixty. Originally the centre had no special programs for the elderly; it was the elderly themselves who joined the centre and pushed for appropriate recreational services. Before long the community centre workers, to their credit, recognized that there was a major need to be met, and looked for ways to do so. They developed special tactics to entice 'the shy, the friendless, the lonely, the poor in spirit, or in cash' out of 'their dreary homes, or from the shelter of relatives' homes or from their self-centered lives.' Such programs showed real concern for the well-being of the individual elderly and, in West Vancouver at least, came quickly to appreciate that not everything should be done *for* the elderly – that the seniors 'wanted to run their own "show."' Through a variety of activities, the common thread was the socializing that reduced the isolation of many elderly.[84] These more general community recreation programs and centres were matched by an increasing number of organizations more specifically directed to the elderly.

There were several purposes to these innovations in programming for seniors, and all reflected fundamentally important new attitudes towards the
elderly and increased sensitivity to some of the problems faced by contemporary senior citizens. Many of the new programs aimed at the elderly themselves sought to end their social and physical isolation, to respond to a
prevalent loneliness that many elderly found difficult to cope with in the
face of the loss of relatives and friends, an increasing inability to pay for
entertainment, and a decreasing mobility. And while there was a new emphasis on facilitating self-help, there remained a powerful 'professional' interest in directing the sort of activity and personal development that
occurred. 'All these services,' commented one social worker to a 1945 Toronto audience, 'are part of a broad community plan to grant older people the
substance of life.'[85] The extended awareness and services were often founded
on a patronizing attitude aimed at 'granting' the elderly a fuller and better
life.

The Old Age Pension program had changed considerably over its twenty-
four-year history, despite the fact that the basic legislation itself had not been
altered. Driven by popular new attitudes about the role of the state in social
programs, and bolstered in the federal civil service by Keynesian economic
theory,[86] new views of the OAP program gained considerable public prominence from the mid-1940s on. But change had been occurring long before
that. Stimulated by the needs and circumstances of the elderly themselves,
and pushed by individual pensioners and by an articulate and organized
'grey lobby,' local and provincial authorities reshaped the program to serve
the interests of the elderly better. That they did so often in the face of determined federal opposition is an indication of how strongly many provincial authorities came to feel about the 'right sort' of pension program. The
result was an OAP that, in practice, had in a number of ways abandoned
the means test as a philosophical basis for such a program and had come
much closer to universality. The adoption of universality in the 1951 Old
Age Security Act was the logical result of a long-term process.
    More than that, the claims of the elderly generated the beginnings of a
new view of the elderly and a variety of other state programs designed to
address the rights and needs of the group. Governments at all levels joined
in the move to meet the financial, physical, and social needs of the elderly.
The 'citizen's wage' expanded beyond a mere financial definition to include
a more complete and fundamental approach to old age and to the new-
found rights of the elderly.

8

Conclusion

The early decades of the twentieth century were of vital importance in redefining old age in modern society. The early focus on the needy and the dependent of whatever age had slowly given way to an increasing association in the public mind between those characteristics and old age. State-operated and charitable residential institutions for the care of the poor had evolved into spartan, authoritarian old age homes that tended to be based on a philosophy of less eligibility. At the same time, economic processes threatened to alter the role and the position of many elderly workers, though the real impact of these processes was probably quite limited for some time. The elderly themselves and their families, as they had traditionally done, adjusted their behaviour to meet these new circumstances – changing their employment patterns, using their assets and resources in new ways, and, where necessary, calling on new sources of potential support.

Voluntary and informal sources of support – family, neighbours, local charities – continued to be of central importance in shaping the lives of the elderly. But the state began to play an ever greater role, both directly and indirectly. Direct assistance occurred in a limited way, through support for a small number of residential institutions and the establishment of a government annuities program. Later, the impact was much more considerable. The state was prodded into the establishment of a limited pension program to assist the needy elderly after they had been forced out of the labour force. The elderly themselves, on the basis of a rising culture of entitlement, played a central role in reshaping that program, so that it met the needs of the elderly better and was less demeaning. Other elements in society responded to the changing perceptions and role of the elderly by taking advantage of those new perceptions. Private capital, big and small, sought to exploit this environment, seeking access to the new funds available for the care of the elderly. Families and neighbours benefited from the significantly greater funds in the hands of individual elderly, adjusting their own behaviour to offer continuing or different forms of assistance. In doing so, these various elements, public and private, condoned and encouraged the continuing redefinition of old age.

In the years immediately following the end of the Second World War, many of Canada's elderly witnessed 'the dawn of a new era.' Not only was this phrase the *Pensioner*'s optimistic masthead statement of the hopes and expectations of the organized elderly, but it was the title of the lead editorial recognizing the fundamental reforms in the Old Age Pension program finally adopted in 1951. The implementation of universality at age seventy, and of a means-tested pension for those aged sixty-five to sixty-nine, marked the end of 'a nightmare to many thousands of our fine people,' commented the *Pensioner*, 'the relief from anxiety due to the stark fear of want that has existed over the past years when advancing years approach them cannot be overestimated.'[1]

Since the OAP payment level was still set at $40 a month, the amount of security offered by the new program was clearly exaggerated in the euphoria of the moment, largely because the *Pensioner* and many others took a great deal of pride in the achievement of these pension reforms.[2] And rightly so. Without underestimating the importance of new conceptions of the state and of social security, new theories of the state's role in economic development, the economic environment of the 1930s and 1940s, and the role played by some politicians and civil servants, the elderly themselves – both through their organizations and in their individual dealings with the developing state programs – pushed and prodded the new programs for the elderly in Canadian society to develop in particular directions with particular characteristics.

This was indeed a new era in the history of the elderly. Most importantly, the state, society at large, and the elderly themselves recognized and accepted the elderly as a distinct and significant social group with legitimate and identifiable needs and demands. Henceforth, and increasingly, some of the inordinate amount of attention paid to children and youth in Canadian (and Western) society would shift to include the elderly as an age group deserving of special consideration, study, and treatment. Societal resources began to be redirected towards the elderly.

Yet, in practice, the dependent elderly and their families were more than just the objects of public policy. As Dominique Jean found in the case of the family allowances program at mid-century, the recipients of these new forms of social welfare were active political agents in the process. The dependent elderly and their families reshaped the OAP program by influencing public attitudes towards the elderly's claims on society, by resisting unattractive or detrimental elements in the program, and by persuading local officials to administer the pensions in ways that best met the needs of the recipients. The elderly and their families, and indeed the broader public, incorporated the idea of a basic level of support into their concept of the rights of the elderly as citizens. In firmly implanting the idea that the state had a financial responsibility for the economic welfare of the elderly, a threshold was set for the citizen's wage and for future claims by the elderly.[3]

The history of state programs for the elderly in the first half of the twentieth century is suggestive regarding the processes involved in the development of the modern welfare state. The state, particularly in a federal system, must be examined not as a monolithic institution, but as a diverse and complex institution. It is not simply a tool in the hands of the bourgeoisie, since it can be used as an instrument by other social groups as well. In the case of the developing citizen's wage in the 1940s, the elderly and their families persuaded some elements of the state, particularly at the local level in urban environments, to adopt their interests and to fight for their cause. These state elements, often with paternalistic motives, accepted the culture of entitlement articulated by the dependent elderly and helped to reshape public policy along those lines.[4]

These processes played a vital role in redefining old age. Singling out the elderly as automatically in need of aid encouraged paternalism and legitimated ageism. The increasing commonality of experience among the elderly reflected what Tamara Hareven has referred to as the growing conjunction of 'family time' and 'historical time.' Regardless of social class or ethnicity or gender, age sixty-five had come to represent the appropriate time to end paid labour. Age became a much more precise element in defining an individual, as accuracy regarding birth date was fundamental to many processes and programs touching individual lives. The culture of entitlement crossed social boundaries and underlined a shared basis of experience and attitudes among the elderly. Public pensions and seniors' benefits pointed towards universality among the elderly.

In the first half of the twentieth century the elderly became a distinct group. In A.M. Rose's classic phrase, they moved from a social category to a social group.[5] It is surely their group consciousness that is of such fundamental importance in understanding the new meanings of old age in the post-industrial world. This study has emphasized the role of the elderly themselves, both individually and collectively, in developing and manifesting this new group consciousness. The state processes and policies directed at an increasingly large proportion of the elderly politicized those Canadians in and approaching old age.[6] Formal and informal public programs and perceptions articulated a view of the elderly that generated responses from the target group. While accepting and using to their advantage many of the limiting elements of this view of old age, the elderly themselves emphasized some characteristics and de-emphasized others. The resulting image of the elderly was fundamental to the culture of entitlement that gained such an authoritative position by mid-century. The 'citizen's wage' recognized the contributions of the elderly to society and their claims to reciprocal benefits now that they were in need. The adoption of a universal state pension program and the extension of other benefits to all elderly accepted their group identity and claims.

The value of these developments is problematic. While the automatic benefits removed some of the stigma of old age, the universality of the programs carried new implications about the allegedly inherent characteristics of the elderly – frailty, economic need, and an age when gender, race, and class were no longer significant factors. The increasing universality of programs inhibited the recognition (much less the ability to act thereon) that old age continued to be very different for some than for others. The elderly were certainly not a monolithic group. The working-class pensioners who formed their own organizations in this period by no means represented all elderly, much less all working-class elderly. The organized elderly were divided by issues as simple as recreational interests, as seen in the discussion of the founding of elderly associations. Fundamental factors, such as gender, race, ethnicity, and social class, continued to play central roles in the history of the elderly. And yet government programs came by 1951 to ignore these vital differences and to treat all elderly as being much the same.

The reality of gender meant that the experience of old age in the first half of the twentieth century was very different for men than for women, particularly among the dependent elderly. Men's entitlement to support was unaffected by their substantially different work history and their ability to accumulate assets, for example; women's entitlement did not reflect their weaker financial position or their greater longevity.

Elderly women's access to financial resources in various forms was considerably more limited than men's: they had fewer opportunities for paid employment, lower levels of remuneration when employed, limited control over resources as long as their husbands were alive, infrequent widows' benefits where their husbands had private pensions. They were much more often left widowed, without the support (economic and otherwise) of a spouse. And yet, given women's greater life expectancy, needy elderly women required more support, and for considerably longer periods, than did men. At no point did the formal programs of state support take such disadvantages into account. Indeed, the reverse is true, as the OAP program adopted numerous measures that discriminated against women and maintained the relative economic power of older men. Throughout the period under study, there was no indication that the organized elderly, the articulate public, or state officials recognized women's disadvantages. Thus, no attempt was made to adapt existing programs or to develop additional, complementary measures to respond to women's particular needs. The public view of old age itself was non-gendered. Women's sole advantage in old age was their greater access to informal resources provided by family and friends, yet even this reflected their greater vulnerability.

At the same time, with the OAP, vast numbers of older women gained access to a secure and direct source of economic support for what was likely the first time in their life. If the OAP was discriminatory, it nevertheless represented a significant step forward for older women.

Nor did social class disappear as a significant factor in the lives of the elderly. This study has tended to concentrate on working-class elderly, those whose poverty forced them to rely on the community and the state for assistance and to struggle for sufficient income or support for mere survival. The middle class employed their greater financial assets, and their often greater flexibility regarding the timing of events such as retirement, to structure their old age in ways that best suited their individual interests, investing in government annuities or life insurance in ever greater amounts to be certain of economic security in their later years. Even the public processes employed by the dependent elderly emphasized the various strata among the working class. While the adoption of universality in 1951 removed much of the stigma earlier associated with the OAP, it retained the stigma by initiating a means-tested support program for those aged sixty-five to sixty-nine. And the greater needs of the poorer elderly aged seventy or more lost any explicit public recognition.

Race and ethnicity, too, played vital roles in shaping old age. The OAP Act, for example, excluded Native peoples (those falling under the 'protection' of the Indian Act), and, by insisting on a twenty-year residency and on British citizenship, tended to exclude immigrants, particularly those from outside the British Empire. People of colour clearly lack a voice in this study, their history being at least partially separate and distinct from that of their more privileged sisters and brothers. The community and state processes responding to the elderly thus confirmed a hierarchy of status and privilege against which there was virtually no public outcry.[7] While the dependent elderly were disadvantaged compared with younger age groups and compared with the middle-class aged, they accepted and condoned a system that legitimated their privileged position vis-à-vis even more disadvantaged others.

Writing about the rise of the welfare state in the United States, Theda Skocpol argued that the extensive system of Civil War pensions there was so characterized by fraud and corruption within the partisan political process that broader schemes of social insurance were repeatedly rejected prior to the 1930s.[8] In Canada, the history of social insurance in the form of old age pensions is markedly different. Though Canada too was late in adopting social insurance for the needy elderly, in contrast with other industrializing states in Europe and Australasia, the evidence of fraud did not inhibit the development of a still more generous and more inclusive program. In part, the difference is that the operation of the Canadian OAP was never enmeshed in partisan politics. The timing, too, is crucial. By the period when Canadians were considering the OAP program and its expansion, attitudes towards the state had changed dramatically. State provision for its needy elderly citizens came to be taken almost for granted in the developing culture of entitlement at mid-century.

The economic gains made by the Canadian elderly through the citizen's wage ought not to be exaggerated. The generally 'progressive' tone of this study reflects the underlying optimism of many senior citizens and their organized groups. But that progressive tone obscures the negative features accompanying the history of the elderly in the early twentieth century. As David Thomson has argued in several articles, twentieth-century senior citizens are not necessarily better provided for than the elderly of the past. The provision of an old age pension enabled the state and the community to withdraw provision of a number of support programs, on the dubious assumption that merely putting minimal funds in the hands of the needy elderly solved their problems or gave them the capacity to do so.[9] Flexible local and provincial programs purchasing room and board for needy elderly from poor relatives or from neighbours ended, for example. In adopting more formal and extensive measures for aid, the elderly lost much. Some of the flexibility and individuality of earlier mechanisms disappeared; some elements of community and family support shrank as these sources gladly relinquished some of their responsibilities or obligations to the state. While this study demonstrates repeatedly that the lot of the needy elderly tended to improve markedly under state assistance programs, many problems remained and a number of traditional discriminatory practices or assumptions were simply incorporated into the new processes.

During the half century under investigation here, the state increasingly responded to some of the perceived needs of the elderly. Primarily, this assistance focused on guaranteeing some element of personal and financial security, by pushing families to look after their own elderly members and by making available minimal amounts of money. As the first great cost-sharing program in Canada, the OAP program brought together all three levels of government, both through sharing the financial burden and through a complex distribution of administrative responsibilities. This interlocking character of state involvement, first established with the OAP program, came to characterize government initiatives addressing the needs of the elderly. As medical and housing programs began in the 1930s and 1940s, they too followed the patterns of cost-sharing and of coordination among the various levels of government.[10] While this multilayered administrative structure was often inefficient, it nevertheless had the advantage of providing multiple access points for those seeking to influence policies or regulations.

The state's assumption of some of the primary obligations for support for the elderly did not undermine the traditional familial responsibilities for elderly relatives. It altered some of the form but not the character of family culture as it pertained to the care of the elderly. Family culture remained of fundamental importance in shaping the lives of the elderly. By relieving families of much of their direct financial obligations for the elderly, state programs ended the most obvious and, in the symbols of the twentieth century, the most demeaning form of control/dependence. The elderly gained or retained a greater degree of financial independence, and their adult children were 'released' to use their financial resources to best fulfil their socialized primary responsibility: to sustain themselves and the next generation. There can be no doubt that in gaining independence, some elderly became isolated from their families. But this was not a new phenomenon; there have always been families that were dysfunctional in assistance to their elderly members. Another result was a greater emphasis on a narrower spectrum of functions for the extended family. Many children have internalized the opportunities of the welfare state and have tended to alter their sense of obligation towards their parents. The new sense of obligation centred around non-monetary and non-residential forms of support. The role of the state made most elderly less reliant on dependency-creating forms of family support and assistance, creating an environment in which emotional attachment could more readily flourish. Families in the twentieth century could concentrate on what they do best: the provision of affective and informal support.[11]

The elderly themselves were poised to play an increasing role in determining their own social and physical environment. They fought hard to place themselves in that position, and they would likely do so again. Many elderly employed a variety of tactics – legal and illegal – that aimed to meet a single, concerted strategy: the acquisition of a significant level of benefits and support for themselves and for others like them.

In the 1990s, discussion of the end of universality is increasingly common as the state faces major fiscal problems. But there is no reason to believe that the modern elderly would act any differently in this regard from those of the 1930s and 1940s. Any attempt to restrict initial access to state support would result not only in very expensive bureaucratic procedures, but also in a repetition of the manipulative tactics of the past designed to ensure maximum access to a 'citizen's wage.' When the Canadian government in 1985 considered ending universality in old age pensions, senior citizens organized a broad-based, intensive public campaign and lobbying effort that forestalled any such government action.[12] It is reasonable to predict that no such restrictions will be effective until the more fundamental culture of entitlement alters. Until then, the 'citizen's wage' will continue to play a vital role in the social construction of old age in modern Western society.

Notes

INTRODUCTION

1 See, for example, A.S. Orloff, *The Politics of Pensions: A Comparative Analysis of Britain, Canada, and the United States, 1880–1940* (Madison, 1993)
2 T.H. Marshall, 'Citizenship and Social Class,' in T.H. Marshall, *Class, Citizenship, and Social Development* (Westport, 1973 [1963]), 65–122
3 J. Myles, *Old Age in the Welfare State: The Political Economy of Public Pensions* (Lawrence, 1989 [1984]), 38–50; M. Kohli, 'Ageing as a Challenge for Sociological Theory,' *Ageing and Society*, 8 (1988), 367–94. Kohli takes issue with the proposition that this structured dependency of the elderly was new, or was enhanced by the new state programs of the twentieth century.
4 D. Jean, 'Familles québécoises et politiques sociales touchant les enfants, de 1940 à 1960: obligation scolaire, allocations familiales, travail juvénile,' PhD thesis, Université de Montréal, 1989; D. Owram, *The Government Generation: Canadian Intellectuals and the State, 1900–1945* (Toronto, 1986), 88–9. Olivier Faure argues that in France the elderly's sense of legitimate claim on societal support had developed in the nineteenth century; see 'Les classes populaires face à l'hôpital à Lyon au XIXe siècle,' *Cahiers d'histoire*, 26 (1981), 259–69.
5 C. Tilly, 'Family History, Social History, and Social Change,' *Journal of Family History*, 12 (1987), 319–30
6 V.M. Marshall, ed., *Later Life: The Social Psychology of Aging* (Beverly Hills, 1986), 12
7 See also J. Struthers, 'Regulating the Elderly: Old Age Pensions and the Formation of a Pension Bureaucracy in Ontario, 1929–1945,' *Journal of the Canadian Historical Association*, 3 (1992), 235–55.
8 Tilly, 'Family History, Social History, and Social Change,' 327–28
9 P. Christianson, 'Patterns of Historical Interpretation,' in W.J. Van Der Dussen

and L. Rubinoff, eds., *Objectivity, Method and Point of View: Essays in the Philosophy of History* (Leiden, 1991), 47–71

CHAPTER 1: Daily Lives

1 P. Laslett, *The World We Have Lost* (London, 1965)
2 L. Stone, 'Walking over Grandma,' *New York Review of Books*, 24 (12 May 1977), 10–16; D.H. Fischer and L. Stone, 'Growing Old: Exchange,' ibid. (15 Sept. 1977), 47–9; P.N. Stearns, ed., *Old Age in Preindustrial Society* (New York, 1982); S. Woolf, *The Poor in Western Europe in the Eighteenth and Nineteenth Centuries* (London, 1986); C. Haber, *Beyond Sixty-Five: The Dilemma of Old Age in America's Past* (Cambridge, 1983), 8–27; S.R. Smith, 'Death, Dying and the Elderly in Seventeenth Century England,' in S.F. Spicker et al., eds., *Aging and the Elderly* (Atlantic Highlands, NJ, 1978), 205–20; R.M. Smith, 'The Structured Dependence of the Elderly as a Recent Development: Some Sceptical Historical Thoughts,' *Ageing and Society*, 4 (1984), 409–28; M. Zimmerman, 'Old-Age Poverty in Preindustrial New York City,' in B.B. Hess, ed., *Growing Old in America* (New Brunswick, NJ, 1980), 65–98
3 W.A. Achenbaum, *Old Age in the New Land: The American Experience since 1790* (Baltimore, 1978), 40, 86, and passim. See also T.R. Cole, *The Journey of Life: A Cultural History of Aging in America* (Cambridge, 1992). For a different view of the timing of attitudinal change see D.H. Fischer, *Growing Old in America* (New York, 1977). For a more extended anlysis of the historiography of old age, see C. Haber and B. Gratton, *Old Age and the Search for Security: An American Social History* (Bloomington, 1994), 1–19.
4 Haber, *Beyond Sixty-Five*, 68, 65, 47–87; H.-J. von Kondratowitz, 'The Medicalization of Old Age,' in M. Pelling and R.M. Smith, eds., *Life, Death, and the Elderly: Historical Perspectives* (London, 1991), 134–64; Cole, *Journey of Life*, 161–211
5 St John's *Evening Telegram*, 23 March 1906, 2
6 Haber, *Beyond Sixty-Five*, 82–107; T.R. Cole, 'The Prophecy of *Senescence:* G. Stanley Hall and the Reconstruction of Old Age in America,' *Gerontologist*, 24 (1984), 360–6; Cole, *Journey of Life*, 191–226
7 Brian Gratton, *Urban Elders: Family, Work, and Welfare among Boston's Aged, 1890–1950* (Philadelphia, 1986)
8 David Thomson offers a somewhat complementary analysis of the elderly in nineteenth- and twentieth-century England; see 'Workhouse to Nursing Home,' *Ageing and Society*, 3 (1983), 43–69; 'The Decline of Social Welfare: Falling State Support for the Elderly since Early Victorian Times,' ibid., 4 (1984), 451–82; 'Welfare and the Historians,' in L. Bonfield et al., eds., *The World We Have Gained* (Oxford, 1986), 355–78.

9 Haber and Gratton, *Old Age and the Search for Security,* chapters 2 and 3; B. Gratton, 'The Labor Force Participation of Older Men, 1890–1940,' *Journal of Social History,* 20 (1987), 689–710; B. Gratton and F.M. Rotondo, 'Industrialization, the Family Economy, and the Economic Status of the American Elderly,' *Social Science History,* 15 (1991), 337–62

10 William Graebner, *A History of Retirement: The Meaning and Function of an American Institution, 1885–1978* (New Haven, 1980). See also L. Hannah, *Inventing Retirement: Occupational Pensions in Britain* (Cambridge, 1986).

11 P. Townsend, 'The Structured Dependency of the Elderly: A Creation of Social Policy in the Twentieth Century,' *Ageing and Society,* 1 (1981), 5–28; A.-M. Guillemard, ed., *Old Age and the Welfare State* (Beverly Hills, 1983), 6–7

12 H.P. Chudacoff, *How Old Are You? Age Consciousness in American Culture* (Princeton, NJ, 1989); T.K. Hareven, 'Family Time and Historical Time,' *Daedalus,* 106 (1977), 57–70

13 J.G. Snell, 'The Newfoundland Old Age Pension Programme, 1911–1949,' *Acadiensis,* 23 (1993), 86–109; *Labour Gazette,* July 1907, 73, and March 1908, 1122–3; K. Bryden, *Old Age Pensions and Policy-Making in Canada* (Montreal, 1974), 46–51; Canada, Committee on Old Age Pensions System for Canada, *Old Age Pensions System for Canada: Memorandum* (Ottawa, 1912)

14 Bryden, *Old Age Pensions,* 61–101, presents a useful, detailed chronology of the implementation of the scheme. See also Canada, *Journals of the House of Commons,* 1924, appendix 4; Canada, Department of Labour, *Old Age Pensions in Canada* (Ottawa, 1929); Social Service Council of Canada, Committee on Research, *Preliminary Report on Old Age Pensions* (Toronto, 1928); A.S. Orloff, *The Politics of Pensions: A Comparative Analysis of Britain, Canada, and the United States, 1880–1940* (Madison, 1993), 240–68.

15 Graebner, *History of Retirement;* Gratton, *Urban Elders,* 4–5

16 Haber, *Beyond Sixty-Five*

17 Public Archives of Newfoundland and Labrador (PANL), GN38/S6–1–9, file 8, clipping and letter of 19 October 1940. For another dimension, obscuring the realities of aging, see V. Strong-Boag, *The New Day Recalled: Lives of Girls and Women in English Canada, 1919–1939* (Toronto, 1988), 179–81.

18 For an overview of the historical demography of the Canadian elderly, see L.O. Stone and S. Fletcher, 'Demographic Variations in North America,' in E. Rathbone-McCuan and B. Havens, eds., *North American Elders: United States and Canadian Perspectives* (New York, 1988), 9–33; N.L. Chappell et al., *Aging and Health Care: A Social Perspective* (Toronto, 1986), 15–32.

19 J. Henripin, *Trends and Factors of Fertility in Canada* (Ottawa, 1972), 21; A. and A.T. McLaren, *The Bedroom and the State* (Toronto, 1986), 11. The general fertility rate is the annual number of births per 1000 women aged 15–49 years.

20 R. Bourbeau and J. Legaré, *Evolution de la mortalité au Canada et au Québec, 1831–1931* (Montréal, 1982), 81–91. See also D. Nagnur, *Longevity and Historical Life Tables, 1921–1981 (abridged)* (Ottawa, 1986); Nagnur and M. Nagrodski, 'Epidemiologic Transition in the Context of Demographic Change: The Evolution of Canadian Mortality Patterns,' *Canadian Studies in Population,* 17 (1990), 1–24; E.M. Gee, 'The Life Course of Canadian Women: An Historical and Demographic Analysis,' *Social Indicators Research,* 18 (1986), 264–5.

21 D. Gagan, *Hopeful Travellers: Families, Land, and Social Change in Mid-Victorian Peel County, Canada West* (Toronto, 1981), 89, 93; Haber, *Beyond Sixty-Five,* 29–30

22 By 1951 the ratio of resident children to elderly-headed households was 1:3.5; see *Census of Canada, 1951* (Ottawa, 1956), III, table 136.

23 E.M. Gee, 'Demographic Change and Intergenerational Relations in Canadian Families: Findings and Social Policy Implications,' *Canadian Public Policy,* 16 (1990), 191–9; E.M. Gee, 'The Changing Demography of Intergenerational Relations in Canada,' in Canadian Association on Gerontology, *The Changing Family in an Aging Society* (Ottawa, 1988); E.M. Gee, 'Life Course of Canadian Women,' 263–83; S.S. Kulis, *Why Honor Thy Father and Mother? Class, Mobility and Family Ties in Later Life* (New York, 1991), 41

24 *Labour Gazette,* March 1908, 1122–3

25 *Census of Canada, 1931,* III, table 1; *Census of Canada, 1941,* III, table 3; *Census of Canada, 1951,* I, table 21

26 *Report of the Commission appointed to consider Old Age Pensions* (Halifax, 1930), 7

27 n=1946. *Report of the Commission Appointed to Consider Old Age Pensions,* 7. The data on proportions self-supporting and on sources of support do not include the elderly in Hants County.

28 *Census of Canada, 1931,* III, table 12; *Census of Canada, 1941,* III, table 7; *Census of Canada, 1951,* II, table 1

29 For an example where such inducements were insufficient to retain the support of adult children, see W.P. Ward, 'Family Papers and the New Social History,' *Archivaria,* 14 (1982), 63–73.

30 Kulis, *Why Honor Thy Father and Mother?* 3, 26; P. Wilmott and M. Young, *Family and Class in a London Suburb* (London, 1960); B. Bradbury, *Working Families: Age, Gender, and Daily Survival in Industrializing Montreal* (Toronto, 1993), 67

31 The anecdotal evidence garnered from the OAP files was supplemented by an appeal to contemporary seniors to write to the author describing the role of the extended family in the lives of their own grandparents and of their grandparents' role within the family.

32 Wilmott and Young, *Family and Class in a London Suburb*, found that in the 1950s urban England, social class was a major factor in determining whether elderly parents moved to children (middle class) or, at an earlier stage, children located near parents (working class).

33 For an earlier period, see A.G. Darroch and M. Ornstein, 'Family and Household in Nineteenth-Century Canada: Regional Patterns and Regional Economics,' *Journal of Family History*, 9 (1984), 158–77; G. Bouchard, 'Family Structures and Geographic Mobility at Laterrière, 1851–1935,' ibid., 2 (1977), 350–69; E.-A. Montigny, 'Perceptions, Realities and Old Age,' PhD thesis, University of Ottawa, 1994, 84–91.

34 Research in some areas, such as the relationships between the elderly and their adult children, indicates similar patterns in Canada and the United States; see C.J. Rosenthal, 'Aging and Generational Relations in Canada,' in V.W. Marshall, ed., *Aging in Canada: Social Perspectives*, 2nd ed. (Markham, Ont., 1987), 311–42.

35 Of the married elderly, 16 per cent resided with a married child and 42 per cent with an unmarried child; for the unmarried elderly, including the widowed, the comparable figures were 38 per cent and 27 per cent, respectively. See M. Dahlin, 'Perspectives on the Family Life of the Elderly in 1900,' *The Gerontologist*, 20 (1980), 100; D.S. Smith, 'Historical Change in the Household Structure of the Elderly in Economically Developed Societies,' in R.W. Fogel, ed., *Aging: Stability and Change in the Family* (New York, 1981), 100, 110; H.P. Chudacoff and T.K. Hareven, 'Family Transitions into Old Age,' in T.K. Hareven, ed., *Transitions: The Family and the Life Course in Historical Perspective* (New York, 1978), 224–7; Gratton, *Urban Elders*, 56. See also R. Wall, 'Relationships between the Generations in British Families Past and Present,' unpublished paper presented at the Tenth International Economic History Conference, Louvain, 1990.

36 For the households of the elderly in the United States of 1900, 73 per cent of the elderly aged 65–69 were heads or the spouse of a head; for those aged 70–74, 65 per cent were still heads or the spouse of the heads, and even for those aged seventy-five or more, a majority (53 per cent) retained their headship status. See D.S. Smith, 'Life Course, Norms, and the Family System of Older Americans in 1900,' *Journal of Family History*, 4 (1979), 286–91; M.R. Haines and A.C. Goodman, *A Home of One's Own: Aging and Homeownership in the United States in the Late Nineteenth and Early Twentieth Centuries* (Cambridge, MA, 1991); Bradbury, *Working Families*, 207. See also Gratton, *Urban Elders*, 39–60; Wall, 'Relationships between Generations.'

37 Grandparenting ms, V. Allen to author, Woodham, Ont., 23 January 1992

38 Grandparenting ms, L. Clement to author, Richmond Hill, Ont., 15 February 1992; ibid., J.L. Salmon to author, Binbrook, Ont., 20 January 1992

39 University of Western Ontario (UWO), London Welfare Records, box B411, file 1912–29 A–D, report of J.W. McCallum, London, 21 November 1912
40 UWO, Lambton County OAP Commission, box B888, application of 31 August 1929
41 UWO, London Welfare Records, box B411, file 1912–29 A–D, individual to J.W. McCallum, Great Falls, Montana, 24 July 1913; report of 30 July 1914
42 UWO, Lambton County OAP Commission, box B886, Clerk's Special Report, 19 September 1935
43 National Archives of Canada (NA), RG 29, vol. 139, no. 208-5–6 pt. 2, C.K. Newcombe to W.C. Clark, Winnipeg, 12 January 1939
44 Grandparenting ms, H.P. Marr to author, Newmarket, Ont., 12 January 1992
45 UWO, Lambton County OAP Commission, box B882, application of 13 November 1929
46 Andrejs Plakans makes a useful distinction between 'stepping down' and 'retirement.' 'Stepping down' connotes an often informal process that did not necessarily include a complete separation from the world of productive work, but rather signalled the beginning of a process of withdrawal from productive work that ended only when one was completely infirm or dead. 'Retirement' suggests a conclusion to one's productive working life and the beginning of another phase of the life course, during which other forms of material support enable the retiree to pursue other activities. Retirement is a very recent phenomenon, dependent on the availability of alternate forms of support other than paid work. See Plakans, 'Stepping Down in Former Times: A Comparative Assessment of "Retirement" in Traditional Europe,' in D.I. Kertzer and K.W. Schaie, eds., *Age Structuring in Comparative Perspective* (Hillsdale, NJ, 1989), 176.
47 R.J. Morris, 'The Middle Class and the Property Cycle during the Industrial Revolution,' in T.C. Smout, ed., *The Search for Wealth and Stability* (London, 1979), 91–113
48 See, for example, E. Rotella and G. Alter, 'Working Class Debt in the Late Nineteenth Century United States,' *Journal of Family History*, 18 (1993), 111–34; T.K. Hareven, *Family Time and Industrial Time: The Relationship between the Family and Work in a New England Industrial Community* (New York, 1982); R.L. Ransom and R. Sutch, 'The Labor of Older Americans: Retirement of Men on and off the Job, 1870–1940,' *Journal of Economic History*, 46 (1986), 1–30; J.R. Moen, 'Rural Nonfarm Households: Leaving the Farm and Retirement of Older Men, 1860–1980,' *Social Science History*, 18 (1994), 55–75.
49 Graebner, *Retirement*, 4–5. The occasion of the speech was Osler's departure from Johns Hopkins University, where he had been professor of medicine since 1889, having previously served for fifteen years on the faculty at McGill University and the University of Philadelphia.

50 British Columbia Archives and Records Service (BCARS), GR1249, box 5, file 4, 'Old Age Pensions in British Columbia,' [mid-1929], 5–6

51 Dahlin, 'Perspectives,' 101–2; N.S. Weiler, 'Industrial Scrap Heap: Employment Patterns and Change for the Aged in the 1920s,' *Social Science History*, 13 (1989), 65–88. For women, the comparable figures are 17 per cent for ages 55–64, 12 per cent for ages 65–74, and 8 per cent for ages seventy-five and over. These figures are for the non-institutionalized elderly population. There has recently been a considerable amount of debate regarding the timing of changes in retirement behaviour; see R.A. Margo, *The Labor Force Participation of Older Americans in 1900: Further Results* (Washington, 1991); R.L. Ransom and R. Sutch, 'Labor of Older Americans'; Ransom and Sutch, 'The Decline of Retirement in the Years before Social Security: U.S. Retirement Patterns, 1870–1940,' in R. Ricardo-Campbell and E.P. Lazear, eds., *Issues in Contemporary Retirement* (Stanford, 1988), 3–26; Gratton, *Urban Elders*, 61–97; D.O. Parsons, 'Male Retirement Behavior in the United States, 1930–1950,' *Journal of Economic History*, 51 (1991), 657–74.

52 Montigny, 'Perceptions, Realities and Old Age,' 109. These calculations were based on the total population of elderly in the three communities, but the reliance on self-reported income renders the figures problematic.

53 M. MacKinnon, 'Providing for Faithful Servants: Pensioners at the CPR,' paper presented at Conference on Quantitative Canadian Economic History, Vancouver, September 1992. The plan set retirement age at sixty-five and the minimum monthly payment at $20; survivor benefits were not introduced until the late 1940s and early 1950s. MacKinnon did not examine the possible shifting of older workers to less skilled and/or lower paid jobs.

54 Canada, Committee on Old Age Pensions System for Canada, *Old Age Pensions System for Canada: Memorandum* (Ottawa, 1912), 24–5; ibid., Minutes of Proceedings, 61. See also Canada, *Journals of the House of Commons*, 1924, appendix 4, 57–8.

55 See, for example, Archives of Ontario (AO), RG 8, Series II–10–F, box 1, file 11, F. Dufresne to OAP Commission, Montreal, 30 November 1929; ibid., box 2, file 3, T. Pierson to H. Ferguson, Brantford, 31 July 1929; BCARS, GR150, box 17, file 6, Rev. A.D. Greene to provincial secretary, Quathiaski Cove, BC, 14 January 1925.

56 AO, RG 8, Series II–10–F, box 2, file 16, J. Eiler to H. Ferguson, Kitchener, 26 June 1929; ibid., box 3, file 19, individual to J.A. Ellis, Toronto, 5 August, 16 July 1929; *Canadian Magazine*, 68 (August 1927), 30

57 BCARS, GR150, box 16, file 11, individual to W. Sloan, Vancouver, 9 June 1925; ibid., deputy provincial secretary to individual, [Victoria], 10 June 1925; ibid., box 15, file 7, individual to deputy provincial secretary, Vancouver, 9 July 1925

58 AO, RG 8, Series II–10–F, box 4, file Timmins (Cochrane), I.E. Dunn to OAP
    Commission, Timmins, 20 January 1930
59 BCARS, GR150, box 3, file 3, R. Hayward to Sir R. McBride, Victoria, 17 July
    1915
60 AO, RG 8, Series II–10–F, box 4, file Oakland Twp. (Brant), J.F. McNally to
    OAP Commission, Scotland, Ont., 8 April 1929; ibid., file Lucknow Twp.
    (Brant), individual to OAP Commission, Lucknow, Ont., 16 January 1930;
    ibid., file Ripley Village (Bruce), individual to OAP Commission, Ripley, Ont.
    [early April 1929]
61 *Census of Canada, 1941* (Ottawa, 1946), VII, table 3; *Census of Canada, 1951*
    (Ottawa, 1953), III, table 3; Strong-Boag, *New Day Recalled*, 185–6
62 AO, RG 8, Series II–10–F, box 12, file Port Colborne (Welland), L.C. Ray-
    mond et al. to OAP Commission, Port Colborne, Ont., 24 September 1929
63 J. Stafford, 'The Class Struggle and the Rise of Private Pensions, 1900–1950,'
    Labour/Le Travail, 20 (1987), 147–71; M.E. McCallum, 'Corporate Welfarism
    in Canada, 1919–39,' *Canadian Historical Review*, 71 (1990), 46–79; J. Naylor,
    *The New Democracy: Challenging the Social Order in Industrial Ontario,
    1914–1925* (Toronto, 1991), 171–2; N.K. Joanette, 'Worn Out: The Origins and
    Early Development of Pensions in Canada,' PhD thesis, University of Waterloo,
    1993
64 There were ethnic variations in the rates of home ownership; among franco-
    phone Montrealers, home ownership tended to be restricted to the small mid-
    dle class and the bourgeoisie. See J.C. Bacher, *Keeping to the Marketplace: The
    Evolution of Canadian Housing Policy* (Montreal, 1993).
65 Gratton and Rotondo, 'Industrialization, the Family Economy, and the Eco-
    nomic Status of the American Elderly'; B. Gratton and F.M. Rotondo, 'The
    "Family Fund": Strategies for Security in Old Age in the Industrial Era,' in M.
    Szinovacz et al., eds., *Families and Retirement* (Newbury Park, CA, 1992),
    51–63; M.R. Haines, 'The Life Cycle, Savings, and Demographic Adaptation:
    Some Historical Evidence for the United States and Europe,' in A.S. Rossi,
    ed., *Gender and the Life Course* (New York, 1985), 43–63; M.R. Haines, 'Indus-
    trial Work and the Family Life Cycle, 1889–1890,' *Research in Economic History*,
    4 (1979), 289–356
66 B. Bradbury, 'Pigs, Cows, and Boarders: Non-Wage Forms of Survival among
    Montreal Families, 1861–91,' *Labour/Le Travail*, 14 (1984), 9–46
67 P. Johnson, 'Self-Help versus State Help: Old Age Pensions and Personal Sav-
    ings in Great Britain, 1906–1937,' *Explorations in Economic History*, 21 (1984),
    332–4; Bryden, *Old Age Pensions and Policy-Making in Canada*, 51–9; F.A. Car-
    man, 'Canadian Government Annuities,' *Political Science Quarterly*, 30 (1915),
    425–47; D. Owram, *The Government Generation: Canadian Intellectuals and*

the State, 1900–1945 (Toronto, 1986), 34–6. Private life insurance companies and fraternal insurance plans already met (and played upon) some of this 'need.' The absolute value and per capita amount of life insurance in Canada had increased remarkably since the mid-nineteenth century, particularly the plans with private companies; the per capita value of private life insurance was $10.01 in 1869, $81.32 in 1900, $636.00 in 1930, and $1148.33 in 1950. See *Canada Year Book, 1933* (Ottawa, 1933), 946–8; *Canada Year Book, 1952–53* (Ottawa, 1953), 1141–9; Strong-Boag, *New Day Recalled,* 186.

68 *Report of the Royal Commission on the Taxation of Annuities and Family Corporations* (Ottawa, 1945), 26; *Labour Gazette,* August 1928, 850

69 A non-systematic examination of one collection of government annuity case files (NA, RG 50, no. 80–81/191) provided some insight into the ways in which the program was used by individuals. A list of the occupations of annuitants to 1925 can be found in Canada, *Report of the Department of Labour, 1925–26* (Ottawa, 1927), 112–13. There is also an occupational breakdown for 1939 in NA, RG 29, vol. 1921, no. R206/100–1/50. The English experience with a similar scheme was much the same; see Hannah, *Inventing Retirement,* 5.

70 F.H. Leacey, ed., *Historical Statistics of Canada* (Ottawa, 1983), K1–7; O.J. Firestone, *Canada's Economic Development, 1867–1953* (London, 1958), 77–82; G.W. Bertram and M.B. Percy, 'Real Wage Trends in Canada 1900–26: Some Provisional Estimates,' *Canadian Journal of Economics,* 12 (1979), 299–312

71 *Census of Canada, 1941* (Ottawa, 1946), VII, table 3; *Census of Canada, 1951* (Ottawa, 1953), III, table 3

72 *Census of Canada, 1951* (Ottawa, 1953), V, table 17. While 6.1 per cent of men aged seventy or older reported themselves to be workers who had earned no wages in the past year, 11.1 per cent of women aged seventy or more placed themselves in that category.

CHAPTER 2: Institutionalizing the Dependent Elderly

1 See, for example, L. Granshaw and R. Porter, eds., *The Hospital in History* (London, 1989); P. Slack, *Poverty and Policy in Tudor and Stuart England* (London, 1988); S.J. Woolf, *The Poor in Western Europe in the Eighteenth and Nineteenth Centuries* (London, 1986); J.B. Williamson, 'Old Age Relief Policy prior to 1900: The Trend toward Restrictiveness,' *American Journal of Economics and Sociology,* 43 (1984), 369–84.

2 The term 'poorhouse' is used here for consistency, where nineteenth-century Canadians used 'poorhouse,' 'almshouse,' and 'House of Industry' interchangeably.

3 The literature on nineteenth-century poor relief is considerable. See, for example, R. Baehre, 'Paupers and Poor Relief in Upper Canada,' Canadian Histori-

cal Association *Historical Papers*, 1981, 57–90; J. Fingard, 'The Relief of the
Unemployed Poor in Saint John, Halifax, and St John's, 1815–1860,' *Acadiensis*,
5 (1975), 32–53; J.M. Whalen, 'The Nineteenth Century Almshouse System in
Saint John County,' *Histoire sociale*, 7 (1971), 5–28; B. Greenhaus, 'Paupers and
Poor Houses: The Development of Poor Relief in Early New Brunswick,' *Histoire sociale*, 1 (1968), 103–28; G. Hart, 'The Halifax Poor Man's Friend Society,
1820–1827,' *Canadian Historical Review*, 34 (1953), 109–23.
4 N. Rudy, *For Such a Time as This: L. Earl Ludlow and a History of Homes for
the Aged in Ontario, 1837–1961* (Toronto, 1987), 18–21; S.E. Stewart, 'The Inmates of the Wellington County, Ontario, House of Industry, 1877–1907,' MA
thesis, University of Victoria, 1990, 51
5 C. Haber, *Beyond Sixty-Five: The Dilemma of Old Age in America's Past* (Cambridge, 1983), 35–6; Stewart, 'Wellington County House,' 75–8. Compare B.
Bradbury, 'The Fragmented Family: Family Strategies in the Face of Death, Illness, and Poverty, Montreal, 1860–1885,' in J. Parr, ed., *Childhood and Family
in Canadian History* (Toronto, 1982), 109–28.
6 S.A. Cook, '"A Quiet Place ... to Die": Ottawa's First Protestant Old Age
Homes for Women and Men,' *Ontario History*, 81 (1989), 25–40
7 Whalen, 'Nineteenth Century Almshouse System,' 14–15; Haber, *Beyond Sixty-
Five*, 91–2; B.G. Rosenkrantz and M.A. Vinovskis, 'The Invisible Lunatics:
Old Age and Insanity in Mid-Nineteenth Century Massachusetts,' in S.S.
Spicker, ed., *Aging and the Elderly* (Atlantic Highlands, NJ, 1978), 95–126. See
also, Rudy, *For Such a Time*, 12
8 Ontario, 2 Geo. V (1912), c.82, s.14 (2); Rudy, *For Such a Time*, 13, 48–9; Stewart, 'Wellington County House,' 65; British Columbia Archives and Records
Service (BCARS), GR624, box 3, file 1, Rules and Regulations for the Government of the Provincial Home, 25 July 1895. See, for example, the rules of the
Kingston House of Industry, Queen's University Archives (QUA), no. 2262,
box 1, file 2. The same loss of voting rights occurred in British Columbia after
1893 and in Nova Scotia.
9 *Thirty-First Annual Report upon the Hospitals and Refuges, Etc. of Ontario for
1900* (Toronto, 1901), 77–81; Haber, *Beyond Sixty-Five*, 86. In 1900 these homes
received $58,226.68 in government aid and $170,002.30 in private contributions; the government funds were for upkeep, but the private funds were for a
variety of purposes.
10 *Thirty-Seventh Annual Report upon the Hospitals and Charities, Etc. of Ontario
for 1906* (Toronto, 1907), 107–16; R.B. Splane, *Social Welfare in Ontario,
1791–1893* (Toronto, 1965), 99–100; D.C. Park and J.D. Wood, 'Poor Relief
and the County House of Refuge System in Ontario, 1880–1911,' *Journal of
Historical Geography*, 18 (1992), 439–55

11 *Census of Newfoundland, 1911,* vol. 3, 13; *Census of Newfoundland, 1921,* vol. 3, 15, 33; Newfoundland, *Journal of the House of Assembly, 1910,* appendix, 33. The institutions were the Rescue Home, the Rescue and Industrial Home, the Poor Man's Shelter, the Women's Industrial and Hostel, the Men's Social, the Anchorage (for women), and the Metropole (for men).

12 Canada, Committee on Old Age Pensions System for Canada, *Old Age Pensions System for Canada: Memorandum* (Ottawa, 1912), 30

13 Ibid., 31–2; ibid., Minutes of Proceedings, 23

14 Ibid., *Memorandum,* 36

15 Ibid., 36–7

16 Ibid., 39; Manitoba, (1916) 6 Geo. V, c.81

17 *Twenty-eighth Annual Report upon the Common Gaols, Prisons and Reformatories of Ontario for 1895* (Toronto, 1896), 53, 57, 60, 68; *Thirty-first Annual Report for 1898* (Toronto, 1899), 11, 77; *Thirtieth Annual Report upon the Hospitals and Refuges, Etc. of Ontario for 1899* (Toronto, 1900), 9; Splane, *Social Welfare,* 101–3

18 BCARS, GR624, box 3, file 1, C. Chisholm to Mayor, Vancouver, 17 December 1906; University of Western Ontario (UWO), London Welfare Records, box B411, file 1912–29 A–D, J.W. McCallum to Welfare Committee, London, 24 February 1923; London Welfare Records, R. Birrell to G.A. Wenige, London, 22 July 1924

19 Archives of Ontario (AO), RG 22, unprocessed records, York, Crown Attorney/Clerk of the Peace, Inquests, 1877–1907, box 74, file A. Scott 1906; box 72, file G. Fielding 1906

20 Ibid., box 59, file A. Stullaford 1903; box 54, file J. Kamm 1902

21 Ibid., box 65, file D. Sanderson 1904

22 See, for example, ibid., box 62, file S. Hastings 1904; file E. Hicks 1904.

23 QUA, no. 2262, box 1, Minutebook 1914–16, 1; M.B. Katz, *In the Shadow of the Poorhouse: A Social History of Welfare in America* (New York, 1986), 85–109; Canada, Committee on Old Age Pensions System for Canada, *Old Age Pensions System for Canada: Memorandum* (Ottawa, 1912), Minutes of Proceedings, 174–5. At the Kingston Home in 1905 there were eight residents under 60 years, sixteen aged 60–69, twenty-two aged 70–79, forty-eight aged 80–89, and two aged 90–100. See QUA, no. 2262, Minutebook 1903–14, 30.

24 The average age at the Wellington County House of Refuge rose from 44.3 for males and 25.5 for females in 1880 to 68.1 for males and 69.2 for females in 1906. Stewart, 'Wellington County House,' 135

25 Ibid., 115, 141

26 T.A. Bishop, 'Peel Industrial Farm and House of Refuge: A Case Study of Institutional Development,' MA thesis, University of Toronto, 1982, 46, 58,

62–3, 69–70; Public Archives of New Brunswick (PANB), MC249, 4/2, 8 April 1940; 4/3, 1 March 1948

27 Stewart, 'Wellington County House,' 75–6

28 Canada, Committee on Old Age Pensions System for Canada, *Old Age Pensions System for Canada: Memorandum* (Ottawa, 1912), appendix 2, 29–30; *Thirtieth Annual Report upon the Hospitals and Refuges, Etc. of Ontario for 1899* (Toronto, 1900), 9

29 O.N. Kardal, 'A Brief Account of the History of Gimli from 1875 to 1955,' 5; *Gimli Saga: The History of Gimli, Manitoba* (Gimli, 1975), 371–2. In Saskatchewan, local ethnic and social organizations began to take a special interest in elderly members of the community who had insufficient family assets. In the 1930s, for example, the Association of Rebekah Assemblies in Estevan contributed $10 a month towards the upkeep of two women at the Wolseley home, until they began to receive the OAP. The German-Canadian Association of Saskatchewan asked the provincial minister responsible to look into the case of a needy old German-Canadian farmer near Cruikshank, giving details of his problems.

30 QUA, no. 2262, box 1, Minutebook 1914–16, 96

31 E. Goffman, *Asylums: Essays on the Social Situation of Mental Patients and Other Inmates* (Chicago, 1961), 1–124

32 Grandparenting ms, G.M. Hully to author, Peterborough, Ont. [late January 1992]

33 BCARS, GR624, box 4, file 2, individual to ?, Vancouver, 26 April 1912. The superintendent brushed off these complaints by dismissing the complainant's credibility and by describing any incidents of his shaking the residents as having being done 'in fun'; see ibid., H. McLean to provincial secretary, Kamloops, B.C., 10 May 1912.

34 QUA, no. 2622, Minutebook 1903–14, 30

35 Cook, 'A Quiet Place … to Die'

36 See, for example, BCARS, GR624, box 4, file 4, H. McLean to provincial secretary, Kamloops, BC, 15 March, 7 April, 25 April, 17 May 1913; ibid., box 6, file 3, 28 June 1917; ibid., to deputy provincial secretary, 8 November 1917

37 BCARS, GR366, box 6, file 18, case report, Salmon Arm, BC, 27 August 1948, and attached documents

38 BCARS, GR624, box 3, file 3, H. McLean to provincial secretary, Kamloops, 17 May 1909; ibid., to Deputy Provincial Secretary, 1 July 1909; ibid., 23 August 1909; ibid., box 5, file 3, E. Kingwell to H.E. Young, Kamloops, 21 June 1915

39 Newfoundland, *Proceedings of the House of Assembly, 1912*, 13, 18; Newfoundland, *Journal of the House of Assembly, 1912*, appendix, 662–5, 'Report of the Poor Asylum, 1911'; Newfoundland, (1911) 1 Geo. V, c.32; Public Archives of

Newfoundland and Labrador (PANL), GN1/3/A, no. 209/1910, colonial secretary to Sir R. Williams, St John's, 16 December 1910. The building was popularly known as the poorhouse throughout the period under investigation, and Sudbury Street was known as 'Poorhouse Lane'; see Memorial University of Newfoundland Folklore Archives ms, 69–015A/p.6.

40 Newfoundland, *Journal of the House of Assembly, 1912,* appendix, 662–5, 'Report of the Poor Asylum, 1911'

41 Ibid., 371; ibid., *1925,* appendix, 532

42 *Census of Newfoundland, 1911,* vol. 3, 31; *Census of Newfoundland, 1921,* vol. 3, 33; Newfoundland, *Journal of the House of Assembly, 1912,* appendix, 664–5, 'Report of the Poor Asylum, 1911'; *Census of Newfoundland, 1921,* appendix, 356; *Census of Newfoundland, 1910,* appendix, 36

43 St John's *Evening Telegram,* 22 January 1934, 5

44 Newfoundland, *Journal of the House of Assembly, 1930,* appendix, 561, 'Report of the Poor Asylum, 1929.' The physical description of the home comes from the Vatcher report, *Evening Telegram,* 22 January 1934, 5.

45 Newfoundland, (1931) 22 Geo. V, c.12, ss.545–70

46 The records of the Saint John Municipal Home are found in PANB, MC249.

47 PANL, GN13/1, box 357, file 'Grand Jury Report'; *Evening Telegram,* 26 December 1933

48 The report is summarized in *Evening Telegram,* 20 January 1934, 4, and printed in full in the 22 January 1934, 5, 7, 10, and 23 January 1934, 5, 7, issues. The following summary and quotes are taken from that version of the full report. The original report is in PANL, GN2/5, file 603, and is also reprinted in the St John's *Daily News,* 22 January 1934, 6–9.

49 PANL, GN38/S6–6–1, file 5, Dr J.St.P. Knight to H.M. Mosdell, St John's, 30 June 1934

50 James Struthers reports a revolt at an Ontario house of refuge. When an elderly couple wished to wed, the authorities objected and discharged the man from the institution, so angering the residents that they subjected the board members to 'yelling and hooting' when they drove away from the refuge. See Struthers, *The Limits of Affluence: Welfare in Ontario, 1920–1970* (Toronto, 1995).

51 PANL, GN38/S6–6–1, file 5, Dr J.St.P. Knight to H.M. Mosdell, St John's, 30 June 1934; ibid., file 6, Mosdell to J.C. Puddester, St John's, 21 May 1934; ibid., Puddester to Mosdell, [St John's], 1 June 1934; ibid., file 5, Mosdell to Puddester, 3 July 1934; *Daily News,* 1 June 1934, 3; *Evening Telegram,* 4 June 1934, 8; 7 June 1934, 6

52 M. Tennant, 'Elderly Indigents and Old Men's Homes, 1880–1920,' *New Zealand Journal of History,* 17 (1983), 3–20, notes a similar ignoring of residents elsewhere.

53 PANL, GN13/2/A, box 446, file 'Grand Jury Reports, 1937–1938'; ibid., file
    'Grand Jury Reports 1939–1940'; ibid., GN38/S6–6–1, file 12. Grand juries per-
    formed similar inquiries elsewhere in Canada and were significant in articulat-
    ing popular attitudes and standards for the care and standard of living of
    senior citizens; see, for example, Toronto *Daily Star*, 30 September 1948, 2
54 *Evening Telegram*, 9 December 1946, 3 January 1948; *Daily News*, 14 December
    1948
55 E.-A. Montigny offers evidence of the long-standing character of community-
    based support for the elderly; see 'Perceptions, Realities and Old Age,' PhD
    thesis, University of Ottawa, 1994, 132–60.
56 BCARS, GR624, box 3, file 3, V. Jany to J.H. Hawthornthwaite, Nanaimo, 7
    January 1909; ibid., box 4, file 3, J.M. Lomprey et al. to ?, Nelson, 12 Septem-
    ber 1912; ibid., file 5, W.A. Pardoe to provincial secretary, Lower Arrow Lake,
    BC, 13 September 1911, and file
57 BCARS, GR366, box 4, file 6, report by Constable F.E. Bradner, Nanaimo,
    BC, 22 September 1925; AO, RG 8, Series II–10–F, box 1, file 6, F. Sturm to
    OAP Commission, Dome Creek, BC, 10 February 1930
58 BCARS, GR624, box 5, file 2, J.T. Bardolph to L. Norris, Lumby, BC, 28 Jan-
    uary 1914
59 See, for example, BCARS, GR150, box 7, file 3, H.H. Docksteader to H.W.
    King, Midway, BC, 16 August 1915; ibid., file 4, J. Simpson to C.S. Campbell,
    Greenwood, BC, 13 March 1917; ibid., file 6, Deputy Provincial Secretary to
    Secretary of Nanaimo Hospital, [Victoria], 21 October 1919; ibid., box 13, file
    6, E. McDougall to J. Oliver, Wellington, BC, 14 June 1920.
60 AO, RG 8, Series II–10–F, box 6, file Hastings County, individual to Parlia-
    ment Buildings, Bonarlaw, Ont., 14 June 1929
61 Ibid., box 7, file Drummond Twp. (Lanark), individual to OAP Commission,
    Balderson, Ont., 8 June 1929. To avoid any misunderstanding, the writer made
    it clear that he did not intend to keep the man once he was able to pay.
62 AO, RG 22, unprocessed records, York, Crown Attorney/Clerk of the Peace,
    Inquests 1877–1907, box 64, file H. Nixon 1904
63 See, for example, ibid., Crown Attorney/Clerk of the Peace, Inquests 1877–1907,
    box 63, file M. Lane 1904.
64 H.J. Dorgan, 'The Old Age Pension Applicant: A Study of 154 Applicants for
    Old Age Pension at the Toronto Department of Public Welfare in December
    1948,' MSW thesis, University of Toronto, 1949, 9
65 PANL, GN37/1, box 2, file no. 2492. On the state programs of support for the
    elderly in Newfoundland, see Snell, 'The Newfoundland Old Age Pension
    Programme 1911–1949,' *Acadiensis*, 23 (1993), 86–109.
66 PANL, GN37/1, box 10, file no. 14591

67 See, for example, ibid., box 11, file no. 13863; ibid., box 5, file no. 5104.
68 Ibid., box 5, file no. 5438. See also, for example, ibid., box 8, file no. 10911; BCARS, GR624, box 4, file 1, G.E. Duncan to ?, Vernon, BC, 13 December 1910; GR366, box 6, file 5, K. McRae to deputy provincial secretary, Nanaimo, BC, 20 February 1939.
69 See, for example, BCARS, GR624, box 3, file 4, W.A. Whitelaw to provincial secretary, Vancouver, 25 May 1910; ibid., box 4, file 1, W.H. Keary to T. Gifford, New Westminster, BC, 18 January 1911; ibid., GR150, box 7, file 6, J. Shaw to provincial secretary, Nanaimo, BC, 17 October 1919; ibid., GR366, box 5, file 27, T. King to F. Hurley, Golden, BC, 18 May 1945; ibid., box 7, file 5; ibid., box 7, file 23, case report, Salmon Arm, BC, 20 August 1947. Hospitals had traditionally been a haven to the needy elderly; see, for example, Woolf, *The Poor in Western Europe*, 93–5.
70 BCARS, GR366, box 7, file 10, case report, Kamloops, BC, 4 March 1948. See, for example, BCARS, GR624, box 3, file 3, B. Brophy to Captain Tatton, Lytton, BC, 5 October 1909; ibid., GR366, box 5, file 40, case report, Alberni, BC, 5 May 1944; ibid., box 7, file 2, K.M. Davies to C.M. Lundy, Quesnel, BC, 6 November 1947
71 BCARS, GR366, box 5, file 28, report of B.J. Shannon, Chilliwack, BC, 28 May 1945
72 For figures on the number of institutionalized elderly in 1931, see *Census of Canada, 1931* (Ottawa, 1935), 9, table 9.
73 Compare E. Shapiro, 'We've Come a Long Way but Are We There?' *Canadian Journal on Aging*, 11 (1992), 206. Ethnic groups and fraternal organizations were both active in founding residential old age institutions in the United States, relying less than Canadians on the initiative of state and quasi-state agencies; see F.E. Parker, E.M. Stewart, and M. Conymgton, comps., *Care of Aged Persons in the United States* (New York, 1976 [1929]), 160–83. There were also a number of private, commercial institutions catering to the elderly; see V. Strong-Boag, *The New Day Recalled: Lives of Girls and Women in English Canada, 1919–1939* (Toronto, 1988), 187.
74 *Census of Canada, 1931* (Ottawa, 1935), 9, tables 12 and 14; C.K. Warsh, *Moments of Unreason: The Practice of Canadian Psychiatry and the Homewood Retreat, 1883–1923* (Montreal, 1989)
75 AO, RG 8, Series II–10–F, box 6, file Hastings County, C. Thompson to OAP Commission, Belleville, Ont., 3 December 1929; ibid., file Huron County, G.W. Holman to Dr Jamieson, Goderich, Ont., 9 December 1929; ibid., Holman to J.A. Ellis, 6 August, 7 November 1929; ibid., file Hastings County, J.W. Haggerty to OAP Commission, 7 November, 2 December 1929; ibid., Holman to Dr. Jamieson, Goderich, Ont., 9 December 1929; ibid., box 10, file

Prince Edward, E.A. Adams to OAP Commission, Picton, Ont., 20 September 1929

76 Canada, *Report of the Department of Labour, 1926–7* (Ottawa, 1927), 93–4. While these figures are clearly of dubious accuracy, they do give some indication of the extent of state support for the indigent elderly.

77 Ibid., 95. In 1926 Ottawa had five institutions specifically for the elderly. They housed 466 residents that year. Three other institutions had small numbers of elderly among their residents. A further 140 elderly in private residences received at least partial support from the city's social service department. Ottawa thus aided 641 elderly citizens. The city's post-sixty-five population was calculated from the 1921 and 1931 censuses, evenly dividing the growth in that population that had occurred over the period. See *Census of Canada, 1921*, II, table 17, 92; *Census of Canada, 1931*, III, table 29, 814–15.

78 On friendly societies, see, A. Mitchell, 'The Function and Malfunction of Mutual Aid Societies in Nineteenth-Century France,' in J. Barry and C. Jones, eds., *Medicine and Charity before the Welfare State* (London, 1991), 172–89; B. Palmer, *Working-Class Experience: The Rise and Reconstitution of Canadian Labour, 1800–1980* (Toronto, 1983), 78–80. The claim in such societies was based on the contribution of the wage-earner, invariably a skilled male, but widows did receive some assistance.

79 Canada, Committee on Old Age Pensions System for Canada, *Old Age Pensions System for Canada: Memorandum* (Ottawa, 1912), 25; Canada, *Journals of the House of Commons*, 1924, appendix 4, 91, 93. For a study of institutionalization of the elderly in more recent years, see W.F. Forbes et al., *Institutionalization of the Elderly in Canada* (Toronto, 1987).

80 AO, RG 8, Series II–10–F, box 2, file 13, individual to OAP Commission, Hamilton, 16 September 1929

81 Canada, Committee on Old Age Pensions System for Canada, *Old Age Pensions System for Canada: Memorandum* (Ottawa, 1912), 26

82 Ibid., 24; PANB, RS24, 1930 RE/2, 'Interim Report of the Commission on Old Age Pensions,' April 1930, 24. This medicalization of aging – the increasingly negative emphasis on the physical characteristics associated with senescence – was best exemplified when the old age pension program was expanded to include pensions for the blind in 1937, linking one 'disability' with another.

83 Canada, Committee on Old Age Pensions System for Canada, *Old Age Pensions System for Canada: Memorandum* (Ottawa, 1912), Minutes of Proceedings, 61

84 Canada, *Journals of the House of Commons*, 1924, appendix 4, 85. On Alberta policies regarding the elderly, see A. Finkel, 'Social Credit and the Unemployed,' *Alberta History*, 31 (spring 1983), 30.

CHAPTER 3: The Family and Intergenerational Support

1 M. Anderson, 'The Impact on the Family Relationships of the Elderly of
Changes since Victorian Times in Government Income-Maintenance Provi-
sion,' in E. Shanas and M.B. Sussman, eds., *Family Bureaucracy and the Elderly*
(Durham, NC, 1977), 36–59; J.S. Quadagno, 'The Transformation of Old Age
Security,' in D.D. Van Tassel, ed., *Old Age in a Bureaucratic Society* (New York,
1986), 142–8
2 Anderson, 'Impact on Family Relationships'; W.A. Achenbaum, *Old Age in the
New Land: The American Experience since 1790* (Baltimore, 1978), 76, 120
3 D. Thomson, 'Welfare and the Historians,' in L. Bonfield et al., eds., *The
World We Have Gained* (Oxford, 1986), 364; D. Thomson, 'The Decline of Social Welfare: Falling State Support for the Elderly Since Early Victorian Times,'
Ageing and Society, 4 (1984), 451–82
4 National Archives of Canada (NA), RG 29, vol. 135, no. 208-5-4 pt. 1, E.A.
Thomas, memo for the deputy minister, Ottawa, 12 October 1932. The basis of
these figures is unknown.
5 V. Strong-Boag, *The New Day Recalled: Lives of Girls and Women in English
Canada, 1919–1939* (Toronto, 1987), 186
6 B. Elliott, *Irish Migrants in the Canadas* (Kingston and Montreal, 1988),
195–232; N. Davies, '"Patriarchy from the Grave": Family Relations in 19th
Century New Brunswick Wills,' *Acadiensis,* 13 (1984), 91–100; W.P. Ward,
'Family Papers and the New Social History,' *Archivaria,* 14 (1982), 64–6
7 M. Anderson, *Family Structure in Nineteenth-Century Lancashire* (Cambridge,
1971); P. Stearns, *Old Age in European Society: The Case of France* (New York,
1976), 21–2. D. Thomson, '"I Am Not My Father's Keeper": Families and the
Elderly in Nineteenth Century England,' *Law and History Review,* 2 (1984),
265–86, argued that families were quite reluctant to accept responsibility for
needy elderly parents.
8 T.K. Hareven, *Family Time and Industrial Time: The Relationship between
Family and Work in a New England Industrial Community* (Cambridge, 1982),
108–9; S.S. Kulis, *Why Honor Thy Father and Mother? Class, Mobility, and
Family Ties in Later Life* (New York, 1991), 38–45, 96, 131
9 Anderson, 'Impact on Family Relationships,' 50–1
10 J.S. Quadagno, *Aging in Early Industrial Society: Work, Family, and Social Policy
in Nineteenth-Century England* (New York, 1982)
11 Anderson, 'Impact on Family Relationships,' 54; Quadagno, *Aging in Early Industrial Society*
12 See, for example, Archives of Ontario (AO), RG 8, Series II–10–F, box 2, file
25, D. Farncomb to J.A. Ellis, Oshawa, Ont., 20 August 1929.

13 University of Western Ontario (UWO), London Welfare Records, box B411, file 1912–29 A–D, J.W. McCallum to mayor, London, 22 November 1915; ibid., McCallum to individuals, London, 23 November 1915; ibid., individual to McCallum, 25 November 1915

14 See also, for example, British Columbia Archives and Records Service (BCARS), GR150, box 9, file 4, deputy provincial secretary to government agent, [Victoria] 14 November 1921; ibid., government agent to deputy provincial secretary, Nelson, BC, 7 December 1921.

15 For more detailed information see J.G. Snell, 'Filial Responsibility Laws in Canada: An Historical Study,' *Canadian Journal on Aging*, 9 (1990), 268–77. Even when prosecutions occurred, magistrates were very reluctant to issue a support order; the Ontario Department of Public Welfare alleged that in more than 90 per cent of such cases, no maintenance order was made K. Bryden, *Old Age Pensions and Policy-Making in Canada* (Montreal, 1974) 232 n.57.

16 BCARS, GR927, vol. 10–13; GR1827, vol. 1–2; ibid., GR1883, vol. 3; ibid., GR1839, vol. 2. The one case is ibid., GR1827, vol. 1, 193–4. As with the Ontario jurisdictions, these courts were selected because of the continuous run of records that were available.

17 Thomson, 'I Am Not My Father's Keeper,' 274–6, found a similar lack of enforcement of such legislation in nineteenth-century England.

18 This is true in Saskatchewan, British Columbia, and Ontario, where detailed welfare records were available. See, for example, Saskatchewan Archives (SA), T.C. Douglas Papers, R33.1, XVII, 633 (17–2).

19 BCARS, GR150, box 16, file 3, deputy provincial secretary to government agent, [Victoria], 18 May 1925. See also, for example, ibid., box 14, file 3, 12 May 1924; ibid., box 15, file 4, 11 February 1925; ibid., box 14, file 11, W.V. Shepherd to A.T. Stephenson, Ladysmith, BC, 2 August 1922.

20 BCARS, GR150, box 17, file 5, deputy provincial secretary to R.H. Neelands, [Victoria], 9 December 1925

21 Indeed, state and familial responsibility for the needy elderly had long been shared and recognized in legislation; see D. Thomson, 'The Welfare of the Elderly in the Past,' in M. Pelling and R.M. Smith, eds., *Life, Death, and the Elderly: Historical Perspectives* (London, 1991), 197.

22 As some commentators have pointed out, another area of compatibility is that state pensions for the elderly have always been at best barely adequate for the recipients' needs; in practice the elderly remained dependent on a wide variety of other sources of support, particularly from female family members. See M. McIntosh, 'The State and the Oppression of Women,' in A. Kuhn and A. Wolpe, eds., *Feminism and Materialism: Women and Modes of Production* (London, 1978), 273.

23 NA, RG 29, vol. 151, no. 208–6–11 pt. 2, 28

24 Ibid., vol. 152, no. 208–7–1 pt. 2, memo of recommendations, 7. See also, for example, ibid., vol. 148A, no. 208–6–7 pt. 1, M.A. MacPherson to R.B. Bennett, Regina, 1 February 1932; ibid., to W.A. Gordon, Regina, 20 February 1932; Saskatoon *Star-Phoenix*, 2 February 1932. As E.-A. Montigny points out, it had long been the practice of state officials to perceive a decline in traditional family behaviour; see 'Perceptions, Realities and Old Age,' PhD thesis, University of Ottawa, 1994.

25 NA, RG 29, vol. 126, no. 208–1–4, S.A. Cudmore, memo on the Proposed Statistics of Old Age Pensioners, [April? 1939]. See also, for example, B.C. Department of Health and Welfare, *The Administration of the Old Age Pensions Act: Annual Report, 1948–49* (Victoria, 1950), 11; 1932 speech of the Ontario minister of welfare, in NA, RG 29, vol. 147, no. 208–6–5 pt. 1; NA, R.B. Bennett Papers, reel M1270, no. 334568–69, J.T. Simpson to Bennett, Ottawa, 4 March 1935.

26 BCARS, GR1249, box 3, file 9, E.S.H. Winn to W.C. Clark, [Vancouver], 30 November 1942

27 NA, RG 29, vol. 135, no. 208–5–4 pt. 1, E.A. Thomas, memo to the deputy minister, Ottawa, 12 October 1932

28 J.E. Laycock, 'The Canadian System of Old Age Pensions,' Ph.D. thesis, University of Chicago, 1952, 280, 287–8

29 NA, RG 29, vol. 151, no. 208–6–11 pt. 2, 27; ibid., vol. 153, no. 208–7–2 pt. 1, vol. 2, 49–50; ibid., vol. 133, no. 208–5–2 pt. 2, C.A. Dunning to A. Macdonald, Ottawa, 24 February 1938

30 Ibid., vol. 127, no. 208–1–13, J.R. Forest to W.C. Clark, Quebec, 14 May 1938; ibid., Forest to J.W. MacFarlane, Quebec, 31 January 1939

31 Ibid., J.W. MacFarlane, memo to W.C. Clark, Ottawa, 13 February 1940; ibid., [Clark] to C.F. Elliott, Ottawa, 17 May 1938

32 Ibid., W.C. Clark to C.F. Elliott, Ottawa, 11 May 1939; ibid., Elliott to Clark, Ottawa, 17 May 1939

33 NA, W.L.M. King Papers, reel C3740, no. 222644; *Windsor Star*, 20 February 1932, clipping in NA, RG 29, vol. 147, no. 208–6–5 pt. 1

34 NA, RG 29, vol. 148A, no. 208–6–7 pt. 1, W.J. Pallinson to C.A. Dunning, Regina, 28 March 1938

35 BCARS, GR1249, box 2, file 7, E.S.H. Winn to J.P. Hogg, [Vancouver], 19 September, 24 October 1940; ibid., box 6, file 6, Winn to G.S. Pearson, [Vancouver], 3 December 1940

36 See, for example, *Vancouver Daily Province*, 23 June 1934, 30 November 1940, 19 November 1941; *Vancouver Sun*, 7 August 1934, 3 December 1940, 24 December 1941; *Victoria Daily Times*, 8 August 1934, 30 November 1940.

37 NA, RG 29, vol. 128, no. 208–2–3 pt. 1, memo from Blackie to V.D. McElary, [Edmonton], 7 June 1938

38 BCARS, GR1249, box 2, file 7, E.S.H. Winn to G.M. Sloan, [Vancouver], 12 December 1932

39 Refusing to accept the implied slur on her children, one seventy-year-old widow answered: 'no failure they can not maintain themselves and families.' UWO, Lambton County OAP Commission, box B887

40 Ibid., box B886

41 NA, RG 29, vol. 131, no. 208–4–3, B.R. King, Report on Inspections of Old Age Pension Payments, 4 February 1935, 6; ibid., vol. 128, no. 208–2–3 pt. 2, V.D. McElary to J.W. MacFarlane, Winnipeg, 16 August 1940; ibid., vol. 139, no. 208–5–6 pt. 3, L.D. McNeill to MacFarlane, Winnipeg, 29 September 1945

42 NA, RG 29, vol. 132, no. 208–5–2 pt. 1, E.H. Blois to J.W. MacFarlane, Halifax, 9 April 1937; ibid., pt. 3, F.R. Davis to J.L. Ilsley, Halifax, 2, 20 March 1942

43 *Annual Report of the Bureau of Child Protection, 1936–37* (Regina, 1937), 21

44 NA, RG 29, vol. 152, no. 208–7–1 pt. 1, E.A. Thomas to H.H. Ward, Winnipeg, 11 October 1928

45 BCARS, GR1249, box 6, file 6, memo re Old Age Pensions – Parents' Maintenance, [np], 15 November 1939. Alberta, Ontario, and Quebec charged $185; British Columbia and Manitoba, $180; Nova Scotia and New Brunswick, $210; PEI's policy is not known.

46 Joint Committee of the Senate and House of Commons on Old Age Security, 1950, *Minutes of Proceedings and Evidence,* 31

47 AO, RG 8, Series II–10–F, box 3, file 6, [J.A. Ellis] to G. Gibbon, [Toronto], 14 October 1929; ibid., file 10, director to H. Tolley, [Toronto], 22 July 1929

48 *St Thomas Times-Journal,* 12 November 1930, clipping in NA, RG 29, vol. 137, no. 208–5–5 pt. 1; Ontario, *Annual Report of the Department of Public Welfare, 1934–35,* 3

49 AO, RG 8, Series II–10–F, box 1, file 2, [OAP Commission] to O.L. Joyce, [Toronto], 20 November 1929

50 Ibid., box 2, file 2, [J.A. Ellis] to H.M. Lynch, [Toronto], 10 October 1929

51 NA, RG 29, vol. 144, no. 208–5–9A, H.H. Ward to P. Williams, Ottawa, 4 February 1932. See also ibid., vol. 147, no. 208–6–5 pt. 1, W.G. Martin to R.B. Bennett, Toronto, 13 March 1933.

52 Grandparenting ms, V. Chrisp to author, St Catharines, Ont., 12 January 1992

53 NA, RG 29, vol. 147, no. 208–6–5 pt. 1, M.F. Hepburn to C.A. Dunning, Toronto, 17 March 1938; ibid., vol. 128, V.D. McElary to J.W. MacFarlane, Toronto, 26 November 1939, 1 June 1940

54 Ibid., vol. 128, V.D. McElary to J.W. MacFarlane, Toronto, 26 November 1939, 1 June 1940; ibid., vol. 137, no. 208–5–5 pt. 3, E.R. Swettenham, memo for J.W. MacFarlane, Ottawa, 18 December 1941, and enclosed tables

55 NA, RG 29, vol. 129, no. 208-2-3 PT. 4, V.D. McElary to J.W. MacFarlane, Toronto, 3 May 1944; ibid., W.C. Clark to McElary, Ottawa, 11 May 1944

56 Ibid., vol. 144, no. 208-5-9A, A.W. Neill to W.A. Gordon, Alberni, BC, 28 July 1932; ibid., vol. 151, no. 208-6-11 pt. 2, 27

57 BCARS, GR1249, box 1, file 8, E.S.H. Winn to G.S. Pearson, [Vancouver], 6 March 1936; ibid., file 9, R.W.L. to A. Bell, [Vancouver], 3 November 1937

58 Ibid., box 5, file 4, memo re Old Age Pensions in B.C., 21 May 1937

59 Ibid., box 1, memo, 29 December 1934; ibid., file 10, E.S.H. Winn, memo re interview with G.S. Pearson, Vancouver, 19 January 1938; ibid., box 6, file 6, E.S.H. Winn, memo, [Vancouver], 3 July 1942. At first, a single child earning $90 a month or more was held liable to support a needy parent, and this rose to $100 in 1938; in 1938 a married child was liable for support once income had reached $125 a month, plus $15 for each child. In 1942 a single child with a net annual income of $1100, or a married child with a net annual income of $1800, was required to contribute all income above that amount until the parent received adequate support; a $300 additional exemption was allowed for each dependent child under the age of eighteen.

60 Ibid., box 6, file 6, E.W. Griffith to E.S.H. Winn, Victoria, 25 June 1942; ibid., Winn to Griffith, [Vancouver], 3 July 1942

61 Ibid., G.S. Pearson to E.S.H. Winn, Victoria, 12 February 1936

62 Ibid., box 2, file 1; ibid., box 1, file 5. The 1939 motion was ruled out of order by the Speaker.

63 Vancouver Daily Sun, 3 December 1940; Vancouver Daily Province, 16 March 1944

64 NA, RG 29, vol. 151, no. 208-6-11 pt. 2, 27

65 The case files are not available for systematic examination; rather, what is available is the correspondence of the Old Age Pension Board (BCARS, GR1249).

66 In Saskatchewan no relevant government records are extant, but considerable material was found in the papers of Premier T.C. Douglas and of cabinet ministers J.M. Uhrich and J.H. Sturdy.

67 NA, RG 29, vol. 144, no. 208-5-9A, H.L. Greenwood to G.H. Brown, Vancouver, 21 March 1933; ibid., A.W. Neill to W.A. Gordon, Ottawa, 7 March, 1 April 1933

68 See also, for example, BCARS, GR1249, box 1, file 8, E.S.H. Winn to G.S. Pearson, [Vancouver], 22 February 1936; ibid., box 2, file 3, G.S. Pearson to E.S.H. Winn, Victoria, 4 April 1941; ibid., Winn to Pearson, [Vancouver], 7 April 1941.

69 BCARS, GR1249, box 1, file 10, E.S.H. Winn to G.S. Pearson, [Vancouver], 6 May 1938

70 See, for example, BCARS, GR1249, box 1, file 10, H.L. Greenwood to G.S. Pearson, [Vancouver], 11 February 1938.

71 Ibid., box 2, file 1, E.S.H. Winn to G.S. Pearson, [Vancouver], 17 January 1939. See also, for example, ibid., box 1, file 10, E.S.H. Winn to G.S. Pearson, [Vancouver], 14 January 1938.

72 See, for example, UWO, London Welfare Records, box B411, file 1912–29 A–D, memo of April 1925, application of 7 August 1923, report of 10 September 1923; AO, RG 8, Series II–10–F, box 2, file 22, [J.A. Ellis] to H. Freeman, [Toronto], 12 November 1929.

73 AO, RG 8, Series II–10–F, box 4, file Timmins (Cochrane), individual to OAP Commission, Timmins, Ont., 16 November 1929

74 BCARS, GR1249, box 6, file 6, E.S.H. Winn to N.W. Whittaker, [Vancouver], 25 July 1941

75 Ibid., box 2, file 10, E.S.H. Winn to Constable F. Broughton, [Vancouver], 14 February 1935; ibid., Winn to Corporal J.F. Johnston, [Vancouver], 13 March 1935; ibid., file 7, Memo, 19 June 1935; ibid., H.L. Greenwood to G.M. Sloan, [Vancouver], 19 June 1935

76 Ibid., box 4, file 3, E.S.H. Winn to R.L. Maitland, [Vancouver], 10 December 1938

77 See, for example, ibid., box 2, file 2, E.S.H. Winn to G.S. Pearson, [Vancouver], 26 January, 9 February, 5 November 1940.

78 Ibid., memo, 20 May 1940

79 UWO, London OAP Committee Record Books, 1931, 125–6

80 See, for example, BCARS, GR1249, box 1, file 10, E.S.H. Winn to G.S. Pearson, 10[?] January 1938; ibid., box 2, file 2, Winn to D. Spurr, [Vancouver], 21 December 1940; ibid., box 4, file 3, Winn to T. Reid, [Vancouver], 1 April 1939; SA, J.H. Sturdy Papers, M14, box 42, Social Welfare Case Files, no. G17 (1), memo [nd].

81 See, for example, UWO, Lambton County OAP Commission, box B882, individual to J.A. Huey, Bothwell, Ont., 29 October 1934; individual to Pension Board, [Forest, Ont.], 12 October 1931; J.A. Huey to OAP Commission, Sarnia, 17 October 1931.

82 Ibid., individual to J.A. Huey, Arkona, Ont., 28 June 1934

83 UWO, London Welfare Records, box B408, E.V. Berry to R.H. Cooper, London, 25 June 1948. Compare ibid., 9 December 1950.

84 M.A. Crowther, 'Family Responsibility and State Responsibility in Britain before the Welfare State,' *Historical Journal*, 25 (1982), 131–45

85 Quadagno, *Aging in Early Industrial Society*, 133–8; J. van Houtte and J. Breda, 'Maintenance of the Aged by Their Adult Children: The Family as a Residual Agency in the Solution of Poverty in Belgium,' *Law & Society Review*, 12 (1977–8), 645–64

86 Montigny, 'Perceptions, Realities and Old Age,' chapter 5

87 J.A. Falconbridge, 'Living Arrangements of Elderly People,' MSW thesis, University of Toronto, 1951, 82. In this study of 100 Toronto elderly, fifteen had moved to their current location in order to be with or near a family member (ibid., 49).

CHAPTER 4: Property and the Culture of Entitlement

1 C. Gaffield, 'Children, Schooling and Family Reproduction in Nineteenth-Century Ontario,' *Canadian Historical Review*, 72 (1991), 183–5; C. Gaffield, 'Labouring and Learning in Nineteenth-Century Canada: Children in the Changing Process of Family Reproduction,' in R. Smandych et al., eds., *Dimensions of Childhood: Essays on the History of Children and Youth in Canada* (Winnipeg, 1991), 18–21

2 As with many collective family processes, when individual interests were considered, the results tended to be highly gendered; women received markedly fewer benefits and less protection than did men, whether in marriage portions, in inheritance, or during old age.

3 For a more extended discussion of maintenance agreements and their adaptation by twentieth-century Canadian elderly, see J.G. Snell, 'Maintenance Agreements for the Elderly: Canada, 1900–1950,' *Journal of the Canadian Historical Association*, new series, 3 (1992), 197–216.

4 The following paragraph is drawn from B.B. Lee-Whiting, *Harvest of Stones: The German Settlement in Renfrew County* (Toronto, 1985), 69–77; B.B. Lee-Whiting, 'Doddy-House Duties Outlined in 1912,' *German-Canadian Yearbook*, 6 (1981), 89–102.

5 M. Verdon, 'The Quebec Stem Family Revisited,' in K. Ishwaran, ed., *Canadian Families: Ethnic Variations* (Toronto, 1980), 105–24; H.M. Miner, *St. Denis: French-Canadian Parish* (Chicago, 1939), 212–14; A. Greer, *Peasant, Lord, and Merchant: Rural Society in Three Quebec Parishes 1740–1840* (Toronto, 1985); W.S. Reid, 'An Early French-Canadian Pension Agreement,' *Canadian Historical Review*, 27 (1946), 291–4

6 National Archives of Canada (NA), RG 29, vol. 128, no. 208-2-3 pt. 2, V.D. McElary to J.W. MacFarlane, Quebec, 3 March 1939. A second son also continued to live with his parents on the property ten years later.

7 University of Western Ontario (UWO), London OAP Committee Record Books 1933, 221. See also, for example, UWO, London Welfare Records, box B408, E.V. Berry to H.E. Copeland, London, 26 April 1949, where the maintenance agreement was with a 'nephew-in-law.'

8 UWO, London Welfare Records, box B419, 'OAP Applications E,' relief officer to S. Baker, London, 21 October 1933

9 NA, RG 29, vol. 128, no. 208-2-3 pt. 2, V.D. McElary to J.W. MacFarlane,

Fredericton, NB, 11 February 1941; *Report of the Commission Appointed to Consider Old Age Pensions* (Halifax, 1930), 8

10 See, for example, British Columbia Archives and Records Service (BCARS), GR624, box 2, file 4, application of 11 June 1903; ibid., file 5, E.M. Carncross to J.A. Anderson, Cloverdale, BC, 1 February 1908; ibid., J. Baird to deputy provincial secretary, Cumberland, BC, 7 April 1904; ibid., file 6, A. McInnes to A.C. Riddle, New Denver, BC, 6 October 1905.

11 UWO, London Welfare Records, box B408, E.V. Berry to City Administration Board, London, 24 March 1944. See also, for example, ibid., box B411, file 1912-29 A-D, E. Davis to City Council, London, 12 April 1917; ibid., J.W. McCallum to mayor, London, 21 April 1917; Grandparenting ms, individual to author, Agincourt, Ont., 18 February 1992.

12 See, for example, UWO, London Welfare Records, box B408, E.V. Berry to N. Toll, London, 8 October 1946; ibid., box B411, file 1912-29 A-D, agreement of 11 February 1915; ibid., file 1929-44 [A-C], F. McKay to individual, London, 25 September 1939; ibid., to Miss Turner, London, 21 August 1940.

13 See, for example, UWO, London Welfare Records, box B408, E.V. Berry to Welfare Board, London, 26 October 1944; ibid., Berry to R.H. Cooper, London, 31 October 1947, 18 August 1948.

14 Ibid., E.V. Berry to R.H. Cooper, London, 18 August, 31 October 1947; Ontario, 2 Geo. V (1912), c.82, s.12(1); BCARS, GR624, box 2, file 5, example of Form F; Ontario, 3 Geo. VI (1939), c.47, s.32; Revised Statutes of Nova Scotia (RSNS), 3rd Series (1864), c.89, s.39; RSNS, 1923, c.48, s.28; Newfoundland, (1931) 22 Geo. V, c.12, ss.550, 554

15 NA, RG 29, vol. 143, no. 208-5-9 pt. 1, A.W. Neill to P. Heenan, Alberni, BC, 14 August [1927]; Archives of Ontario (AO), RG 8, Series II-10-F, box 2, file 22, H. Freeman to OAP Commission, North Bay, Ont., 23 September 1929; ibid., box 3, file 6, G. Gibbon to OAP Commission, Port Arthur, Ont., 10 October 1929; ibid., box 5, file Leamington (Essex), OAP Commission to individual, 20 December 1929; ibid., box 8, file Lincoln county, C. Wismer to J.A. Ellis, St Catharines, 5 October 1929. That officials had not thought out OAP policies in the early years is effectively demonstrated by the fact that answering this question in the affirmative did not constitute a transfer, nor were there any follow-up procedures leading to transfer.

16 Some applicants were clever enough to try to turn this process to their own advantage. Understanding that the state would not throw them out of their homes, they answered 'yes' to the question in the belief that this constituted transfer and that the state would thereafter have to pay the taxes on the property. See AO, RG 8, Series II-10-F, box 6, file Haliburton County, individual to OAP Commission, Gelert, Ont., mid-January 1930.

17 AO, RG 8, Series II–10–F, box 3, file 1, individual to OAP Commission, Owen
    Sound, Ont., 2 December 1929; ibid., box 5, file Grey County, 23 October 1929
18 See, for example, AO, RG 8, Series II–10–F, box 3, file 19, individual to OAP
    Commission, Toronto, 19 November 1929.
19 There were some instances in which the state nevertheless proceeded with its
    claim. In one court case, for example, a woman's estate (valued at $1808.50)
    was divided evenly between her husband and her son; provincial officials
    pushed the state's claim of $544.93 against both heirs (rather than waiting for
    the husband's death), and the claim was upheld in the Supreme Court of
    British Columbia. Counsel for the British Columbia board argued that the
    Pension authorities were the sole judge of whether the contribution made by
    an heir had been 'reasonable.' See BCARS, GR1249, box 6, file 1; ibid., C.W.
    Craig to OAP Department, Vancouver, 12, 18 December 1934.
20 NA, RG 29, vol. 127, no. 208–1–15, W.S. Edwards to J.D. O'Neill, Ottawa,
    6 February 1928. When the OAP Act was amended in 1947, the federal govern-
    ment deleted the clause empowering provincial boards to recover from Pen-
    sioners' estates, but the federal-provincial agreements were amended requiring
    each provincial government to confer that power on the provincial board.
21 Ibid., vol. 153, no. 208–7–2 pt. 1, vol. 2, 45
22 Ibid., vol. 145, no. 208–6–2 pt. 1, E.H. Blois to A.L. Macdonald, Halifax,
    12 March 1938
23 Ibid., vol. 133, no. 208–5–2 pt. 3, Memo for J.W. MacFarlane, Ottawa, 12 March
    1942
24 AO, RG 8, Series II–10–F, box 3, file 18, director to G. Whitworth, [Toronto],
    19 July 1929; ibid., box 4, file Brant County board, OAP Commission to I.
    Montgomery, [Toronto], 14 October 1929
25 See, for example, UWO, Lambton County OAP Commission, box B883, D.
    Jamieson to J.A. Huey, Toronto, 27 June 1934, and file.
26 Ibid., box B882
27 Ibid. See also, box B883.
28 Ibid., box B883
29 Ibid., box B888, individual to J.A. Huey, Petrolia, Ont., 5 February 1940
30 Ibid., box B882, J.A. Huey to individual, Sarnia, 26 June 1936
31 BCARS, GR1249, box 6, file 1
32 NA, RG 29, vol. 130, no. 208–3–5, W.K. Esling to E.N. Rhodes, Rossland, BC,
    16 December 1932; ibid., J. Stuart to F. Boyes, London, Ont., 25 October 1932
33 Ibid., vol. 138, no. 208–5–6 pt. 1, J.W. MacFarlane to B.J. Roberts, Ottawa,
    14 February 1936
34 Ibid., vol. 147, no. 208–6–5 pt. 2, G.S. Tattle to J.W. MacFarlane, Toronto,
    16 March 1943

35 *Dixon* v. *Workman's Compensation Board* (1935), 49 BCR 407 (BCSC); *Old Age Pensions Branch of the Workman's Compensation Board of Manitoba* v. *Jacobs,* [1937] 3 WWR 657 (Man. KB); *Re Ethier,* [1946] 1 DLR 272 (Ont. CA); *Re: the Old Age Pension Board of Nova Scotia and Estate of Margaret Murphy* (1944), 18 MPR 84 (NSSC)

36 NA, RG 29, vol. 132, no. 208–5–1 pt. 1, memo for J.W. MacFarlane, [Ottawa], 14 August 1937

37 Though there had been an income tax in some municipalities, the first federal income tax was initiated in 1917; in its early years it did not affect a large proportion of income earners, and most elderly poor of the 1930s and early 1940s may have escaped its impact, though this was less likely the case for those with income in the 1940s. See J.H. Perry, *Taxes, Tariffs and Subsidies: A History of Canadian Fiscal Development,* 2 vols (Toronto, 1955).

38 n=794. No identifiable social characteristics – age, sex, marital status, number of living children – distinguished these applicants from the other applicants.

39 NA, W.L.M. King Papers, reel C4867, no. 264868–71, individual to King, Toronto, 28 April 1941. The woman had been a trained nurse who had cared for King's mother during a lengthy illness.

40 NA, RG 29, vol. 148A, no. 208–6–7 pt. 1, M.A. MacPherson to R.B. Bennett, Regina, 1 February 1932; A. Meighen Papers, reel C3447, individual to Meighen, Vancouver, 7 September [1925]

41 UWO, Lambton County OAP Commission, box B885, Clerk's Special Report, 8, 9 May 1946

42 AO, RG 8, Series II–10–F, box 6, file Marmora and Lake Twp. (Hastings), C. Jones to J.A. Ellis, Marmora, Ont., 17 August 1928

43 Women could, however, be found employing this justification; see, for example, UWO, Lambton County OAP Commission, box B882, individual to J.A. Huey, Bothwell, 29 October 1934.

44 NA, S.H. Knowles Papers, vol. 1, file 1.16, individual to Knowles, Toronto, 27 April 1948. See also, for example, ibid., file 1.18, individual to Knowles, Winnipeg [1 November 1949].

45 NA, RG 29, vol. 127, no. 208–1–15, memos by J.W. MacFarlane, Ottawa, 22 May 1940, 26 November 1942

46 House of Commons, *Debates,* 1944, 1742–3; NA, RG 29, vol. 129, no. 208–2–3 pt. 4

47 NA, RG 29, vol. 148, no. 208–6–6 pt. 2, J. McLenaghen to W.C. Clark, Winnipeg, 6 October 1944; ibid., Clark to McLenaghen, Ottawa, 13 October 1944; ibid., vol. 150, no. 208–6–9 pt. 3, G.F. Davidson to E.W. Griffith, Ottawa, 3 February 1949; ibid., Davidson to J.H. Creighton, Ottawa, 25 April 1950; ibid., vol. 135, V.D. McElary to J.W. MacFarlane, Fredericton, 21 February 1949

48 Ibid., vol. 154, no. 208-7-3 pt. 2, 1946 Proceedings of the Interprovincial Advisory Board, 574
49 Ibid., pt. 3, 1946 Proceedings of the Interprovincial Advisory Board, 327–8; ibid., vol. 2282, no. 232-9-1 vol. 1, British Columbia OAP Board, Serial no. 57P, 9 September 1944; Violet McNaughton Papers (VM), A1, no. 46(2), D.E. Chalmers to McNaughton, Regina, 22 May 1946
50 In fiscal year 1941-2, the state recovered $402,781 from Pensioners' estates; by 1944-5 this amount peaked at $605,386 and fell to $428,172 by 1948-9. See NA, RG 29, vol. 130, no. 208-4-2; Joint Parliamentary Committee on Old Age Security, *Minutes of Proceedings and Evidence* (Ottawa, 1950), 35.
51 NA, RG 29, vol. 143, no. 208-5-9, pt. 1, A.M. Manson to P. Heenan, Victoria, 12 January 1928; ibid., RWL to individual, [Vancouver] 26 November 1928; AO, RG 8, Series II-10-F, box 11, file Victoria, individual to OAP Commission, Minden, Ont., 16 January 1930; UWO, London Welfare Records, box B408, F. McKay to W.J. Brown, London, 27 January 1941
52 NA, RG 29, vol. 129, no. 208-3-1, individual to 'Gentlemen,' Indianapolis, 8 March 1949; ibid., individual to Department of Old Age Pensions, Islip, NY, 4 November 1950; UWO, Lambton County OAP Commission, box B883, J.A. Huey to OAP Commission, Sarnia, 24 March 1933
53 J.E. Norris and J.A. Tindale, *Among Generations: The Cycle of Adult Relationships* (New York, 1994), 6
54 BCARS, GR1249, box 2, file 1, E.S.H. Winn to G.S. Pearson, [Vancouver], 1 May 1939
55 See, for example, NA, RG 29, vol. 148A, no. 208-6-7 pt. 2, J.S. White, 'Brief for Submission to the Legislative Committee on Social Welfare,' [Regina] March 1943.
56 Ibid., vol. 154, no. 208-7-3 pt. 3, 1946 Proceedings of the Interprovincial Advisory Board, 383
57 BCARS, GR1249, box 1, file 10, memo, Victoria, 30 May 1938
58 Ibid., box 2, file 2, memo, 2 December 1940
59 Ibid., box 6, file 7, P.N. to A.W. O'Neill, [np], 21 November 1935. The use of a solicitor by OAP applicants was not systematically recorded, so it is not possible to estimate how many employed such services, though they undoubtedly represented a minority of applicants. Nevertheless, the use of a solicitor is another sign of the growing sense of entitlement.
60 See, for example, PANL, GN 37/1, box 2, file no. 1810.
61 See, for example, NA, S.H. Knowles Papers, vol. 1, file 1.16, individual to Knowles, Winnipeg, 29 May 1948; VM, A1, no. 46(2), H. Graham to McNaughton, Regina, 14 May 1947. Liens against real estate were bureaucratically simple because of the central registry of real estate ownership in land registry offices.

62 See, for example, BCARS, GR1249, box 2, file 3, E.S.H. Winn to G.S. Pearson, [Vancouver], 30 January 1941. Winn explained how this process operated legally in the context of another example in NA, RG 29, vol. 144, no. 208-5-9 pt. 4, Winn to J.W. MacFarlane, Vancouver, 8 January 1943.

63 The evidence for this particular tactic comes from the early 1940s. It is likely that many municipalities developed liberal property tax forgiveness policies in the 1930s to avoid any greater strain on local welfare budgets. On Vancouver's attempt to deal with the problem of property tax arrears in the 1930s, see J. Wade, *Houses for All: The Struggle for Social Housing in Vancouver, 1919–1950* (Vancouver, 1994), 53–5.

64 NA, RG 29, vol. 150, no. 208-6-9 pt. 2, J.A. Craig to W.C. Clark, Victoria, 16 March 1944, appendix B

65 Ibid., vol. 125, no. 208-1-1 pt. 1, official to F.P. Varcoe, Ottawa, 20 December 1941; ibid., vol. 142, no. 208-5-8 pt. 4, memo for G.F. Davidson, Ottawa, 9 August 1946; ibid., vol. 148A, no. 208-6-6 pt. 3, L.D. McNiell to J.W. MacFarlane, Winnipeg, 14 January 1949

66 C.M. Arensberg, *The Irish Countryman* (Gloucester, MA, 1937), 86–7

67 An analysis of a random sample of 379 OAP applications in Lambton County, Ontario, found that 91.2 per cent of the applicants admitted no property transfer in the past five years, but the process was biased in favour of underreporting. Of the thirty-three applicants reporting such transfers, four were to married daughters, six to married sons, two to unmarried sons, two to nephews, two to other relatives, and seventeen to non-relatives. The results were similar for a random sample of 413 OAP applicants in London, Ontario, where 91.3 admitted no property transfer. Compare the thirty-six applicants reporting thirty-eight transfers, two were to married daughters, seven were to unmarried daughters, two to married sons, two to unmarried sons, one to a brother, one to another relative, twenty-two to non-relatives, and one to an institution.

68 NA, RG 29, vol. 128, no. 208-2-3 pt. 2, V.D. McElary to 'Ernie,' Quebec, 1 February 1939

69 Saskatchewan Archives (SA), T.C. Douglas Papers, R33.1, XVII, 636 (17–5k), D.E. Chalmers to E. Loehr, Regina, 2 January 1948

70 Toronto *Daily Star*, 24 April 1950, 6

71 BCARS, GR1249, box 4, file 1, individual to K.C. MacDonald, Vernon, 26 January 1938; ibid., E.S.H. Winn to MacDonald, [Vancouver], 15 March 1938

72 Ibid., E.S.H. Winn to N.W. Whittaker, [Vancouver], 19 February, 3 March 1938

73 Ibid., file 4, E.S.H. Winn to F.H. Putnam, [Vancouver], 4 May 1939

74 NA, S.H. Knowles Papers, vol. 1, file 1.18, individual to Knowles, Winnipeg, 20 September 1950

75 Ibid., individual to Knowles, Winnipeg, 30 March 1949. See also, for example, ibid., letters of 6 April, 19 July 1949.
76 NA, RG 29, vol. 142, no. 208–5–8 pt. 2, V.W. Wright to W.C. Clark, Edmonton, 8 May 1939. See also V. Strong-Boag, 'Janey Canuck': Women in Canada, 1919–1939 (Ottawa, 1994), 25.
77 J.G. Snell, 'The Gendered Construction of Marriage among the Canadian Elderly, 1900–1951,' Canadian Journal on Aging, 12 (1993), 509–23
78 BCARS, GR1249, box 3, file 9
79 UWO, Lambton County OAP Commission, box B885, A. Lamont to OAP Board, [np, nd] and passim. See also, for example, UWO, London Welfare Records, box B408, E.V. Berry to Old Age Pension Commission, London, 10 September 1948, 28 June 1949.
80 NA, RG 29, vol. 144, no. 208–5–9a, E.S.H. Winn to T. Reid, [Vancouver], 7 April 1933; Grandparenting ms, S. Laird to author, Oshawa, Ont., 6 February 1992; ibid., B. Leithwood to author, Agincourt, Ont., 23 January 1992
81 AO, RG 8, Series II–10–F, box 6, file Carpenter Twp. (Kenora), individual to OAP Commission, Pinewood, Ont., 21 April 1929
82 Ibid., box 2, file 9, individual to OAP Commission, 13 April [1929]; ibid., [nd]; ibid., to J.A. Ellis, [nd]
83 In a study of intergenerational support in Britain in this period, R. Wall concludes: 'It is not possible to detect any major change in the frequency with which the elderly were supported by relatives following the introduction of state [old age] pensions early in the twentieth century.' See Wall, 'Relationships between the Generations in British Families Past and Present,' unpublished paper delivered at the Tenth International Economic History Conference, Louvain, 1990, 28.
84 V.G. Cicirelli, 'Adult Children's Attachment and Helping Behavior to Elderly Parents: A Path Model,' Journal of Marriage and the Family, 45 (1983), 815–24; L. Thompson and A.J. Walker, 'Mothers and Daughters: Aid Patterns and Attachment,' ibid., 46 (1984), 313–22
85 Norris and Tindale, Among Generations, 5–14; I.A. Connidis, Family Ties and Aging (Toronto, 1989), 45–70; E.M. Brody, Women in the Middle: Their Parent-Care Years (New York, 1990)
86 UWO, Lambton County OAP Commission, box B885, Clerk's Special Report, 12 February 1947
87 BCARS, GR1249, box 1, file 9, G.S. Pearson to E.S.H. Winn, Victoria, 21 July 1937
88 UWO, Lambton County OAP Commission, box B883, Clerk's Special Report, 16 July 1936
89 UWO, London Welfare Records, box B419, 'OAP Applications F,' Administrator to K.G. Crawford, London, 4 May, 5 May 1936. See also, for example, AO, RG 8, Series II–10–F, box 9, file Peel, individual to OAP Commission, Chel-

tenham, Ont., 30 January 1930; UWO, Lambton County OAP Commission, box B888, Clerk's Special Report, 12 January 1935.

90 See, for example, M.B. Katz, *In the Shadow of the Poorhouse: A Social History of Welfare in America* (New York, 1986), 20; B. Bradbury, 'The Fragmented Family: Family Strategies in the Face of Death, Illness, and Poverty, Montreal, 1860–1885,' in J. Parr, ed., *Childhood and Family in Canadian History* (Toronto, 1982), 109–28.

91 AO, RG 8, Series II–10–F, box 3, file 19, individual to J.A. Ellis, Toronto, 11 June 1929

92 NA, A. Meighen Papers, reel C3550, no. 88744, H. Wilson Sr to Meighen, Edmonton, 4 July 1926

93 Similarly, the needy elderly became a more attractive target for local businesses. With regular income to spend, a number of businesses sprang up, particularly boarding houses and nursing homes, aimed at meeting the perceived needs of the target group.

94 VM, A1, no. 47, E. Baker to McNaughton, Calgary, 11 July 1942. F.M.L. Thompson, *The Rise of Respectable Society: A Social History of Victorian Britain* (Cambridge, MA, 1988), 200, commented that 'the ultimate disgrace for a Victorian worker's family was a pauper burial'; that stigma clearly continued well into the twentieth century.

95 See, for example, AO, RG 8, Series II–10–F, box 3, file 19, B.D. Savage to OAP Commission, Toronto, 5 November 1929; Strong-Boag, *New Day Recalled*, 188; UWO, Norfolk County OAP Commission Miscellaneous Administration File, secretary to OAP Commission, [np], 15 June 1940; NA, S.H. Knowles Papers, vol. 1, file 1.16, individual to Knowles, Winnipeg, 30 September 1948; NA, RG 29, vol. 138, no. 208-5-5 pt. 4, C.H. Green to J.W. MacFarlane, Toronto, 11 April 1946; UWO, Lambton County OAP Commission, box B884, application of 19 March 1935.

96 UWO, London Welfare Records, box B419, 'OAP Applications A,' Administrator to K.G. Crawford, London, 2 March 1937; ibid., box B411, file 1912–29 A–D, administrator to Welfare Committee, London, 18 October 1937; ibid., individual to F.W. McKay, Hamilton, 20 April 1941; Queen's University Archives (QUA), no. 2262, box 1, minutes 1940–5, 27 September 1944; NA, RG 29, vol. 129, no. 208-2-3 pt. 4, memo to commissioner, Winnipeg, 12 July 1944; ibid., vol. 150, no. 208-6-9 pt. 2, J.A. Craig to W.C. Clark, Victoria, 16 March 1944, appendix D

CHAPTER 5: Agency among Old Age Pensioners

1 There is no evidence that any elderly organized to articulate their views in any Canadian province before the local adoption of the OAP program.

2 'Interim Report of Commission Appointed to Consider Old Age Pensions,'
  April 1930, 17–18; 'Final Report of the Commission Appointed to Consider Old
  Age Pensions,' [September 1930], 4. The 1931 census (volume 3, table 27)
  recorded 17,124 persons aged seventy or older in the province, and a further
  12,611 persons aged 60–69.
3 C. Haber, *Beyond Sixty-Five: The Dilemma of Old Age in America's Past* (Cambridge, 1983), 47–87
4 For a discussion of these samples, see the Note on Sources.
5 This information is supplemented by scholarly investigations of local pensioners carried out by two social work students in the late 1940s: H.J. Dorgan,
  'The Old Age Pension Applicant: A Study of 144 Applicants for Old Age Pension at the Toronto Department of Public Welfare in December 1948,' MSW
  thesis, University of Toronto, 1949; and M.S. Jewett, 'An Evaluation of the
  Old Age Pension System in Canada: An Analysis Based on the Socio-Econom-
  ic Needs of One Hundred Aged Clients of the Family Welfare Association of
  Montreal,' MSW thesis, McGill University, 1949. A third study done at the
  same time was not useful for these purposes: E.W. Mathewson, 'Old Age Pensions in British Columbia: A Review of Trends in Eligibility,' MSW thesis,
  University of British Columbia, 1949.
6 This figure corresponds with the percentage of childless found in Nova Scotia
  in 1930; see chapter 1. However, in a small, non-random sample of Montreal
  pensioners, almost half were childless; where pensioners had living adult children, they were much more likely to contribute to a parent's support once the
  parent had been widowed. See Jewett, 'OAP System: Montreal,' 40–1, 48–51.
7 Percentage of pensioners with living children:

No. of children	0	1	2	3	4	5+	n
Female pensioners	30.4	12.2	14.0	12.7	8.7	22.0	401
Male pensioners	25.3	13.6	11.7	13.1	11.7	24.5	367
All pensioners	28.0	12.9	12.9	12.9	10.2	23.2	768

Source: Combined sample of Lambton and London OAP applicants, 1929–51

  There were slightly more applicants in the sample with daughters (476) than
  with sons (455).
8 For both sexes combined in the combined sample, 75.6 per cent (n=555) of
  those with living children had at least one child residing in the same municipality as the pension applicant. The increase in propinquity with the age of the
  parent presumably reflected rising perceived parental dependence; see L.M.
  Crawford, J.B. Bond Jr, and R.F. Balshaw, 'Factors Affecting Sons' and Daugh-

ters' Caregiving to Older Parents,' *Canadian Journal on Aging*, 13 (1994), 454–69.

9 In the combined sample, the following cohorts of pensioners with living children had at least one child living within the same municipality:

Men	Women
<75 = 69.6% (n=184)	<75 = 76.2% (n=193)
75.0–79.11 = 73.6% (n=53)	75.0–79.11 = 90.4% (n=52)
80.0–84.11 = 57.9% (n=19)	80.0–84.11 = 96.0% (n=25)
85+ = 83.3% (n=18)	85+ = 72.7% (n=11)

10 In the combined sample for those applicants having children in the specific category being tested, the following had at least one child in the specific category living in the same municipality:
parents: sons = 57.1 per cent (n=455); daughters = 64.7 per cent (n=476); *fathers:* children = 70.4 per cent (n=274); *mothers:* children = 80.4 per cent (n=281).

11 Urban pensioners were just as likely to live near married sons as were their rural counterparts.

12 P. Wilmott and M. Young, *Family and Class in a London Suburb* (London, 1960)

13 Dorgan, 'OAP Applicants: Toronto,' 47–54; Jewett, 'OAP System: Montreal,' 46

14 In the combined sample, 10.8 per cent of the children gave money, 7.0 per cent housing, 1.8 per cent kind, and 7.4 per cent some combination of the above.

15 In the combined sample, 32.3 per cent of the children of the women applicants (n=1045) had given support, compared with 21.5 per cent of the men's children (n=1030). The support increased with each age cohort: 24.5 per cent for applicants under age 75 (n=1382); 30.2 per cent for those aged 75–79 (n=427); 33.1 per cent for those aged 80–84 (n=172); and 36.2 per cent for those aged 85 or more (n=94).

16 In the combined sample, 18.9 per cent of married children (n=829) aided their fathers, while 28.4 per cent (n=885) helped their mothers; 31.6 per cent of single children (n=187) aided their fathers, while 47.9 per cent (n=165) gave substantial support to their mothers.

17 In the combined sample, the following percentages of children gave reported support to each parent: *daughters* – to fathers, 23.0 (n=535); to mothers, 35.5 (n=519); *sons* – to fathers, 21.7 (n=475); to mothers, 30.1 (n=512).

18 University of Western Ontario (UWO), London Welfare Department, box B419, 'OAP Applications R,' 2 November 1937. See also UWO, London OAP Committee Record Books, 1929, 133–4.

19 J.E. Norris and J.A. Tindale, *Among Generations: The Cycle of Adult Relation-*

ships (New York, 1994), 8–9; E.M. Brody, *Women in the Middle: Their Parent-Care Years* (New York, 1990)

20 These trends are confirmed by more general figures. See, for example, National Archives of Canada (NA), RG 29, vol. 133, no. 208–5–2 pt. 2, 'Old Age Pensions, Province of Nova Scotia: Social Statistics'; ibid., vol. 154, no. 208–7–3 pt. 2, 1946 Proceedings of the Interprovincial Advisory Board, 456; BC Department of Health and Welfare, *The Administration of the Old Age Pensions Act: Annual Report, 1948–49* (Victoria, 1950), 7.

21 On the other hand, Dorgan reported that Toronto women were more likely to apply immediately for the OAP compared with men. In 1948, 45 per cent of women's applications were at the age of seventy, compared with just 25 per cent for men, whose rate of application was higher for those aged seventy-one to seventy-five. As one observer pointed out, one of the few advantages open to women through their unpaid domestic labour was that they tended to be eligible for the OAP earlier than men, who found it more profitable to avoid retirement as long as possible. See Dorgan, 'Toronto OAP Applicants,' 48, 63.

22 Dorgan, 'OAP Applicants: Toronto,' 3–4, 11–42. See also Jewett, 'OAP System: Montreal,' 41–2.

23 UWO, London Welfare Records, box B419, 'OAP Applications A,' Administrator to K.G. Crawford, London, 24 August 1936

24 See, for example, UWO, Lambton County OAP Commission, box B884, Petrolia, Ont., 15 November 1947; ibid., Thedford, Ont., 17 April 1942.

25 UWO, London Welfare Records, box B408, F. McKay to F. Clark, London, 8 November 1940

26 UWO, Lambton County OAP Commission, box B882, 28 November 1938

27 Ibid., Clerk's Special Report, 9 January 1939. See also, for example, ibid., Clerk's Special Report, Courtwright, Ont., 8 April 1941; ibid., box B888, Clerk's Special Report, 10 April 1935.

28 See, for example, ibid., box B886, Clerk's Special Report, Forest, Ont., 12 August 1946, 10 October 1947; ibid., Watford, Ont., 12 March 1936; ibid., box B885, Clerk's Special Report, 7 January 1937.

29 See, for example, ibid., box B882, Clerk's Special Report, 9 April 1936; ibid., box B888, Clerk's Special Report, 25 April 1936; Saskatchewan Archives (SA), J.M. Uhrich Papers, R97, no. 27 (2), W.C. Mills to J.M. Uhrich, Regina, 31 August 1937. The English OAP reflected some of the same discrimination, barring those imprisoned within the past ten years and those guilty of an habitual failure to work; see A. Deacon and J. Bradshaw, *Reserved for the Poor: The Means Test in British Social Policy* (Oxford, 1983), 7.

30 UWO, London Welfare Department, box B419, 'OAP Applications F,' administrator to secretary, London, 17 February 1936

31 Archives of Ontario (AO), RG 8, Series II–10–F, box 2, file 13, D. Jamieson to Bruce, Counsell & Boyds, Toronto, 1 November 1929; Bruce, Counsell & Boyds to OAP Commission, Hamilton, 28 October 1929; ibid., to J.A. Ellis, 19 November, 22 November 1929

32 NA, RG 29, vol. 126, no. 208-1-4, memo on the Proposed Statistics of Old Age Pensioners, 8–9

33 NA, R.B. Bennett Papers, reel M1401, no. 437741

34 UWO, Lambton County OAP Commission, box B882, Clerk's Special Report, 28 January 1938

35 UWO, London Welfare Records, box B411, file 1912–29 A–D, individual to mayor, London, 18 June 1924; R.H. Sanders to Welfare Committee, London, 21 June 1924

36 R.J. Deachman, 'Judgement Reserved,' Canadian Magazine, 89 (June 1938), 39; UWO, Lambton County OAP Commission, box B888, Investigator's Report, 20 September 1943 and passim

37 NA, RG 29, vol. 131, no. 208-4-3, B.R. King to Department of Finance, Ottawa, 12 March 1937; vol. 140, no. 208-5-7 pt. 1, J.W. MacFarlane, 'Report of Inspection of OAP Branch,' [Ottawa] 7 January 1936. See also Toronto Star, 6 February 1933.

38 NA, RG 29, vol. 134, no. 208-5-3 pt. 1, 'Report on Pensions Listed by Dominion Auditors 25 July 1938,' Fredericton, 15 September 1938; vol. 140, no. 208-5-7 pt. 1, J.W. MacFarlane, 'Report of Inspection of OAP Branch,' [Ottawa] 7 January 1936

39 Ibid., vol. 129, no. 208-2-3 pt. 4, J.W. MacFarlane to V.D. McElary, Ottawa, 5 September 1944

40 Ibid., vol. 134, no. 208-5-3 pt. 1, 'Report on Pensions Listed by Dominion Auditors 25 July 1938,' Fredericton, 15 September 1938

41 T.K. Hareven, 'Family Time and Industrial Time,' Daedalus, 106 (1977), 57–70

42 NA, RG 29, vol. 140, no. 208-5-7 pt. 2, W.C. Clark to G. Beckett, Ottawa, 4 January 1940. And not knowing his age, no OAP could be granted, according to Clark.

43 See, for example, British Columbia Archives and Records Service (BCARS), GR1249, box 4, file 4, E.S.H. Winn to W.J. Asselstine, [Vancouver], 31 October 1939

44 AO, RG 8, Series II–10–F, box 10, file Rainy River, individual to OAP local board, Emo, Ont., 24 October 1929

45 NA, RG 29, vol. 138, no. 208-5-6 pt. 1, J.W. MacFarlane to B.J. Roberts, Ottawa, 14 February 1936. See also, for example, BCARS, GR1249, box 1, file 9, memo, 31 December 1936.

46 See, for example, UWO, London OAP Committee Record Books, 1948, no. 117.

47 The gendered character of such social insurance programs is developed in L. Gordon, 'Social Insurance and Public Assistance: The Influence of Gender in Welfare Thought in the United States, 1890–1935,' *American Historical Review,* 97 (1992): 19–54.

48 See, for example, AO, RG 8, Series II–10–F, box 1, file 2, L.S. Day to provincial secretary, Ypsilanti, Mich., 5 December 1929; ibid., T. Odlum to OAP Commission, Elmira, NY, 26 November 1929; ibid., box 2, file 13, J. Leith to D. Jamieson, Hamilton, 14 October 1929.

49 NA, RG 29, vol. 137, no. 208–5–5 pt. 1, D. Jamieson to director of Provincial Savings Office, [Toronto], 1 June 1933

50 BCARS, GR1249, box 1, file 10, E.S.H. Winn to G.S. Pearson, [Vancouver], 3 January 1938

51 Ibid., file 9, memorandum, 21 April 1937

52 J.G. Snell, *In the Shadow of the Law: Divorce in Canada, 1900–1939* (Toronto, 1991), 232 and passim

53 NA, RG 29, vol. 154, no. 208–7–3 pt. 3, 1946 Proceedings of the Interprovincial Advisory Board, 212

54 Ibid., vol. 2282, no. 232–9–1, *Vancouver Sun* clipping, 21 April [1951]

55 Ibid.

56 Ibid., vol. 126, no. 208–1–5, memo by J.W. MacFarlane, Ottawa, 15 July 1940

57 Ibid., vol. 127, no. 208–1–12, C.F. Needham to J.W. MacFarlane, Ottawa, 20 November 1943

58 Ibid., vol. 125, no. 208–1–1 pt. 2, memo on Employment of Old Age Pensioners on Farms, Ottawa, 1 September 1943

59 BC Department of Health and Welfare, *Administration,* 10–11

60 C.N. Forward, 'The Development of Victoria as a Retirement Centre,' *Urban History Review,* 13 (1984), 116–20

61 C.N. Forward, 'The Elderly Population in Canadian Metropolitan Areas,' in M.C. Brown and G. Wynn, eds., *The Bellingham Collection of Geographical Studies,* British Columbia Geographical Series, no. 27 (Vancouver, 1979), 41–61; NA, RG 29, vol. 153, no. 208–7–3 pt. 1, 1946 Proceedings of the Interprovincial Advisory Board, 687, 847; BC Department of Health and Welfare, *Administration,* 7. In 1946–7, 1947–8, and 1948–9 the net influx of pensioners was 570, 306, and 487. See also *Vancouver Sun,* 8 July 1948.

62 The OAP legislation provided that each participating province paid its share of each pension in proportion to the amount of the previous twenty years (at the point of application) that the pensioner had lived in that province. This resulted in a good deal of bureaucratic squabbling and paperwork, as the responsibilities for each pensioner were established.

63 Hamilton *Herald,* 9 September 1930; NA, RG 29, vol. 148A, no. 208–6–7 pt. 1,

E.A. Thomas, memo to deputy minister, Ottawa, 24 November 1932. See also Toronto *Globe,* 9 February 1933.
64 NA, RG 29, vol. 152, no. 208-7-1 pt. 2, summary of the 1937 Interprovincial OAP Board meeting, 21-7
65 Ibid., vol. 125, no. 208-1-1 pt. 2, C.D. Allan to J.W. MacFarlane, Ottawa, 2 October 1950. Instead, for the most part the Manitoba authorities relied on written statements of the elderly themselves, occasionally employing a private firm (the Retail Credit Association) to check on questionable information.
66 Ibid., vol. 131, no. 208-4-3, B.R. King to Department of Finance, Ottawa, 12 March 1937; ibid., vol. 137, no. 208-5-5 pt. 1, E.A. Thomas, memo to Mr Brown, Ottawa, 27 April 1933; London *Advertiser,* 1 December 1930
67 NA, RG 29, vol. 135, no. 208-5-3 pt. 3, J.G. Robichaud to W.C. Clark, Fredericton, 29 January 1942; ibid., Clark to Robichaud, Ottawa, 14 February 1942
68 See, for example, ibid., vol. 131, no. 208-4-3, Report on Inspection of Old Age Pension Payments, 17 March 1936.
69 *Pensioner* (P), October 1950, 2
70 BCARS, GR1249, box 2, file 3, E.S.H. Winn to G.S. Pearson, [Vancouver], 28 June 1941
71 AO, RG 8, Series II-10-F, box 2, file 9, individual to OAP Commission, 13 April [1929]
72 Ibid., box 10, file Rainy River, individual to OAP local board, Emo, Ont., 24 October 1929
73 BCARS, GR1249, box 6, file 5, G.S. Pearson to E.S.H. Winn, Victoria, 26 June 1941
74 Reprinted in *British Columbia's Welfare,* 8 (February 1950), 9

CHAPTER 6: Organizing Politically

1 A.M. Rose, 'The Subculture of the Aging,' in A.M. Rose and W.A. Peterson, eds., *Older People and Their Social World* (Philadelphia, 1965), 13; A.M. Rose, 'Group Consciousness among the Aging,' ibid., 19; Dahrendorf, cited in P.K. Ragan and J.J. Dowd, 'The Emerging Political Consciousness of the Aged: A Generational Interpretation,' *Journal of Social Issues,* 30 (1974), 140
2 On the Second Mile Club, see M.F. Kennedy, 'Recreation for the Aged,' MSW thesis, University of Toronto, 1952, 13-15; M. Royce, *Eunice Dyke: Health Care Pioneer* (Toronto, 1983), 209-20; National Archives of Canada (NA), MG 28 I441, vol. 38, file 25, 'The Second Mile Club of Toronto,' 1 February 1950; *Pensioner* (P), May 1947, 1. For elsewhere, see H. Anderson, 'Victoria's Sixty-Up Club,' *British Columbia's Welfare,* 6 (July 1949), 17-18; *P,* May 1947, 1. According to Kennedy, 'Recreation for the Aged,' 26-7, by 1951 there were

thirty-eight such clubs nationally, located in Victoria (4), Vancouver (4), Edmonton (3), Calgary (1), Medicine Hat (1), Regina (1), Winnipeg (9), Toronto (6), Barrie (1), Weston (1), Oro Station (1), Hamilton (2), Kingston (1), Montreal (2), and Halifax (1).

3 R.H. Binstock, 'Interest Group Liberalism and the Politics of Aging,' *Gerontologist*, 12 (1972), 265–80, argued that these traits are characteristic of seniors' political groups in general.

4 R.H. Binstock, 'The Politics of Aging Interest Groups,' in R.B. Hudson, ed., *The Aging in Politics: Process and Policy* (Springfield, IL, 1981), 47–73

5 A. Blaikie, 'The Emerging Political Power of the Elderly in Britain, 1908–1948,' *Ageing and Society*, 10 (1990), 17–39; A. Holtzman, *The Townsend Movement: A Political Study* (New York, 1963); J. Putnam, *Old-Age Politics in California: From Richardson to Reagan* (Stanford, 1970); F. Piner, P. Jacobs, and P. Selznick, *Old Age and Political Behavior: A Case Study* (Berkeley, 1959). There is no indication of direct contact among the organized elderly of Canada, the United States, or the United Kingdom; each movement appears to have been indigenous to its own jurisdiction, though the general factors giving rise to the movements were similar. The British Columbia OAPO branches occasionally noted having a speaker from a nearby Washington State organization; see, for example, City of Vancouver Archives (CVA), clipping file, fiche no. 6938-1, 26 September 1941. The *Pensioner*, the OAPO's journal, exchanged with similar magazines in Australia, Scotland, New Zealand, Wales, and England, occasionally reprinting items.

6 The American example is chosen for comparison because the studies of the organized elderly there have been much more detailed than the study of those elsewhere.

7 C.L. Day, *What Older Americans Think: Interest Groups and Aging Policy* (Princeton, NJ, 1990), 22

8 Violet McNaughton Papers (VM), A1, no. 46(3), the Old Age Pensioners' Organization of B.C. (Vancouver, [1938])

9 While the early OAP set a total annual income level of $365, this consisted of a maximum $240 in OAP payments and $125 in income; the 1930s OAPO wanted to raise the pension itself to $365.

10 In British Columbia alone these other groups included the Happier Old Age Club, the Old Age Pensioners' Benevolent Association, the B.C. Pensioners' Friendly Aid Society, the Victoria Aged Pensioners' Association, the Canadian Pensioners' Union, the Retired Employees' Association from one large company, the Canadian Social Security Association, the Senior Citizens Community Club, the E.V. Sturdy Happy Friendly Society Inc., and the Old Age and Invalid Pensioners' Association.

11 For examples, see J.G. Snell, 'The Old Age Pensioners' Organization of British

Columbia, 1932–1951,' *BC Studies,* 102 (1994), 10 n20. Ethel Baker was active in the Social Credit Party, and several of the OAPOS leaders were members of the CCF or had been active in the farmers' movement.

12 VM, A1, no. 49(2), Whiting to McNaughton, Vancouver, 6 May 1942; C.G. Gifford interview with Nurse, Saskatoon, 5 August 1981; VM, A1, no. 47, Baker to McNaughton, Calgary, 29 September 1941

13 Piner, Jacobs, and Selznick, *Old Age and Political Behaviour,* 69–80, 91, 160; A.H. Miller, P. Gurin, G. Gurin, and O. Malanchuk, 'Components of Group Consciousness,' *American Journal of Political Science,* 25 (1981), 494–511

14 N. Babchuk, G.R. Peters, D.R. Hoyt, and M.A. Kaiser, 'The Voluntary Associations of the Aged,' *Journal of Gerontology,* 34 (1979), 579

15 Saskatchewan Archives (SA), T.C. Douglas Papers, R33.1, XVII, 636 (17–5k), secretary of OAPOS to W.L.M. King, Saskatoon, 6 March 1948, and enclosure; SA, N. Medd Papers, A176, minute book of the OAPOS White Fox, Saskatchewan branch no. 12, 3 May 1947; *P,* January 1947, 1; *P,* February 1947, 4–7. By 1947 some branches had changed the words to 'Onward Senior Citizens.'

16 *P,* February 1951, 3

17 National Archives of Canada (NA), RG 29, vol. 1940, no. R249/108, OAPOS

18 *Western Producer (WP),* 1 April 1943, 12

19 One case challenging the provincial OAP board's calculation of fictive income was one of the very earliest class action suits (itself an indication of the growing sense of group identity among the elderly). The case of James E. Murray listed Murray and six other nameless OAP applicants, and also claimed action on behalf of 'all persons having a similar grievance'; see *Vancouver Sun,* 24 December 1941, 9.

20 On tag days, OAPO members solicited contributions from the public, usually on the main streets of Vancouver and elsewhere, often using the carnation as the public symbol of support.

21 For a detailed discussion of these tactics and of the OAPOBC, see Snell, 'The Old Age Pensioners' Organization,' 3–29.

22 VM, A1, no. 46(1), J.W. Moorhouse to McNaughton, New Westminster, BC, 27 July 1942; *P,* January 1948, 12, February 1948, 2

23 *Vancouver Sun,* 12 June 1942, 16, 27 July 1942, 4; *Cowichan Leader,* reprinted in *Victoria Daily Times,* 16 January 1942, 4; VM, A1, no. 46(3), W.S. Simpson to *WP,* Sweetwater, BC, [28 October 1941]

24 *Vancouver Sun,* 28 July 1941, 5; *Victoria Daily Times,* 7 April 1942, 2; VM, A1, no. 47, E. Baker to McNaughton, Calgary, 12 April 1942. See also NA, R.B. Bennett Papers, reel M1270, no. 334586–7; Snell, 'The Old Age Pensioners' Organization.'

25 VM, A1, no. 47, E. Baker to McNaughton, Calgary, 31 July 1942. See also ibid., E. Fisher to McNaughton, Edmonton, 14 April 1942.

26 Ibid., no. 46(2), McNaughton to B.S. Kennedy, [Saskatoon], 27 April 1943
27 Ibid., no. 46(1), McNaughton to W.M. Wray, [Saskatoon], 20 November 1941; ibid., no. 46(2), McNaughton to B.S. Kennedy, [Saskatoon] 12 March 1943; ibid., A.H. Kennedy to McNaughton, Strawberry Hill, BC, 21 September 1945
28 *WP,* 2 March 1939, 24
29 Whether accurate or not, there was a perception among the needy elderly that retribution by the OAP bureaucracy was a real possibility if pensioners complained directly to OAP officials, much less publicly. Whiting quoted an unsigned letter received from seven pensioners in Padockwood, Saskatchewan, who stated that they were afraid to complain about the board's treatment, in their words, 'because they had been told that if they did they would lose what pension they were then getting.' *WP,* 30 November 1939, 24. The fears underlined the vulnerability and dependency of pensioners.
30 See, for example, *WP,* 18 January 1940, 11, 28 November 1940, 11, 9 January 1941, 11, 23 October 1941, 11.
31 Ibid., 30 November 1939, 11, 4 January 1940, 9, 25 January 1940, 11, 8 February 1940, 11, 15 February 1940, 11, 29 February 1940, 11, 25 April 1940, 11; VM, A1, no. 46(1), McNaughton to J.R.L. Ward, [Saskatoon], 10 February 1940
32 VM, A1, no. 46(1), McNaughton to T. Johnson, [Saskatoon], 5 March 1940; *WP,* 7 March 1940, 11
33 VM, A1, no. 46(1), J.R.L. Ward to editor, Veteran, Alta, 5 February 1940; ibid., I. Campbell to McNaughton, Ruthilda, Sask., April 1940
34 Ibid., McNaughton to *Saskatchewan Commonwealth,* [Saskatoon], 11 May 1940; ibid., McNaughton to C. Biesick, [Saskatoon], 17 May 1940
35 *WP,* 20 June 1940, 11, 11 July 1940, 11
36 VM, A1, no. 49(1), J.J. Whiting to McNaughton, New Westminster, BC, 2 November 1941
37 SA, N. Medd Papers, A176, minute book of OAPO White Fox, Saskatchewan branch no. 12, 9 April 1948; *P,* January 1953, 1. Benjamin Stone Kennedy was born in 1872 in Fort Langley, British Columbia, the youngest son of Mr and Mrs James Kennedy, who moved to New Westminster in 1859. Raised in New Westminster, Stone Kennedy had lived in that area all his life. He had worked in the newspaper trade, first as a printer at the *British Columbian,* owned by his three older brothers, and later as a reporter and publisher. A clipping of his obituary for his death on 7 March 1944 is in VM, A1, no. 46(2).
38 SA, T.C. Douglas Papers, R33.1, XVII, 636 (17–5k), secretary of OAPOS to W.L.M. King, Saskatoon, 6 March 1948, enclosure
39 VM, A1, no. 46(1), B.S. Kennedy to McNaughton, New Westminster, BC, 16 February 1942
40 *P,* November 1950, 11

41 VM, A1, no. 48, J.W. Hope to A. Douglas, Vancouver, 30 June 1946; *P*, July 1949, 3

42 VM, A1, no. 47, E. Baker to McNaughton, Calgary, 11 June 1942; ibid., no. 49(2), J.J. Whiting to McNaughton, New Westminster, BC, 6 July 1943; ibid., no. 46(3), Report of Second Annual Meeting of OAPOS, Saskatoon, 18 October 1945, 1; SA, N. Medd Papers, A176 (1), minutes of board of directors, 24 May 1945; NA, RG 29, vol. 130, no. 208–3–4, old age pensioners' organizations in Canada, [March 1947]; *WP*, 8 February 1945, 12; Public Archives of Manitoba (PAM), RG 18, A4, box 38

43 *WP*, 10 September 1942, 12

44 VM, A1, no. 49(2), J.J. Whiting to McNaughton, New Westminster, BC, 12 September 1943, 20 February 1944; ibid., McNaughton to Whiting, [Saskatoon], 3 April 1944; ibid., A1, no. 48, J.W. Hope to all pensioner societies, Vancouver, 23 September 1943

45 VM, A1, no. 46(3), 'Suggestion from the General Council, OAPO Vancouver' [summer 1945]

46 Ibid., N.W. Medd to OAP organizations, Saskatoon, 25 June 1945

47 Ibid., OAPO Western Conference, Saskatoon, 16–17 October 1945; Saskatoon *Star-Phoenix*, 17 October 1945, 3

48 G.A. Dyson, in Victoria *Daily Colonist*, 22 November 1945, 4

49 VM, A1, no. 46(2), McNaughton to A.J. Blackwell, [Saskatoon], 29 May 1943; ibid., McNaughton to C.H. Geefbeght, [Saskatoon], 13 January 1944; ibid., J.J. Whiting to McNaughton, New Westminster, BC, 13 June 1943; *WP*, 14 November 1946, 12

50 *Vancouver Sun*, 21 February 1945, 11; VM, A1, no. 49(2), J.J. Whiting to McNaughton, New Westminster, BC, 11 October 1946; J. Wade, *Houses for All: The Struggle for Social Housing in Vancouver, 1919–50* (Vancouver, 1994), 151–3

51 *Vancouver Sun*, 1 February 1947, 5; *WP*, 20 February 1947, 11. Other suicides were publicly blamed on other facets of the state's response (or lack of response) to the dependent elderly; see *Vancouver Sun*, 13 April 1942, 1; *P*, January 1948, 15–16.

52 VM, A1, no. 49 (2), J.J. Whiting to McNaughton, New Westminster, BC, 13 November 1942; *Vancouver Daily Province*, 26 June 1948, 9; *P*, August 1947, 3

53 W. Partridge, Victoria, in *P*, March 1950, 8

54 *WP*, 19 September 1946, 12; *Vancouver Sun*, 24 June 1944, 5; *Vancouver Daily Province*, 26 June 1948, 9

55 PAM, RG 18, A4, box 38, J.W. Hope and E. Navey to E.F. Willis, Vancouver, 28 August 1946; *P*, June-July 1947, 2–3, September 1947, 2–3

56 *P*, October 1946, 7

57 *P*, January 1947, 2

58 See, for example, *P,* May 1947, 2.
59 *P,* August 1947, 1, 14, November 1947, 1, December 1947, 13. By contrast, the *Western Producer* and other supporters of the pensioners (*P,* August 1947, 12–14), along with many of the less militant elderly, one suspects, judged the legislation to be 'a step in the right direction.'
60 *P,* November 1947, 9
61 *P,* January 1949, 2, June 1949, 1
62 NA, S.H. Knowles Papers, vol. 1, file 1–18, C.N. Ward to all clergy, Springhill, NS, [November 1949]; *P,* September 1949, 11, October 1949, 13, December 1949, 13, January 1950, 13, February 1950, 14
63 J. Struthers, 'Regulating the Elderly: Old Age Pensions and the Formation of a Pension Bureaucracy in Ontario, 1929–1945,' *Journal of the Canadian Historical Association,* 3 (1992), 235–55
64 VM, A1, no. 46(2), McNaughton to B.S. Kennedy, [Saskatoon], 27 April 1943; *P,* June–July 1947, 16, December 1948, 10, August 1950, 13, November 1951, 13, December 1951, 11, November 1952, 6. The founder of the OAPO at the Lakehead was Allan Gray, a Scottish emigrant and a retired CNR conductor; after retirement, Gray served on the Port Arthur City Council, 1938–40, and on the Public Utilities Commission. *P,* March 1949, 14–15
65 *WP,* 16 August 1945, 12, 10 January 1946, 11; *P,* November 1946, 7, January 1947, 4, and March 1951, 3
66 *P,* September 1947, 12
67 Calculated from *P,* September 1951, 4
68 *P,* November 1951, 10
69 *P,* October 1947, 1–2
70 *P,* September 1951, 8, August 1950, 4
71 The Alberta organized elderly were divided. The Alberta Pensioners' Society, centred in Edmonton, refused to alter its stance of a $40 OAP at the age of sixty-five, and thus did not fit with the congress's demands. The Alberta Old Age Pensioners' Association, centred in Calgary, argued that there were insufficient finances to support a national movement and that the provincial organizations were having a very successful impact on federal politicians. *P,* November 1947, 8
72 *P,* November 1946, 7, December 1946, 3, June-July 1947, 4, November 1947, 8, December 1948, 12; *Vancouver News-Herald,* 26 June 1948, 5; *Victoria Daily Times,* 2 July 1948, 5; *Prince Albert Daily Herald,* 9 October 1947, 3, 10 October 1947, 1, 6; *WP,* 23 October 1947, 12. In 1947, for example, the congress received $150 each from the OAPOBC and the OAPOS, and $25 from the Ontario OAPO at the Lakehead. *P,* December 1947, 9
73 *P,* March 1950, 2
74 *Prince Albert Daily Herald,* 5 November 1949, 5

75 *Vancouver Daily Province,* 18 February 1950, 21; *P,* August 1950, 1,4, September 1950, 2, October 1950, 2, January 1951, 2, September 1951, 6–7, 10–11, October 1951, 9, November 1951, 3, 13–14, January 1952, 6, May 1952, 9, August 1952, 3–4, December 1952, 6. The proposed national body, now calling itself the National Pensioners' Federation, limped along, proclaiming a new constitution but lacking meaningful support.

76 *P,* December 1950, 11, January 1951, 2, February 1951, 3; C.G. Gifford, *Canada's Fighting Seniors* (Toronto, 1990)

77 *P,* September 1951, 9. In contrast, organized labour responded much more assertively, organizing a national campaign to end the means test; see NA, S.H. Knowles Papers, vol. 78, file no. 78–6, *Canadian Railway and Employees' Monthly,* 36 (February 1950), back cover; NA, MG 28 I215, vol. 27, file 'Pensions – Campaign for Abolition of the Means Test for OAP, 1950.'

78 Canada, Joint Committee of the Senate and House of Commons on Old Age Security, *Minutes of Proceedings and Evidence* (Ottawa, 1950), I, 8, II, 987–8, 990–1

79 Joint Committee, *Minutes,* II, 1259

80 *P,* June 1950, 5, August 1950, 3, November 1950, 2, December 1950, 8, September 1951, 9, October 1951, 5, January 1952, 4; SA, N. Medd Papers, A176(2). See also, for example, *P,* February 1951, 2, August 1951, 3.

81 J.J. Whiting died in 1951; E.R. Vipond died in 1945; Fred A. Anderson, the long-time president of the Calgary branch of the AOAPS, died in 1951; G.M. Dyson, the founder of the Victoria branch of the OAPOBC, died in 1952. The *Pensioner* announced the government acceptance of the new OAP reforms with an article entitled 'The Fruits of Their Labours' (July 1951, 1–2), suggesting a sense of final victory.

82 Day, *What Older Americans Think,* 24, 74, 76

83 K. Bryden, *Old Age Pensions and Policy-Making in Canada* (Montreal, 1974), 196; K. Kernaghan, 'Politics, Public Administration and Canada's Aging Population,' *Canadian Public Policy,* 8 (1982), 69–79; K. Kernaghan and O. Kuper, *Coordination in Canadian Governments: A Case Study of Aging Policy* (Toronto, 1983); D. Lewis, cited in M. Novak, *Aging and Society: A Canadian Perspective* (Scarborough, 1988), 328

84 VM, A1, no. 46 (3), Old Age Pensioners' Organization of B.C.

85 VM, A1, no. 46(1), A. Watson to editor, Nutana, Sask., 2 January 1942; ibid., A. Strawson to McNaughton, Tawatinaw, Alta, 23 April 1942; *WP,* 9 May 1946, 21, 24 April 1947, 11, 9 June 1949, 13

CHAPTER 7: Shifting Policies of Old Age Pensions

1 F.H. Leacey, ed., *Historical Statistics of Canada* (Ottawa, 1983), K1–7

2 National Archives of Canada (NA), RG 29, vol. 128, no. 208–2–3 pt. 1, J.W. MacFarlane to B.J. Roberts, Vancouver, 22 November 1935; vol. 150, no. 208–6–9 pt. 3, draft memo to Dr Davidson [July 1950]

3 In 1949 the Manitoba government opted to end this levy against municipalities; see NA, RG 29, vol. 148A, no. 208–6–6 pt. 3, L.D. McNeill to J.W. MacFarlane, Winnipeg, 17 October 1949.

4 NA, RG 29, vol. 138, no. 208–5–6 pt. 1, J.W. MacFarlane to B.J. Roberts, Ottawa, 14 February 1936. In 1945, administration of the OAP program was transferred to the Welfare section of the provincial Department of Health and Public Welfare.

5 British Columbia Archives and Records Service (BCARS), GR1249, box 4, file 1, E.S.H. Winn to C.H. Tupper Jr, [Vancouver], 17 May 1938; ibid., box 5, file 6, memo, 23 June 1931; ibid., file 7, Winn to G.S. Pearson, [Vancouver], 17 November 1934; P. Reid, 'Looking Backward,' *British Columbia's Welfare*, 5 (December 1948), 6–7; *British Columbia's Welfare*, 8 (January 1950), 20. Mrs Reid was the widowed niece of G.A. Walkem, a former premier of the province.

6 For a detailed analysis of the changing administration and of provincial government policies in Ontario regarding old age pensions, see the chapter in James Struthers, *The Limits of Affluence: Welfare in Ontario, 1920–1970* (Toronto, 1995).

7 University of Western Ontario (UWO), Lambton County OAP Commission, box B882, W. Culbert to J.A. Huey, Wyoming, Ont., 2 March 1932

8 NA, RG 29, vol. 137, no. 208–5–5 pt. 2, J.W. MacFarlane to B.J. Roberts, Ottawa, 19 August 1936; ibid., vol. 147, no. 208–6–5 pt. 1, M.F. Hepburn to C.A. Dunning, Toronto, 17 March 1938; ibid., vol. 138, no. 208–5–5 pt. 5, memo with regard to information obtained in Ontario, 22 June 1949

9 In Manitoba for January 1939, for example, fully 90 per cent of all pensioners were paid in multiples of $5 a month, 75 per cent alone receiving $20. In the same month in Nova Scotia, 47 per cent were paid in multiples of $5. In Ontario, 97 per cent of all pensioners received cheques in multiples of $5, 75 per cent receiving the full $20. Calculated from NA, RG 29, vol. 139, no. 208–5–6 pt. 2; ibid., vol. 133, no. 208–5–2 pt. 2, 28 February 1939; ibid., vol. 137, no. 208–5–5 pt. 2

10 NA, RG 29, vol. 134, no. 208–5–3 pt. 2, W.P. Jones, 'Memo re Conversation with J.W. MacFarlane,' Fredericton [May 1939]. New Brunswick's population was 68 per cent rural, while British Columbia's was just 33 per cent.

11 UWO, Lambton County OAP Commission, box B886, Clerk's Special Report, Brigden, Ont., 20 November 1940

12 NA, RG 29, vol. 137, no. 208–5–5 pt. 1, E.A. Thomas, memo to the minister, Ottawa, 4 April 1930

13 Archives of Ontario (AO), RG 8, Series II–10–F, box 4, file Dufferin county, W.H. Hunter to J.A. Ellis, Orangeville, Ont., 18 January 1930

14 n = 747
15 NA, RG 29, vol. 134, no. 208-5-3 pt. 2, W.P. Jones to J.W. MacFarlane, Fredericton, 9 June 1939
16 This reinforcement of local hierarchies was further entrenched by the selection of local 'worthies,' almost always male, as trustees of an individual's OAP funds in cases where the individual was felt to be incapable of handling the funds effectively.
17 A. Finkel, *Business and Social Reform in the Thirties* (Toronto, 1979), 81–99. See also J. Struthers, *No Fault of Their Own: Unemployment and the Canadian Welfare State, 1914–1941* (Toronto, 1983).
18 AO, RG 8, Series II–10–F, box 2, file 12, W. Stephens to J.A. Ellis, Guelph, Ont., 17 September 1929; NA, RG 29, vol. 152, no. 208-7-1 pt. 1, J.D. O'Neill et al. to P. Heenan, Ottawa, 16 January 1930
19 NA, RG 29, vol. 145, no. 208-6-1, E.A. Thomas, memo to deputy minister, Ottawa, 22 September 1933; ibid., J.W. MacFarlane, 18 April 1939
20 BCARS, GR1249, box 2, file 5, J.W. Jones to H.L. Greenwood, Victoria, 7 February 1933; ibid., to E.S.H. Winn, 8 July 1932, 3 May 1933; ibid., box 6, file 6, Winn to G.S. Pearson, [Vancouver], 27 January 1936. In 1938 the personal income tax form was amended so that when individuals claimed a dependent, they were required to indicate whether the dependent received the OAP; the government assumption was that since the OAP was of considerably more value than the dependency claim, such identification would be sufficiently intimidating to prevent misuse. It was too costly to crosscheck on individual claims with OAP records. See ibid., box 3, file 8, W.C. Clark to Winn, Ottawa, 21 August 1941.
21 NA, RG 29, vol. 133, no. 208-5-2 pt. 3, E.H. Blois to J.W. MacFarlane, Halifax, 22 May 1940. Charles Dunning was the federal minister of finance, 1935–9.
22 NA, RG 29, vol. 129, no. 208-2-3 pt. 3, V.D. McElary to J.W. MacFarlane, Vancouver, 7 October 1941; ibid., vol. 144, no. 208-5-9 pt. 4, memo on criticism of old age pension scheme by Vancouver papers, [1942?]; ibid., W.C. Clark to H.L. Greenwood, Ottawa, 26 November 1942
23 Manitoba Legislative Assembly, 18 February 1943
24 NA, RG 29, vol. 148, no. 208-6-6 pt. 1, J. McLenaghen to J.L. Ilsley, Winnipeg, 4 and 7 September 1943
25 See, for example, NA, W.L.M. King Papers, vol. 405, no. 365471, G. Myers to King, Vancouver, 1946; ibid., vol. 426, no. 387402, A. Mogridge to King, Toronto, 5 March 1947; ibid., vol. 408, no. 368253-56, J. McDonald to King, Calgary, 14 November 1946. I would like to thank Alvin Finkel for bringing these references to my attention.
26 Canadian Institute of Public Opinion, poll of 25 November 1942

27 Ibid., polls of 29 May 1943, 30 November 1946, 24 February 1951

28 Canadian Institute of Public Opinion, polls of 23 November 1946, 14 October 1950. A similar change in attitude towards the means test has been reported for England; see A. Deacon and J. Bradshaw, *Reserved for the Poor: The Means Test in British Social Policy* (Oxford, 1983), 5–50.

29 In 1937 the OAP Act had been amended to include a pension for the visually disabled, but this did not affect the benefits or policies for persons aged seventy or over. That the disabled and the elderly were so closely linked is suggestive of the official perception of aging.

30 See, for example, NA, RG 29, vol. 127, no. 208–1–12, W.C. Clark to W.S. Edwards, Ottawa, 12 August 1941; ibid., vol. 125, no. 208–1–1 pt. 2.

31 BCARS, GR1249, box 3, file 13, memo by H.L. Greenwood, 13 May 1937

32 Ibid., box 1, file 4, E.S.H. Winn to W.C. Clark, [Vancouver], 22 January, 2 November 1942; NA, RG 24, vol. 2076, no. HQ54–275–11 vol. 2; NA, RG 29, vol. 128, no. 208–2–3 pt. 2, V.D. McElary to J.W. MacFarlane, Regina, 6 September 1940; ibid., vol. 145, no. 208–6–2 pt. 1, E.H. Blois to W.C. Clark, Halifax, 13 January 1942; ibid., vol. 129, no. 208–2–3 pt. 3, McElary to MacFarlane, Edmonton, 20 September 1942; UWO, Norfolk County OAP Miscellaneous Administration File, secretary to OAP Commission, [np], 15 April 1944

33 NA, RG 29, vol. 145, no. 208–6–2 pt. 1, E.H. Blois to W.C. Clark, Halifax, 13 January 1942. See also ibid., vol. 133, Blois to J.W. MacFarlane, Halifax, 22 May 1940.

34 SA, J.H. Sturdy Papers, M14, box 44, no. L30 (3), D. Lane to T.C. Douglas, Craven, Sask. [30 October 1945]

35 NA, RG 29, vol. 129, no. 208–2–3 pt. 3, V.D. McElary to J.W. MacFarlane, Regina, 9 November 1941; ibid., McElary to MacFarlane, Edmonton, 6 and 20 September 1942; NA, RG 24, vol. 1596, file 1, pt. 9, 2, pt. 14, 9–10

36 NA, RG 29, vol. 152, no. 208–7–1, pt. 2, memo regarding upcoming meeting of Interprovincial Board, 1946

37 R.M. Dinkel, 'Attitudes of Children toward Supporting Aged Parents,' *American Sociological Review*, 9 (1944), 379

38 There was an elderly population of 652,146 in the census of that year, and two months earlier the annual report on pensions stated that there were 308,825 pensioners across the country.

39 Calculated from NA, RG 29, vol. 126, no. 208–1–4

40 *Gartley* v. *Workman's Compensation Board* (1932), 57 BCR 217 (BCCA); *R ex rel Lee* v. *Workman's Compensation Board*, [1942] 3 WWR 352 (BCSC), [1942] 2 WWR 129 (BCCA); *Commission des Pensions de Vieillesse de Quebec* v. *Poirier* (1940), 69 Que. QB 11 (Que. QB); *Re Rowe and Province of Manitoba*, [1942] 3 WWR 433 (Man. KB); *Mitchell* v. *Mitchell,* [1946] 3 WWR 670 (Alta SC); *Re Ethier,* [1946] 1 DLR 272 (Ont. CA)

41 *Gartley* v. *Workman's Compensation Board* (1932), 57 BCR 217 (BCCA); *Commission des Pensions de Vieillesse de Quebec* v. *Poirier* (1940), 69 Que. QB 11 (Que. QB); *Old Age Pensions Branch of the Workman's Compensation Board of Manitoba* v. *Jacobs,* [1937] 3 WWR 657 (Man. KB); *Re Ethier,* [1946] 1 DLR 272 (Ont. CA); *R ex rel Lee* v. *Workman's Compensation Board,* [1942] 3 WWR 352 (BCSC), [1942] 2 WWR 129 (BCCA)

42 NA, RG 29, vol. 145, no. 208-6-2 pt. 1, J.W. MacFarlane to B.J. Roberts, Ottawa, 9 October 1935; ibid., W.C. Clark to E.H. Blois, Ottawa, 11 April 1938. On Clark's role in the federal bureaucracy, see D. Owram, *The Government Generation: Canadian Intellectuals and the State, 1900–1945* (Toronto, 1986); J.L. Granatstein, *The Ottawa Men: The Civil Service Mandarins, 1935–1957* (Toronto, 1982).

43 A similar tension and contest for power between local and central authorities was taking place over England's old age pensions program at this time; see Deacon and Bradshaw, *Reserved for the Poor,* 11.

44 NA, RG 29, vol. 145, no. 208-6-2 pt. 1, E.H. Blois to W.C. Clark, Halifax, 21 July 1938; ibid., WER to Blois, Ottawa, 13 July 1938; ibid., Clark to Blois, Ottawa, 18 August 1938. See also, for example, ibid., Blois to J.W. MacFarlane, Halifax, 15 June 1937.

45 Ibid., J.W. MacFarlane to B.J. Roberts, Ottawa, 9 October 1935

46 Ibid., vol. 128, no. 208-2-3 pt. 1, J.W. MacFarlane to B.J. Roberts, Vancouver, 22 November 1935

47 Ibid., vol. 149, no. 208-6-8 pt. 1, V.W. Wright to W.C. Clark, Edmonton, 15 February 1937

48 Ibid., pt. 2, memo for the deputy minister, [np], 26 December 1942

49 BCARS, GR1249, box 1, file 2, E.S.H. Winn to W.C. Clark, [Vancouver], 20 May 1938

50 Ibid., E.S.H. Winn to E.H. Blois, [Vancouver], 21 March 1938

51 Ibid., box 3, file 9, memo, 5 November 1942; *P,* June-July 1947, 2, 6

52 NA, RG 29, vol. 146, no. 208-6-4 pt. 1, memo, Ottawa, 4 September 1937; J.R. Forest to W.C. Clark, Quebec, 17 September 1937

53 Ibid., W.C. Clark, memo to the minister, Ottawa, 3 March 1937; ibid., J.W. MacFarlane, memo to deputy minister, Ottawa, 2 May, 9 November 1940, 6 August 1941

54 Ibid., vol. 134, no. 208-5-3 pt. 1, W.P. Jones to E.H. Blois, Fredericton, 2 March 1937

55 Ibid., vol. 129, no. 208-2-3 pt. 3, V.D. McElary to J.W. MacFarlane, Regina, 4 November 1942; ibid., [MacFarlane] to McElary, Ottawa, 11 November 1942

56 UWO, London Welfare Department, box B408, E.V. Berry to OAP Commission, London, 4 January 1944; ibid., Berry to paymaster general, London,

17 January 1944. See also, for example, ibid., Berry to OAP Commission, London, 3 January, 4 August 1949.

57 NA, RG 29, vol. 145, no. 208–6–0, R.R. Roberts to E.R. Swettenham, St John's, 30 June 1949

58 Ibid., vol. 141, no. 208–5–7 pt. 4, D.E. Chalmers to J.W. MacFarlane, Regina, 12 December 1946

59 UWO, Lambton County OAP Commission, box B882, OAP Application Files, County Clerk's Report, 6 June 1935; ibid., box B883, Clerk's Special Report, Arkona, Ont., 6 August 1941

60 Ibid., box B883, J.A. Huey to OAP Commission, Sarnia, 15 March 1941

61 NA, RG 29, vol. 143, no. 208–5–9 pt. 2, E.S.H. Winn to B.J. Roberts, Vancouver, 7 October 1936

62 Ibid., vol. 145, no. 208–6–2 pt. 1, W.C. Clark to E.H. Blois, Ottawa, 27 September 1938; ibid., Blois to Clark, Halifax, 4 October 1938; ibid., Blois to J.W. MacFarlane, Halifax, 1 April 1939

63 L. Marsh, *Report on Social Security for Canada* (Ottawa, 1943), 68–79. See also H.M. Cassidy, *Social Security and Reconstruction in Canada* (Toronto, 1943), 155.

64 NA, RG 29, vol. 125, no. 208–1–1 pt. 2, G.F. Davidson to J.W. MacFarlane, Ottawa, 18 March 1946

65 Ibid., vol. 138, no. 208–5–5 pt. 4, memo to J.W. MacFarlane, Ottawa, 6 May 1946

66 See, for example, NA, RG 29, vol. 130, no. 208–3–2, Dr D.A. Carmichael to Old Age Pension Department, Ottawa, 4 December 1950.

67 See, for example, *Canadian Unionist*, 11 (1938), 341; 16 (1943), 241; 19 (1945), 118; 20 (1946), 87; 23 (1949), 80, 86; 24 (1950), 53, 130–2.

68 *Vancouver Daily Province*, 27 February 1946, 3. See also *Western Producer* (WP), 17 February, 1944, 11, 14, 16 March 1944, 23; *Pensioner* (P), October 1943, 5 (reporting a motion by the Union of B.C. Municipalities that the name of the OAP be changed to Senior Citizens' Pension), June–July 1947, 7. In some OAPO branches the words of the recruiting song were changed to 'Onward Senior Citizens.'

69 NA, RG 29, vol. 125, no. 208–1–1 pt. 2, memo by G.F. Davidson on Old Age Pensions, Ottawa, 14 September 1945. Many doctors already provided free care for those who could not afford it, including the dependent elderly, but these new state programs gave pensioners such benefits as a right. A motion in favour of state medical aid for pensioners was first introduced in the British Columbia legislature on 10 November 1939.

70 Ibid., vol. 144, no. 208–5–9 pt. 4, [?] to J.W. MacFarlane, Vancouver, 19 July 1943; ibid., pt. 5, 'British Columbia Medical Services Plan'; Violet McNaughton Papers (VM), A1, no. 49(2), J.J. Whiting to McNaughton, New

Westminster, BC, 26 April 1943; ibid., no. 46(2), 13 June 1943; *Vancouver Sun*, 23 November 1940, 19. Where no municipal organization had been formed, the provincial government absorbed the entire cost. In several municipalities these services were already available to pensioners through the local relief department.

71 W.L. Wariner, 'Medical Services for Old Age Pensioners in Ontario,' MSW thesis, University of Toronto, 1950, 14–18, 26; *P*, September 1950, 10; UWO, London Welfare Records, box B408, E.V. Berry to C.H. Greene, London, 31 December 1943; H.J. Dorgen, 'The Old Age Pension Applicant: A Study of 144 Applicants for Old Age Pension at the Toronto Department of Public Welfare in December 1948,' MSW thesis, University of Toronto, 1949, 71–88

72 Saskatchewan Archives (SA), T.C. Douglas Papers, R33.2, xviii, 354 (19–3–1); NA, RG 29, vol. 1940, no. R249/109, 'Alberta O.A.P. Scheme,' [1948]; vol. 138, no. 208–5–5 pt. 5, memo with regard to information obtained in Ontario, 22 June 1949; NA, MG 28 I10, acc. no. 83/275, box 174, file 'Old Age - Medical Care & Mental Health'

73 NA, Canadian Council on Social Development, Acc. no. 83/275, box 174, 'Old Age – Medical Care & Mental Health'; *Calgary Herald*, 6 February 1947

74 Toronto *Daily Star*, 12 August 1948, 6; *P*, February 1951, 11

75 Quoted in 'The Rights of Old Age,' *Canadian Welfare*, 15 April 1947, 23; M.S. Jewett, 'An Evaluation of the Old Age Pension System in Canada,' MSW thesis, McGill University, 1949, 36. See also *British Columbia's Welfare*, 9 (November 1951), 9–10.

76 B.R. Leydier, 'Boarding Home Care for the Aged: A Study of the Social Welfare Aspects of Licensed Homes in Vancouver,' MSW thesis, University of British Columbia, 1948, 17–25

77 University of Toronto Archives, P78–0055, Department of University Extension, *Living in the Later Years* (Toronto, 1951); W. Main, 'A Study of Lambert Lodge, Home for the Aged,' MSW thesis, University of Toronto, 1951, 4

78 J.H. Creighton, 'Life Begins at 70,' *British Columbia's Welfare*, 4 (June 1947), 6–7; *WP*, 13 December 1951, 6. See also M.W. Wagner, *Modern Old Age in a New World* (Toronto [1946]), 2, 5. Canadian social work journals began to reprint American articles on gerontology; see, for example, *British Columbia's Welfare*, 5 (October 1948), 1; ibid., 9 (November 1951), 1.

79 E. Page, 'Places Where Old People Are Happy and Understood,' *British Columbia's Welfare*, 4 (March 1948), 12–14

80 See, for example, Ontario, 1949, 13 Geo. VI, c.41; Ontario, 1947, 11 Geo. VI, c.46; Toronto *Daily Star*, 10 December 1948, 29, 51.

81 *P*, February 1951, 1

82 E. Dixon, 'Recreation for Old People,' in *Living in the Later Years*, 20. See also Wagner, *Modern Old Age*, 2; *P*, November 1951, 6.

83 M.F. Kennedy, 'Recreation for the Aged,' MSW thesis, University of Toronto, 1952, 3; V. McNaughton, 'Spending Our Time After 60,' *WP*, 24 April 1947, 11. At times, however, the recreational philosophy became one of simply entertaining the elderly; see, for example, the comments of Dr Henrietta Anderson of the Recreation Council of Victoria in *P*, October 1946, 6.
84 K. Gorrie, 'Age Comes into Its Own,' *British Columbia's Welfare*, 5 (October 1948), 4–6
85 Wagner, *Modern Old Age*, 10
86 Owram, *Government Generation*

CHAPTER 8: Conclusion

1 *Pensioner* (*P*), August 1951, 1
2 After the 1951 OAP reforms, the three most western provinces continued to pay a cost-of-living bonus to all pensioners – $10 a month in British Columbia and Alberta, and $2.50 a month in Saskatchewan. *P*, November 1952, 1
3 D. Jean, 'Family Allowances and Family Autonomy: Quebec Families Encounter the Welfare State, 1945–1955,' in B. Bradbury, ed., *Canadian Family History: Selected Readings* (Toronto, 1992), 401–37
4 See, for example, B. Curtis, *Building the Educational State: Canada West, 1836–1871* (London, 1988); E. Tucker, *Administering Danger in the Workplace: The Law and Politics of Occupational Health and Safety Regulation in Ontario, 1850–1914* (Toronto, 1990). Compare with A.S. Orloff, *The Politics of Pensions: A Comparative Analysis of Britain, Canada, and the United States, 1880–1940* (Madison, 1993), chapter 8.
5 A.M. Rose, 'The Subculture of the Aging,' in A.M. Rose and W.A. Peterson, eds., *Older People and Their Social World* (Philadelphia, 1965), 13
6 One of the results of broadening state attention and activity is that the targets of that attention tend to become politicized in order to protect themselves and to alter the state's activities so that they take into account the needs and interests of the target groups; implicit in such developments is a positive view of the state, a sense that the state, or some elements of the state apparatus, can be made accessible and at least partially amenable to the interests of the traditionally 'powerless.' See, for example, P. Tennant, *Aboriginal Peoples and Politics: The Indian Land Question in British Columbia, 1849–1989* (Vancouver, 1990).
7 For exceptions, see *Western Producer* (*WP*), 2 July 1942, 24, 17 September 1942, 25; *P*, September 1950, 6.
8 T. Skocpol, *Protecting Soldiers and Mothers: The Political Origins of Social Policy in the United States* (Cambridge, MA, 1992), 248–310
9 D. Thomson, 'The Welfare of the Elderly in the Past,' in M. Pelling and R.M.

Smith, eds., *Life, Death, and the Elderly: Historical Perspectives* (London, 1991), 194–221

10 K. Kernaghan and O. Kuper, *Coordination in Canadian Governments: A Case Study of Aging Policy* (Toronto, 1983)

11 S.S. Kulis, *Why Honor Thy Father and Mother? Class, Mobility, and Family Ties in Later Life* (New York, 1991), 38–45

12 See C.G. Gifford, *Canada's Fighting Seniors* (Toronto, 1990).

A Note on Sources

The OAP cases were examined in two major ways. First, government records, provincially and federally, were thoroughly canvassed for the information they could provide about both government policy and the responses of the elderly. Though the records of the relevant provincial government boards and/or departments are often no longer extant, the federal records (RG 29) are particularly strong. In British Columbia, the records of the OAP Board of the Workmen's Compensation Board (GR1249) were very rich, adding an important local dimension to my information. In Saskatchewan, the private papers of T.C. Douglas, A.T. Proctor, J.M. Uhrich, and J.H. Sturdy, all members of the CCF Government in the 1940s, proved particularly helpful. In Ontario, several collections provided scattered coverage of the provincial administration of the OAP: the early correspondence of the secretary of the OAP Commission (RG 8, Series II-10-F) for 1928–30; the files of a deputy minister of public welfare, Dr James Band (RG 29-74); and OAP correspondence from the office of the minister of public welfare (RG 29–59, microfilm MS728, reels 2 and 3). The records of the Lambton County and London city OAP commissions, held at the University of Western Ontario, were very rich in revealing the behaviour and attitudes of the elderly themselves. The Ottawa records were the most complete and were very useful, but for the most part they dealt exclusively with problems between the two levels of pension bureaucracy rather than with pensioners themselves.

Second, two sets of OAP applications were systematically examined to determine the characteristics of those applying. The records for Lambton County (located in southwestern Ontario, across the border from Port Huron, Michigan, and centring on the city of Sarnia) are held at the Regional History Collection, University of Western Ontario (boxes B882–B887); they cover the years 1929–51 and include all applications received from county residents outside the city of Sarnia. These rural applications were randomly sampled (using a random numbers table), producing a total of 379 cases and representing 28.5 percent of the extant files. For an urban set, I selected the records for London, Ontario (Regional History Collection, boxes B1153–B1154), in the hope that these might demonstrate some links with the data obtained through that city's welfare records. Here a random sample of 415 applicants represented 8.5 per cent of the total number of cases covered in the London records for the period 1929 through 1948.

Welfare records and state programs were particularly dispersed. It was essential to find some ways of containing the research, so that the project could be brought to a conclusion within a reasonable amount of time. Here the selection of particular provinces for analysis was very important. British Columbia was selected for analysis initially because that province was in the forefront of the movement for an OAP program; that selection was strengthened when it early became apparent that it was in that province that the elderly were particularly active organizationally and politically. It was simply fortuitous that the records for relevant aspects of the provincial welfare system, particularly as regards the Provincial Home for Aged and Infirm Men (GR 150, 366, and 624), were as rich as they were for the purposes of this study. Saskatchewan was selected as another province for special analysis, particularly because of the innovative role of the CCF government in the 1940s and the early indications of useful sources for elderly organizations. The provincial printed records proved useful as well regarding state-operated residences. Beyond general sources for Ontario as a whole, there were quite rich sources for the city of London, as a case study of local welfare support for the elderly. The city welfare department's case files are extant for the period 1935–41; though the period is limited and covers years unusual for the level of economic distress and the beginning of the Second World War, this collection is unique in Canada and allows a glimpse of how the elderly were being affected by the changing welfare system. These files were systematically analysed, using a random sample of 1843 and representing some 39.3 per cent of the total case files; such a large group was necessary to ensure that there were sufficient elderly in the sample for an analysis of the character and extent of elderly participation. As well, files of the municipal welfare system and of the local homes for the aged were examined for qualitative evidence; in the latter regard, the records of the Woman's Christian Association were also helpful. The intended case study of the elderly in London was dropped from the final manuscript because of excessive length.

No significant large collections of records regarding the elderly were uncovered in any of the five most easterly provinces. In none of these jurisdictions were the records of the provincial OAP commissions retained. Occasionally, small groups of records for institutions were available. In the absence of such records, it was not possible to concentrate on any one or two of these provinces. Research was undertaken in all five provinces, with an emphasis on Newfoundland, which, given its separate political existence prior to 1949, offered some opportunity for contrast with the other provinces. Two royal commissions on the state of the elderly in the absence of old age pensions reported in Nova Scotia and New Brunswick around 1930 and were helpful, though the information they contained was limited.

To supplement the anecdotal evidence regarding informal and familial methods of supporting the elderly in the above records, I arranged for a brief article about this project to be published in *Especially for Seniors* (January 1992, 4), a publication of the Ontario Advisory Council on Senior Citizens which went to all seniors in that province. In this article I invited readers to write to me about how their grandparents or great-grandparents were cared for within their families, hoping that the reliability of such accounts would be increased by founding them within their own experience and removed from the contemporary context of state aid. Unsolicited by me, the article was repeated in several small-circulation periodicals. The result was a large number of responses of great variation in character, and many of these responses were quite helpful.

In the initial stages of the research, the evidence of the organizational and political initiatives of the elderly in the 1930s and 1940s was limited to occasional files in the federal records regarding the OAP. But beyond Ottawa, the sources became very rich. The Violet McNaughton Papers in Saskatoon were not only very extensive in this regard, but also pointed to several other sources. Most importantly, here I first learned of the existence of the *Pensioner*, the newspaper voice of many of the organized elderly; this was followed shortly by copies of two individual issues of the paper (one in the Douglas Papers and the other in the Proctor Papers), one of which I found nowhere else. The only other extant copies of the *Pensioner* were located in the Library of Congress, Washington, DC. No Canadian libraries are known to hold copies of this paper, so to facilitate further research by others my copies of the paper have been deposited in the University of Guelph Archives. Violet McNaughton's role as women's editor for the *Western Producer* made that paper, too, a vital source for the activities of the grey lobby. These records were supplemented by interviews with Josephine Arland, Philip Grabke, and Stanley Knowles; C.G. Gifford of Halifax generously shared with me the transcripts of his earlier interviews with a number of prominent figures in seniors' organizations.

Index

citizen's wage, xiv, xvi–xvii, 10–11, 98, 165, 184–5, 187, 194, 197–203, 212–14, 217, 220–1, 225; and citizenship, xiii–xiv, xviii, xx, 39, 165, 176, 236 n8
Clark, W.C., 203–4
community, 44–5, 60–7, 69, 103, 121, 133, 138–41, 143, 146–7, 152, 205, 218–19, 223, 240 n55
Conservative Association of British Columbia, 31
courts, 111–12, 201–3, 251 n19, 264 n19
Crown, M. (pseud.), 152–3

demographics, 5–6, 12–18, 20, 28, 35, 103, 131, 230 n22, 249 n87, 257–8 nn7–10
dependants' allowances, 198–200
Depression, xv, 34, 135, 187, 192, 203–4, 254 n63
Dominion Bureau of Statistics, 67, 81
dominion–provincial relations, royal commission on, 84
Douglas, A., 171, 178
Dyson, G.M., 268 n81

Eagles, Fraternal Order of, 164
elderly, definition of, xx
Elice, M. (pseud.), 127–8
Emigrant Society of Fredericton, 37
England, 5, 8, 36, 74–7, 104, 115, 206, 244 n17, 263 n5, 271 n28, 272 n43
entitlement, culture of, xv–xvi, xviii, 92, 97, 100–29, 139, 147–8, 154–5, 162, 164–5, 186–7, 194, 213, 220, 253 n59
ethnicity, xvi, xix, 8, 35, 46, 101–2, 124–5, 191, 215, 220–2, 234 n64, 241 n73
Everett, G. and E. (pseud.), 96

family allowances, xv, 194, 197, 200, 219

family and the elderly, xvi–xvii, 5–8, 10, 18–26, 32–3, 36, 43–4, 59, 69–70, 73–99, 101–11, 114, 120–1, 126, 141–2, 145–6, 151, 154, 186, 192, 197–9, 206, 218–20, 222–3, 255 n83, 257 n6, 258 nn14–17; culture of, 19–22, 33, 36, 75, 78, 82, 98–102, 117–29, 134–5, 138, 224; and the OAP, 10, 80–99, 131–9. See also filial responsibility
Family Welfare Association of Montreal, 213
filial responsibility, 19, 21, 74–99, 113–4, 123, 125, 127, 141, 246 n39. See also family and the elderly
Finkel, A., 192
First World War, xv, 9, 34, 198
Fisher, E., 170
fraud, 113, 119–20, 133, 140–55, 186
friendly societies, 69
Friendship Club of Edmonton, 157
funeral, 129, 139, 256 n94

Gagan, D., 14, 102
gender, xviii, 8, 15, 20, 22, 25, 29, 31, 34–5, 48–9, 53, 59, 66, 68, 70, 73, 93–5, 100, 102, 124, 131–6, 139, 178–9, 191, 215, 221–2, 249 n2, 258 nn15–17, 259 n21, 261 n47, 270 n16
gerontology, 3, 214
Goffman, E., 47
Golden, L. (pseud.), 104
Graebner, W., 6–7, 11
Gratton, B., 5–7, 10–11
Gray, A., 267 n64

Haber, C., 11
Halifax City Asylum, 41
Halifax Poor Man's Friend Society, 37
Happier Old Age Club, 263 n10
Hareven, T., 220

health care programs, xiv, xvii, 150, 187, 211–12, 224, 273 n69
historiography, 3–7
Hope, J.W., 167, 176
housing, 17, 20–4, 32, 60, 65, 76, 87, 92–3, 101–5, 109, 136–8, 150, 208, 210, 223–4, 231 n35, 256 n93, 258 n14
Hull, M., 97

income, fictive, 9, 83, 105, 264 n19
income tax, xv, 83, 112, 198, 210, 252 n37, 270 n20
independence, 76, 98–9, 114, 118, 124, 126–9, 137, 150–1, 224
industrialization, 5–6, 27–30, 32, 69
inheritance, 18, 25, 75, 102, 107, 110, 118, 121, 131, 153, 249 n2
insurance, 75, 97, 235 n67
Interprovincial OAP Board, 81, 83, 107, 192
Ireland, 121–2

jail, 39, 42, 44, 58, 152
Jean, D., 219

Kamloops Provincial Home for the Aged, 39, 41–2, 48–9, 60–1, 66–7, 71
Kennedy, A.H., 168, 175, 178
Kennedy, B.S., 168–9, 265 n37
Kessler, C. and E. (pseud.), 114
Kielly, A. (pseud.), 125
King, W.L.M., 113, 147
Kingston Home for Aged, Friendless and Infirm, 44, 47, 49
kinship. See family
kinship, fictive, 103
Knowles, S., 182
Kohli, M., xiv

labour, organized, 6–7, 9, 34, 195, 210, 268 n77
Lebrun, F. (pseud.), 122
liens, 108, 111, 116, 120, 123, 253 n61
Lovell, S., 171, 178
Lynch, G. (pseud.), 153

maintenance agreement, 101–5, 121–2
Manitoba Commonwealth, 168
Manitoba Pensioners' Society, 171, 181
marriage, among elderly, 18–19, 132, 190; of adult children, 86, 89, 93–4, 132–4, 247 n59, 254 n67, 258 n16
Marsh, L., 209
Marshall, T.H., xiii
McAlton, J. (pseud.), 102–3
McCormick Home of London, 142
McGill University, 214
McNaughton, V., 161, 165–7, 177
McWhinney, Mr, 180
Medd, N., 180
mobility, 150–1
Montigny, E.-A., 28
Montreal Council of Social Agencies, 213
Morton, D., xix
mothers' allowances, xv, 112, 200
Myles, J., xiv, xvi

National Pensioners' Federation, 268 n75
New Brunswick royal commission of 1930, 130
New Zealand, 263 n5
Nova Scotia Pensioners' Union, 179, 213
Nova Scotia royal commission of 1908, 8, 15; of 1928–30, 15–18, 103
Nurse, A., 161, 171, 178

Old Age and Invalid Pensioners' Association, 263 n10